Contemporary Strategy Analysis

Contemporary Strategy Analysis

Concepts, Techniques, Applications

Robert M. Grant

Copyright © Robert M. Grant 1991
The right of Robert M. Grant to be identified as author of this work has been asserted in accordance with the Copyright, Designs and Patents Act 1988.

First published 1991
Reprinted 1992 (three times), 1993

Blackwell Publishers
238 Main Street
Cambridge, Massachusetts 02142, USA

108 Cowley Road, Oxford OX4 1JF, UK

Library of Congress Cataloging in Publication Data
Grant, Robert M.
    Contemporary strategy analysis: concepts, techniques, applications/Robert M. Grant.
    Includes index.
    ISBN 1–55786–242–7 (Hardback): ISBN 1–55786–243–5 (Paperback)
    1. Strategic planning.
  HD30.28.G72 1991
  658.4′012 – dc20
90–36559 CIP

British Library Cataloguing in Publication Data
A CIP catalogue record for this book is available from the British Library.

Typeset in 11 on 13pt Sabon
by Butler & Tanner Ltd, Frome and London
Printed in Great Britain at The Alden Press, Oxford

This book is printed on acid-free paper.

Contents

Preface

The objective of this book is to provide a guide to business strategy analysis which combines *rigor* with *relevance and applicability*.

The book has been developed in the course of MBA teaching of business policy at UCLA, California Polytechnic, University of British Columbia, and London Business School, and it is addressed primarily towards MBA students. At the same time, its content and approach have been determined, not by the requirements of syllabus, but by the need for more effective strategic management in the corporate sector. Since the content and style of the book are directed towards improving the formulation and implementation of strategies within companies it is intended that this book will prove as useful for practicing managers as it is for business students. Indeed, parts of the book have been developed and used within short courses for executives.

The primary distinguishing feature of the book is its quest for a deeper level of analytic rigor without any loss of relevance or practicality. My primary motivation in writing the book was the belief that most books in the strategy field, both student texts and practitioner manuals, were unstimulating, analytically flabby, and failed to provide penetrating insight into the central issues of business success and failure. While practitioner manuals have tended to rely upon checklists, buzzwords, and fad-ideas as a substitute for clear thinking, student texts have failed to communicate the intellectual and practical excitement of strategic management.

My book is determinedly up-to-date in its effort to combine the latest thinking in the subject area. As a result it is eclectic in approach, drawing in particular upon industrial economics, organization theory, and financial analysis. At the same time, the book is selective and integrated. The integrating theme of the book is *competitive advantage*. I uncompromisingly take the view that the primary purpose of strategy is superior profitability through the establishment of sustainable competitive advantage. Among the concepts and theories which are central to the book's analysis of competitive advantage are:

- The resource-based theory of strategy (R. Rumelt, J. Barney), with particular emphasis on the role of firm-specific, intangible assets (O. E. Williamson, Hiroyuki Itami), and organizational routines (R. Nelson and S. Winter)
- Transaction costs (O. E. Williamson) and their impact upon the scope of the firm (D. Teece)

- Value chain analysis (M. Porter, McKinsey & Company)
- Dynamic approaches to the analysis of competition (J. Schumpeter, J. Williams), including ecological analysis of competitive strategy (B. Henderson, M. Hannan and J. Freeman)
- The creation and sustainability of competitive advantage (P. Ghemawat) including the role of isolating mechanisms and uncertain imitability (R. Rumelt)
- Agency problems (M. Jensen)
- Reputation effects (C. Camerer, D. Kreps)
- Rent appropriation (D. Teece)
- Industry recipes (J.-C. Spender)
- Cooperative strategies and strategic alliances (J. Bower, G. Hamel and C. K. Prahalad)
- The contribution of financial theory to strategy analysis including: value maximization, the role of free cash flow, and option theory (A. Rappaport, M. Jensen, S. Myers)
- Transnational approaches to global advantage (C. Bartlett and S. Ghoshal)

My focus upon analysis means that the book is concerned primarily with strategy formulation. Issues of implementation are raised, particularly where strategy formulation is inextricably linked to strategy implementation. However, detailed issues of implementation are left to books on organizational design and the management of specific functions such as production, marketing, human resources, and so on. The analytic focus of the book also implies a "rationalist" approach. This is not because I wish to play down the importance of intuition, creativity, and political processes in strategy formulation – these are important influences and critical to flexibility and opportunism. However, the first stage which a company must go through in developing a successful strategy is objective appraisal of how it will compete and develop its business over the long term.

Finally, the book is international in scope. This is achieved through explicit consideration of international competition, through incorporating Japanese and European contributions to strategic management theory and practice, and including examples of European, and Asian, as well as North American companies.

Robert M. Grant

[handwritten margin note: emphasis a rationalist approach. emphasis is on business rather than corporate strategy. (see p. 22)*]*

The Role of Strategy in Success

- Early in 1962 the Beatles were an undistinguished rock 'n' roll band playing at Liverpool's Cavern Club for around 25 shillings ($3) a session each. Two years later, in February 1964, the Beatles arrived in the US to a tumultuous reception at Kennedy Airport, their records captured the top five places in the Billboard chart, and a frenzied condition known as "Beatlemania", infected the youth of America.
- In April 1975, the Americans pulled out of Saigon. A 30-year struggle by the Vietnamese communist forces culminated in the reunification of the country under the government of the Democratic Republic of Vietnam. In the process, first the Japanese, then the French and, finally, the Americans were expelled from Vietnamese soil.
- A more recent US venture to the other side of the Pacific met greater success. Dennis Connor became the first man in history both to lose and to regain the America's Cup. In February 1987 at Fremantle, Australia, Connor and his Sail America team reestablished US seamanship and US marine technology at the forefront of international competitive sailing.

The Case Notes on the following pages describe in greater detail these three stories of outstanding success in quite different areas of endeavor. The issue I wish to explore here is whether, behind these diverse examples of achievement, there is any common explanation for the success of these three organizations. In none can success be attributed to overwhelmingly superior resources:

- The Beatles possessed originality, zest, and humor but, even during the peak of their popularity in 1964–5 could not be regarded as brilliant singers, instrumentalists or writers of popular music; their musical development took place mainly in the later 1960s.
- The military, human and economic resources of the Vietnamese communists were dwarfed by those of the US and South Vietnam. The only area where the Vietnamese communists could claim superiority was in the dedication and commitment of their leaders and soldiers.
- Dennis Connor has been acclaimed an outstanding helmsman. Yet, the America's Cup is a competition requiring diverse and sophisticated technical expertise and large sums of finance. Connor's cup challenge was built initially from scratch.

Nor can success be attributed either exclusively or primarily to luck. In all three stories, lucky breaks provided opportunities at critical junctures. But none of the three organizations was subject to a consistent run of good fortune. More important was the ability of all three to recognize opportunities when they presented themselves and to have the clarity of direction and the flexibility necessary to exploit these opportunities.

It is my contention that the key common ingredient in all three success stories is the presence of a soundly-formulated and effectively-implemented strategy.

Case Note 1.1 Brian Epstein and the Beatles

On a Saturday afternoon in October 1961 a teenager walked into a Liverpool record store and asked the manager, Brian Epstein, for a German recording by a local band called the "Beatles". This was the first time that Epstein had heard of the band and was the starting point of one of the most remarkable success stories in the history of popular music.

During the lunchtime of November 9, Epstein visited the Cavern Club, a converted basement warehouse in Matthew Street, Liverpool to hear the band play. They had recently returned from a three-month stint at a Hamburg strip-joint and were eager for the 25 shillings ($3.00) a session each which the Cavern paid. Epstein was impressed by the band's loud rock 'n' roll music; he liked their witticisms, their audience rapport and their relaxed, off-hand style, and was fascinated by the bass guitarist, John Lennon. In December 1961, Epstein offered to manage the Beatles and began planning the development and the marketing of the group.

Brian Epstein was an unlikely candidate for the manager of a successful pop group. Before taking over the family's Liverpool record store, his life had been one of failure and disappointment. Unable to settle at any of his seven schools, he left school at 16 with no academic qualifications. He dropped out of acting school and was discharged from the army on medical grounds. He was homosexual at a time when homosexuality was both socially unacceptable and illegal. Beyond his record store, he had little interest in rock music.

Yet as manager of the Beatles he was able to successfully guide them from obscurity to stardom. Although a shy and retiring man, he was ambitious for success and acclaim and was attracted to the glamour and camaraderie of the showbiz world. This ambition was supported by a firm belief that the Beatles could make it in a market which had been largely dominated by American singers and musicians.

Despite lack of experience in the music business, Epstein had a keen sense for the determinants of success in the world of pop music. In particular, he appreciated Sir Thomas Beecham's diagnosis of the perennial popularity of certain operas: "They survive because they consist of bloody good tunes." He also recognized the importance of other ingredients of success in the competitive world of popular music: an identifiable "image", broad-based personal appeal, charm, and acceptability to the executives, producers, and promoters who controlled access to the channels of distribution in the music industry. He was struck by Colonel Tom Parker's role in adjusting Elvis Presley's image to one which was more acceptable to the mainstream tastes of the late 1950s.

A key merit of Epstein's guidance of the band's development was his ability to improve the marketability of the band without constraining their spontaneity, wit, and natural charm. A key factor in marketing was packaging. Epstein designed stage uniforms that featured the characteristic lapel-less "Beatle-jackets", topped by the mop-like, Beatle haircut. The Beatle's stage act became more formalized, while both on and off stage, Epstein established clear rules of behavior based around politeness, media availability, and prohibition of swearing, marriage, comment on politics, religion and drugs. Epstein took a leading role in changing the membership of the band – with the approval of John, Paul, and George, drummer Pete Best was replaced by Richard Starkey who was renamed Ringo Starr.

The coexistence of the group image ("The Fab Four") with the individual identities of the band members was a key feature of the Beatles' broad appeal. Unlike contemporary American groups which tended to suppress individuality in favor of internal homogeneity, each Beatle developed a differentiated appeal: Paul, the gentle choirboy; John, the intellectual live-wire with an aggressive wit; George, the introspective musician; Ringo, the clown.

The promotion of the Beatles was carefully managed by Epstein. To obtain access and visibility for the band, Epstein tirelessly pursued record producers, concert promoters, disk-jockeys and TV producers. The Beatles' first British record release, "Love me do", was pushed into the lower echelons of the charts largely by Epstein's own purchases. Persuading Ed Sullivan to feature the Beatles on his show was a key element in Epstein's promotion of the Beatles in America.

At Kennedy Airport on February 7, 1964, the Beatles' arrival in the US was greeted by 10,000 fans. Their Carnegie Hall concert was a sell-out, and an infectious hysteria known as "Beatlemania" began to take grip on the youth of America. By the time the group departed, their records held the top five places in the singles chart. The Beatles were the highest paid, most widely-acclaimed performers in the history of popular music.

The Beatles' music spearheaded the British invasion of the world pop music market and Epstein was quick to consolidate on the Beatles' success. Hit records and sell-out concerts were followed by two full-length movies. In addition, a whole industry of Beatle merchandise sprang up, which included Beatle clothing accessories, Beatle wigs, and Beatle dolls. Epstein followed up by launching a number of new singers and bands collectively known as the "Merseybeat sound." These included Gerry and the Pacemakers, Cilla Black, and Billy J. Kramer.

Epstein provided far more to the Beatles than pro-motion and management of their finances and external relationships. In their rise to success and during their heyday, Epstein held the band together through disappointment, acclaim, crisis, adulation, and exhaustion. He provided leadership, counselling, and friendship. He mediated disputes between the band members, helped them resolve problems in their private lives, and guided them through moods. On several occasions it was their loyalty to him and their knowledge of his affection for them that kept them together. After Epstein's death from a drug overdose in 1968, the Beatles never again played together in public.

Sources: Brian Epstein, *A Cellarful of Noise* (Doubleday, New York, 1964); Peter Brown and Steve Gaines, *The Love You Make: An Insider's Story of the Beatles* (Signet, New York, 1984).

Case Note 1.2   General Giap and the Vietnam Wars, 1948–75

"As far as logistics and tactics were concerned we suc-ceeded in everything we set out to do. At the height of the war the army was able to move almost a million soldiers a year in and out of Vietnam, feed them, clothe them, house them, supply them with arms and ammunition and gen-erally sustain them better than any army had ever been sustained in the field ... On the battlefield itself, the army was unbeatable. In engagement after engagement the forces of the Vietcong and the North Vietnamese Army were thrown back with terrible losses. Yet, in the end, it was North Vietnam, not the United States that emerged victorious. How could we have succeeded so well yet failed so miserably?"[1]

Despite having the largest army in South-East Asia, North Vietnam was no match for South Vietnam so long as it was backed by the world's most powerful military and industrial nation. South Vietnam and its US ally were defeated not by superior resources but by a superior strategy. North Vietnam achieved what Sun Tzu claimed was the highest form of victory: the enemy gave up.

The prime mover in the formulation of North Viet-nam's military strategy was General Vo Nguyen Giap. In 1944, Giap became head of the Vietmihn guerrilla forces and remained Commander-in-Chief of the North Vietnamese Army until 1974 and Minister of Defence until 1980. Giap's strategy was based upon Mao Tse Tung's three-phase theory of revolutionary war: passive resistance during which political support is mobilized; guerrilla warfare aimed at weakening the enemy and building military strength; general counter-offensive.[2] In 1954, Giap felt strong enough to begin the final stage in the war against the French and the brilliant victory at Dien Bien Phu fully vin-dicated the strategy. Against South Vietnam and its US ally, the approach was similar. Giap explained his strategy as follows:

Our strategy was ... to wage a long-lasting battle ... Only a long-term war could enable us to utilize to the maximum our political trump cards, to overcome our material handi-cap, and to transform our weakness into strength. To main-tain and increase our forces was the principle to which we adhered, contenting ourselves with attacking when success was certain, refusing to give battle likely to incur losses ...[3]

The strategy built upon the one resource in which the Communists had overwhelming superiority: their will to fight. As Clausewitz, the nineteenth-century military theorist, observed: war requires unity of purpose between the government, the military, and the people. Such unity was never achieved in the US. The North Vietnamese, on the other hand, were united in a "people's war." Capitalizing upon this strength necessitated "The Long War." As Prime Minister Pham Van Dong explained: "The United States is the most powerful nation on earth. But Americans do not like long, inconclusive wars . . . We can outlast them and we can win in the end." Limited military engagement and the charade of the Paris peace talks, helped the North Vietnamese prolong the conflict, while diplomatic efforts to isolate the US from its Western allies and to sustain the US peace movement accelerated the crumbling of American will to win.

The effectiveness of the US military response was limited by two key uncertainties: what were the objectives and who was the enemy? Was the US role one of supporting the South Vietnamese regime, fighting Vietcong terrorism, inflicting a military defeat on North Vietnam, or combatting world communism? Lack of unanimity over goals translated into confusion as to whether America was fighting the Vietcong, the North Vietnamese, the communists of South-East Asia, or whether the war was military or political in scope? Diversity of opinions and a shifting balance of political and public opinion over time, was fatal for establishing a consistent long-term strategy.

The consistency and strength of North Vietnam's strategy allowed it to survive errors in implementation. In particular, Giap was undoubtedly premature in launching his general offensive. The heavy infiltration and mounting guerrilla actions by North Vietnamese regulars during 1965–7, was followed in 1968 by the Tet Offensive and in 1972 by the Easter Offensive. Both these offensives on South Vietnamese and US positions were beaten back and huge losses sustained. General Giap was replaced as Commander-in-Chief by General Van Tien Dung, who recognized that the Watergate scandal had so weakened the US presidency that an effective American response to a new communist offensive was unlikely. On April 29, 1975 Operation Frequent Wind began to evacuate all remaining Americans from South Vietnam, and the next morning North Vietnamese troops entered the Presidential Palace in Saigon.

1 Col. Harry G. Summers Jr., *On Strategy* (Presidio Press, Novato, CA, 1982), p. 1.
2 G.K. Tanham, *Communist Revolutionary Warfare* (Praeger, New York, 1961), pp. 9–32.
3 Russell Statler (ed.), *The Military Art of People's War: Selected Writings of General Vo Nguyen Giap* (Monthly Review Press, New York, 1970).

Case Note 1.3   Dennis Connor and Sail America's Campaign for the Cup

Dennis Connor's campaign for the recapture of the America's Cup began the day of his final defeat as skipper of the New York Yacht Club's *Liberty* to the challenger *Australia II* off Rhode Island in 1983. From that day until February 1987 when he held the Cup in his hands, Connor's life was devoted to a single goal.

His campaign was dominated by a single realization: he had been beaten in 1983 not by a better sailor, but by a better boat. *Australia II* had benefits of speed from its revolutionary winged keel and better information from its on-board computer system. The game had changed. Up until 1983, it had been assumed that 12 meter sail boats had been perfected. The case against technology was reinforced by the disastrous performance of the innovatory *Mariner* boat in 1974.

Australia II's victory reignited the quest for a superior performance through innovatory design. Connor knew that to beat the Australians in 1987 required not just imitating Australia II's advantages, but leapfrogging their technical lead. To do this would require expertise and money.

In February 1984, having failed to reach agreement with the wealthy and prestigious New York Yacht Club over forming a syndicate to challenge for the Cup, Connor went it alone forming a new syndicate, Sail America, based at his own San Diego Yacht Club. From then on Connor's campaign combined three elements: the quest for money, the building of a design team that would harness the best technical expertise available, and training a crew.

Money was the most pressing need. The effort would require an estimated $10 million (in fact the syndicate spent over $15 million). For much of 1984 Connor travelled corporate America knocking on doors and trying to get access to some of America's richest and most powerful business leaders. By mid-1986, Sail America had attracted seven major sponsors: Allied-Signal, Anhauser-Busch, Atlas Hotels, Ford Motor Co., Henley Group, Merrill Lynch, and the electronics company, SAIC.

Finding and integrating the ideal combination of technical talent was the biggest challenge. A presentation by SAIC which used computer simulation to analyze the hydrodynamic performance benefits of *Australia II*'s winged keel, convinced Connor of the potential of computer-aided design. John Marshall, the coordinator of Sail America's design team explained the process: "In order to make technology work you have to have both proper methodology and creativity. We lacked both in 1983 ... Any concept of a really radical boat was dealt with strictly in the abstract. We were unable at that time to quantify these abstractions and single out the effects of each trade-off ... Lexcen [designer of *Australia II*] and his team in Holland worked up a methodology for predicting a boat's performance. A lot of data go into the program: model towing, meteorological records, information on lift and drag, input from ship hydrodynamics, resistance in different conditions, the integration of the hull and keel, various building materials, a whole array of factors. This is where computer modelling is particularly helpful."

Marshall's technical team included Britton Chance (yacht designer, working with Grumman Aerospace on keel design), Bruce Nelson, expert in computer simulation of boat designs but with no experience of 12 meter yachts, and Dave Pedrick, a highly-analytic naval architect. A meteorologist was hired to analyze weather conditions at the race site, Fremantle, for the previous ten years, and Rob Hoskins, former US Olympic yachting coach was recruited to provide a bridge between the design team and the sailing team.

The design problem for the computer to solve was complex in the extreme. Among the key inputs were:

1 data on the wind and sea conditions off Western Australia;
2 key aerodynamic and hydrodynamic relationships;
3 the "12 Meter Rule" which is a formula relating the boat's length, sail area, depth and weight — the solution of which must equal 12 meters;
4 the performance requirements which the nature of the race determined, in particular, the fact that the America's Cup is a series of one-on-one contests which requires that a boat has the maneuverability and acceleration to exploit opportunities to dominate the rival;
5 Connor's own preference for a boat with high straight speed.

The analysis pointed to the advantages of a long boat. The application of existing technical knowledge, including the winged keel concept resulted in the team's first boat, *Stars and Stripes 1985*, which, although fast, did not represent a technological breakthrough. Intelligence reports revealed that competitor syndicates were also working on innovatory hull and keel designs — more was called for. Subsequent computer simulation followed by tank testing of a one-third scale model, resulted in the development of an innovative "stepped-bow" design which greatly reduced drag. However, the team's next boat, *Stars and Stripes 1986* failed to translate the new features into superior performance. Only by hectic redesign, testing, and additional funds, was the final boat, *Stars and Stripes 1987* ready for the competition. The final innovation was the application to the hull of a grooved, plastic skin, developed by 3M Corporation in cooperation with NASA, to reduce friction with the water.

Crew selection and training was the responsibility of Connor. On crew selection Connor was clear about his priorities:

The three major factors to consider in a successful crew are attitude, attitude and attitude. What we required of everyone was a total commitment to the commitment ... By and large, those who made the team did so because they were prepared to devote themselves 100 percent to the job. I made it clear to everyone from the beginning that no one would make the team unless he or she put winning the Cup ahead of everything else: families, social lives, money, sex, religion, friendships. It had to be give all or give nothing at all.

Early in 1984 the Sail America team set up camp on Hawaii, selected because of similar wind and sea conditions to Western Australia. There followed nearly three years of intensive and relentless training. A key element of this, explained Connor, was developing the team as winners:

Although, unlike the Australians, we never went in for sports psychologists, there were times when I spoke to the guys collectively and individually about how to lift their game ... I told them they had made it into the program because they were winners, because they had earned the right to be there through sheer hard, relentless work. But to stay at the top they had to continue to see themselves as winners.

I never allowed negativity to enter our thinking. I never criticized them in front of their peers or friends. They were my crew and they knew I would fight like hell to support them just as I expected them to support me. I told them that was what a champion team was all about ... But this wasn't just talk. I believed they had to go out and experience things for themselves. Beating a sailor as good as Harold Cudmore in 20 knots of wind does more for a crew's psychology than a room full of shrinks could do.

Sources: Dennis Connor, *Comeback: My Race for the America's Cup* (St. Martins Press, New York, 1987); "The America's Cup: May the Best Technology Win", *Business Week*, February 2, 1987, p. 74; "In the Grooves", *Yachting*, April 1987, pp. 67, 126, 127.

Fundamental to the successful launching of the Beatles was the strategic role played by their manager Brian Epstein. Epstein, shy, insecure, and inexperienced, was an unlikely pop music entrepreneur, yet, in guiding the Beatles from a Liverpool cellar to international adulation, he was brilliant. From the beginning he had clear objectives of commercial and popular success for the band. It was his vision of managing a successful rock band that raised the Beatles' own aspirations. Although an outsider to the pop music business, he showed remarkable insight into the determinants of success, both in terms of what appealed to teenager consumers, and in how to gain access to the showbiz industry. He clearly recognized the Beatles' abilities, both in terms of musical potential and as appealing extroverts with great reserves of vitality and humor. Under his direction the Beatles were transformed from a bunch of scruffy beatniks into a well-groomed, smartly-uniformed, carefully stage-managed group of avant-garde youngsters who not only appealed to the teenagers of the world, but were also acceptable to their parents and to the industry. He put the strategy into effect with flair, resolution, attention to detail, and sensitivity to the personalities and needs of each of the four band members.

The victory of the Vietnamese forces over the French and then the Americans is a classic example of how, despite inferior resources, a sound strategy pursued with total commitment over a long period can achieve final victory. Apart from a few lapses (such as the near-disastrous Tet Offensive), Giap pursued a protracted war of limited engagement. So long as the American forces were constrained by domestic and international opinion from using their full military might, the strategy was unbeatable once it had begun to sap the willingness of the American government to fight. Giap's strategy of a three-stage war successfully exploited North Vietnam's nationalist will-power and his military leaders' superior understanding of the environment while protecting against weaknesses of military resources. In addition, the Vietnamese strategy combined long-term planning with the short-term flexibility needed to adjust tactics to changing circumstances. The persistence of the Vietnamese communists in implementing their strategy was in marked contrast to the ambiguity and dissent which characterized American and South Vietnamese conduct of the war.

Single-minded devotion to a single goal was also the driving force behind the challenge of Dennis Connor and his Sail America syndicate for the 1987 America's Cup. The basis of Connor's campaign between 1984 and 1986 was a clear recognition that in order to win the Cup he needed, first, the best technical expertise that America could offer to design a boat that was at least as fast as anyone else's; secondly, a crew that was unrivalled in terms of commitment, fitness, and coordination. Having determined what was needed, the task was to acquire the key resources of technology and sailing ability, to integrate them, and to match them to the requirements for victory under the rules of the game and the specific environmental conditions of the race venue.

Despite the differences between the three organizations and their activities, clear similarities can be discerned in their strategies. In none of the three was strategy a detailed plan of action; it was primarily a sense of direction which was founded upon three key elements:

- *Objectives which were long-term, simple, and agreed.* Epstein wanted to develop a band that would be "bigger than Elvis". The North Vietnamese leadership wanted to expel Western powers from South Vietnam and reunify Vietnam under communist rule. Connor wanted to recapture the America's Cup.
- *Profound understanding of the competitive environment.* Epstein possessed intuitive understanding of the combination of music and image necessary to appeal to the newly-affluent teenagers of the 1960s. Giap understood his enemy and the battlefield conditions under which he would engage them. Connor appreciated the essence of the game: to combine seamanship with technology.
- *Objective appraisal of resources.* The image which Epstein established for the Beatles built upon the band members' youth, humor, spontaneity, and irreverence. Epstein and record producer George Martin encouraged the Beatles to move away from conventional American popular music style and themes and develop a sound which exploited their own creativity and individualities. Giap's strategy was carefully designed to protect against his weaknesses in arms and equipment, while exploiting the commitment and loyalty of his troops. Connor recognized his own sailing skills, but was acutely aware of the need for advanced technology.

Not only were the strategies sound, but their implementation was effective. Epstein, Giap, and Connor were leaders of quite different styles, but all demonstrated enthusiasm, involvement, and effectiveness in developing commitment and unity of purpose. They developed organizational structures which were appropriate to the type of organization and to the tasks to be performed. A feature of all three was their exploitation of the specialist skills of individual organization members matched by integration through effective coordination and communication.

These observations about the role of strategy in success can be made in relation to most fields of human endeavor. Whether we look at military warfare, political campaigns, sport, or business, the successful organizations are not selected by some random process, nor is superiority of initial endowments of skills and resources typical. It is strategies which build upon commitment to clear objectives, upon understanding of the environment, and the appreciation of strengths and weaknesses that, in the long term, prevail.

The same goes for people. What do Margaret Thatcher, Ken Olsen of Digital Equipment, golfer Jack Nicklaus, army general Ariel Sharon, and pop star Michael Jackson have in common, other than remarkable success in their chosen area of activity? What about the "high achievers" among your own circles of friends and acquaintances? My own observations support the view that these successful individuals in terms of recognition, power, and material rewards are not necessarily, nor most commonly, those with the greatest innate abilities. Central to the success of individuals within each of their highly competitive spheres is the pursuit of strategies which share the elements identified above:

- *They have clear, long-term career objectives.* Equally importantly, those career goals take primacy over the multitude of life's other goals – friendship, love, leisure, knowledge, spiritual fulfillment – which the majority of us spend most of our lives contemplating, juggling, and reassessing.
- *They know their environment.* They are adept in selecting the careers which offer the best opportunities and, once in, they tend to be fast learners in terms of understanding "the game", namely, what needs to be done to secure advancement in a particular career or organization.
- *They know themselves well.* In particular they appreciate their strengths and weaknesses in terms of what activities they can perform well and those they cannot.
- *They pursue their careers with commitment, consistency and determination.*

These four ingredients of successful strategies: clear objectives, understanding the environment, resource appraisal, and effective implementation will form the key components of our analysis of business strategy. These principles are not new, over 2,000 years ago Sun Tzu wrote:

> Know the other and know yourself:
> Triumph without peril.
> Know Nature and know the Situation:
> Triumph completely.[1]

As a preliminary to developing our analysis of business strategy, let us trace the historical development of strategy.

The Development of Business Strategy

Origins and military antecedents

Business enterprises, successful ones in particular, have always had strategies, yet, before the early 1960s, business strategy scarcely existed as a distinct area of business analysis. Many of the concepts and theories of business strategy have their antecedents in military strategy, which extend back to principles enunciated by Julius Caesar and Alexander the Great[2] and beyond to Sun Tsu's classic treatise written around 300 BC.[3]

The applicability of the principles of military strategy to business is a subject of continuing controversy. What is agreed, however, is that military strategy yields important insights into business management, the most basic being the military distinction between strategy and tactics:

- Strategy is the overall plan for deploying resources to establish a favorable position.
- A tactic is a scheme for a specific action.

While tactics are concerned with the maneuvers necessary to win battles, strategy is concerned with winning the war. Strategic decisions, whether in the military or the business sphere, share three characteristics:

- they are important;
- they involve a significant commitment of resources;
- they are not easily reversible.

Armies and business enterprises have similar needs for strategy, both possess objectives. For the army, they are established by the government; for the enterprise, they are established by its board of directors. For both, the competitive situation arises from the incompatibility between the objectives of different organizations. For example, both Britain and Argentina wanted control of the Falkland Islands in 1983; both Coca Cola and Pepsi Cola wanted the largest share of the US cola market during the 1980s. Resources are similar in an army and a business enterprise: Both possess people, capital equipment, and technical skills that they must deploy to achieve their objectives. Both face external environments determined partly by exogenous factors (the terrain in military conflict, the market in business competition) and partly by the strategies pursued by the rivals.

Hence, the general framework for the formulation of military strategy in terms of the basic trinity of objectives, resources, and an external environment, is similar to that facing business firms.

At the more detailed level, there are specific theories of military strategy that can be applied to business situations. These theories concern the principles that determine advantage under different environmental circumstances and for adversaries with different relative resources. They can therefore be used to formulate appropriate strategies. A number of attempts have been made to apply theories of military strategy to business situations. Arithmetic theories of numerical superiority – for example, Lanchester's theories of the outcome of battles as a function of number of troops, firepower, and rate of reinforcement – have been applied, notably by Japanese business strategists to predicting critical levels of market share.[4] Military theories of the relative strengths of offensive and defensive strategies; of the merits of outflanking as opposed to frontal assault; of the roles of flexible and graduated responses to aggressive initiatives; and the potential for deception, envelopment, escalation and attrition all have been used to justify and to guide business strategies.[5] Some military analysts have formulated general principles of superiority, for example, Liddell Hart, the military historian, observed: "The principles of war can be condensed into a single word *concentration*. But for truth this needs to be amplified as the *concentration of strength against weakness*."[6]

On a more analytic basis, Schelling's classic study, *The Strategy of Conflict*, formulates the major elements of a theory of strategy common to war and business.[7] This theory deals with the principles of bargaining, threats, mutual distrust, and the balance between cooperation and conflict.

Management practices in the military have had a powerful influence upon strategy implementation by business firms. The traditional features of corporate organizational structure – vertical hierarchy, functional specialization, and line and staff distinction – have their origins in the organization of the modern army. Ideas about leadership and the generation and maintenance of commitment and morale have similar military antecedents. Such similarities are not surprising. Before the establishment of business schools, the military provided the primary training ground for those aspiring to senior management in the private sector.

At the same time, there are some clear differences in the nature of competition between military warfare and business enterprise. The usual objective of war is to defeat the enemy. The purpose of business strategies is seldom so aggressive: most business firms impose limits on their competitive ambitions in seeking coexistence with rather than destruction of competitors. Hence, a closer analogy may be between international relations and business strategy. International relations is concerned with the management of peace and war; only when diplomacy breaks down do nations resort to war. Similarly, business relations typically comprise a duality between cooperation and competition. Competition at times may be intense, but seldom between established rivals does it become destructive.

The development of business strategy analysis

The shift in the focus of strategy from military to business applications reflects a movement over time in the principal medium of competition between nations and groups. Until the early twentieth century the wealth of nations and individuals was determined primarily by ownership and control over land. Competition between countries mainly involved a quest for territory which was pursued through military conflict. Industrial development and the growth of trade has changed the basis of competition from the quest for land to the quest for customers. The consequences are twofold: first, economic competition has displaced military rivalry; secondly, the front-line players in world competition are companies rather than governments.[8]

Explicit interest in business strategy emerged in the US during the late 1950s and early 1960s in response to the problems of managing large, complex corporations. The main problem for large, complex enterprises was coordinating individual decisions and maintaining top management's overall control. The development of annual financial budgeting procedures provided a vital vehicle for such coordination and control, but coordinating capital investment decisions required a longer planning horizon. The emphasis on longer-term planning during the 1960s reflected concern with achieving coordination and consistency of purpose during an expansionary period. The post-war period was one of unprecedented stability and growth which was conducive to the expansion of large enterprises. As companies sought efficiency and control of risk through scale-efficient production, mass marketing, vertical integration, and large long-term investments in technology, so long-term planning based upon medium-term economic and market forecasts became popular. The typical format was a five-year corporate planning document which set goals and objectives, forecast key economic trends, established priorities for different products and business areas of the firm, and allocated resources. A central issue in corporate planning was diversification. During the 1960s and 1970s diversification was perceived as the main route to corporate growth and profitability and the principal stategic responsibility of corporate management. Indeed, Igor Ansoff defined strategy in terms of the firm's diversity: "Strategic decisions are primarily concerned with external rather than internal problems of the firm and specifically with selection of the product-mix which the firm will produce and the markets to which it will sell."[9] During the 1970s, portfolio planning matrices (see chapter 13) came into vogue as frameworks for selecting strategies and allocating resources within the diversified corporation.

The enthusiasm for corporate planning during the 1960s and early 1970s paralleled the infatuation of governments and public authorities with economic, social, and investment planning. In both private and public sectors this interest in planning reflected the development of new "scientific" techniques of decision making and policy formulation: cost-benefit analysis, discounted cash flow techniques, linear programming, econometric forecasting, and Keynsian macroeconomic management. The transition of business enterprise from entrepreneurial capitalism to managerial "technocracy" was analyzed by J. K. Galbraith.[10] In Galbraith's view, the size, risks, and time-scale of new investment implied the superiority of planning by firms over the haphazard workings of markets.

However, by the mid-1970s, attitudes and circumstances had changed. Accumulating evidence on the failure of diversification to yield the synergy gains predicted by strategy analysis resulted in a slowing down in the drive towards conglomeration. At the same time, increasing macroeconomic instability (associated in particular with the oil price explosion of 1974–5) discredited the elaborate planning systems installed by many leading corporations during the previous decade. As the world entered a period of turbulence, firms were forced to abandon their medium-term corporate plans in favor of more flexible approaches to strategic management. The increase in international competition during the 1970s and 1980s was a further factor rquiring fundamental redirection of companies' approaches to strategy. As US firms' preeminence across a wide range of world industries from steel to banking was increasingly challenged, so interest shifted away from issues of diversification and the matching of new capacity to anticipated increases to demand, towards the critical issue of competitiveness in individual industries and markets. In consequence, top management now perceive their strategic role in terms of strategic management rather than corporate planning. The key features of this new approach to strategy are:

- a central concern with building competitive advantage by combining monitoring and analysis of the industrial environment with appraisal and development of internal resources;
- a rejection of the rigidity of detailed corporate plans and an embracing of flexibility;
- disillusion with corporate planning departments as the primary source of strategy formulation, and a relocation of strategy formulation in the hands of the same managers who are responsible for its implementation.

The evolution of strategic planning between the 1950s and 1980s has been divided into four stages by senior management consultants with McKinsey & Company. These are shown in Exhibit 1.2.

Exhibit 1.2   The four stages in the evolution of strategic planning systems

	Phase 1 Basic financial planning	Phase 2 Forecast-based planning	Phase 3 Externally-orientated planning	Phase 4 Strategic management
Dominant priority	Operational control	More effective planning for growth	Increasing response to markets and competition	Orchestration of resources to create competitive advantage
Main features	Annual budget Functional focus	Environmental medium-term forecasts Static resource allocation	Competitive analysis Evaluation of strategy alternatives Dynamic resource allocation	Strategically chosen planning framework Creative, flexible planning processes. Supportive value system.
Value system	Meet the budget	Predict the future	Think strategically	Create the future

Source: F. W. Gluck, S. P. Kaufman, A. S. Walleck, "Strategic management for competitive advantage", *Harvard Business Review*, July–August 1980, pp. 154–61.

[handwritten margin note: New approach to strategy.]

The Nature of Strategy

Competition provides the rationale for strategy. Without competition strategy is empty; it is concerned only with establishing objectives, forecasting the external environment, and planning resource deployments. The essence of strategy is the *interdependence* of competitors. Because actions by one player affect outcomes for other participants, each player's decisions must take account of other players' expected reactions. Games of strategy like poker and chess are thus radically different from games of chance such as bingo and games of skill such as archery.

Competition occurs whenever resources are finite and competitors' objectives are mutually inconsistent. What separates competition in human society from competition among other species is strategy. The evolutionary process is driven by natural competition which involves no strategy. Genetic mutation results in variety and those varieties which are best adapted to the prevailing environment multiply their numbers. Varieties which are less well adapted to their environment die out.

Among humans and the organizations they create, competition is different. Unlike other living organisms, human beings have the capacity to anticipate competitors' actions and, on the basis of their expectations, to adjust their behavior and characteristics. In contrast to natural competition, which is governed by an environmentally-determined selection process, the capacity for strategic behavior results in *strategic* or *rational* competition. The essential requirements for strategic competition have been specified by Bruce Henderson, founder of the Boston Consulting Group:[11]

- a critical mass of knowledge concerning the competitive process;
- the ability to integrate the knowledge and understand cause and effect;
- the imagination to foresee alternative actions and logic to analyze their consequences;
- the availability of resources beyond current needs in order to invest in future potential.

Although strategic competition is a feature of many fields of human interaction, comparatively little progress has been made in establishing general theories of competition. One reason is that economic analysis has been dominated by the concept of *perfect competition* and *monopoly*. Both these limiting cases of competition lack any competitive rivalry. In the case of pure monopoly this is because there are no rivals and no risk of entry. In the case of perfect competition there are so many competitors that each firm is unconscious of rivalry. In reality, most industries comprise a fairly small group of leading firms; to use the jargon of economic theory they are *oligopolies*. In these industries, the complexity of the interactions between firms has meant competitive behavior and industry outcomes can only be predicted with precision in highly abstract models based on very restrictive assumptions.[12]

This complexity and indeterminacy of competitive behavior and performance in oligopoly industries with closely-matched competitors has an important implication for the emphasis of our strategy analysis in this book. The priority will be less on "playing competitive games" through anticipating competitors' moves and engaging in bluff and counterbluff, threat, and deterrence, and much more on seeking insulation from the uncertainties of competitive interaction through establishing a position of sustainable advantage over rivals. This notion that the primary goal for strategy is the establishment of unique advantages over competitors is consistent with an ecological approach to business strategy. Bruce Henderson argues that the implication of Gause's Principle that competitors who make their living in the same way cannot coexist implies that each business must differentiate itself:

Strategy is a deliberate search for a plan of action that will develop a business's competitive advantage and compound it. For any company, the search is an iterative process that begins with a recognition of where you are now and what you have now. Your most dangerous competitors are those that are most like you. The differences between you and your competitors are the basis of your advantage. If you are in business and are self-supporting, you already have some kind of advantage, no matter how small or subtle . . . The objective is to enlarge the scope of your advantage, which can only happen at someone else's expense.[13]

The starting-point for analysis: the goal of the firm

The strategy literature is littered with a multitude of alternative definitions of business strategy. I shall not attempt to compete here, but simply offer a small sample of definitions proposed by leading authorities (see Exhibit 1.3). Rather than start with some prior definition of strategy, my approach is to define strategy in terms of what we want it to do.

The goal of business strategy has been succinctly stated by Alfred P. Sloan Jr., architect of the world's largest industrial enterprise, General Motors, "The strategic aim of a business is to earn a return on capital, and if in any particular case the return in the long run is not satisfactory, then the deficiency should be corrected or the activity abandoned for a more favorable one."[14]

In practice, companies pursue a wide range of goals. This diversity of goals is a reflection of the variety of different interest groups that make up the firm. Cyert and March viewed the firm as a coalition in which different operational goals were associated with different functional interests. For example, sales and marketing would favor seeking increases in sales revenue and market share; production would pursue goals related to the level and stability of output. More recent approaches have taken a "stakeholder" approach – viewing the corporation as a coalition of a number of interests including shareholders, managers, and other employees.

While strategies can be formulated by taking explicit account of multiple goals, the need to establish priorities and tradeoffs results in excessive

Exhibit 1.3 Some
definitions of strategy

The determination of the long run goals and objectives of an enterprise, and the adoption of courses of action and the allocation of resources necessary for carrying out these goals.

Alfred Chandler, *Strategy and Structure: Chapters in the History of American Industrial Enterprise.*

A strategy is the pattern or plan that integrates an organization's major goals, policies, and action sequences into a cohesive whole. A well-formulated strategy helps to marshal and allocate an organization's resources into a unique and viable posture based upon its relative internal competences and shortcomings, anticipated changes in the environment, and contingent moves by intelligent opponents.

James Brian Quinn, *Strategies for Change: Logical Incrementalism.*

Strategy is the pattern of objectives, purposes or goals and the major policies and plans for achieving these goals, stated in such a way as to define what business the company is in or is to be in and the kind of company it is or is to be.

Kenneth Andrews, *The Concept of Corporate Strategy.*

complication.[15] The case for adopting a single overriding goal for the firm is supported by the fact that, in most industries, the pressure of competition, particularly of international competition, has increased over time. The result has been the apparently conflicting interests of the different constituencies in the firm. The underlying common interest of all stakeholders is the firm's survival. Survival requires that, over the long term, the firm earns a rate of profit which covers its cost of capital. During the 1980s decreasing numbers of business firms had the luxury of being able to diverge substantially from the goal of long-run profit maximization imposed by the need for survival.

The key assumption upon which this book is based therefore is that the purpose of strategy is to increase the long-term profitability of the corporation. This assumption goes a long way to simplifying strategy analysis. At the same time it does not succeed in eliminating ambiguity. What is the firm to maximize: total profit, margin on sales, return on equity, return on invested capital or what? Over what period? With what kind of adjustment for risk? And what is profit anyway: are we concerned with accounting profit, cash flow, or economic rent?

The valuation of firms and strategies

Resolving these problems of the definition of profits, the period over which profits are measured, and the influence of risk calls for a value-maximizing approach. By maximizing the present value of the firm, management maximizes the wealth of the owners of the firm. The present value of the firm (V) is the sum of the future net cash flows of the firm (C) in each period t, discounted at the firm's cost of capital (k). Hence:

$$V = C_0 + \frac{C_1}{1+k} + \frac{C_2}{(1+k)^2} \cdots + \frac{C_n}{(1+k)^n} = \sum_t \frac{C_t}{(1+k)^t}$$

Net cash flow (C), also known as "free cash flow", is the after-tax cash flow generated by the company that is available to all providers of the company's capital, both shareholders and creditors. Starting with earnings before interest and tax ($EBIT$), net cash flow can be calculated as follows:

$$C = EBIT - \text{Taxes} + \text{Depreciation} - \text{Capital expenditure} - \text{Increase in working capital}$$

The net present value of the firm (V) is not an abstract concept. The net present value of the company is equal to the market value of its securities including both equity (E) and debt (D):

$$V = E + D$$

Discounted cash flow (DCF) analysis was developed for the appraisal of individual investment projects; however, it is equally applicable to valuing groups of investment projects, individual business units, or the firm itself. In appraisal of individual projects, the incremental cash flows associated with the project are discounted. The adoption of a strategy for a firm or business unit has implications for all the investment projects undertaken within the firm or business unit. Hence, appraisal of business strategies must be based upon the valuation of the firm or business unit as a whole. The main steps in appraising business strategies are to:

- identify strategy alternatives (the simplest approach is to compare the current strategy with the preferred alternative strategy);
- estimate the cash flows and cost of capital associated with each strategy;
- select the strategy that generates the highest net present value.

Compared to the appraisal of individual investment projects, special problems arise from DCF analysis of strategies. While individual investment projects have finite lives, the firm (or the business unit) is much longer living, and strategies must also be chosen for the long term; hence, forecasting cash flows over long periods of time gives rise to particular difficulties. The Appendix to this chapter discusses in more detail the forecasting of cash flows and the choice of discount rates. Despite the problems, recent years have seen increasing interest in the application of investment valuation techniques to corporate and business strategies in the form of "value approaches" to strategy.[16] A group of consultants from McKinsey and Company explain this trend:

In the last decade, two separate streams of thinking and activity – corporate finance and corporate strategy – have come together with a resounding crash. Corporate finance is no longer the exclusive preserve of financiers. Corporate strategy is no longer a separate realm ruled by CEOs. The link between strategy and finance has become very close and clear. Participants in the financial markets are increasingly involved in business operations through leveraged buyouts, hostile takeovers, and proxy contests. At the same time, chief executives have led their companies to become increasingly active players in the financial markets through self-generated restructurings, leveraged recapitalizations, leveraged buyouts, share

[handwritten margin note: DCF concept is used to assist decision making between options]

repurchases and the like. Financing and investing are now inextricably linked. This new reality presents a challenge to business managers: the need to manage value. They need to focus as never before on the value their companies are creating.[17]

When it comes to issues of multibusiness strategy, the valuation of business units is particularly important since the critical issue in the management of the corporate portfolio is the contribution which individual business units make to the overall value of the corporation. We shall return to this discussion of company valuation in chapter 13. Moreover, the valuation of individual business units within a corporate portfolio is an easier task than the valuation of alternative business strategies for a firm or business unit. Quantitative evaluation of business strategy alternatives in terms of net cash flows discounted at an appropriate cost of capital is made difficult by the fact that most strategies involve a stream of resource-allocation decisions over time, where subsequent investment decisions are contingent upon the performance and information generated by initial investments. As we have already noted, in an increasingly turbulent environment, strategy is less a predetermined program of investment plans and more a positioning of the firm to permit it to take advantage of profitable investment opportunities as they arise. Within this view of strategy, investments in early stages of projects are essentially *options* – they offer the firm the option of further investments in later stages of the projects. For example, investments in research and development typically do not offer direct returns, their value is in the option to invest in new products and processes which may arise from the R&D. DCF does not accurately value investments where there is a significant option value. Conversely, standard option pricing models are applicable only to the specifics of the option contracts offered on the world's major securities markets. In order to assess the value of strategic options it is necessary to specify the successive stages of the investment process, to identify the alternatives available at each stage, and to specify the possible outcomes together with their probabilities.[18]

This discussion of the valuation of firms and strategies has established principles and explored issues, but has made only limited progress in recommending specific techniques. While DCF analysis is the appropriate technique to use in the valuation of firms and investment projects, its application to strategic decision making is limited, first, by the problems of forecasting cash flows for long periods into the future, and second, by the option-like character of most strategic investments. For certain types of strategic decisions (for example, portfolio decisions within the diversified corporation and strategy formulation in stable, mature environments) we shall be utilizing value-maximizing approaches based upon DCF appraisal. Given, however, the broad equivalence of decision rules based upon net present value and those based upon internal rate of return, and given the ability to draw inferences about internal rates of return from accounting rates of return,[19] we can simplify our financial appraisal of business strategies by the adoption of two basic guidelines:

- on existing resources, the firm should seek to maximize the post-tax rate of return earned;
- on new investment, the firm should seek a post-tax rate of return which exceeds its cost of capital.

Sources of profit and the distinction between corporate and business strategy

2 Sources of Superior Performance (handwritten)

If we accept that the fundamental goal of the firm is to earn a return on its capital that exceeds the cost of its capital, what determines the ability of the firm to earn such a rate of return? There are two routes. First, the firm may locate in an industry where favorable industry conditions result in the industry earning a rate of return above the competitive level. Secondly, the firm may attain a position of advantage *vis-à-vis* its competitors within an industry allowing it to earn a return in excess of the industry average.

These two sources of superior performance define the two basic levels of strategy within an enterprise: corporate strategy and business strategy (Exhibit 1.4). Corporate strategy defines the industries and markets in

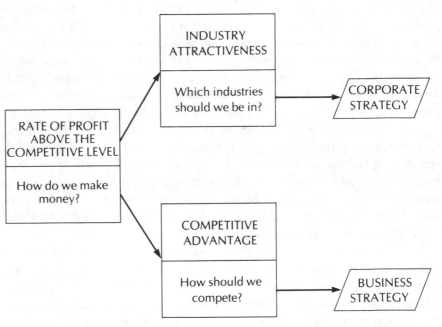

Exhibit 1.4 The sources of superior profitability

which the firm competes, comprising decisions over diversification, vertical integration, acquisitions, divestments and new ventures. It is concerned with the *balance* of the enterprise's portfolio of businesses which is adjusted by corporate decisions over the allocation of resources between the individual businesses.

Business strategy is concerned with how the firm competes within a particular industry or market. If the firm is to win, or even to survive, within an industry, it must adopt a strategy which establishes a competitive advantage over its rivals. Hence, this area of strategy is also referred to as *competitive strategy*.

While business strategy defines the overall approach of the firm to achieving a competitive advantage that is sustainable over time, the detailed deployment of resources at the operational level is the concern of *functional strategies*. This third level of strategy comprises policies towards production, R&D, marketing, personnel, and finance at the industry or at the product level.

In the single-business firm there is no distinction between corporate and business strategy, and in the small, entrepreneurial firm there is unlikely to be any organizational separation of business and functional strategies, or, for that matter, between strategic and operating decisions. In the larger corporation the three levels of strategy are typically separated. Corporate strategy is formulated and implemented at corporate head office. Business strategy is typically formulated jointly by corporate and business unit management, and is implemented at business unit level. Functional strategies are, for the most part, dictated by business strategies, but their elaboration and implementation is primarily the responsibility of the functional departments. Exhibit 1.5 depicts the three levels of strategy and their location within the typical organization structure of the large firm.

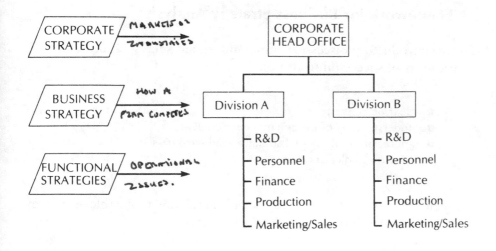

Exhibit 1.5 Levels of strategy

We can view the primary tasks of strategy and the two principal levels of strategy in even simpler terms. The purpose and the content of a firm's strategy is defined by the answer to a single question: How can the firm make money?

On the basis of the two sources of profit, we can elaborate this basic question by two further questions:

- What business should we be in?
- How should we compete?

NB rationalit
approach to business
strategy.

The first of these questions addresses the primary concern of corporate strategy; the second defines the scope of business strategy.

For the greater part of this book my emphasis will be on business rather than corporate strategy. This is justified by my conviction that the key to successful performance is establishing competitive advantage. A consequence of the increasing intensity of competition is that there are few industries where satisfactory profitability is assured for all participants, hence competitive advantage is a prerequisite for long-term profitability. A second reason is that in the development firms, issues of business strategy generally precede those of corporate strategy. Once the firm is established, its survival and success is dependent upon building competitive advantage in a single market. Only when it is successful in one product market can it contemplate diversification into other areas. Hence, issues of diversification and the allocation of resources between different business activities are typically the concern of mature organizations that have already achieved success as specialist enterprises. Even for the diversified corporation, business strategy must take precedence over corporate strategy: Issues of resource allocation between different activities are redundant if the firm is unable to establish competitive advantage in any of its activities.

A Framework for Business Strategy Analysis

In the introductory discussion of organizational success, I identified four ingredients of successful strategies:

- clear objectives;
- understanding of the external environment;
- appreciation of internal strengths and weaknesses;
- effective implementation.

Exhibit 1.6 displays these four ingredients in relation to the role of strategy as the link between the firm and its environment.

Exhibit 1.6   Strategy: The link between the firm and its environment

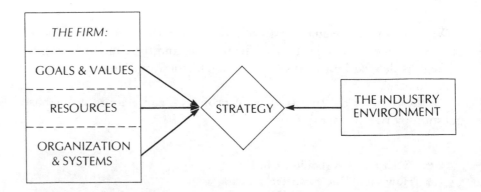

The firm is a complex institution, but for analytic purposes it is useful to distinguish just three key characteristics:

- its goals and values;
- its resources;
- its organization and systems.

The external environment of the firm comprises all external influences which influence the firm's performance and decisions. These include the economy, the political structure, the social system, and the state of technology. However, for most business strategy decisions, the relevant part of the firm's environment is its industry and is defined by the firm's network of relationships with competitors, suppliers and customers.

The task of business strategy, then, is to determine how the firm will deploy its resources within its environment, to select the organizational structure and management systems needed to effectively implement that strategy, and so satisfy its long-term goals.

The analysis that I shall be developing in this book is mainly concerned with the role of strategy in linking the firm's resources with its environment. Limited attention is given to the goals and values of the firm: these are matters for managers to identify rather than to analyze, and, in any event, I have already assumed the basic goal of the firm to be the pursuit of profit.

The prerequisite for a strategy to be successful is that of *fit*: a strategy must be consistent with the firm's goals and values, with its organization and systems, with its resources, and with its environment. Let us examine these four aspects of strategic fit in a little more detail.

Strategic fit

Consistency with goals and values So far we have viewed the primary objective of the firm as long-run profitability. But, on its own, the goal of profitability provides little in the way of direction as to the strategy which a firm should pursue. Also, the quest for profit is a goal which is unlikely to inspire the wholehearted commitment of the organization's members. For both these reasons, companies may need a more precise idea of their purpose which can guide strategy, provide unity among disparate personal motivations, and, ultimately, give meaning to the existence of the company. This concept of organizational purpose is typically based upon the personal "vision" of the company founder – how the company will develop and what contribution it will make to the unfolding of the future. Examples of such visions include Steve Jobs' idea of "one person–one computer" which provided the motivating vision behind Apple Computer's early development, and the vision of a truly reliable mail service which inspired Fred Smith to found Federal Express.

The value of such a vision is that it communicates the motivation of the founding entrepreneur or the top management team to the organization as a whole, and, more importantly, it relates the objectives of the firm to a set of personal values which can harness the diverse interests and aptitudes of the organization's members and motivate them in a common direction. Profit, although essential for the long-run survival of the firm, cannot provide inspiration. Values on the other hand can offer the meaning required to unite and motivate the organization's members and, in Peters and Waterman's terminology, to yield "extraordinary performance from otherwise ordinary people."[20] The phenomenal success of Apple Computer in developing innovatory personal computers of unsurpassed user-friendliness owed much to Steve Jobs' vision of "one person–one computer." The power of the vision was its revolutionary implications. To the extent that information is the basis of power in modern society, widespread ownership of computers meant a transfer of power from corporations and government to the people, and to the young in particular. The enthusiasm, dedication, and gruelling team-work of Apple's young workforce in designing and bringing to market the uniquely user-friendly Apple II and Macintosh computers was dependent upon the inspiration which Jobs' vision gave to a group of brilliant young engineers and designers. Similarly, McDonald's ability to sell 60 billion hamburgers in 86 countries and in doing so make huge profits both for itself and its franchisees cannot be explained by reference just to low costs, quality control or advertising. The organization is driven not by profit alone, nor by the desire to sell hamburgers, but by a philosophy that transcends social class and national culture and is enshrined in the values of "quality, consistency, cleanliness, and value."

To communicate and make a vision explicit and action-orientated, many companies have adopted what is known as "mission statements" which define the goals, values, and overall direction of the company.

American Express's mission is simple: to be the best at what it does. This means a never-ending search for excellence by attracting outstanding people who embrace entrepreneurship and flexibility in managing change; creating premium products with strong brand names that are provided through carefully targeted marketing channels; an individual and corporate commitment to community involvement and citizenship; and, above all, consistent and uncompromising quality in all we do.

American Express Company, 1988 Annual Report, p. 6.

The Golden Rule of L. L. Bean: Sell good merchandise at a reasonable profit, treat your customers like human beings, and they'll always come back for more.

Extract from L. L. Bean Inc. magazine advertisement.

MCI's mission is leadership in the global telecommunications services industry. Profitable growth is fundamental to that mission so that we may serve the interests of our stockholders and our customers.

MCI Communications Inc.

Consistency with the industry environment   Industries differ according to the nature of customer requirements, the characteristics of the product, and competitive structure. These factors determine the principal sources of competitive advantage. Unless a strategy is directed towards exploiting the opportunities for competitive advantage offered by the industry, the firm will not succeed. In resource-based industries producing semi-finished producers' goods such as steel bars, petrochemical feedstocks, and wood pulp, the potential for product differentiation is limited and strategies must be directed towards minimizing costs through scale efficiency and well-coordinated vertical integration. In a highly segmented industry, such as the garment industry, a number of different strategies may be viable. For non-fashion garments products with comparatively stable demand (e.g. socks, T-shirts), a low-cost strategy based on long production runs might be appropriate. In the high quality and fashion segments of the market, a large number of niche positions are available to firms which differentiate their products by quality, style, branding, and exclusivity.

Fit between strategy and the business environment also requires that strategy is adjusted in response to or, preferably, in anticipation of environmental change. It took the best part of a decade for the US automobile manufacturers to respond to the growing domestic demand for smaller cars. In the meantime the "Big Three" (Ford, GM, and Chrysler) yielded this growth sector of the market to European and Japanese imports.

Consistency with resources   Strategy decisions are investment decisions involving the long-term commitment of resources. The resource demands of a strategy must be consistent with the resource availability of the firm in terms of the *amount* and the *types* of resources. Some of the most spectacular corporate failures are the result of a mismatch between strategy and resources. The aero engine and luxury car manufacturer, Rolls Royce, was driven into bankruptcy in 1971 as a result of insufficient financial resources to support the ambitious RB211 jet engine project. More often, however, it is not financial resources or the firm's tangible assets that determine the success or failure of its strategy, but the firm's skills and competences. Some of the most spectacular failures of diversification strategy, such as Exxon's move into computers and office automation, have been due to the diversifying firm not having the right blend of management skills for developing its new venture. During different stages of a firm's development, different strategies are likely to require different resources. Hence strategy changes are frequently associated with changes in top management. The transformation of Apple Computer between 1984 and 1986 was provoked by a maturing of the personal computer industry that necessitated a change of strategy by Apple. This in turn required different resources: management changes, including the replacement of Steven Jobs by John Scully (former President of Pepsi Cola) reflected the need for more conventional marketing, production, and financial skills to supplement Apple's innovative zeal.

Consistency with organization and systems Successful implementation of a strategy also requires that organization and systems are appropriate to the strategy being pursued. Changes in corporate strategy normally necessitate changes in organizational structure. Thus, product diversification typically involves a functional structure being replaced by a multidivisional structure. Changes in business strategy may also require changes in structure. At General Motors during the 1920s, semi-autonomous product divisions each selling their own range of branded automobiles fitted Alfred Sloan's strategy of product differentiation. By the 1980s GM's strategy had changed radically: the company was then fighting to close the cost differential between itself and its Japanese competitors. In the interests of economies of scale and administration it moved in 1984 to a more centralized structure by combining its six automobile divisions into two.

The firm's management systems also need to be consistent with its strategy. General Electric is consistently regarded as one of America's best managed companies on the grounds of the sophistication and effectiveness of its management systems which have effectively reconciled the pursuit of innovation with cost efficiency and have ensured the continuing success of this highly diverse corporation. In general, different management systems are appropriate to different types of business strategy. Innovation at 3M is encouraged by management systems that permits the "bootlegging" of time and materials for unauthorized research and development projects.

Similarly, cost leadership strategies directed towards short- and medium-term financial targets are likely to require management systems that implement very detailed and rigorous central monitoring of all aspects of operations. In the food-processing industry, Conagra Inc. in the US and Hillsdown Holdings in Britain have achieved remarkable growth of profits from acquiring well-established but poorly performing food processors and implementing rigorous cost-cutting and strict financial control.

Internal consistency Finally, a strategy must be internally consistent. Functional strategies must be consistent with business strategy and the business strategies of the individual business units must be consistent with the corporate strategy of the enterprise as a whole. Achieving such consistency is no easy matter. Consistency between functional strategies requires overcoming the propensity for functional specialists to optimize locally. Bruce Henderson, the founder of the Boston Consulting Group, has observed that: "Every production man's dream is a factory that always runs at capacity making a single product that requires no change ... every salesman would like to give every customer whatever he wants immediately."[21]

Attaining consistency of objectives and decisions between the various departments, units and members of the corporation may be an important function of strategy. While the emphasis of this book is on the *external* role of strategy, through the creation of competitive advantage in the firm's industry, strategy may also fulfill an important *internal* role in so far as strategy formulation provides a mechanism for reconciling divergent goals and plans within the organization.

The Strategy-making Process: Criticisms of the "Rationalist Approach"

As indicated by its title, the concern of this book is analysis. The implicit belief is that the senior management of the organization is able to make an objective appraisal of the enterprise and its environment. To formulate an optimal strategy for the organization and then to implement that strategy. The primary concern of this book is the formulation phase.

This "rationalist" approach to business strategy makes implicit assumptions about the strategy-making process. First, strategy formulation is the preserve of top management: It is the Chief Executive Officer (CEO), possibly assisted by his senior managers, who analyze the current situation, then determine the appropriate direction for the organization. Once formulated, the desired strategy is then passed down for implementation by the lower level of managers.

For most organizations, such a picture is a fiction: the process is less structured, more diffused, and the dichotomization of formulation and implementation is less apparent. Empirical research by Henry Mintzberg and his colleagues at McGill University of the long-term development of strategy in a number of organizations, has identified a number of features of the strategy-making process.[22]

The rational, top-down strategy formulation of the type that I have envisaged in this chapter, is what Mintzberg terms "deliberate strategy". Even here, however, the strategy is unlikely to be the result of decisions by a single person or group, and is likely to reflect a complex political process of negotiation, bargaining, compromise, and window-dressing. However, the strategy we observe in the pattern of decisions of the organization, what Mintzberg terms "emergent strategy", is likely to deviate substantially from deliberate strategy. Deviation occurs for several reasons. To begin with, no CEO has sufficient information to make his or her intended strategy fully explicit: implementation necessitates formulation of the details. Secondly, no CEO has full control over the organization: inevitably the decisions and activities of subordinates deviate from the edicts from above. Thirdly, even in the most rigidly hierarchical organizations, strategy formulation is never the exclusive preserve of top management. Top management has no monopoly over good ideas or decisions; discoveries of better ways of doing things occur at all levels of the organization. Moreover, involvement of middle management in strategy formulation may be essential to gain their commitment to subsequent implementation.

An example of the process by which strategy emerges is Richard Pascale's account of Honda's successful invasion of the US motorcycle market during the 1960s. According to the Boston Consulting Group's analysis, Honda's strategy was an exemplar of the analytic approach to strategy formation based upon the exploitation of the experience curve to attain an unassailable position of cost leadership in the world motorcycle industry.[23] However, Pascale's examination of the facts revealed otherwise.[24] The initial decision to enter the US market was based upon little analysis and comprised no clear plan of how Honda would build a market position. The outstanding success of the Honda 50cc model was a surprise; Honda had believed that its main opportunities lay with its larger bikes. As Mintzberg observes: "Brilliant as its strategy may have looked after the fact, Honda's managers made almost every conceivable mistake until the market finally hit them over the head with the right formula."[25]

Not only is the "rationalist approach" a distortion of the actual process of strategy formulation, it is a rather poor way of making strategy, declares Mintzberg: "The notion that strategy is something that should happen way up there, far removed from the details of running an organization on a daily basis, is one of the great fallacies of conventional strategic management."[26] The problem is that a divide between formulation and implementation precludes learning. In practice the two must go hand in hand, with strategy constantly being adjusted and revised in the light of experience.

Mintzberg uses two images to contrast his conception of strategy formulation from the conventional rationalist approach, that of *planning* and that of *crafting*:

Imagine someone planning strategy. What likely springs to mind is an image of orderly thinking: a senior manager, or a group of them, sitting in an office formulating courses of action that everyone else will implement on schedule. The keynote is reason – rational control, the systematic analysis of competitors and markets, or company strengths and weaknesses, the combination of these analyses producing clear, explicit, full-blown strategies.

Now imagine someone *crafting* strategy. A wholly different image likely results, as different from planning as craft is from mechanization. Craft invokes traditional skill, dedication, perfection through the mastery of detail. What springs to mind is not so much thinking and reason as involvement, a feeling of intimacy and harmony with the materials at hand, developed through long experience and commitment. Formulation and implementation merge into a fluid process of learning through which creative strategies emerge.[27]

My approach here is to follow the "planning" rather than the "crafting" approach advocated by Mintzberg. This is not because I regard planning as necessarily superior to crafting or because I wish to downplay the role of skill, dedication, involvement, harmony, and creativity; such qualities are essential ingredients of successful strategies and successful enterprises. Strategy development is a multidimensional process which must involve both rational analysis and evolution through implementation and experience. But, whatever process of strategy formulation is chosen as most appropriate and whatever the emphasis between analysis and implemen-

the reality of
strategy
development

tation, there can be little doubt as to the importance of systematic analysis as a vital input into the strategy process. Without analysis, the process of strategy formulation, particularly at the senior management level, is likely to be chaotic with no basis for the comparison and evaluation of alternative strategies. The concepts, theories, and analytic frameworks are not alternatives or substitutes for experience, commitment, and creativity. But they do provide useful frames for organizing and assessing the vast amount of information available on the firm and its environment and for guiding decisions, and may even act to stimulate rather than repress creativity and innovation.

Moreover, the two approaches are not antithetical. Clearly the purely-rational, ex-ante approach to strategy formulation is impractical; the strategy process must involve intuition and learning from experience. Yet good strategy analysis can allow the wisdom of experience and implementational issues to be fed into the analysis. Similarly, good analysis can encourage the development of intuition, can promote harmony and involvement, and stimulate creativity. Even though strategy formulation must involve the organization as a whole and occurs through the linking of analysis with action, top management must play a leadership which requires that they are equipped with the appropriate analytic tools for the job. The right analytic tools not only provide the basis for selecting the right strategy, they also provide a framework for rational discussion of alternative ideas and the means to communicate the strategy throughout the organization.

The Role of Analysis in Strategy Formulation

A further reason for not distinguishing too sharply between the role of "scientific" analysis and that of intuition, tacit knowledge, and learning-by-doing is the nature of strategy analysis. Unlike mathematical analysis or chemical analysis, strategy analysis is not firmly based upon an agreed, internally-consistent, empirically-validated body of theory. While it employs theory and theoretical concepts, these are drawn mainly from longer-established social and administrative sciences, particularly from economics, psychology, and organization theory. In this respect it is similar to engineering whose methods and techniques rest heavily upon the principles of physics.

However, even as an applied science, strategy differs substantially from engineering and most other technically-orientated managerial and scientific disciplines in its analytic techniques. The main feature of analytic techniques based upon scientific theory is their ability, once the appropriate data has been entered, to generate solutions to complex problems and to choose between alternatives on the basis of preselected criteria. For instance, linear programming can determine optimal production scheduling, discounted cash-flow analysis can select between alternative investment projects, sampling theory can determine the appropriate size and structure of a market research activity.

A major feature of the techniques that I introduce in this book is that they do not provide solutions. Just as in our personal lives no decision technique can be relied upon to make strategic decisions such as getting married, having children, changing career, or migrating, the same is true in business strategy. There are simply too many variables to reduce strategy analysis to a programmed algorithm.

The purpose of strategy analysis is not to provide answers but to help us to understand the issues. Many of the analytic techniques introduced in the book are simply frameworks to assist us to identify, classify, and understand the principal factors which impinge upon strategy decisions. Such frameworks are invaluable in getting to grips with the complexities of strategy decisions: The infinite complexity of the firm's environment, and the tangle of people, resources, structures, and traditions that make up the business enterprise. In some instances the most useful contribution may be in assisting us to make a start on the problem: by guiding us to the questions which we need to answer and providing a framework for fitting the information gathered into, we are in a superior position to a manager who relies exclusively upon experience and tacit knowledge. Finally, analytic frameworks and techniques can assist our flexibility as managers. The analysis in this book is general in its applicability, it is not specific to particular industries, companies or situations. Hence, it can help increase our confidence and effectiveness in understanding and responding to new situations and new circumstances.

Summary

We have established a number of key propositions concerning business strategy and introduced issues and areas of analysis that will be explored in subsequent chapters.

Strategy is an important determinant of success in most areas of human activity. In military conflict, sport, business, and in our individual careers, a good strategy can create success out of initial weakness. Successful strategies typically comprise four key ingredients:

- they are directed towards unambiguous long-term goals;
- they are based on insightful understanding of the external environment;
- they are based on intimate self-knowledge by the organization or individual's internal capabilities;
- they are implemented with resolution, coordination, and effective harnessing of the capabilities and commitment of all members of the organization.

We are concerned here with the use of systematic analysis in the formulation of winning strategies. Consequently, we shall concentrate upon two of the above ingredients of successful strategies: analysis of the external environment and analysis of internal capabilities.

An important assumption is that the underlying goal of the business enterprise is profit. Hence, our approach is based upon the sources of profit available to the firm. The firm can achieve superior profitability either by locating in a profitable industry or by establishing competitive advantage over rivals. Hence, the firm's strategy is defined by the answers to two basic questions: "Which business should we be in?" and "How should we compete?" The answer to the first question defines *corporate strategy* which is concerned with issues of diversification, entry and exit, and the allocation of resources within the diversified corporation. The answer to the second question defines *business strategy*: How the firm will compete within a specific industry.

The two ingredients of our strategy analysis – environmental analysis and resource analysis – form the basis of both corporate and business strategy decisions, although our primary emphasis for most of this book will be business strategy.

Notes

1. R. L. Wing, *The Art of Strategy: A New Translation of Sun Tzu's Classic "The Art of War"* (Doubleday, New York, 1988), p. 135.
2. V. J. Varner and J. I. Alger (eds), *History of the Military Art: Notes for the Course* (US Military Academy, West Point, NY., 1978).
3. Wing, *The Art of Strategy*, p. 135.
4. For a survey, see Nigel Campbell, "Market share patterns and market leadership in Japan," (Paper presented at Strategic Management Workshop, Brussels, June 7, 1984).
5. For an interesting and informed survey, see Barrie G. James, *Business Wargames* (Penguin Books, Harmondsworth, 1985).
6. B. H. Liddell Hart, *Strategy* (Praeger, New York, 1968).
7. Thomas C. Schelling, *The Strategy of Conflict*, 2nd edn (Harvard University Press, Cambridge, Mass., 1980).
8. George Gilder in *Microcosm: The Quantum Revolution in Economics and Technology* (Simon & Schuster, New York, 1989) argues that this shift of competitive activity from the military to the business sphere is only one aspect of a more fundamental transition from wealth based upon physical resources to wealth based upon ideas and technologies.
9. Igor Ansoff, *Corporate Strategy* (Penguin Books, London, 1985), p. 18.
10. John K. Galbraith, *New Industrial State* (Penguin, Harmondsworth, 1969).
11. Bruce Henderson, *The Logic of Business Strategy* (Ballinger, Cambridge, Mass., 1984), pp. 31–6.
12. Franklin M. Fisher, "Games economists play: a noncooperative view," *RAND Journal of Economics*, 20 (Spring 1989), pp. 113–24.
13. Bruce D. Henderson, "The origin of strategy," *Harvard Business Review*, November–December 1989, pp. 139–43.
14. Alfred P. Sloan Jr, *My Years with General Motors* (Sidgwick and Jackson, London, 1963).

15. See Kenneth R. MacCrimmon, "An overview of multiple objective decision making," in *Multiple Criteria Decision Making*, eds J. L. Cochrane and M. Zeleny (University of South Carolina Press, 1973).

16. A. Rappaport, *Creating Shareholder Value: The New Standard for Performance* (Free Press, New York, 1986).

17. Tom Copeland, Tim Koller and Jack Murrin, *Valuation: Measuring and Managing the Value of Companies* (John Wiley, New York, 1990), p. ii.

18. Option pricing theory is outlined in R. A. Brealey and S. C. Myers, *Principles Corporate Finance* 3rd edition (McGraw-Hill, New York, 1988), chs 20 and 21. For a discussion of option valuation approaches to strategic investments see Stewart C. Myers, "Finance theory and financial strategy," *Interfaces* 14 (January–February 1984), pp. 134–6; and Tom Copeland, Tim Koller and J. Murrin, *Valuation: Measuring and Managing the Value of Companies* (John Wiley, New York, 1990), ch. 12.

19. See: John A. Kay, "Accountants, too, could be happy in a golden age: the accountant's rate of profit and the internal rate of return," *Oxford Economic Papers*, 28 (1976), pp. 447–60; and John A. Kay and Colin Meyer, "On the application of accounting rates of return," *Economic Journal*, 96 (1986), pp. 199–207. For an alternative view see, F. M. Fisher and J. J. McGowan, "On the misuse of accounting rates of return to infer monopoly profit," *American Economic Review*, 73 (1983), pp. 82–7.

20. Tom Peters and Robert Waterman, *In Search of Excellence* (Harper and Row, New York, 1982).

21. Bruce D. Henderson, *The Logic of Business Strategy* (Ballinger, New York, 1984), pp. 26–7.

22. See Henry Mintzberg, "Of strategies: deliberate and emergent," *Strategic Management Journal*, 6 (1985), pp. 257–72 and *Mintzberg on Management: Inside our Strange World of Organizations* (Free Press, New York, 1988).

23. Boston Consulting Group, *Strategy Alternatives for the British Motorcycle Industry* (HMSO, London, 1975).

24. R. T. Pascale, "Perspective on strategy: the real story behind Honda's success," *California Management Review*, May–June 1984 pp. 47–72.

25. H. Mintzberg, "Crafting strategy," *Harvard Business Review*, July–August 1987, p. 70.

26. Ibid., p. 70.

27. Ibid., p. 66.

APPENDIX: Valuing a Company or a Business Unit[1]

The net present value of a company or business unit (V) is the free cash flow (C) in each period t discounted at the cost of capital (k):

$$V = \Sigma_t \frac{C_t}{(1 + k)^t}$$

Using this basic formula involves two problems: first, forecasting cash flows in each period over the lifetime of the firm; secondly, estimating the appropriate cost of capital.

THE CONCEPT OF STRATEGY

The problem of forecasting cash flows a long way into the future can be simplified in several ways.

If the firm is in a static business situation and is expected to earn a constant cash flow into perpetuity, then:

$$V = \frac{C}{k}$$

In such a situation, the firm's invested capital is constant, hence depreciation is equal to capital investment and it is possible to express our valuation formula in terms of accounting profits:

$$V = \frac{C}{k} = \frac{EBIT - Tax}{k} = \frac{I.r}{k}$$

Where: $EBIT$ is earnings before interest and tax,
I is invested capital,

r is post-tax, pre-interest return on invested capital $= \dfrac{EBIT - Tax}{I}$

If cash flows are growing at a constant rate g into infinity, then:

$$V = \frac{C}{k - g}$$

Since: $C = EBIT - Tax + Depreciation - Replacement$ investment expenditure $-$ New investment expenditure
and, Replacement investment expenditure $=$ Depreciation
and, New investment expenditure $= g.I$
then:

$$V = \frac{I(r - g)}{k - g}$$

In general, however, it is not possible to make any reliable forecast of cash flows beyond a certain valuation horizon. Hence, a more practical approach to valuing the firm may be to estimate the cash flows up to the valuation horizon (H), then to calculate the value of the firm at time H (V_H) which is called the "horizon value" or "continuing value":

$$V = \underbrace{C_0 + \frac{C_1}{1 + k} + \frac{C_2}{(1 + k)^2} + \dots \frac{C_H}{(1 + k)^H}}_{\text{Present value of cash flows}} + \underbrace{\frac{V_H}{(1 + k)^H}}_{\substack{\text{Present value of} \\ \text{horizon value}}}$$

Horizon values can be calculated in different ways. Two simple alternatives are:

(1) *Book value.* If the firm is to be wound up at the end of period H, or if it is anticipated that returns will fall to a level that just covers the firm's cost of capital, then it is reasonable to assume that the book

value of the firm's capital is a reasonable indicator of value at time H.

(2)　*Zero growth after period*. If cash flows become constant after period, then the present value of the horizon value is:

$$\frac{C_H}{k(1+k)^H}$$

Even within a finite horizon period estimating cash flow in each period can be difficult and it may be simpler to apply a forecast growth rate g to current returns. Thus, if a firm grows at a constant rate g over H years at which time its value is equal to its book value, then:

$$V = \frac{I(r-g)}{k-g}\left[1 - \left(\frac{1+g}{1+k}\right)^H\right] + \frac{I(1+g)^H}{(1+k)^H}$$

Estimating cost of capital

The appropriate cost of capital to a firm or to a business unit is the opportunity cost of capital which is the rate of return which the providers of capital could earn on alternative investments of similar risk. The cost of capital to the firm is the *weighted average cost of capital* (k) which is the weighted average of the cost of equity (k_E) and cost of debt (k_D):

$$k = (1 - T)\, L\, K_D + (1 - L)\, k_E$$

Where T is the tax rate on corporate profits and L is leverage:

$$L = \frac{D}{D+E}$$

The cost of debt financing is reduced relative to equity financing by the fact that interest on debt is tax deductible whereas dividends on stock are not. However, this does not imply that debt financing is always preferable to equity financing. As leverage increases, the cost of debt rises due to the increasing risk of bankruptcy, while the cost of equity also rises due to increasing cyclicality of return on equity.

The cost of equity is determined by two factors: the risk-free rate of interest (i) and the risk premium for the firm or for the individual business. The capital asset pricing model predicts that:

$$k_E = i + \beta(R_m - i)$$

Where β is the *beta coefficient* or *coefficient of systematic risk* for the firm or for the business unit, while R_m is the return on the stock market as a whole.

Note

1.　For a more detailed and explicit exposition see R. A. Brealey and S. C. Myers, *Principles of Corporate Finance*, 3rd edn (McGraw-Hill, New York, 1988), especially pp. 59–66 and 173–99.

TWO

Industry Analysis: Assessing Profit Prospects

The reinsurance business has the defect of being too attractive-looking to new entrants for its own good and will therefore always tend to be the opposite of, say, the old business of gathering and rendering dead horses which always tended to contain few and prosperous participants.

Charles T. Munger, Chairman, Wesco Financial Corp.,
extract from the 1986 Annual Report

Introduction

The profitability of a firm, we have observed, is the outcome of two factors: the profitability of the industry in which it is located, and the firm's ability to establish a competitive advantage over its rivals. The choice of the industry or industries in which the firm competes (which business should we be in?) is the concern of corporate strategy. The establishment of advantage within a particular industry (how should we compete?) is the concern of business strategy. In both of these areas of strategy formulation, the analysis of the firm's industry environment plays a central role.

Corporate strategy is concerned with deciding which industries the firm should be engaged in, and the allocation of corporate resources between them. To make such decisions, it is vital that the firm can evaluate the attractiveness of different industries in terms of their likely future profitability. The primary objective of this chapter is to analyze the determinants of industry profitability. Once the determinants of industry profitability are understood, it will then be possible to forecast the future profitability of an industry. Our analysis concentrates upon the role of industry structure in determining competition within the industry, which in turn determines the level of profitability.

Understanding the links between industry structure, competitive behavior, and profitability is critical to the formulation of business strategy. First, understanding the determinants of industry profitability can indicate how strategy can be used to change industry structure in order to improve the balance of competitive forces and improve the industry's profit prospects. Secondly, by understanding the determinants of competition in an industry and the characteristics of customers' demand, we can identify the basis upon which competitive advantage can be established in an industry. Our analysis of competitive advantage will be limited here to the discussion of *key success factors* – the prerequisites for survival and success within an industry. In subsequent chapters we shall analyze the sources of competitive advantage in greater detail.

Consider the brief account of the US tire industry contained in Case Note 2.1. Using this information on the structure of the tire industry, the analysis in this chapter will enable us to understand why competition in the industry has been intense and why profitability has been so low. It will enable us to identify the structural changes in the industry which are likely to be critically important in influencing competition, and what the impact of these structural changes will be on industry profitability. The analysis will direct us to the strategies which may be effective both in improving profitability in the industry and in establishing a competitive advantage over rivals.

Case Note 2.1 The US Tire Industry during the 1980s

Between 1986 and 1987, the US tire industry (SIC 3011) underwent extensive restructuring. In 1986, B. F. Goodrich and Uniroyal combined their tire businesses to form a jointly-owned venture. In 1987–8, Pirelli of Italy acquired 80 percent of Armtek Corporation's subsidiary Armstrong Tire Company, Gencorp (formerly General Tire and Rubber) sold its tire interests to Continental AG of Germany, Firestone Tire and Rubber was bought by Bridgestone of Japan, while the market leader, Goodyear, narrowly avoided acquisition by Sir James Goldsmith. In 1989, Uniroyal Goodrich was bought by Michelin.

The spate of consolidations and acquisitions in the industry were in response to the dismal financial performance of most participants caused by the industry's intensely competitive conditions.

Despite a steady increase during the 1980s in the motor vehicle population of the US and an increase in mileage driven per vehicle, tire demand was depressed by the adoption of longer-lasting radial

Table 2.1

	Shipments (m.)	Value of shipments ($m. 1982)	Imports/ sales (%)	Price index (radials)	Operating income/sales (%)	Return on book value (%)
1978	241	11,924	10.3	86.3	8.31	4.12
1980	181	9,103	12.6	93.6	7.34	2.74
1982	204	9,047	12.5	100.0	8.26	4.45
1984	246	10,777	15.4	92.1	9.04	10.33
1986	246	10,346	17.5	89.9	9.21	2.43
1987	259	10,653	18.8	88.0	10.60	11.05
1988	269	10,973	19.7	87.8	9.80	10.20
1989	257	10,598	19.6	87.5	8.70	7.60

Sources: US Industrial Outlook, S&P Industrial Surveys, 1990.

tires. Apart from cyclical fluctuations, shipments of tires were virtually static. But, due to increased productivity in existing plants, capacity additions by foreign entrants such as Michelin (French), Bridgestone (Japanese), and Continental (German), and rising imports, the industry suffered from a large overhang of excess capacity. Because fixed costs make up a large proportion of the total costs of tire production, there is considerable pressure on the manufacturers to maintain high levels of capacity utilization. This, together with the lack of differentiation in the products of the leading manufacturers and weak customer brand loyalty, is conducive to heavy price competition.

About 25 percent of the market is original equipment. Here, the tire companies sell primarily to the "Big Three" US automobile manufacturers, which in recent years have put intense pressure on their suppliers for higher quality, more frequent delivery, and lower prices. In August 1987, Firestone announced that it had agreed unspecified price reductions on OEM (original equipment manufacturers) tires for 1988 models. Margins are higher in the replacement market, but here too the tire manufacturers contend with the strong bargaining power of the leading tire retailers which include Sears, Montgomery Ward, and the major oil companies such as Exxon and Shell. Many retailers sell under their own brand names.

Raw materials account for about one-third of total production cost. The cost of synthetic rubber is closely linked to the price of oil; the cost of natural rubber is determined in part by the forces of supply and demand and in part by the effectiveness of the producer governments' cartel.

At the beginning of 1990, it was unclear how far structural changes would help to restore the industry's prosperity. Consolidation and plant closures (28 plants closed in the decade to 1989) had brought capacity more closely into line with demand. But some recent entrants were adding new capacity: Bridgestone's acquisition of Firestone was followed by a $1.5 billion program of capital investment. Demand was forecast to grow at between 1 and 2 percent – partly dependent upon the performance of the US automobile manufacturers. Exchange rate movements would largely determine whether this growth would translate into increased output by US factories. Prospects for competition also depended upon the intentions of the foreign-owned producers, Michelin, Continental, Bridgestone, and Pirelli. Would they aggressively pursue market share through further price cutting? A further uncertainty concerned the impact of technology. Would it offer profitable opportunities for new product innovation or would it squeeze profits by making tires longer lasting or improving the quality of retread tires?

From Environmental Analysis to Industry Analysis

A feature of this chapter is that it limits consideration of the firm's environment to its industry environment. Yet, the environment of the firm comprises all the external influences which impinge upon the firm's behavior and performance. The problem for managers is that, given the vast number and range of external influences, how can the firm hope to monitor, let alone analyze environmental conditions? The starting-point is some kind of system or framework for organizing information about the environment. For example, environmental influences can be classified by source into economic, technological, demographic, social, and governmental factors. Another approach is to study the firm's environment at differing levels of aggregation: the "microenvironment" or "task environment" is distinguished from the wider influences which form the "macroenvironment."

Such wide-ranging, systematic, and continuous approaches to environmental scanning may be appropriate for the large, multibusiness corporation. But for most firms, extensive environmental analysis is unlikely to be cost effective and can create information overload. One of the world's largest companies, the Royal Dutch/Shell Group, probably invests more heavily in the monitoring and analysis of its business environment than any other company. Its scenario planning exercises are ambitious and farsighted. Nevertheless, the scope of its environmental scanning and analysis is focussed upon factors which are directly relevant to the group's strategic planning: the price of crude oil; the growth of demand for oil-based products; political developments in OPEC and consumer countries; the changes in technology in energy production; and automobile design.[1]

The prerequisite for effective environmental analysis is to distinguish the vital from the merely important. From the point of view of the firm, the core of its environment is its network of business relationships. These relationships comprise transactions with suppliers and customers, and competitive interactions with rival producers. Hence, the core of the firm's environment is formed by competitors, suppliers, and customers. This arena is the firm's *industry environment*.

This is not to say that macrolevel factors such as general economic trends, changes in demographic structure, or such social and attitudinal trends as the decline of the family and the rise of the "new morality" are unimportant to strategy analysis. These factors may be critical determinants of the threats and opportunities a company will face in the future. However, these more general environmental factors affect the firm through their impact upon the demand for the firm's products, upon its costs, and upon its competitive position relative to its rivals. By focussing on the industry environment we can determine which of the general environmental influences are important for the firm and which are not.

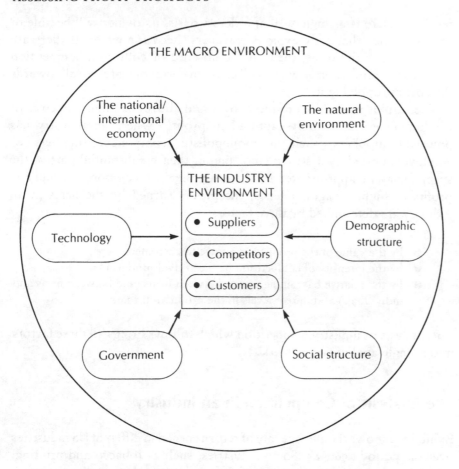

Exhibit 2.1 The business environment

The Determinants of Profit: Demand and Competition

The approach to strategy analysis here is guided by the simple assumption that the purpose of strategy is to help the firm to survive and make money. Hence, the starting-point for industry analysis is to ask: "What determines the level of profit in an industry?"

The basic source of profit is the creation of value for the customer. Production transforms inputs into goods and services for the customer. For production to be profitable, the first criterion is that the value of the product or service created (as measured by the price that the customer is willing to pay) exceeds the cost of the inputs used in its creation. The greater the surplus of value over cost, the greater the potential for profit in an industry. The value of a product or service to a customer is dependent upon the intensity of his or her need and the availability of substitutes.

But potential profit is not actual profit. The surplus of value over cost is distributed between customers and producers by the forces of competition. The stronger the competition between producers, the greater the proportion of the surplus gained by customers ("consumer surplus") and the less is earned by producers ("producer surplus" or "economic rent"). If there is a single well at a desert oasis, its owner will be able to charge a price that fully exploits travellers' need for water. If there are many wells at the oasis, then, in the absence of collusion, competition between their individual owners will cause the price of water to fall towards the cost of supplying it.

The surplus earned by producers over and above the minimum costs of production is not entirely captured in profits. Where an industry has powerful suppliers, such as monopolistic component suppliers or employees united by a strong labor union, then a substantial part of the surplus may be appropriated by these suppliers (in component suppliers' profits or higher wages). Hence, the profits earned by the firms in an industry are determined by three factors:

- by the value of the product or service to customers;
- by the intensity of competition between rival producers;
- by the relative bargaining power between firms (and between firms and individuals) at different levels in the production chain.

The analysis of industry competition which follows brings all three factors into a single analytic framework.

The Analysis of Competition in an Industry

Exhibit 2.2 shows the average rate of return earned in different US industries over the period 1960–85. Some industries, such as tobacco and printing, earned comparatively high rates of profit; others, such as textiles, primary metals, and stone, glass and clay, earn consistently low rates of profit. The basic premise of industry analysis is that the level of industry profitability is neither an historical accident nor the result of entirely industry specific influences, but is determined by the characteristics of *industry structure*. Across the whole range of manufacturing and service industries the nature and intensity of competition is a product of common structural factors.

The underlying theory of the relationship between industry structure, competitive behavior, and industry profitability is provided by the Structure–Conduct–Performance approach to industrial economics which seeks to relate the characteristics of industry structure to the nature of competitive behavior and to the level of industry profitability. The two reference points are the theory of monopoly and the theory of perfect competition, which represent the two ends of the spectrum of industry structures. Where there is a single firm in an industry and new firms are unable to enter, *monopoly* exists: competition is absent and the monopolist can fully exploit customers' need for the product to earn the maximum level of profit available. Where there are many firms in an industry, all producing an identical product, and with no restrictions upon entry, *perfect competition* exists: price competition causes profits to fall to "the

Industry	1960–85 (%)	1981–5 (%)
Scientific instruments	9.1	4.2
Printing	8.6	7.3
Tobacco	8.1	9.5
Miscellaneous manufacture	6.1	5.6
Apparel	7.0	7.4
Electrical machinery	7.0	4.5
Chemicals	6.9	3.8
Transportation equipment	6.6	5.4
Paper	6.6	3.8
Leather	6.4	4.3
Non-electrical machinery	6.1	2.1
Food	6.0	6.1
Fabricated metals	5.7	3.7
Rubber	5.4	2.1
Petroleum	5.3	2.8
Lumber	5.0	0.9
Furniture	4.3	4.3
Stone, glass, clay	4.3	1.1
Textiles	4.2	1.8
Primary metals	2.8	− 2.2

Exhibit 2.2 The after-tax rate of return on invested capital in US manufacturing industries, 1960–85

After-tax return on invested capital is measured as inflation-adjusted, after-tax net income divided by the inflation-adjusted capital stock (net plant and equipment plus investments and intangibles).
Source: Lawrence F. Katz and Lawrence H. Summers, "Industry rents: evidence and implications," *Brookings Papers: Microeconomics 1989* (3), p. 214.

competitive level", a level that just covers the firms' cost of capital. In the real world, industries fall between these two extremes. Exhibit 2.3 identifies some key points on the spectrum. For any particular industry, it is possible to predict the type of competitive behavior likely to emerge and the resulting level of profitability by examining the principal structural features and their interactions.

A particularly useful framework for diagnosing competition in an industry is that developed by Michael Porter of Harvard University.[2]

Structural characteristics	Perfect competition	Oligopoly	Duopoly	Monopoly
No. of firms	Many	Few	Two	One
Barriers to entry/ exit	None	Moderate/ high	Moderate/ high	Very high entry barriers
Product differentiation	None	High	Moderate/ high	Varies

Exhibit 2.3 The spectrum of industry structures

Porter's "five forces of competition model"

The rate of return on invested capital (ROI) in an industry, relative to the industry's cost of capital, is determined by five sources of competitive pressure which impinge upon the firms within the industry (see Exhibit 2.4). These five forces of competition include three sources of "horizontal" competition – competition from the suppliers of substitutes, the threat of competition from entrants, and competition from established producers; and two sources of "vertical" competition – the bargaining power of suppliers and buyers. The strength of each of these competitive forces is determined by a number of key structural variables as shown in Exhibit 2.5.

Exhibit 2.4   Porter's "five forces of competition" framework

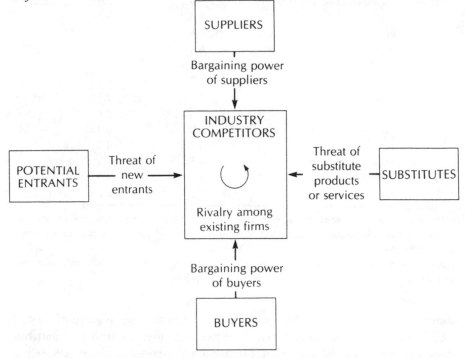

Competition from substitutes

We observed earlier that the potential for profit in an industry is determined by the maximum price that customers are willing to pay. This depends primarily on the availability of substitutes. Where there are few substitutes for a product, as in the case of gasoline or cigarettes, then consumers are willing to pay a potentially high price. In other words, demand is *inelastic* with respect to price. If there are close substitutes for a product then there is a limit to the price that customers are willing to pay and any increase in price will cause some customers to switch towards substitutes. In other words, demand is *elastic* with respect to price. Thus an important constraint upon the pricing policies of the suppliers of frozen foods is the prices of canned and fresh produce.

The extent to which the threat of substitutes constrains industry pricing depends upon two factors:

● the propensity of buyers to substitute;
● the price-performance characteristics of substitutes.

Exhibit 2.5 The structural determinants of competitive pressure

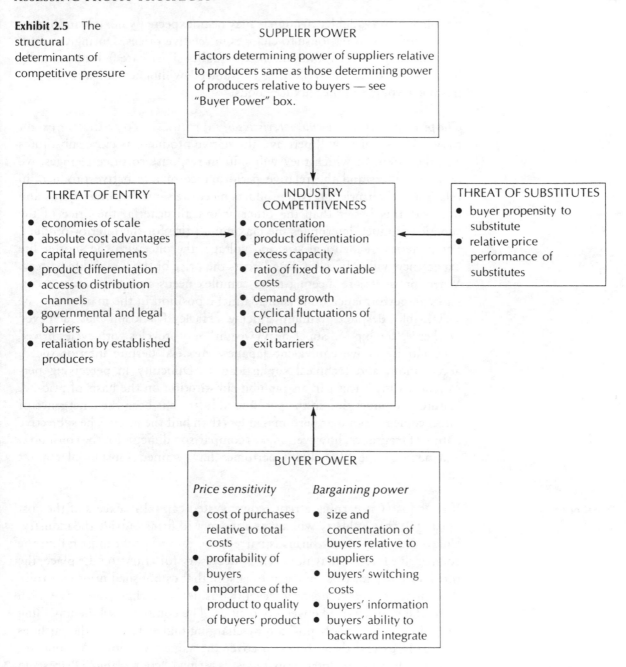

SUPPLIER POWER

Factors determining power of suppliers relative to producers same as those determining power of producers relative to buyers — see "Buyer Power" box.

THREAT OF ENTRY

- economies of scale
- absolute cost advantages
- capital requirements
- product differentiation
- access to distribution channels
- governmental and legal barriers
- retaliation by established producers

INDUSTRY COMPETITIVENESS

- concentration
- product differentiation
- excess capacity
- ratio of fixed to variable costs
- demand growth
- cyclical fluctuations of demand
- exit barriers

THREAT OF SUBSTITUTES

- buyer propensity to substitute
- relative price performance of substitutes

BUYER POWER

Price sensitivity

- cost of purchases relative to total costs
- profitability of buyers
- importance of the product to quality of buyers' product

Bargaining power

- size and concentration of buyers relative to suppliers
- buyers' switching costs
- buyers' information
- buyers' ability to backward integrate

The propensity of buyers to substitute Are there close substitutes for the product or service and how willing are customers to shift their purchases on the basis of changes in relative prices? The critical issue is the willingness to substitute; even though substitutes exist, customers may be unresponsive to changes in relative prices. For example, efforts by city planners to relieve traffic congestion either by charging the motorist or by subsidizing public transport have been remarkably ineffective in encouraging motorists to forsake their cars for buses. Conversely, even when close substitutes are not obviously available, customers may be unexpectedly flexible in shifting their purchases in response to changes in relative prices. During the peak of silver prices in 1980, the demand for quality silverware fell substantially in the US and Europe reflecting consumers' willingness to allocate disposable income to other luxury goods.

The price-performance characteristics of substitutes   To predict the extent to which customers will perceive alternative products as close substitutes and the extent to which they will shift in response to price changes, we need to understand the relative performance of alternative products in relation to their price. If two products meet the same customer needs and one performs better than the other across all criteria, the price of the superior product determines the maximum price for the inferior product. For batteries of identical size and voltage, the one with the shorter life expectancy will only sell if it undercuts the price of the longer-life battery. Where products are meeting more complex needs and no product dominates all performance dimensions, a niche position in the market may be sustainable despite premium pricing. Harley-Davidson has achieved market leadership in "super-heavyweight" motorcycles with cycles priced substantially above equivalent Japanese models, despite inferior speed, acceleration, and technical sophistication. Difficulty in perceiving performance differences can also inhibit substitution on the basis of price. A feature of competition in the perfume industry has been the emergence of direct copies of popular perfumes at less than half the price. The subjective nature of fragrance, however, makes comparison difficult for the consumer, and none of the "knockoff" perfumes have gained substantial market share.

Threat of entry

If an industry is earning a return on invested capital in excess of the cost of capital, that industry will act as a magnet to firms outside the industry. Unless the entry of new firms is barred, the rate of profit must fall to the competitive level. It may not even be necessary for entry to take place, the threat of entry may be sufficient to ensure that established firms constrain their prices to the competitive level. Consider an airline company which offers the only service between two cities. The company will be unwilling to exploit its monopoly position by charging higher fares if other airlines can easily extend their routes to cover the same two cities. An industry where no barriers to entry or exit exist is termed "contestable": Prices and profits will remain at the fully competitive level, irrespective of the number of firms within the industry.[3] Contestability depends critically upon the absence of "sunk costs." Sunk costs exist where entry requires investment in industry-specific assets which cannot be recovered on exit. An absence of such sunk costs implies that the industry is vulnerable to "hit-and-run entry": whenever established firms raise their prices to earn profits in excess of the competitive level, entrants will move in and will compete away excess profits before leaving the industry.

However, in most industries, new entrants cannot enter on equal terms to those of established firms. The size of the advantage of established over entrant firm (in terms of unit costs) measures the height of barriers to entry, which determines the extent to which the industry can, in the long run, enjoy profit above the competitive level. The principal sources of barriers to entry are:

- capital requirements;
- economies of scale;
- absolute cost advantages;
- product differentiation;
- access to channels of distribution;
- governmental and legal barriers;
- retaliation.

Capital requirements   The capital costs of getting established in an industry can be so large as to discourage all but the largest companies. Between 1980 and 1984, Exxon spent over $600 million in a vain attempt to establish Exxon Information Systems as a major player in the office computer systems market. In television broadcasting, Rupert Murdoch spent over $200 million in capital costs and operating losses to establish his Fox Broadcasting as a fourth US national network; while his Sky TV required a similar-sized investment in Europe.

Economies of scale   In some industries, particularly those which are capital intensive or research intensive, efficiency requires producing at a very large scale. In jet engines for commercial airliners, the importance of scale economies has resulted in the survival of just three producers in the world: General Electric, Pratt and Whitney, and Rolls Royce. Moreover, the costs of developing new engine designs are such that these big three are increasingly cooperating through joint ventures. In telecommunications equipment, the economies in spreading large system development costs over large volumes of business has resulted in the industry becoming concentrated around six companies: AT&T, Northern Telecom, Alcatel, Seimens, NEC, and Ericcson. Economies of scale in the development and manufacture of cars have squeezed out small independents such as Jaguar and Saab, and made it a very difficult industry to enter. New entrants are faced with the choice of entering either on a small scale and accepting high unit costs or a large scale and running the risk of drastic underutilization of capacity while they build up sales volume.

Absolute cost advantages   Irrespective of scale economies, established firms may have a cost advantage over entrants across all levels of output. Such advantages are usually associated with "first-mover advantages": By being early into the industry the established firms may have been able to acquire low-cost sources of raw materials and by being in the industry for longer they benefit from economies of learning. For example, in the international petroleum industry, a major barrier to entry was the ownership by the established majors of low-cost sources of crude oil, particularly in the Middle East. In small gasoline engines, Honda and Briggs and Stratton are so far down the experience curve that it is doubtful whether any new entrant could compete on cost.

Product differentiation   In an industry where products are differentiated, established firms possess an advantage over new entrants by virtue of brand recognition and customer loyalty. The percentage of US consumers loyal to a single brand varies from under 30 percent in batteries, canned vegetables and garbage bags, up to 61 percent in toothpaste, 65 percent in mayonnaise, and 71 percent in cigarettes.[4] New entrants into highly differentiated markets must spend disproportionately heavily on advertising and promotion to gain similar levels of brand awareness and brand goodwill as established suppliers. Alternatively, the new entrant can either accept a small market share which can be gradually expanded over the long term or seek to compete by undercutting the established firms on price. In producer goods, too, bonds between suppliers and their customers based on loyalty and understanding of reciprocal needs are often strong. Establishing credibility and goodwill by a new entrant can be slow and costly. It took Apple from 1984 to 1987 to get its Macintosh computer accepted by corporate customers as a serious business computer. In business services such as auditing, advertising, and investment banking, established reputations and relationships create formidable entry barriers.

Access to channels of distribution   Product differentiation barriers relate to the preferences of final customers for established products. However, for consumer goods manufacturers, the biggest barrier may be distributors' preferences for established firms' products. Limited capacity within distribution channels (e.g. shelf space), risk aversion, and the fixed costs associated with carrying an additional product result in distributors' reluctance to carry a new manufacturer's product. In the US and Britain, food and drink processors are increasingly required to make lump-sum payments to the leading supermarket chains in order to gain shelf space for a new product. One study found that, compared to early entrants, late entrants into consumer goods markets incurred additional advertising and promotional costs amounting to 2.12 percent of sales revenue.[5]

Governmental and legal barriers   It has been claimed, notably by economists of the Chicago School, that the only really effective barriers to entry are those created by government. In industries such as taxi-cab services, banking, telecommunications, and broadcasting, entry may require the granting of a license by a public authority. In knowledge-intensive industries, patents, copyrights, and trade secrets are frequently the most effective barriers to entry. Xerox Corporation's near-monopoly position up to the mid-1970s, in the world plain-paper copier business was protected by a wall of over 2,000 patents relating to its xerography process. In industries subject to heavy government involvement through regulation, procurement, and environmental and safety standards, new entrants may be at a disadvantage to established firms because of government officials' preferences for established firms, because of the costs of becoming listed as an "approved supplier", or because the costs of compliance weigh more heavily on newcomers.

Retaliation The effectiveness of all these barriers to entry in excluding potential entrants depends upon the entrants' expectations as to possible retaliation by established firms. Retaliation against a new entrant may take the form of aggressive price-cutting, increased advertising, or a variety of legal maneuvers. Proposals to launch new newspapers frequently lead to threats of advertising rate cuts and increased promotion by the incumbent. In 1987, IBM used threats of litigation over patent and copyright infringement to deter competitors from cloning its PS2 range of personal computers. The likelihood of retaliation also depends upon industry conditions. If entrants restrict themselves, initially at least, to market segments where they do not compete directly with established firms, then reaction is less likely. In the US automobile and television markets, the Japanese entrants initially introduced small products, segments which had been written-off by the domestic producers as inherently unprofitable. The effectiveness of threats of retaliation as an entry barrier depends upon their credibility. It has been argued that threats of aggressive price competition against new entrants are only credible when backed by excess capacity, excess inventories, or a reputation for aggression.[6]

A number of empirical studies have measured the impact of entry barriers on industry profitability. Studies by Bain[7] and Mann[8] found return on equity to be, on average, five percentage points higher in industries with "very high entry barriers" than those with "substantial" or "moderate to low" barriers. Studies using capital intensity and advertising intensity as proxies for scale economy and differentiation barriers respectively, show both variables to be positively related to profitability.[9]

The effectiveness of barriers to entry in deterring potential entrants depends upon the resources of the would-be entrants. Barriers which are effective in impeding the entry of new companies may be ineffective in preventing the entry of firms which are established in other industries. A study by George Yip[10] found, contrary to expectation, that entry barriers had no observable effect in deterring entry. Entrants were able to successfully overcome entry barriers for one of two reasons. They either possessed resources and skills in terms of finance, expertise and transferable brand images, which permitted them to compete effectively with firms already established in the industry using similar strategies, or successfully circumvented entry barriers by adopting different strategies from those of incumbent firms. Examples of firms which used their strong resource bases in existing markets to enter new markets include American Express's use of its brand name to enter a broad range of financial services industries, and Proctor and Gamble's reliance on its product development and marketing strengths to enter health product markets.[11] Examples of how new approaches to competing can negate or circumvent entry barriers include:

- the emergence during the late 1980s of Drexel Burnham Lambert Inc. as a major player in investment banking was a result of its exploiting new approaches to acquisition financing based upon "junk bonds";[12]
- the entry of People's Express into transatlantic air travel on the basis of a low-cost, low-service strategy;
- Japanese entry into US consumer electronics market avoided the distribution barriers built by US firms by initially supplying retailers' own brand products, and by focussing on market segments that domestic producers viewed as unattractive, such as monochrome and portable TVs. From then on they adopted a strategy of "cascading segment expansion" to move from market niches to market dominance.[13] Japanese incursion was facilitated by a lack of vigilance by US manufacturers in leaving "windows of opportunity" open to importers, and lack of quick, aggressive responses to initial entry.[14]

Rivalry between established competitors

For most industries, the major determinant of the overall state of competition and the general level of profitability is competition among the firms within the industry. In some industries, firms compete aggressively, sometimes to the extent that prices are pushed below the level of costs and industry-wide losses are incurred. In others, price competition is muted and rivalry focusses on advertising, innovation, and other non-price dimensions. Among the major factors determining the nature and intensity of competition between established firms are:

- concentration;
- diversity of competitors;
- product differentiation;
- excess capacity and exit barriers;
- cost conditions – scale economies and the ratio of fixed to variable costs.

Concentration   Seller concentration refers to the number of competitors in an industry and their relative sizes. Seller concentration is most commonly measured by the *concentration ratio* which is the combined market share of the leading producers. For example, the four-firm concentration ratio (conventionally denoted "CR4") measures the combined market share of the four largest producers in an industry. An industry dominated by a single firm, such as Xerox's dominance of plain-paper copiers during the early 1970s, displays little competition and the dominant firm can exercise considerable discretion over the prices it charges. Where an industry comprises a small group of leading companies (an oligopoly), price competition may also be restrained, either by outright collusion or, more commonly through "parallelism" of pricing decisions. In markets dominated by two suppliers, such as Duracell and Ever Ready in alkaline batteries and Kodak and Fuji in color film, prices are set at similar levels and competition focusses upon advertising, promotions, and product improvements. Even where there are several competitors, as in the US airline industry and supply of gasoline in Britain, prices tend to be closely coordinated.[15] In general, the fewer the number of firms in an industry, the easier is coordination of pricing behavior, and the smaller the chance that one firm will initiate aggressive price competition.

Diversity of competitors   The ability of the firms in an industry to avoid competition depends not only upon the number of firms, but also on their similarities in terms of origins, objectives, costs, and strategies. The cozy atmosphere of the US steel industry before the advent of overseas competition and the new minimills was possible because of the similarities of the companies and the outlooks of their senior managers. By contrast, the inability of OPEC to maintain oil prices during the 1980s was due, in part, to differences between member countries in objectives, production costs, language, politics, and religion.

Product differentiation   The more similar are the offerings of rival firms, the more willing are customers to substitute between them, and the greater is the incentive for firms to cut prices in order to expand business. Where the products of rival firms are virtually indistinguishable, the product is a commodity and the sole basis for competition is price. The markets for commodities, whether they are raw materials, such as crude oil, wheat and gold bullion, or finished products, such as 256K DRAM chips and US Treasury Bills, are the closest real-world approximations to the economist's concept of perfect competition. By contrast, in industries where products are highly differentiated, such as perfumes, pharmaceuticals and management consulting services, price competition is limited by customers' unwillingness to shift their purchases simply on the basis of small price differentials. Even though these industries may comprise many producers, firms' lack of price competition can result in relatively high profitability.

Excess capacity and exit barriers   The propensity of firms in an industry to resort to aggressive price competition depends critically upon the balance between capacity and output. The presence of unused capacity encourages firms to compete for additional business in order to spread fixed costs over a greater sales volume. Excess capacity is most commonly the result of declining market demand, which may be long term, as in steel, or cyclical, as in building materials. Overinvestment may also lead to periodic excess capacity, as there was with personal computers in 1984–5 and petrochemicals during 1977–83. The period during which excess capacity overhangs an industry depends upon the ease with which firms and resources can leave the industry. Costs and other impediments to leaving an industry are termed "barriers to exit." Where resources are durable and specialized or where employees are entitled to job protection, barriers to exit may be substantial.[16] The prolonged depression of profits in the world copper industry during the 1980s was reflected in the high costs of mine closure which encouraged firms to maintain operation despite heavy losses. Conversely, when demand exceeds available capacity, price competition wanes and margins grow. In the market for memory chips (DRAMs), excess capacity during 1985–6, resulting in low prices and widespread losses, was quickly reversed during 1987–8 when capacity shortage pushed the price of 256K DRAMs from $2 to $11.50, providing a short-term profit bonanza for NEC, Toshiba, Micron Technology, and other manufacturers.[17]

Cost conditions: scale economies and the ratio of fixed to variable costs
The aggressiveness with which rivals compete for market share is crucially dependent upon the cost conditions which they face. The more important the scale economies in an industry, the greater are the incentives for expanding sales at the expense of competitors. The higher the ratio of fixed to variable costs, the greater is the willingness of firms to reduce prices in order to utilize spare capacity. The devastating impact of excess capacity on profitability in petrochemicals, tires, and steel during 1975–82 reflected the fact that total costs were much the same at 60 percent capacity utilization as at full capacity; while the eagerness of the companies for extra business resulted in prices being cut down to the level of variable costs. Similar cost conditions explain the willingness of airlines to offer heavily-discounted tickets to "consolidators" when excess capacity emerges.

Despite considerable empirical research into the relationship between industry structure and profitability, the results are far from conclusive. Most contentious is the impact of seller concentration on profitability.[18] The impact of other variables on profitability is clearer. Studies using the PIMS (Profit Impact of Market Strategy) data base[19] show that rate of market growth is positively associated with profitability, although cash flow declines with higher growth, reflecting the greater investment needs of growing businesses (see Exhibit 2.6). Excess capacity has a strongly depressing effect on both ROI and ROS (return on invested capital), this is particularly so in capital-intensive businesses.[20]

Exhibit 2.6 The relationship between real market growth and profitability

	Real annual rate of market growth (%)				
	< −5	−5–0	0–5	5–10	>10
Gross margin on sales	23.5	25.6	26.9	25.7	29.7
Return on sales	7.8	8.3	9.1	8.3	9.4
Return on investment	20.6	23.0	23.2	22.2	26.6
Cash flow/investment	6.0	4.9	3.5	2.4	−0.1

Source: Based upon R. D. Buzzell and B. T. Gale, *The PIMS Principles* (Free Press, New York, 1987), pp. 56–7.

The firms in an industry operate in two types of market: The markets for *inputs* and the market for *outputs*. In the markets for inputs they purchase raw materials, components, finance, and labor services from the suppliers of these factors of production; in the markets for outputs they sell their products and services to customers, who may be distributors, consumers, or other manufacturers. In both these markets the relative profitability of the two parties to a transaction depends upon relative economic power. Dealing first with the sales to customers, two sets of factors are important in determining the strength of buying power:

Bargaining power of buyers

- buyers' price sensitivity;
- relative bargaining power.

Buyers' price sensitivity   The sensitivity of buyers to price depends, first, upon the importance of the item as a proportion of their total cost. The buyers of metal cans are primarily beverage manufacturers and food-processing companies. Because cans are one of the largest single items in their purchases of materials, they are highly sensitive to the prices they are charged and take every opportunity to resist price increases and press for favorable discounts. Conversely, specialized items such as electronic sensors and other types of control instruments typically account for a very small proportion of the machines and appliances into which they are assembled, hence, the manufacturers of such items are comparatively free from strong pressure on prices.

Secondly, the less differentiated are the products of the supplying industry, the more willing is the buyer to switch suppliers on the basis of price. In the food-processing industry, manufacturers of such standardized products as packaged white bread are particularly vulnerable to the buying power of supermarket chains. Hence, the incentive for food processors to differentiate their products by increasing advertising and new product introductions.

Thirdly, the greater the competition between buyers, the lower their profit margins, and the greater their eagerness to achieve price reductions from their sellers. One consequence of intense international competition in the automobile industry has been the increased pressure that the manufacturers have placed upon their component suppliers for lower prices, higher quality, and faster delivery.

Finally, the greater the importance of the industry's product to the quality of the buyer's product or service, the less sensitive are buyers to the prices they are charged. As competition in the personal computer industry has become increasingly focussed on the range and sophistication of software available, so has the bargaining power of the leading software houses, Microsoft and Ashton-Tate, increased relative to that of the PC manufacturers. A central strategic weakness of IBM's position in the personal computer industry is its dependence upon Microsoft's operating systems.

Relative bargaining power Bargaining power rests, ultimately, upon refusal to deal with the other party. The balance of power between the two parties to a transaction depends on the credibility and effectiveness with which each makes this threat. The key determinants are, first, the relative costs which each party sustains as a result of the transaction not being consummated and, secondly, the expertise of each party in leveraging its position through gamesmanship. Three factors are likely to be important in determining the bargaining power of buyers relative to that of sellers:

- size and concentration of buyers relative to suppliers;
- buyers' information;
- vertical integration.

With regard to size and concentration, the smaller the number of buyers, the less easy is it for a supplier to find alternative customers if one is lost. The bigger the purchases of the customer, the greater is the damage from losing the customer. The larger the size of the buyer relative to the supplier, then the better able is the buyer to withstand any financial losses arising from failure to reach agreement. To lever their bargaining power, independent retailers in both Europe and North America have formed buying groups to pool their orders and so match the buying power of the major chains.

Secondly, the better informed are buyers about suppliers and their products and costs, the better able are they to effectively bargain over prices and terms of business. The first essential for the exercise of bargaining power by buyers is that they are able to compare the prices and qualities of different suppliers' products or services. Doctors and lawyers do not normally display the prices they charge, nor do traders in the bazaars of Tangier and Istanbul. Keeping customers ignorant of relative prices is an effective constraint upon their buying power. But knowledge of price is of little value if the quality and attributes of the product are unknown. In industries where the characteristics of a product or service are not easily ascertained before purchase, such as for baldness treatments, investment advice, and management consulting, buying power is weak.

Finally, there is the ability to enter the other party's business through vertical integration. In refusing to deal with a supplier, the alternative is to find another supplier or to do-it-yourself. Large food processors such as Heinz and Campbell's Soup have reduced their dependence upon the oligopolistic suppliers of metal cans by manufacturing their own. The leading retail chains have increasingly displaced the brands of the major manufacturers with their own-label products. Backward integration need not necessarily occur; a credible threat may suffice.

The tendency for buyer concentration to depress prices and profits in supplying industries has been well documented in the empirical literature.[21] PIMS data show that the larger the average size of customers' purchases and the larger the proportion of customers' total purchases that the item represents, the more price sensitive customers become, and the lower is the profitability of supplying firms (see Exhibit 2.7).

	ROI (%)	ROS (%)
Typical size of customers' purchase:		
< $1,000	27	10
$1,000–$10,000	22	7
> $10,000	21	6
Purchase importance (as % of customers' total purchases):		
< 1%	25	10
1–5%	23	9
> 5%	20	8

Exhibit 2.7 The impact of customers purchases on profitability

Source: Based upon R. D. Buzzell and B. T. Gale, *The PIMS Principles: Linking Strategy to Performance* (Free Press, New York, 1987), pp. 64–5.

Analysis of the determinants of relative power between the producers in an industry and their suppliers is precisely analogous to the analysis of the relationship between producers and their buyers. Since the factors which determine the effectiveness of supplier power against the buying power of the industry are the same as those which determine the power of the industry against that of its customers, they do not require a separate analysis.

Bargaining power of suppliers

To the extent that the suppliers of raw materials, semi-finished products, and components to manufacturing companies are smaller than their customers and their products are comparatively undifferentiated, their bargaining power tends to be weak. As a result, the suppliers of inputs to manufacturing firms often seek to boost their bargaining power through forming cartels. For example, raw material suppliers have formed such cartels as OPEC in oil and the International Coffee Organization in coffee beans; workers have united into labor unions; farmers have formed co-operatives and agricultural marketing boards.

PIMS studies of the impact of supplier's bargaining power upon firms' profitability is complex. Increasing concentration of a firm's purchases is initially beneficial since it permits certain economies of purchasing. Thereafter, increasing concentration among purchasers results in profitability becoming depressed because of increased supplier power. Supplier power is significantly increased by forward integration into its customer's own industry. When a firm faces its suppliers as competitors within its own industry, its ROI is reduced by two percentage points. The effect of unionization on profitability, on the other hand, is relatively straightforward: increased unionization is unambiguously associated with decreasing profitability. Exhibit 2.8 shows some of these findings.

Exhibit 2.8 The
impact of supplier
power on profitability:
PIMS estimates

Supplier power (%)	ROI (%)	ROS (%)
Total purchases from the three biggest suppliers:		
< 25	21	8.9
25–50	24	9.8
> 50	23	8.9
Employees unionized:		
None	25	10.8
1–35	24	9.0
35–60	23	9.0
60–75	18	7.9
> 75	19	7.9

Source: Based upon R. D. Buzzell and B. T. Gale, *The PIMS Principles: Linking Strategy to Performance* (Free Press, New York, 1987), pp. 62 and 67.

Applying Industry Analysis

**Forecasting industry
profitability**

Decisions to commit resources to a particular industry must be based upon anticipated returns five or ten years ahead. In the case of new ventures by established firms, one study found that "new ventures need, on average, eight years before they reach profitability."[22] Over periods of five years or more, industry profitability cannot simply be forecasted by projecting current industry profitability. Indeed, at any point in time, available data on an industry's profitability are at least six months out of date.

But while we cannot directly forecast industry profitability, we can predict with some accuracy changes in the underlying structure of an industry. By monitoring current changes in product and process technology we can determine whether costs of entry are changing and whether competition from substitutes is increasing. Changes in the structure of supplying and customer industries and in the unionization of the industry's labor force can indicate the likely trends of supplier and buyer bargaining power. Macroeconomic forecasts of general economic activity can indicate future changes in capacity utilization and the implications for price competition in the industry.

Consider the US tire industry shown in Case Note 2.1. During the period 1981–8 return on investment had been depressed, almost certainly below the average cost of capital for the industry. What is the outlook for competition and profitability in the industry during the early 1990s?

Identifying changes in industry structure and the likely impact of each of these changes on competition and industry profitability is fairly easy. Exhibit 2.9 lists the principal structural changes occurring in the tire industry and the predicted direction of the effect. However, predicting the *quantitative* impact on profitability of each of these changes is far more difficult. While the results of cross-sectional empirical studies, such as those of the PIMS data base or those using SIC (Standard Industrial Classification) data, provide estimates of the quantitative impact of changes in structural variables on profitability, these estimates are across all industries and are unlikely to be reliable for changes within a particular industry. An even greater problem is evaluating the net effect of changes in a number of structural variables. In the tire industry different factors are working in opposite directions. Because of the complex interaction between the different structural variables, the overall outcome cannot be predicted with accuracy. In some industries, seemingly small changes in industry structure and market conditions can reinforce one another and so have a major impact on profitability. For instance, the slowdown in the demand for personal computers during 1989–90 combined with competition for market share among the leading producers led to discounting and a severe reduction in industry profits. Where several elements of market structure are changing simultaneously, intimate understanding of the particular industry based upon careful observation and study of past patterns of competition and performance in the industry is likely to be particularly valuable in providing insight into the relationships between structure, competitive behavior, and profitability.

Factors likely to increase price competition and reduce profitability	Factors likely to reduce price competition and increase profitability
Decline in demand for new cars during 1989–90 intensified by general recession	Industry capacity being reduced by mergers and plant closures
Switch to radial tires reducing rate at which tires are replaced	Potential increased produce differentiation due to innovation
Increasing concentration and price sensitivity among tire retailers	Increased global concentration of the tire industry conducive to weaker price competition
Big 3 automobile producers increasingly cost sensitive over components	
Overseas tire producers in US likely to promote more aggressive competition in seeking market share	
Increasing imports from low-cost manufacturing countries	
Weak brand loyalty of customers inducing price competition by tire producers	

Exhibit 2.9 Structural factors affecting competition and profitability in the US tire industry, 1988–92

In other situations, the principal structural changes may all be pointing in the same direction making forecasting comparatively easy. For example, the changes in the oil industry at the beginning of the 1980s, such as heavy investment by the majors in non-OPEC sources of crude, declining world oil demand, and increasing disunity in the Arab world, all pointed to increasing competition in the oil market and weakening prices for crude. During the latter half of 1989, a combination of weakening demand, heavy investment in new US capacity by Japanese automobile companies, declining product differentiation as manufacturers adopted similar designs and technologies, and a rising US dollar against the yen and Korean won, all pointed towards declining profitability for the US automobile industry.

Strategies to improve the balance of competitive forces

Understanding how the structural characteristics of an industry determine the intensity of competition and the level of profitability provides a basis for identifying opportunities for adjusting industry structure in order to increase the hospitality of the industry environment. The first issue is to identify the key structural features of an industry that are responsible for depressing profitability. The second is to consider which of these structural features are amenable to change through appropriate strategic initiatives. Opportunities by which a firm, either individually or in cooperation with other firms in the industry, can modify industry structure and competitive behavior can then be identified. Consider two examples.

During the early 1980s the European market for welding equipment was shrinking at the rate of 5–10 percent a year. Profitability was depressed both by the overhang of excess capacity and by the industry's fragmentation. Between 1980 and 1984, the leading Swedish producer of welding equipment, Elektriska Svetsningsaktiebolaget AB (ESAB) began acquiring competitors in West Germany, Britain, Switzerland, and the Netherlands. By consolidating the industry and cutting back capacity, the whole industry moved into profitability during 1983–4.[23]

Capacity rationalization may be achieved by a series of bilateral agreements rather than by acquisition. In the Western European petrochemicals industry, a series of plant exchanges between producers during the 1980s facilitated capacity rationalization and the stabilization of prices and profits.[24]

Entry barriers are particularly susceptible to manipulation by established firms. Various strategies have been adopted by incumbents to restrict entry. For example, in instant photography, Polaroid's construction of a wall of patents around its camera designs and its aggressive enforcement of them was effective in reestablishing its 30-year-old monopoly by driving out its sole competitor, Kodak. In TV receivers, Zenith also used litigation as a means of restricting Japanese suppliers' access to the US market.

Professional associations of doctors, lawyers, accountants, and architects tend to press for more and more stringent entry standards into their professions. The tendency for professional examination requirements to rise, and for the all-graduate entry to give way to demands for additional higher degrees, reflects the desire by existing members to protect their incomes through building barriers to entry.

Similarly, control over distribution outlets is a particularly potent means of restricting entry into consumer-product industries. In gasoline, automobiles, and consumer electrical appliances, manufacturers have used exclusive-dealing arrangements to restrict entrants' access to distribution.

Opportunities for a firm to influence industry structure and so improve the balance of competitive forces are usually limited either to large firms which occupy strong positions within their industries or to industries where firms are able to cooperate effectively. Hence, for most firms the primary objective for business strategy is not to improve overall industry conditions, but to establish a competitive advantage over rivals. A comprehensive analysis of competitive advantage follows in chapters 5, 6, and 7. However, with the tools of industry analysis outlined in this chapter, we can look ahead and identify the potential for competitive advantage in a particular industry in terms of the factors which are important in determining a firm's ability to survive and prosper. These are referred to as *key success factors*, which were defined by Chuck Hofer and Dan Schendel as:

Identifying key success factors

those variables which management can influence through its decisions and which can affect significantly the overall competitive positions of the firms in an industry … Within any particular industry they are derived from the interaction of two sets of variables, namely, the economic and technological characteristics of the industry … and the competitive weapons on which the various firms in the industry have built their strategies.[25]

To survive and prosper in an industry a firm must meet two criteria: It must supply what customers want to buy, and it must survive competition. Hence, our approach in identifying key success factors is to ask two questions:

- What do our customers want?
- What does the firm need to do to survive competition?

To answer the first question we need to look more closely at customers of the industry and to view them, not so much as a source of bargaining power and hence as a threat to profitability, but more as the basic rationale for the existence of the industry and as the source of profit for the industry. The first criterion for profitability, we noted at the outset, is that the firm provides customers with a product or service for which they are willing to pay a price that exceeds the cost of production. This implies that we must identify customers' needs and establish the basis on which they select the offerings of one supplier in preference to those of another.

The second question requires that we examine the basis of competition in the industry. How intense is competition, and what are the key dimensions of competition? If the industry supplies a commodity product where there is limited scope for differentiation, then the focus of competition is likely to be price. To survive and prosper in the face of price competition requires that the firm establishes a low-cost position. Examination of cost conditions in the industry, for example, the importance of scale economies, the extent of excess capacity, the ratio of fixed to variable costs, can then indicate the major opportunities of a cost advantage.

The basic framework for identifying key success factors is depicted in Exhibit 2.10. Exhibit 2.11 shows the application of the framework to identifying key success factors.

Exhibit 2.10
Identifying key success •
factors

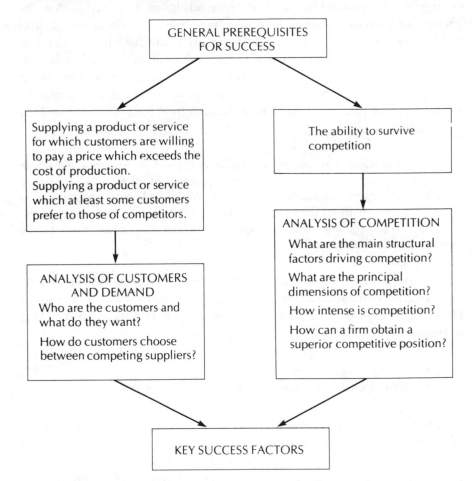

In most industries there are likely to be a small number of factors which are critical determinants of why some firms are more successful than others. Once the basic factors have been identified, further analysis and elaboration can build a detailed understanding of the appropriate strategies to be pursued in that industry. In Case Note 2.2, Kenichi Ohmae, the Senior Vice-President of McKinsey and Company's Tokyo office, explains how an initial identification of key success factors can be elaborated into a more sophisticated strategy analysis.

Exhibit

2.11 Identifying key success factors: some examples

Industry	What do Customers Want? + (Analysis of Demand)	How do Firms Survive Competition? = (Analysis of Competition)	Key Success Factors
Steel	Customers include automobile, engineering, and container industries. Customers acutely price sensitive. Also require product consistency and reliability of supply. Specific technical specifications required for special steels.	Competition primarily on price. Competition intense due to declining demand, high fixed costs and low-cost imports. Entry and exit barriers high. Strong union bargaining power. Transport costs high. Scale economies important.	Cost efficiency through scale-efficient plants, low-cost location, rapid adjustment of capacity to output, low labor costs. In special steels and some special uses, scope for differentiation through quality.
Fashion Clothing	Demand fragmented by garment, style, quality, color. Customers willing to pay price premium for fashion, exclusivity and quality. Retailers seek reliability and speed of supply.	Low barriers to entry and exit. Low seller concentration. Few scale economies. International competition strong. Retail buying power strong. Price and non-price competition strong.	Need to combine effective differentiation with low-cost operation. Key differentiation variables are speed of response to changing fashions, style, reputation with retailers or consumers. Low wages and overhead costs important except in less price-sensitive segments.
Grocery supermarkets	Low prices. Convenient location. Wide range of products.	Markets localized, concentration normally high. But customer price sensitivity encourages vigorous price competition. Exercise of bargaining power a key determinant of purchase prices. Scale economies in operations and advertising.	Low-cost operation requires operational efficiency, scale efficient stores, large aggregate purchases to maximize buying power, low wage costs. Differentiation requires large stores (to allow wide product range), convenient location, easy parking.

Case Note 2.2   Probing for Key Success Factors

As a consultant faced with an unfamiliar business or industry, I make a point of first asking the specialists in the business, "What is the secret of success in this industry?" Needless to say, I seldom get an immediate answer, and so I pursue the inquiry by asking other questions from a variety of angles in order to establish as quickly as possible some reasonable hypotheses as to key factors for success. In the course of these interviews it usually becomes quite obvious what analyses will be required in order to prove or disprove these hypotheses. By first identifying the probable key factors for success and then screening them by proof or disproof, it is often possible for the strategist to penetrate very quickly to the core of a problem.

Traveling in the United States last year, I found myself on one occasion sitting in a plane next to a director of one of the biggest lumber companies in the country. Thinking I might learn something useful in the course of the five-hour flight, I asked him, "What are the key factors for success in the lumber industry?" To my surprise, his reply was immediate: "Owning large forests and maximizing the yield from them."

The first of those key factors is a relatively simple matter: the purchase of forest land. But his second point required further explanation. Accordingly, my next question was: "What variable or variables do you control in order to maximize the yield from a given tract?"

He replied: "The rate of tree growth is the key variable. As a rule, two factors promote growth: the amount of sunshine and the amount of water. Our company doesn't have many forests with enough of both. In Arizona and Utah, for example, we get more than enough sunshine but too little water, and so tree growth is very low. Now, if we could give the trees in those states enough water, they'd be ready in less than fifteen years instead of the thirty it takes now. The most important project we have in hand at the moment is aimed at finding out how to do this."

Impressed that this director knew how to work out a key factor strategy for his business, I offered my own contribution: "Then under the opposite conditions, where there is plenty of water but too little sunshine – for example, around the lower reaches of the Columbia River – the key factors should be fertilizers to speed up the growth and the choice of tree varieties that don't need so much sunshine."

Having established in a few minutes the general framework of what we were going to talk about, I spent the rest of the long flight very profitably hearing from him in detail how each of these factors was being applied.

Source: Kenichi Ohmae, *The Mind of the Strategist* (McGraw-Hill/Penguin Books, London 1982), p. 85.

The Problem of Where to Draw Industry Boundaries

Because it is logical, systematic, and commonsense, Porter's five forces of competition model is remarkably simple and straightforward to apply to the analysis of competition and profitability in an industry. The greatest difficulty is in defining the industry. No industry has clear boundaries either in terms of products or geographical areas. In analyzing the industry environment of Chrysler, should we examine the "transportation equipment" industry (SIC 37), the "motor vehicles and equipment" industry (SIC 371), or the automobile industry (SIC 3712)? Should we view the industry as international, national, or regional? There is no easy or unique answer. The major criterion that needs to be applied is that of *substitutability,* both on the demand side and the supply side.

From a demand perspective, if customers consider the products of two firms to be close substitutes for one another, then the two firms should be viewed as competing within the same industry. If customers substitute between the automobiles of Chrysler, Ford, and General Motors on the basis of price differentials, then the firms fall within the same industry. If customers are unwilling to substitute Mack's trucks for Chrysler automobiles then we should regard automobiles and trucks as falling into separate industries. However, the criterion of demand substitutability does not always yield sensible results. A golfer wanting to buy a set of left-handed clubs would be unlikely to purchase a set of right-handed clubs just because they were on special offer. Yet it would be a nonsense to categorize a manufacturer of left-handed golf clubs as a separate industry. An additional criterion is needed.

If two manufacturers find it easy to switch their production facilities to manufacture one another's products, then such supply-side substitutability would suggest classifying the two firms to the same industry. If trucks and cars are manufactured on the same equipment using the same technology and labor skills, then the ease of switching would make Chrysler and Mack potential competitors who should be included in the same industry. Consumers do not readily substitute between full-fat and skimmed milk, yet, because both products use the same raw materials, equipment, labor, and distribution, we regard both products as falling within the liquid milk industry.

The same criteria of demand-side and supply-side substitutability can be used to determine an industry's geographical boundaries. If customers in the US and Italy are willing to substitute between Chrysler and Fiat cars, or if Fiat and Chrysler are willing and able to produce cars for both the American and Italian markets, then the market is international.

However, the issue of substitutability is one of degree. Judgement is important and judgement needs to take account of the purposes of the analysis. For some issues we may need to define the industry broadly; in order to examine more specific matters, we may want to define the industry much more narrowly. Fortunately, if industry analysis is based on Porter's five forces model the delineation of an industry's boundaries is not usually critical to the analysis. For example, if Chrysler's industry is defined very narrowly to include only US automobile producers, other actual and potential competitors, such as European automobile producers and manufacturers of trucks and motorcycles, can be included in the analysis either as producers of substitutes or as potential entrants.

Analyzing Competitive Dynamics

One of the chief criticisms levelled at the Structure–Conduct–Performance approach to industry analysis which underlies the Porter framework is that it fails to take account of the dynamic nature of competition and industry structure. The analysis begins with an industry's structure which determines the nature and intensity of competition which determines profitability. But industry structure is not exogenously determined. A key feature of the competitive process is that industry structure is continually being changed both consciously by firms' strategic decisions and as an outcome of the competitive interaction between firms.

The key danger in using the Porter framework is that it can encourage us to make our predictions about competitive behavior and profitability on the assumption that industry structure is exogenous and is constant over time. Yet the essence of competition is that it is a dynamic process in which equilibrium is never reached and in the course of which industry structures are continually being reformed. Recognition of the dynamic interaction between competition and industry structure is associated with the writings of Joseph Schumpeter. In Schumpeter's view, innovation is the key element of competition in transforming industrial structures. Innovation represents a "perennial gale of creative destruction" through which favorable industry structures, monopoly in particular, contain the seeds of their own destruction by providing incentives for firms to attack established positions through new approaches to competing.[26]

The key issue raised by Schumpeter for our analysis is whether we can use current industry structures as a reliable guide to the nature of competition and industry performance in the future? The relevant consideration is the speed of structural change in industry. Clearly no industry structure is a constant over time. Indeed, we have already explored how business strategy can be used to alter industry structure to the firm's advantage. However, if the pace of transformation is rapid, if entry rapidly undermines the market power of dominant firms, if innovation speedily transforms industry structure by changing process technology, creating new substitutes, and by shifting the basis on which firms compete, then there is little merit in using industry structure as a basis for analyzing competition and profit.

Most empirical studies of changes over time in industry structure and profitability show Schumpeter's process of "creative destruction" to be more of a breeze than a gale. Studies of US and Canadian industry[27] have found entry to occur so slowly that profits are undermined only slowly. One survey commented that "the picture of the competitive process ... is, to say the least, sluggish in the extreme."[28] Overall, the studies show a fairly consistent picture of the rate of change of profitability and structure. At both the firm and the industry level, profits tend to be highly persistent in the long run.[29] Structural change, notably concentration, entry, and the identity of leading firms, also appears to be, on average, slow.[30]

The competitive interaction of firms

A second major limitation of the Structure–Conduct–Performance approach to industry analysis is that it takes little or no account of the competitive interaction between firms. In chapter 1 we noted that the essence of strategic competition is that the players are involved in an interactive game: decisions made by one player are dependent upon the actual and anticipated decisions of the other players. The assumption that competitive behavior is determined by industry structure placed too strict a limitation on the role of competitive interaction. Observation shows that, in most markets, the outcome of the competitive process is determined not just by industry structure but also by the sequence, timing, and mutual perceptions of each firm's competitive moves. The competitive process is unstable. Evidence from gasoline retailing shows that intense local price wars can erupt as a result of a modest price cut by one gas station, by personal animosity between adjacent retailers, or by misjudgement by one retailer.[31] The airline industry displays similar speed of competitive reactions which cause unstable competitive conditions.[32]

Two approaches can be used to model and predict the outcome of competitive interactions between small groups of competing firms: game theory and catastrophe theory.

Game theory   Game theory is the longest and best established approach. It seeks to identify the strategy options of the different players, estimates the outcomes of alternative combinations of strategy choices by the players, and predicts players' choices. Game theory offers insights into a number of aspects of strategic behavior. Most illuminating are:

- the prisoners' dilemma, which shows that seemingly rational decision making by players who fail to cooperate leaves both worse off than had they cooperated;[33]
- the analysis of reputation, which demonstrates the value of a firm's reputation in making threats credible and in conferring competitive advantage in markets characterized by uncertainty.[34]

In general, however, game theory has not developed either the generality or the sophistication to enable realistic modeling of the complexity of real business situations or to generate insights and predictions that are useful to managers facing strategic decisions.[35]

Catastrophe theory   Catastrophe theory is another area of potentially valuable theoretical development. The great merit of catastrophe theory is that it permits modeling of unstable processes. In particular, it permits the analysis of:

- discontinuity – sudden shifts in competitive behavior or in performance outcomes;
- divergence – small movements from an initial position can result in quite different competitive outcomes;
- hysteresis – reversals of behavior typically do not cause a return to the initial situation.

Nevertheless the potential is considerable. The earlier discussion on forecasting industry profitability identified the tendency for quite small changes in industry structure to have devastating consequences for competition and profitability. Catastrophe theory offers a useful approach to such apparent instability. The cusp catastrophe model offers interesting insights into the role of strategic investments and industry inertia in determining a firm's competitive position.[36]

Summary

Every industry is unique in terms of the competitive behavior observed during any period. At the same time, the different patterns of competition across industries can be explained and predicted within a common analytical framework. The premise of this chapter is that the structural characteristics of an industry play a key role in determining the nature and intensity of competition within it. Competition, in turn, determines the overall rate of profit in an industry.

This premise is of crucial importance for managers and students of management. It means that to understand competition and profitability within a particular industry we over a long period need not rely exclusively on the acquisition of knowledge specific to that industry, but we can utilize a general framework of cause and effect to understand past patterns of competitive activity and to predict the course of competition and profitability in the future.

The principal framework used in this chapter is Porter's "five forces of competition model." The merit of this model is that it provides a simple, yet powerful, organizing framework for classifying the relevant information about an industry's structure and for predicting what the implications of these structural features are for competitive behavior.

By understanding the links between industry structure, competition, and profitability, it is possible to analyze three important strategic issues:

- to predict industry profitability – the key questions of corporate strategy, such as the appropriate level of investment in an industry, the choice of directions of diversification require a forecast of the attractiveness of industry environments;
- to indicate how the firm can influence industry structure in order to moderate competition and improve profitability;
- to identify key success factors – the prerequisites for survival and success in a particular industry; their identification is an essential step in determining how the firm can establish a position of competitive advantage.

The framework suffers from some critical limitations. In particular it fails to take account of the dynamic character of competition. Competition is not determined wholly by industry structure, it is a complex social process of action and reaction where the objectives, perceptions, and personalities of the players occupy important roles. The competitive process is also one which changes industry structure.

In subsequent chapters we shall draw heavily upon the frameworks, concepts, and techniques described in this chapter. We shall also be extending the analysis to deal with some of its limitations and to make it more applicable to the dynamics of competitive situations. The next chapter examines the internal complexity of industries in terms of segmentation and the characteristics and behavior of individual competitors. Chapter 5 returns to the dynamics of competitive interactions, and chapter 8 considers the evolution of industries over time.

Notes

1. See, for example, J. P. Leemhuis, "Using scenarios to develop strategies", *Long Range Planning*, pp. 30–7, and Pierre Wack, "Scenarios, shooting the rapids," *Harvard Business Review*, November–December 1985, pp. 139–50.

2. Michael E. Porter, *Competitive Strategy: Techniques for analyzing Industries and Competitors* (Free Press, New York, 1980), ch. 1. For a summary see his article, "How competitive forces shape strategy," *Harvard Business Review*, 1979, pp. 86–93.

3. W. J. Baumol, J. C. Panzar and R. D. Willig, *Contestable Markets and the Theory of Industry Structure* (Harcourt, Brace, Jovanovich, New York, 1982).

4. "Brand loyalty is rarely blind loyalty," *Wall Street Journal*, October 19, 1989, p. B1.

5. Robert D. Buzzell and Paul W. Farris, "Marketing costs in consumer goods industries," in Hans Thorelli (ed.), *Strategy + Structure = Performance* (Indiana University Press, Bloomington, 1977), pp. 128–9.

6. For a discussion and empirical evidence, see: Martin B. Lieberman, "Excess capacity as a barrier to entry," *Journal of Industrial Economics* 35 (June 1987), pp. 607–27.

7. J. S. Bain, *Barriers to New Competition* (Harvard University Press, Cambridge, Mass., 1956).

8. H. Michael Mann, "Seller concentration, entry barriers and rates of return in thirty industries," *Review of Economics and Statistics* 48 (1966), pp. 296–307.

9. See, for example, the studies by W. S. Comanor and T. A. Wilson, *Advertising and Market Power* (Harvard University Press, Cambridge, Mass., 1974); and L. Weiss, "Quantitative studies in industrial organization," in M. Intriligator (ed.) *Frontiers of Quantitative Economics* (North Holland, Amsterdam, 1971).

10. G. Yip, "Gateways to entry," *Harvard Business Review* September–October 1983, pp. 85–93.

11. "Proctor and Gamble goes on a health kick," *Business Week*, June 29, 1987, pp. 90–2.

12. "Now Drexel Burnham is Fighting on Two Fronts," *Business Week*, February 16, 1987, pp. 90–6.

13. Marc Particelli, "The Japanese are Coming," *Outlook*, Spring, 1981, pp. 35–44.

14. Gary E. Willard and Arun M. Savara, "Patterns of entry: pathways to new markets," *California Management Review* 30 (1988), pp. 57–76.

15. See "U.S. probes whether airlines colluded on fare increases," *Wall Street Journal*, December 14, 1989, p. B1; and "A tank full of trouble," *Economist*, December 16–22, 1989, p. 57.

16. The problems caused by excess capacity and exit barriers are discussed in Charles Baden Fuller (ed.), *Strategic Management of Excess Capacity* (Blackwell, Oxford, 1990).

17. "When the chips are down," *Business Week,* June 27, 1988, pp. 28–9.

18. See, for example, R. Schmalensee, "Inter-industry studies of structure and performance," and T. F. Bresnahan, "Empirical studies of industries with market power," in R. Schmalensee and R. D. Willig (eds.), *Handbook of Industrial Organization* (North Holland, Amsterdam, 1988).

19. The PIMS (Profit Impact of Market Strategy) data base is developed, maintained and analyzed by the Strategic Planning Institute. The PIMS data base comprises information provided by over 3,000 business units in North America and Western Europe. PIMS uses multiple regression analysis to estimate the impact of a variety of strategy and industry structure variables on business unit profitability. The development of PIMS and the application of its analytic techniques to strategy formulation is discussed in chapter 13.

20. R. D. Buzzell and B. T. Gale, *The PIMS Principles* (Free Press, New York, 1987), pp. 273–84.

21. S. H. Lustgarten, "The impact of buyer concentration in manufacturing industries," *Review of Economics and Statistics,* 57 (1975), pp. 125–32, and R. M. Grant "Manufacturer–retailer relations: the shifting balance of power," in G. Johnson (ed.), *Business Strategy and Retailing* (John Wiley, Chichester, 1987).

22. Ralph Biggadike. "The risky business of diversification," *Harvard Business Review*, May–June 1979, pp. 103–11.

23. "Exploiting the shakeout in Europe's welding industry," *International Management,* April 1984, pp. 56–8.

24. See Joe Bower, *When Markets Quake* (Harvard Business School Press, Boston, 1986).

25. Chuck Hofer and Dan Schendel, *Strategy Formulation: Analytical Concepts* (West Publishing, St Paul, 1977).

26. Joseph A. Schumpeter, *The Theory of Economic Development* (Harvard University Press, Cambridge, Mass., 1934).

27. R. Masson and J. Shaanan, "Stochastic dynamic limit pricing: an empirical test," *Review of Economics and Statistics,* 64 (1982), pp. 413–22.

28. P. A. Geroski and R. T. Masson, "Dynamic market models in industrial organization," *International Journal of Industrial Organization* 5 (1987), pp. 1–13.

29. D. Mueller, *Profits in the Long Run* (Cambridge University Press, Cambridge, 1986).

30. R. Caves and M. Porter, "The dynamics of changing seller concentration," *Journal of Industrial Economics,* 19 (1980), pp. 1–15; P. Hart and R. Clarke, *Concentration in British Industry* (Cambridge University Press, Cambridge, 1980).

31. Ralph Cassidy, *Price Warfare in Business Competition* (Michigan State University, East Lancing, 1963); R. M. Grant, "Pricing behavior in the U.K. wholesale market for petrol: a structure–conduct analysis," *Journal of Industrial Economics* 30, (1982).

32. The argument for less emphasis on industry structure and more emphasis on the dynamics of competitive processes is made by Bo Carlsson, "Reflections on industrial dynamics," *International Journal of Industrial Organization* 5 (1987), pp. 135–48.

33. F. M. Scherer, *Industrial Market Structure and Economic Performance*, 2nd edn, (Rand McNally, Chicago, 1980), pp. 160–4.

34. K. Weight and C. Camerer, "Reputation and corporate strategy: a review of recent theory and applications," *Strategic Management Journal* 9 (1988), pp. 137–42.

35. For applications of game theory to business situations see: B. K. Dutta and W. R. King, "Metagame analysis of competitive strategy," *Strategic Management Journal*, 1 (1980), pp. 357–70; and H. Mills, "Notes on game theory in marketing competition – marketing as a science," *Harvard Business Review*, Sept.–Oct. 1961, pp. 137–42. For a critical assessment of the usefulness of game theory see Franklin M. Fisher, "Games economists play: a noncooperative view," *RAND Journal of Economics*, 20 (1989), pp. 113–24.

36. For a discussion of the application of catastrophe theory to competitive situations see Terence A. Olivia, Diana L. Day and Ian C. MacMillan, "A generic model of competitive dynamics," *Academy of Management Review* 13 (1988), pp. 374–89.

THREE

Intra-industry Analysis: Segmentation and Competitor Appraisal

We are not competing for the whole pie, just for certain slices.
James Robinson III, Chairman, American Express Company

Introduction

An "industry" is an artificial construct. Companies exist, but an industry is a group of companies where the boundaries depend upon the classification scheme adopted by the observer. Unlike other forms of classification, such as species of plants or birds, industry classifications suffer from the problem that there is limited internal homogeneity within each industry category and little agreement between individuals as to the boundaries which separate industries. The retailing sector includes such companies as J. C. Penney, Safeway Foodstores, Tiffany's, Shell filling stations, and Mad Mike's Video Emporium. Each of these retailers inhabits a different environment and none competes directly with another.

Such heterogeneity poses serious problems for industry analysis. In the last chapter we viewed the industry as something real with definite structural features which determined competition and profitability. However, if the concept of the industry is a simplification of reality, then, as with all generalizations, industry analysis can lead to misleading distortion. For example, industry analysis tells us that the bread industry is one of declining demand, excess capacity, and low brand loyalty which leads to strong competition and low margins, both of which are exacerbated by the buying power exerted by the major supermarket chains. Yet, Jean-Louis Vilgrain, president of France's leading milling group, established the Vie de France chain of mini-bakeries in the US and achieved an average annual growth of sales of 53 percent and net earnings growth of 72 percent. By 1985, Vie de France was seeking growth opportunities in Japan, Hong Kong, Indonesia, South Africa, and even back in France. Clearly, the fresh-baked, specialty bread segment of the bread industry is substantially different from the industry in general.[1]

To understand competition more intimately and to predict profit prospects more accurately a more detailed analysis of an industry may be needed. This requires two important extensions to our analysis of industries.

- segmentation analysis;
- competitor analysis.

First, to examine in greater detail the competitive environment of particular firms, we need to divide the industry into smaller competitive arenas. We shall use segmentation analysis to disaggregate an industry into more narrowly-defined segments, and to analyze the competitive characteristics, attractiveness, and key success factors of each segment. In analyzing segments, we will use the same tools of industry analysis which were outlined in the previous chapter.

Secondly, we shall examine the competitive interactions between individual firms within industries. In the last chapter competition was analyzed as an outcome of industry structure. To understand and predict competitive behavior more precisely, investigation of the objectives, values, and strategies of the individual competitors is required. The more concentrated an industry is, the greater is the importance of individual firms' decisions and behavior in understanding industry competition. For Pepsi Cola, the key feature of its industry environment is the competitive strategy of Coca Cola, and vice versa. In the computer industry the most important features of the industry environment for Apple, Unisys, HP, and others, are the policies of IBM with regard to new products, technical standards, and pricing. Competitor analysis is concerned with identifying the strategy, objectives, assumptions, and capabilities of a rival in order to predict its likely future behavior.

Segmentation Analysis[2]

The uses of segmentation

If the nature and intensity of competition varies within an industry, then it is useful to partition an industry into segments and analyze the structural characteristics of different industry segments. Such analysis is useful in appraising the attractiveness of different segments, not only for the new entrant determining which part of the industry to enter, but also for the established firm deciding which segments to enter, which to withdraw from, and how to allocate its resources between segments.

Differences in structure and competition between segments may also mean differences in key success factors between segments. In the bread industry, competing effectively in the market for standard, packaged, sliced bread requires cost-efficient operation in the form of large-scale, automated production with well-organized distribution through large-volume retail outlets. In the market for specialty bread, success is far more dependent upon quality, freshness, variety, and presentation. This would require small-batch, localized production of a wide variety of breads.

Segmentation analysis proceeds in five principal stages:

Stages of segmentation analysis

1 Identify key segmentation variables and categories:
  - identify segmentation variables;
  - reduce the number of segmentation variables by selecting the most significant segmentation variables and combining closely correlated segmentation variables;
  - identify discrete categories for each segmentation variable.
2 Construct a segmentation matrix.
3 Analyze segment attractiveness:
  - segment size;
  - segment growth rate
  - intensity of competition within the segment.
4 Identify key success factors in each segment.
5 Analyze attractions of broad versus narrow segment scope:
  - potential for sharing costs and transferring skills across segments;
  - similarity of key success factors between segments;
  - product differentiation benefits of segment specialization.

Case Note 3.1 discusses the segmentation of the US brewing industry.

Case Note 3.1 Segmentation of the US Brewing Industry

During the 1960s and 1970s, the increasing dominance of the US beer industry by a small number of nationally-competing brewers was assisted by increasing convergence of preferences among American beer drinkers. Until World War II, beer production was mainly localized with over 500 breweries serving an enormous diversity of beer types. Pasteurization and improved transportation increased each brewery's marketing area, while national TV advertising increased the appeal of the national brands. At the same time the brewers directed their appeal to majority preferences by reducing the distinctiveness of their beers' flavors. Progressive reduction in the hop and malt content of beers resulted in beers which were light-colored, smooth-tasting, and bland in contrast to the heavier-bodied,

more bitter European brews. The rise of branded mediocrity was indicated by the increasing four-firm concentration ratio:

1947	1962	1972	1982
21%	29.6%	53.4%	75.8%

Yet despite the near-indistinguishable characteristics of the leading brands of beer, in many respects, the US beer industry remained deeply segmented.

There are two main brewing processes which result in two distinct types of beer: top-fermentation resulting in lager or bottom-fermenting resulting in ale. Virtually all US produced beer was lager; most ales consumed in the US were imported from Europe. Among the lager beers the principal distinction was between the standard pale lagers and the more recently-introduced light beers which were even lighter in color, flavor and, most importantly, calories than the standard lagers. Apart from these two major types, there was also a small proportion of heavier beer with higher malt and hop content which was produced either by small local breweries or as imported brands produced under license in the US.

Apart from production method, color and taste, beers were differentiated by alcoholic content. Lowest were near-beers (less than 0.5 percent alcohol) and alcohol-free beers; next were the light beers, followed by standard beers. Malt liquor was a classification of beers whose alcoholic content was too high to be legally referred to as "beer" under state law.

Beers could also be classified by price/quality category. Five price ranges were apparent: luxury priced, which comprised mainly imported brands; super-premium, such as Anheuser-Busch's Michelob and Miller's Lowenbräu; premium-priced beers, which comprised the leading national brands such as Budweiser, Miller High Life, Coors, Stroh and Schlitz; the popular-priced beers which included Anheuser Busch's "Busch", Miller's "Old Milwaukee", and Heileman's "Stag", and were distinguished from the premium beers more by their lower advertising than lower quality; and budget beers which were mainly no-name brands and generic beer. Table 3.1 shows market shares by type of beer.

The changing composition of beer sales corresponded to changes in the composition of beer drinkers. Beer drinking was becoming less heavily concentrated among male, blue-collar workers. The growing market share for light beers was associated with growing consumption by women and the more health-conscious white-collar workers; while the primary market for the expensive import beers was among status-conscious, high-income groups.

Table 3.1 Market shares by type of beer

Type of beer	1975	1982
Luxury-priced imports	1.1	3.1
Super-premium	3.4	6.1
Premium beers (except light)	47.0	46.6
Light beers	1.9	17.1
Popular and budget-priced	44.0	23.8
Malt liquor	2.6	3.3

Apart from types of beer and types of beer drinker, the industry could also be segmented by distribution channel and by region. The two principal distribution channels were retail outlets and on-premises consumption in bars and restaurants. A large proportion of sales to bars and restaurants were in kegs of beer. A major feature of the retail market was the powerful buying power exercised by the leading supermarket chains as compared to the more fragmented structure of liquor and convenience stores.

Regional differences arose primarily through different market shares, the presence of regional and local brewers, and differences in consumer preferences. Beer drinking was heaviest in the Mid-West, while the heaviest consumption of super-premium, luxury, and light beers was on the Eastern and Western seaboards. Coor's strength was primarily in the West; Heileman's in the Mid-West; while Stroh's brand strength was mainly in the East. Regional brands were important in parts of the South, while in several metropolitan areas, most notably San Francisco and Boston, recently-established micro-breweries established loyal local followings.

Identifying key segmentation variables   The first stage of segmentation analysis is to decide the basis of industry segmentation. What is the most appropriate basis for dividing up the industry: Different types of products, different groups of customers, different price ranges, or different geographical areas? For most industries there are numerous criteria which can be applied. These mostly relate to characteristics of the product or characteristics of the customers. Exhibit 3.1 shows a number of segmentation variables. The most appropriate segmentation variables are those which yield the most distinct categorization in terms of our *substitutability* criteria. Just as we used substitutability on the customer side and on the supplier side, as the basis for defining industry boundaries, the same criteria can be applied to determining industry segments.

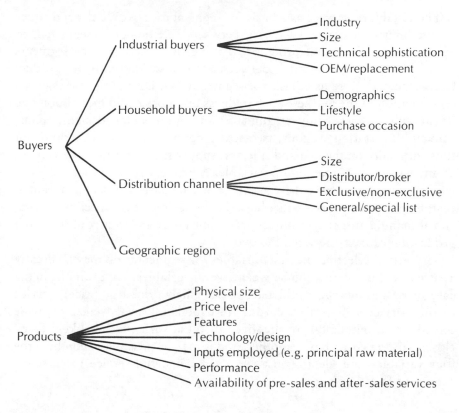

Exhibit 3.1 The basis for segmentation: Customer and product characteristics

For example, the automobile industry can be segmented on the basis of many different variables. In the early 1920s, Alfred Sloan Jr. established General Motors' view of the US automobile market as a number of price segments which were to form the basis of GM's product policy until the 1960s:

The product policy we proposed is the one for which General Motors has now long been known. We said first that the corporation should produce a line of cars in each price area, from the lowest price up to one for a strictly high-grade quantity-production car, but we would not get into the fancy-price field with small production; second, that the price steps should not be such as to leave wide gaps in the line, and yet should be great enough to keep their number within reason, so that the greatest advantage of quantity production could be secured; and third, that there should be no duplication by the corporation in the price fields or steps . . .

It also recommended that the policy of the corporation should be to produce and market only six standard models, and that as soon as practicable the following grades should constitute the entire line of cars:

(a) $450–$600
(b) $600–$900
(c) $900–$1,200
(d) $1,200–$1,700
(e) $1,700–$2,500
(f) $2,500–$3,500.[3]

The suitability of price as a basis for segmentation would depend either on the limited customer switching between different price segments, or upon different groups of producers serving the different price segments with limited ability to switch between segments. Alternatively, product features may be used as a basis for segmentation. During the 1960s GM's segmentation of the market was based less upon price and more upon size of car (subcompact, compact, full-size) and upon vehicle design (sedans, convertibles, station wagons, two-seater coupés). Again, the criteria of substitutability on the demand side and supply side determine the validity of any particular segmentation variable. A product feature such as front-wheel versus rear-wheel drive is not a useful basis for segmentation if customers are willing to switch between front- and rear-wheel drive cars, and if manufacturers typically supply both types and can readily switch production capacity between the two.

The task of selecting the best variables for segmentation may be greatly assisted by close correlation between several variables. For example, in the case of restaurants we could select price (high price/low price), service (waiter service/self-service), cuisine (fast-food/full meals), alcohol (wine served/soft drinks only). In practice, all these variables are likely to be closely correlated with one another, and it may be possible to combine the four variables and identify just three segments: full-service restaurants, cafes, and fast-food outlets.

Constructing a segmentation matrix   Once the segmentation variables have been selected and discrete categories for each determined, the individual segments may be identified using a two- or three-dimensional matrix. For example, an analysis of the British frozen food industry[4] used types of food and distribution channel as the basis for segmentation (see Exhibit 3.2). Where firms are specialized by their geographic area, or where customer preferences differ by country or region, then geography may be a useful basis for segmentation. Exhibit 3.3 shows a three-dimensional segmentation of the US beer industry. Note that just three variables, each with four separate categories give us a total of 64 segments – a rather large number when it comes to evaluating the attractiveness of each. However, for most industries, it is likely that many categories will be empty, and it may be possible to combine others. But, because a segment is "empty" – that is, there are no firms supplying within it – does not mean that we can ignore it completely. Some of these empty segments might provide opportunities for future development. Thus, in the early 1960s, microwave ovens and dishwashing machines were manufactured almost exclusively for the catering trade, a segmentation analysis of the appliance industry might have alerted the firms established in these segments to opportunities for developing these products for the consumer market.

Analyzing segment attractiveness   Competition and the profit potential of an industry segment can be analyzed using the same structural analysis

		DISTRIBUTION CHANNELS				
		Supermarkets		Independent grocery retailers	Specialist freezer stores	Caterers
		Producers' brands	Retailers' brands			
P R O D U C T T Y P E S	Vegetables					
	Fruits					
	Meat Products					
	Desserts					
	Convenience Ready Meals					

Exhibit 3.2
Segmenting the British frozen food industry

Note: The above matrix identifies five categories of frozen food, and five distribution channels. While the basic distinction of customers is between retail and catering, within retailing there are three distinct categories of outlet: Supermarkets, independent grocery stores, and specialist retailers of frozen foods ("home freezer centers"). In addition different market conditions exist for processors supplying frozen foods for sale under their own brand names from those supplying frozen foods for sale under the brand name of the retailer.

Source: Monopolies and Mergers Commission, Frozen Foods (HMSO, London 1976); and P. Geroski and T. Vlassopoulos, "The rise and fall of a market leader: Frozen foods in the UK," London Business School, Case series 9, 1989.

that was applied to the analysis of an industry. Just as the pressure of competition and the prospects for profit in the frozen food industry can be analyzed by determining the strength of each of the five forces of competition, so can the same analysis be applied to the supply of frozen vegetables to the catering trade.

However, there are a few differences. First, when analyzing the pressure of competition from substitute products, we are concerned not only with substitutes from other *industries*, but also with substitutes from *other segments* within the same industry. For example, in analyzing competition in the supply of frozen vegetables to the catering trade, we must take account not only of caterers' willingness to purchase fresh vegetables as an alternative, but also to purchase frozen vegetables from supermarkets and discount stores.

Secondly, when considering entry into the segment, the major source of entrants is likely to be producers established in other segments within the industry. Thus, in discussing the threat of entry into the segment we must focus primarily upon the barriers which restrict the incursion of firms from

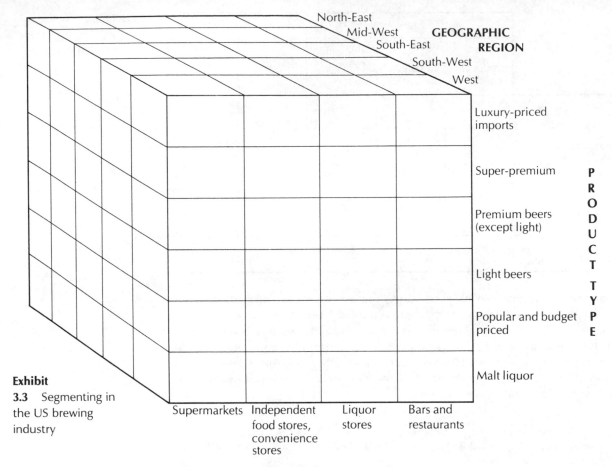

Exhibit
3.3 Segmenting in the US brewing industry

DISTRIBUTION CHANNEL

other segments: these are termed "barriers to mobility" to distinguish them from the barriers to entry which offer protection from outside the industry. Barriers to mobility are a key factor in determining the ability of a segment to offer superior returns to those available elsewhere in the industry. Unless there are significant barriers to the mobility of firms from other segments there is no basis for the preservation of superior profitability.[5] In most industries, the increased flexibility of design and production made possible by computer-aided design and flexible manufacturing systems has had the effect of reducing barriers to mobility. In the automobile industry the luxury car and sports car segments were regarded as high-margin niches relatively free from the intense competition which characterized the mass market. However, up-market penetration by large-scale producers such as Honda (Acura), Volkswagen (Audi), Toyota (Lexus), and Nissan (Infiniti) has greatly increased competition in the luxury car segment and severely dented the profits of BMW, Mercedes, Jaguar, and Volvo.[6]

The value of segmentation analysis is revealed in the diversity in structure and competition between different segments of the same industry.

For example, in the chemical industry during the late 1970s and early

1980s, the differences in competition and profitability between bulk chemicals and specialty chemicals were startling. Bulk chemicals were commodity products subject to substantial excess capacity, scale economies, and high fixed costs; elements which contributed to ruinous price competition. Specialty chemicals were differentiated, patent and technical barriers limited entry, and capacity and demand were better balanced. Chemical producers who quickly shifted from bulk to specialty chemicals (such as Dow and ICI) were much more profitable during the 1980s than those which were heavily concentrated on bulk chemicals.

In automobile parts, there are substantial differences in margins between the original equipment (OEM) segment and the replacement segment. In the former, prices are forced down by the bargaining power of the car manufacturers. In the replacement market, there is less buyer power and the final purchaser is less able to substitute between one component manufacturer and another. An inquiry by the British Monopolies Commission in the early 1960s found that Champion spark plugs, which retailed at 5 shillings ($0.70) each were supplied as original equipment for one-tenth of that price.[7]

Identify the segment's key success factors Differences in competitive structure and in customer preferences between segments also imply differences in the basis of competitive advantage. Examination of differences between segments in buyers' purchase criteria and the ways in which firms compete can reveal clear differences in key success factors. For example, the US bicycle industry can be segmented on the basis of customer age, price, branding and distribution channel. Combining these segmentation variables, four major segments can be identified within which key success factors differ considerably (see Exhibit 3.4).

Narrow versus broad segment scope A final issue concerning the choice of which segments to enter and how to compete in each concerns the relative advantages of *segment specialization* versus *segment diversity*. The advantages of a broad over a narrow segment focus are dependent upon two major factors: Similarity of key success factors and the presence of shared costs. In an industry where key success factors are similar between segments, a firm can adopt a similar strategic approach in relation to different segments. If different strategies need to be adopted for different segments then, not only does this pose organizational difficulties for the firm, but the credibility of the firm in one segment may be adversely affected by its strategy in another. The introduction by Harley-Davidson of a range of lightweight motorcycles during the 1960s was a failure, not only because Harley-Davidson could not compete with the Japanese in this segment, but also because of the damage to the firm's reputation in the heavyweight motorcycle segment.

Shared costs between segments are important because their presence means that broad-segment suppliers can achieve lower costs than their

Exhibit

3.4 Segmentation and key success factors in the US bicycle industry

Segment	Key success factors
Low-price bicycles sold primarily through department and chain stores, mainly under the retailer's own brand (e.g. Sears' "Free Spirit").	The key requirement is low-cost manufacture combined with consistency of quality and sufficient financial security to guarantee a long-term supply relationship. Manufacturers must be responsive to the design and supply requirements of their retailers. Most of this segment was occupied by Taiwanese assemblers, although some US manufacturers, such as Murray Ohio, had survived rigorous cost control and supplemented domestic production by imported components and complete bicycles.
Medium-priced bicycles sold primarily under the manufacturer's brand name and distributed mainly through specialist bicycle stores.	Success requires cost-efficient manufacture, which depends upon scale-efficient manufacture and either low wage rates or automated manufacturing techniques. Success also requires a reputation for quality and effective marketing both to dealers through the provision of information and dealer-support services, and to final customer through advertising. Scale-efficient production and national (and increasingly international) distribution and advertising, give large firms an advantage. Leading companies include Schwinn (US), Raleigh (UK), Peugeot (France), and Fuji (Japan).
High-priced enthusiasts' bicycles.	Success requires high quality components and assembly, innovation in design and materials (primarily in order to achieve speed through minimizing weight and wind resistance) and market appeal through competitive success in racing and advertising through the specialist cycling press.
Children's bicycles and tricycles sold primarily through toy retailers (both department stores and specialist toy stores).	Manufacturers can compete either on basis of low price (offshore manufacture) or strong brand name backed by good design and reputation for safety and quality.

narrow-segment competitors. The vulnerability of narrow-segment specialists to competition from broad-line competitors is constantly being revealed:

- In soft drinks, 7-Up's reliance on a single lemon-lime drink places it in a weak position against its broader-line competitors Coca Cola, Pepsi Cola, and Schweppes.
- One of the problems that Zenith faces in competing in the US consumer electronics industry is that its narrow segment focus (it competes only in televisions and video recorders and almost entirely in the North American market) places it at a disadvantage to companies like Philips,

Matsushita, and Toshiba which are able to spread their costs of R&D, manufacturing, and brand advertising across most countries in the world and across a wide range of consumer electronic products.

● The acquisition of specialist automobile producers such as Saab, Lancia, Jaguar, AMC-Jeep, and Lotus, by larger, broad-line automobile producers reflects the latter companies' ability to spread the costs of R&D, tooling, marketing, and distribution across a number of market segments.

In service industries, William Davidow and Bro Uttal have argued that economies from specialization and differences in key success factors in different customer segments favor a narrow segment focus. By specializing in hernia surgery, Shouldice Hospital near Toronto achieves remarkable levels of productivity and quality. Segment-focussed banks such as University National Bank and Trust, Palo Alto, outperform broad-based competitors such as Bank of America and Wells Fargo. The fall of People's Express can be traced to its decision to broaden its segment focus from its core clientele of backpack travelers to business and upper-income travelers.[8]

Many of the issues which arise in relation to the relative attractiveness of broad or narrow segment strategies are identical to those which arise when considering the merits of specialization versus diversification. Issues of shared costs and transferable skills will be discussed in more detail in chapter 12.

An alternative approach to segmenting the firms within an industry is that of *strategic groups*. The concept originated at Harvard[9] and was developed and applied in empirical research at Purdue.[10] A *strategic group* is "the group of firms in an industry following the same or a similar strategy along the strategic dimensions."[11] These "strategic dimensions" include product market scope (in terms of product range and geographical breadth); choice of distribution channels; level of product quality; degree of vertical integration; cost position; extent of technological leadership; and so on. By selecting the most important strategic dimensions and locating each firm in the industry along them it is usually possible to identify one or more groups of company which have adopted more or less similar approaches to competing within the industry. Exhibit 3.5 identifies strategic groups within the world automobile industry.

Strategic group analysis has been proposed (notably by Michael Porter) as the basic framework to be used in diagnosing competition, positioning, and profitability of firms and types of firm within an industry. Unfortunately, the approach suffers from fundamental flaws as a means of analyzing competition. Most serious is the fact that the members of a strategic group, while pursuing similar strategies, are not necessarily in competition with one another. For example, in the strategic group map of the world automobile industry, the member firms within the nationally-focussed groups may be pursuing a similar strategic focus, but are differentiated by location. Hence, it is not possible to analyze strategic groups

Strategic groups

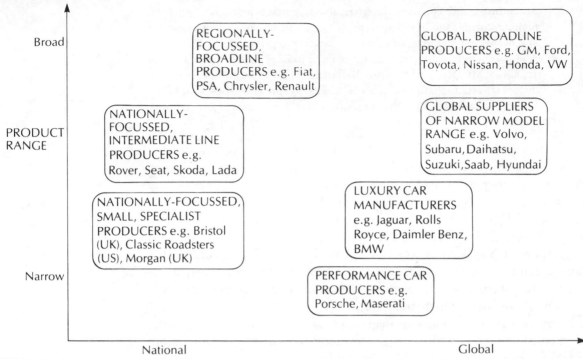

Exhibit 3.5 Strategic groups in the world automobile industry

GEOGRAPHICAL SCOPE

as competing groups of firms whose profitability depends upon the internal structure of the group and protection from other strategic groups by barriers to mobility.

This is not to imply that the strategic group is not a useful concept, but that the value of strategic group analysis is more a descriptive than a predictive tool. Strategic group analysis is unlikely to offer much insight into why some firms in an industry are more profitable than others. However, as a means of gaining a broad picture of the types of firms within an industry and the kinds of strategy which have proven viable, strategic group analysis can contribute to an understanding of the structure, competitive dynamics, and evolution of an industry, and to the issues of strategic management within it.[12]

Competitor Analysis

The importance of competitor analysis to a company depends upon the structure of its industry. In a fragmented industry where firms produce an undifferentiated product, as in the case of most agricultural commodities, market competition is the outcome of the strategies and decisions of so many producers that there is little point in analyzing the behavior of one or two individual firms. In such industries, analysis of an individual firm's competitive behavior is only useful if it is representative of the behavior of other firms. Hence, by understanding a single firm it is possible to predict the behavior of the industry as a whole. In other industry environments, particularly concentrated industries or those where there is substantial product differentiation, the competitive environment of a company may depend critically upon the behavior of a few rivals. In household detergents, the industry environment is dominated by the competitive interaction of Proctor and Gamble, Colgate-Palmolive, and Lever Brothers (Unilever). In jumbo-jets, the major feature of the global competitive environment is the interaction between Boeing and Airbus Industrie.

In other industries, although concentration may be only modest, the extent of differentiation in the goods and services offered by different firms may mean that a company faces just one or two close competitors whose strategies impact substantially upon its profitability. For example, in the world soft drinks industry, despite the large number of national, international, and local suppliers of soft drinks, the main feature of competition is the struggle between Coca Cola and Pepsi Cola for dominance in cola drinks. Each company's obsessive interest in obtaining a market share advantage over the rival is reflected in the monitoring and prediction by each firm of the other's marketing strategies, and the constant quest for advantage over the other whether by comparative taste tests ("The Pepsi Challenge"), the use of popular entertainers in commercials (Michael Jackson by Pepsi; Elton John by Coca Cola), and the quest for new markets through political influence (e.g. Coca Cola's mobile bottling plants for General Eisenhower's advancing army in Western Europe in 1944–5; Pepsi Cola's entry into China on the coat-tails of President Nixon's visit in 1972).

Similarly in the US automobile market, although there are over 20 suppliers, of which GM, Ford, Chrysler, Honda, and Toyota have the leading shares, Jaguar's competitive environment is most strongly influenced by the product, pricing, and promotional policies of Mercedes Benz and BMW.

It is not only through marketing activities that firms' competitive strategies are interdependent. In industries where plant capacity is large relative to the total market, investment decisions are highly interdependent. In the petrochemical industry, for example, any single firm's calculation of the returns on investment in a new plant must take careful account of other firms' investment plans. Research and development activities show similar interactions. In the pharmaceuticals industry, the returns to R&D depend crucially upon being the first company to apply for a patent on a new drug. Expenditures on R&D require a careful appraisal of whether other firms are pursuing similar avenues of research and, if so, their stage of development.

Competitor analysis has three major purposes:

- to forecast competitors' future strategies and decisions;
- to predict competitors' likely reactions to a firm's strategy and competitive initiatives;
- to determine how competitors' behavior can be influenced to the benefit of the initiating firm.

For all three purposes, the key requirement is to understand competitors in order to predict their choices of strategy and tactics and likely reactions to environmental changes and any competitive moves initiated by one's own company.

A framework for predicting competitor behavior

Exhibit 3.6 shows the basic framework for competitor analysis. There are four main inputs into the analysis:

- the competitor's current strategy;
- the competitor's objectives;
- the competitor's assumptions about the industry;
- the competitor's capabilities.

Exhibit 3.6 A framework for competitor analysis

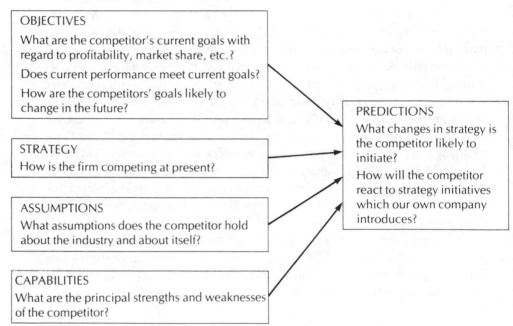

OBJECTIVES
What are the competitor's current goals with regard to profitability, market share, etc.?
Does current performance meet current goals?
How are the competitors' goals likely to change in the future?

STRATEGY
How is the firm competing at present?

ASSUMPTIONS
What assumptions does the competitor hold about the industry and about itself?

CAPABILITIES
What are the principal strengths and weaknesses of the competitor?

PREDICTIONS
What changes in strategy is the competitor likely to initiate?
How will the competitor react to strategy initiatives which our own company introduces?

Identifying current strategy   The starting-point is an identification of the company's current strategy. In the absence of any forces for change, a reasonable assumption is that the company will continue to compete in the future in much the same way as it competes at the present. A company's strategy may be identified on the basis of what the firm says and what it does. These two are not necessarily the same; as Mintzberg has pointed out, there may be a divergence between *intended strategy* and *realized strategy*.[13] Major sources of explicit statements of strategy intentions are likely to be found in the annual reports of companies, particularly in the chairman's message to shareholders, and in other public statements by senior managers. With regard to realized strategy, this can be inferred from the answers to our two key questions: "Where is the firm competing?" and "How is the firm competing?" Further insight can be gained by examining functional strategies: "What are the firm's policies with regard to products, marketing, human resources, production, finance, and technology?"

Identifying *changes* in a competitor's strategy is of crucial importance.

Here, the principal clues to the direction of change are likely to be current decisions over resource deployment. What capital investments have been recently announced? In which divisions and plants are redundancies and layoffs taking place? What new personnel are being hired? What new products have been announced? What advertising campaigns have been commissioned?

Such information can offer considerable insight into future priorities and the likely responses of the competitor to our own company's strategic initiatives. For example, US Steel's diversification during the 1980s culminated in the company changing its name in 1986 to "USX". The signal to other companies in the industry was that US Steel no longer regarded steel as its core business and its priorities were its diversified businesses. In these circumstances, the new USX might be a less aggressive competitor in the steel industry than the old US Steel. In particular, when faced by competitive threats from other steel companies, instead of fighting for its market position, it might be willing to relinquish market share and transfer resources to its more attractive businesses. By contrast, Zenith's sale of its computer division in 1989 was a clear indication to its competitors of its commitment to long-term survival in the US television industry.

Identifying the competitor's objectives   To determine likely changes in a competitor's strategy and competitive stance, some knowledge of the company's goals is crucial. Identifying basic financial and market objectives is particularly important. A company with short- and medium-term ROI objectives, such as ITT or Hanson, is likely to be a very different competitor than a company with long-term market share goals such as Proctor and Gamble or Komatsu. A company with a short-term ROI objective is unlikely to react aggressively to the competitive initiative of a rival. Such a reaction would be financially costly. The company is more likely to withdraw from competition and retreat to market segments where profits are more secure. Thus, when Hanson acquired Ever Ready, it withdrew from most European markets on the basis that, due to strong competition, they were financially unattractive. Not only did Ever Ready give up ground to its arch-rival Duracell, it actually sold several of its overseas subsidiaries to Duracell. Compare the reaction of Proctor and Gamble to emerging competition. When meeting competition in any market it is renowned for its willingness to finance long-lasting competitive warfare using price cuts, promotions, and advertising. In the case of new products, P&G is willing to accept losses for up to nine years while building its market position.

If the competitor is a subsidiary of a larger corporation, it is important to comprehend the goals of the parent, since these will be the major determinant of the goals of the subsidiary. The means by which the parent controls the subsidiary is also important. How much autonomy does the subsidiary have? In the case of a highly-centralized corporation, the ability of the subsidiary to respond to competitive assaults may be restricted by slow corporate decision-making procedures.

The level of current performance in relation to the competitor's objectives is important in determining the likelihood of strategy change. The more a company is satisfied with present performance, the more likely it is to continue with the present strategy. If, on the other hand, the competitor's performance is falling well short of target, then the likelihood of radical strategic change, possibly accompanied by a change in top management is increased.

Particular problems arise when a competitor is not subject to commercial objectives at all. In small business situations, competition is sometimes dominated by the personal animosities between rival entrepreneurs. Such situations are extremely dangerous since they can give rise to destructive competition that threatens the financial viability of both companies. In international business, the presence of state-owned corporations provides a similarly serious challenge. The willingness of governments to support state-owned enterprises, particularly if they are viewed as "national champions", means that these corporations are not subject to normal commercial constraints. The establishment of Airbus Industrie as a heavily-subsidized vehicle for reestablishing the Western European aircraft industry in the world market for large passenger jets was a serious threat to the US aircraft industry and undoubtedly hastened the exit of Lockheed from jet airliners.

Competitors' assumptions about the industry   A competitor's future strategy changes and its likely reactions to competitive initiatives by our own company also depend upon its assumptions about the industry. It has been observed that the top managers of a firm typically hold a set of deep-seated beliefs about success factors within the industry which change only slowly over time. Moreover, within an industry, different firms tend to adhere to very similar beliefs, these industry-wide beliefs have been described by J-C Spender as "industry-recipes."[14]

The importance of these industry recipes is that they may limit the ability of a firm, and indeed an entire industry, to respond either to external change, or to an aggressive and innovative strategy move by an intruder. For example, during the 1960s, the Big Three US automobile manufacturers firmly believed that small cars were unprofitable. This belief was based upon their own experiences, which were, in part, a result of their own cost allocation procedures. A major consequence of this belief was their willingness to yield the fastest-growing segment of the US automobile market to Japanese and European imports.

In the motorcycle markets of the US and Britain during the 1960s, similarly rigid beliefs inhibited powerful domestic manufacturers from responding effectively to the growth of Japanese imports, spearheaded by Honda. The leading British and US manufacturers discounted the Japanese threat, principally because they discounted the importance, the profitability, and the longevity of the small motorcycle segment. Eric Turner, Chairman of BSA Ltd (manufacturer of Triumph and BSA motorcycles) commented in 1965:

The success of Honda, Suzuki and Yamaha has been jolly good for us. People start out by buying one of the low-priced Japanese jobs. They get to enjoy the fun and exhilaration of the open road and they frequently end up buying one of our more powerful and expensive machines.[15]

Similar complacency was expressed by William Davidson, President of Harley-Davidson:

Basically, we do not believe in the lightweight market. We believe that motorcycles are sports vehicles not transportation vehicles. Even if a man says he bought a motorcycle for transportation, it's generally for leisure time use. The lightweight motorcycle is only supplemental. Back around World War I, a number of companies came out with lightweight bikes. We came out with one ourselves. We came out with another in 1947 and it just didn't go anywhere. We have seen what happens to these small sizes.[16]

By the end of the 1970s, BSA and Triumph had ceased production and Harley-Davidson was barely surviving. The world motorcycle industry, including the large bike segments was dominated by the Japanese.

Identifying the competitor's capabilities   Predicting a competitor's future strategic initiative must be followed by an evaluation of the seriousness of the potential challenge. The extent to which a competitor threatens a company's market position depends upon the competitor's capabilities. Detailed analysis of resources and capabilities is deferred to the next chapter; suffice to say at this stage, that the key elements are an examination of the firm's principal categories of resources including financial reserves, capital equipment, work force, brand loyalty, and management skills, together with an appraisal of capabilities within each of the major functions: R&D, production, marketing, distribution, and so on.

Circumspection in the evaluation of a competitor's capabilities is essential before embarking upon any strategy that is likely to provoke a competitor. Many brilliant and innovative new companies have failed to withstand the aggressive reactions of well-entrenched, established firms. In the airline industry both Laker and Peoples Express aroused powerful competitive reactions that ultimately overwhelmed them. Conversely, established giants frequently underestimate the threat from newer and smaller rivals. It was not until Fuji negotiated photographic sponsorship of the 1984 Los Angeles Olympic Games, that Kodak began to respond to Fuji's challenge to its global dominance.

Predicting competitors' behavior   The first question we want to answer is: "What strategy shifts is the competitor likely to make?" This requires that we carefully identify current forces that are likely to provoke a change in strategy. These may be external, a shift in consumer preferences or regulatory change that may have important consequences for the firm, or

Applying competitor analysis

they may be internal – a failure to achieve current financial or market share targets, or factional conflict within the company. Whatever the sources, a careful identification of current strategy and goals, the company's assumptions about the industry, and its capabilities, will provide a sound basis on which to forecast the direction of change.

Secondly, we may wish to forecast a competitor's likely reactions to a proposed strategy change which our own company is initiating. If this strategy change involves an attack upon the competitor's market base, then that competitor's reactions may be crucial in determining the desirability of the strategy change. The same four elements will together provide useful guidance as to the nature, likelihood, and seriousness of a defensive reaction by the competitor. When Honda first attacked BSA/Triumph and Harley-Davidson directly with the introduction of a large-capacity motorcycle it knew that:

- both companies pursued medium-term financial goals rather than market share goals;
- both firms were benefiting from an upsurge in motorcycle demand and hence, were not unduly sensitive to losses in market share;
- both firms believed that due to their own customer loyalty and brand image, the Japanese producers were not a serious threat in the big-bike market;
- even if BSA/Triumph and Harley-Davidson did react aggressively, the effectiveness of their response would be limited by their weak financial positions and by their lack of innovative and manufacturing capabilities.

Influencing competitors' behavior: signalling and deterrence   By understanding its competitors, a firm may also be able to influence their behavior to its own advantage. Such influence may be directed towards discouraging aggressive competition from rivals; of ensuring that their competitive initiatives are misdirected. *Signalling* refers to the strategic use of information by a firm in order to influence the behavior of competitors. Jean Tirole describes such manipulation of rivals' perceptions so as to influence their subsequent behavior as "investments in disinformation."[17] Such manipulation is well developed within the military sphere. Sun Tzu placed heavy emphasis on the art of illusion:

The location we take to initiate a challenge must not be made known. When opponents do not know our location, they must prepare in many places. When opponents must prepare in many places, there will be few at the location where we initiate a challenge.

The ultimate Positioned Strategy is to be without apparent Position. Without position even the deepest intelligence is unable to spy; and those who are clever are unable to plan.[18]

In 1944, Allied deception was so good that even after the D-Day landings in Normandy had begun, the Germans believed that the main invasion would occur near Calais.

Signalling is viewed primarily as a means of threatening competitors and thereby dissuading them from competitive initiatives or reactions. The essence of the threat is a promise to take retaliation against any firm encroaching upon our own market position. For example, a firm holding a dominant position within a market may signal to potential entrants its intention to fight entry by aggressive price cutting. For a threat to be effective in deterring a competitive challenge, it must be credible. Since carrying out a threat is usually costly to both the threatener and the victim, it needs to be supported by commitment.[19] Thus, the threat of aggressive price cuts needs to be backed either by excess capacity or by excess inventories.[20] The classic example of a dominant firm investing in excess capacity in order to warn off potential entrants is Alcoa in the US aluminum industry during the 1930s and 40s (US versus Alcoa, 1945). However, subsequent studies have cast doubt upon the prevalence of this practice.[21]

The credibility of a threat also depends upon the reputation of the firm which issues it. Hence, even though carrying out a threat can be costly and seemingly irrational, we can regard such punishment as an investment in reputation which will yield returns from deterring competitive challenges in the future.[22] *Fortune* magazine identified Perrier in mineral water, Gillette in razors and razor blades, Anheuser-Busch in beer, and Emerson-Electric in sink disposal units as examples of companies whose aggressive quest for market share has gained them reputations as "killer competitors" which has encouraged a number of rivals to give up the fight.[23] The benefits of building a reputation for aggressiveness may be particularly great for diversified companies where reputation can be transferred from one market to another; hence, diversified firms may be able to exploit "economies of scope" in reputation.[24] Thus, the protracted market share wars that Proctor and Gamble fought in disposable diapers and household detergents have established a reputation for toughness that protects P&G's market position across a range of products and countries.

Signalling is not exclusively concerned with issuing threats. An equally important function of signalling may be to avoid aggressive competition. In the case of an established firm facing the possibility of entry, the incumbent may find that deterring entry is either too costly, in which case the incumbent may wish to signal its intention to accommodate rather than to fight entry. Jean Tirole characterizes the strategic choices as "top dog" and "puppy dog" alternatives.[25] Signalling mechanisms can also be used to avoid price competition between established firms within an industry. A common means by which firms avoid price competition is to follow a pattern of price leadership the success of which depends critically upon establishing consensus between competitors. In the UK gasoline market, the initiation of a price increase by a firm is normally preceded by a period of consensus building during which the price leader tests the water by means of press releases which announce "the unsatisfactory level of margins in the industry", the "need for a price increase to recoup recent cost increases", and the likelihood that "a price increase will become necessary in the near future."[26]

Game theory shows that in simple, single-period games with equally-matched players, the problem of *"prisoners' dilemma"* arises. This refers to the propensity for independent decision making by players to result in each selecting competitive strategies and arriving at a position which is undesirable for all concerned since each would have been better off through cooperation. Thus, equilibrium of military power between the United States and the Soviet Union results in each country building enormously-expensive nuclear arsenals. Similarly the economies of the OPEC countries suffer from the inability of the member countries to cooperate in restricting their oil sales to their allocated quotas. Moving towards a cooperative solution requires the building of trust between the players so that each player is sufficiently confident that it can adopt a cooperative strategy without it being stabbed in the back by another player. Signalling, either by direct communication between the players, or through adaptation of competitive behavior over time, provides a mechanism for avoiding competitive behavior which, while seemingly rational at the individual level, results in an outcome which is collectively undesirable.[27]

A firm can deter would-be competitors by other means. While threats deter through reducing the incentives for competition, *preemption* limits the opportunities for competition. Preemptive strategies involve a closing off by the incumbent firm of the investment opportunities available to competitors. Preemption may take various forms. Proliferation of product varieties by a market leader can leave new entrants and smaller rivals with few opportunities for establishing a market niche. Between 1950 and 1972, the six leading suppliers of breakfast cereals introduced 80 new brands into the US market.[28] Large investments in production capacity ahead of growth of market demand also preempt opportunities for rivals. Du Pont's aggressive expansion of its capacity for producing titanium dioxide paint whitener during the 1970s was aimed at exploiting the company's first-mover advantage and making it unattractive for competitors to invest.[29] To protect competitive advantage built upon proprietary technology, patent proliferation can limit competitors' opportunities. In 1974, Xerox's dominant market position was protected by a wall of over 2,000 patents. When IBM introduced its first copier in 1970, Xerox sued it for infringing 22 of these patents.[30]

Summary

The industry analysis of chapter 2 provided a first-stage analysis of a company's industry environment. But for a company to outperform the industry average, environmental analysis at the level of the industry is too aggregated. Superior performance requires that the company applies a more detailed analysis of its industry environment in order to target more precisely where it will position itself within the industry, and how it will out-maneuver rivals. Hence, segmentation analysis and competitor analysis are critical components of industry analysis.

Segmentation analysis applies the framework of industry analysis to specific portions of an industry. Such analysis permits a company to:

- identify which segments have the most attractive profit prospects within the industry;
- identify the strategies which are likely to be effective in increasing the profit potential of a segment and exploiting the Key Success Factors within a segment;
- evaluate the merits of a niche strategy involving specialization in one or a few segments, as compared with a broad-based multisegment strategy.

The ability to identify and occupy attractive segments of an industry is critical to success. Hewlett Packard's superior performance in the office electronics industry during the late 1980s was primarily due to its ability to quickly identify slowing sales and falling margins in the minicomputers segment, and swiftly shift its emphasis towards personal computers (desktops and workstations) and PC peripherals such as laser printers.[31] Location of attractive industry segments must be supported by clear understanding of key success factors within those segments. In clothes retailing, both Benetton and Marks & Spencer are highly successful companies, but their strategies are quite different, reflecting the different requirements of their respective market segments.

Even the industry segment is too high a level of aggregation for most firms. To gain an intimate understanding of competition, to predict competitive threats, and to influence competitors' behavior, analysis must extend down to the level of individual competitors. In industries where a company faces a few close competitors, it is not possible to understand competition without understanding the competitors themselves. Understanding competitors requires identification of:

- the competitor's goals;
- the competitor's current strategy;
- the competitor's assumptions;
- the competitor's capabilities.

"Getting inside" competitors in order to understand and influence competitive interaction lies at the heart of strategy analysis. An essential characteristic of successful strategists, whether corporate chief executives, military commanders, political leaders, or chess players, is their ability to insightfully analyze their opponents.

Notes

1. "How America took to France's baguettes," *Financial Times*, November 22, 1985, p. 26.

2. This section draws heavily upon the approach used by Michael E. Porter, *Competitive Advantage*, (Free Press, New York, 1985), ch. 7.

3. Alfred P. Sloan, *My Years with General Motors* (Sidgwick and Jackson, London, 1963), pp. 65–7.

4. Robert M. Grant, *Birds Eye and U.K. Frozen Food Industry*, mimeo, 1986 (available from the author).

5. For a formal analysis of mobility barriers, see R. E. Caves and M. E. Porter, "From entry barriers to mobility barriers: conjectural decisions and contrived deterrence to new competition," *Quarterly Journal of Economics* 91 (1977), pp. 241–62.

6. "The motor industry," *Financial Times*, October 20, 1988, Section III.

7. Monopolies Commission, *Report on the Supply of Electrical Equipment for Mechanically-Propelled Land Vehicles* (HMSO, London, 1963).

8. William H. Davidson and Bro Uttal, "Service companies: focus or falter," *Harvard Business Review*, July–August, 1989, pp. 77–84.

9. See, for example, Michael Hunt, *Competition in the Major Home Appliance Industry*, doctoral dissertation, Harvard University, 1973; and Michael E. Porter, "Structure within industries and companies' performance," *Review of Economics and Statistics* 61 (1979), pp. 214–27.

10. Kenneth Hatten, Dan Schendel and Arnold Cooper, "A strategic model of the U.S. brewing industry, 1952–71," *Academy of Management Journal* 21, (1978), pp. 592–610; Karel Cool, *Strategic Groups in the U.S. Pharmaceuticals Industry*, PhD dissertation, Krannert School of Business, Purdue University, 1987.

11. Michael E. Porter, *Competitive Strategy* (Free Press, New York, 1980), p. 129.

12. For further discussion of strategic groups and their role in strategy analysis see John McGee and Howard Thomas, "Strategic groups: theory, research and taxonomy," *Strategic Management Journal* 7 (1986), pp. 141–60.

13. Henry Mintzberg, "Opening up the definition of strategy", in J. Quinn, H. Mintzberg and R. James, *The Strategy Process: Concepts, Contexts and Cases* (Prentice-Hall, Englewood Cliffs, 1988), pp. 14–20.

14. J-C Spender, *Industry Recipes: The Nature and Sources of Managerial Judgement* (Blackwell, Oxford, 1989).

15. *Advertising Age*, December 27, 1965, quoted by Richard T. Pascale, *Honda A* (Harvard Business School, Case 9–384–049, 1983).

16. *Forbes*, September 15, 1966.

17. Jean Tirole, *The Theory of Industrial Organization* (MIT Press, Cambridge, Mass., 1988), p. 361.

18. R. L. Wing, *The Art of Strategy: A New Translation of Sun Tzu's Classic "The Art of War"* (Doubleday, New York, 1988), pp. 85–7.

19. The role of commitment is discussed in detail by Thomas Schelling in his classic study *The Strategy of Conflict* (Harvard University Press, Cambridge, Mass., 1980), pp. 35–41.

20. For a formal analysis of the role of excess capacity and inventories in deterring entrants see: E. Maskin and J. Tirole, "A theory of dynamic oligopoly II: Price competition, kinked demand curves and Edgeworth cycles,"

Econometrica 56 (1988), pp. 127–40; and J. Rotemberg and G. Saloner, "Strategic inventories and the excess volatility of production," Discussion Paper (MIT, Cambridge, Mass., 1985).

21. Marvin B. Leiberman, "Excess capacity as a barrier to entry: an empirical appraisal," *Journal of Industrial Economics* 35 (1987), pp. 607–27.

22. Keith Weigelt and Colin Camerer, "Reputation and corporate strategy: a review of recent theory and applications," *Strategic Management Journal* 9 (1988), pp. 443–54.

23. "Companies that compete best," *Fortune*, May 22, 1989, pp. 36–44.

24. P. Milgrom and J. Roberts, "Predation, reputation and entry deterrence," *Journal of Economic Theory* 27 (1982), pp. 280–312.

25. Jean Tirole, *The Theory of Industrial Organization* (MIT Press, Cambridge, Mass., 1988), pp. 323–8.

26. Robert M. Grant, "Pricing behavior in the UK wholesale market for petrol," *Journal of Industrial Economics* 30 (1982), pp. 271–92

27. For a non-technical discussion of prisoners' dilemma in particular and game theory in general, see Sharon M. Oster, *Modern Competitive Analysis* (Wiley, New York, 1990), ch. 12.

28. R. Schmalensee, "Entry deterrence in the ready-to-eat breakfast cereal industry," *Bell Journal of Economics* 9 (1978), pp. 305–27.

29. Pankaj Ghemawat, "Sustainable advantage," *Harvard Business Review*, September–October 1986, pp. 55–6.

30. Monopolies & Mergers Commission, *Indirect Electrostatic Reprographic Equipment* (HMSO, London, 1975), pp. 35, 56.

31. "Hewlett-Packard's screeching turn towards desktops," *Business Week*, September 11, 1989, pp. 106–12.

FOUR

Analyzing Resources and Capabilities

Analysts have tended to define assets too narrowly, identifying only those that can be measured, such as plant and equipment. Yet the intangible assets, such as a particular technology, accumulated consumer information, brand name, reputation, and corporate culture, are invaluable to the firm's competitive power. In fact, these invisible assets are often the only real source of competitive edge that can be sustained over time.

Hiroyuki Itami, *Mobilizing Invisible Assets*

Introduction

In this chapter we shift our focus from the firm's industry environment to the characteristics of the firm itself. Our interest in the firm is very specific: we wish to identify the firm's potential for establishing competitive advantage by assessing the resources and capabilities which the firm owns or has access to. Specifically, this chapter has five objectives:

- to outline the role which a company's resources and capabilities play in the formulation of its strategy and to explain their crucial importance in establishing competitive advantage;
- to show how the firm can identify, classify, and explore the characteristics of its base of resources and capabilities;

- to develop a set of criteria for analyzing the potential for the firm's resources and capabilities to yield long-term profit returns;
- to show how strategy is concerned not only with deploying the firm's resources to yield returns over the long term but also with augmenting and strengthening the firm's resources and capabilities;
- to develop a framework for resource analysis which integrates the above themes into a practical guide to formulating strategies that build competitive advantage.

Let us begin by explaining why a company's resources and capabilities are so important.

The Role of Resource Analysis in Strategy Formulation

Strategy, we have observed, is concerned with matching a firm's capabilities to the opportunities which arise in the external environment. So far, the emphasis of the book has been the firm's relationships with its external environment. This focus upon external analysis is common to the strategy literature in general. During the past two decades, most of the developments in strategy analysis have concentrated upon the industry environment of the firm and its competitive positioning in relation to rivals. The analysis of industry and competition has been based primarily on the concepts and theories of microeconomics and has been closely associated with the work of Michael Porter. The analysis of the relative competitive positions of the firms within an industry has been developed primarily by consulting companies. For example, the Boston Consulting Group's use of the experience curve as the primary determinant of relative cost position, and the Strategic Planning Institute's linking of market share, quality, and other positional variables to profitability through its PIMS project.

By contrast, strategic analysis of the firm's internal environment is surprisingly underdeveloped. Analysis of the internal environment has, for the most part, been concerned with issues of strategy implementation. Internal characteristics of the firm such as organizational structure, systems of control and incentives, and top management skills and style, have been viewed primarily as consequences of the strategy adopted, and to some extent as constraints upon the range of strategies that can be adopted.[1] This comparative neglect of internal resources by business strategists contrasts sharply with the approach of military strategy which has always given primacy to resource analysis. Liddell Hart, a prominent military historian, argued that there is only one underlying principle of war, "concentration of strength against weakness."[2] Military strategy's preoccupation with resources is also reflected in the central importance of "balance of power" in military analysis. Over time, only the elements in the arithmetic equations have changed. During World War I, the military strategy of the allied forces was underpinned by the premise that, since the combined population of the Allies exceeded that of the Axis countries, ultimate victory was assured. For most of the post-war period, defense strategies were based upon calculations of the balance of nuclear and conventional armaments between the NATO and Warsaw Pact countries and the underlying logic of Mutually Assured Destruction (MAD).

The case for making the resources and capabilities of the firm the foundation for its long-term strategy rests upon two premises. The first concerns the role of resources in defining the identity of the firm. The starting-point for the formulation of strategy must be some statement of the firm's identity and purpose; this takes the form of a *mission statement* which answers the question: "What is our business?" Conventionally, the definition of the business has been in terms of the served market of the firm: "Who are our customers?" and "Which of their needs are we seeking to serve?" But if the external environment is in a state of flux, if different technologies vie to serve the same customer needs, or if the identity of customers quickly change, then an externally-focussed orientation does not provide the constancy of direction to act as a secure foundation for formulating long-term strategy. When external conditions are changing, the firm itself in terms of the resources and capabilities which it comprises may be a much more stable basis on which to define its identity.

Resources and capabilities as the foundation for strategy

Thus, the basis of a resource-based approach to strategy is a definition of the firm, not in terms of the needs it is seeking to satisfy, but in terms of what it is capable of. The primary issue for strategy is determining what the firm can do. The second issue is deciding in which industries and through what types of competitive strategy the firm can best exploit these capabilities.

This approach rejects that proposed by Ted Levitt in his classic article "Marketing myopia."[3] When markets are changing, argued Levitt, the key to successful adjustment is for the firm to define its served market broadly rather than narrowly; hence, by defining themselves as railroad businesses rather than transportation businesses, the railroad companies became prisoners of a declining industry. However, those companies which have defined their businesses as serving broad-based customer needs have frequently failed through their inability to master the breadth of capabilities which correspond to their target markets. By contrast, firms whose strategies have been based upon the development and application of specific capabilities have frequently shown a remarkable capacity to adjust to external changes. Exhibit 4.1 gives some examples.

The second reason for focussing upon resources as the foundation for an enterprise's strategy is that profits are ultimately a return to the resources owned and controlled by the firm. In chapter 2 we identified the profits of the firm as deriving from two sources: the attractiveness of the industry in which the firm is located, and the achievement of competitive advantage over other firms within the industry. However, if we probe deeper into

Resources as the source of corporate profitability

Exhibit 4.1 Firm's capabilities versus served market as a basis for strategy

Company	Strategic focus	Comments
Companies pursuing market-focussed strategies		
Allegis Corp.	Serving the needs of the traveler.	Formed in 1986 from the merger of United Airlines, Westin Hotels, Hertz car rental. Non-airline businesses divested in 1987.
Merrill Lynch	Serving the investment and financial needs of individual and institutional clients.	Between 1976 and 1982 diversified from stockbroking into insurance, retail and investment banking, real estate broking and relocation services. Financial performance during the 1980s was well below industry average and some activities were divested.
Sears Roebuck	"Sears is where America shops."	During the 1980s, Sears' attempt to "expand its special franchise with the American consumer" ran into trouble. In attempting to compete across a vast range of merchandise, for all ages and groups of people, while expanding aggressively into financial services, Sears was unable to develop the specialized resources and expertise needed to compete with more focussed rivals.
Companies with strategies based upon specific capabilities		
Honda Motor Co.	Technical leadership and manufacturing excellence in 4-cycle gasoline engines.	Dominated the world's motorcycle industry during 1960s. Successfully expanded into automobiles, generators, lawnmowers and other engine-powered products during 1970s and 80s.

Company	Strategic focus	Comments
3M Corp.	Competence in the development and marketing of innovatory new products based upon technical expertise in adhesives and tapes.	Initially manufactured abrasives. Expanded into broad range of adhesives and tapes and disks for industrial and domestic use.
Hanson	Competence in acquiring, restructuring, and managing mature, low-technology businesses.	Diversified into broad range of mature businesses in UK and US. Acquisitions have included Ever Ready, SCM, Imperial Group, Kidde. One of the fastest-growing and most profitable British companies of the 1980s.

both competitive advantage and industry attractiveness, we can trace the origins of both sources of profit back to the firm's resources.

Take competitive advantage. The ability to establish a cost advantage over competitors rests upon the possession of scale-efficient plant, superior process technology, ownership of low-cost sources of raw materials, or locational advantages in relation to low-wage labor or proximity to markets. Differentiation advantage is similarly based upon the ownership or control over certain resources: brand names, patents, or a wide distribution and service network. Hence, the superior profits which a firm gains as a result of competitive advantage over rivals are really returns earned by these resources. Once these resources depreciate, become obsolete, or are replicated by other firms, so these returns disappear.[4]

The superior profits associated with attractive industry environments are typically thought of as accruing to the industry rather than to individual firms. Profitability above the competitive level is typically the result of market power. But what is the source of market power? Contemporary industrial economics regards barriers to entry as the fundamental prerequisite for market power.[5] Barriers to entry have their basis in scale economies in capital equipment, patents, experience, brand loyalty, or some other resource which incumbent firms possess but which entrants can acquire only slowly or at disproportionate expense.

Most of the resources upon which market power is based are privately owned by individual firms, but some may be owned jointly. For example, industry standards are set jointly by the member firms of an industry. A standard may be viewed as a jointly-owned asset which confers market power upon incumbent firms by increasing the costs of entry. A cartel can also be regarded as a resource which is jointly owned by the participant firms.[6] Exhibit 4.2 summarizes these basic relationships.

Thus, the case for resource analysis rests not only upon the observation

Exhibit 4.2 Resources
as the basis of superior
profitability

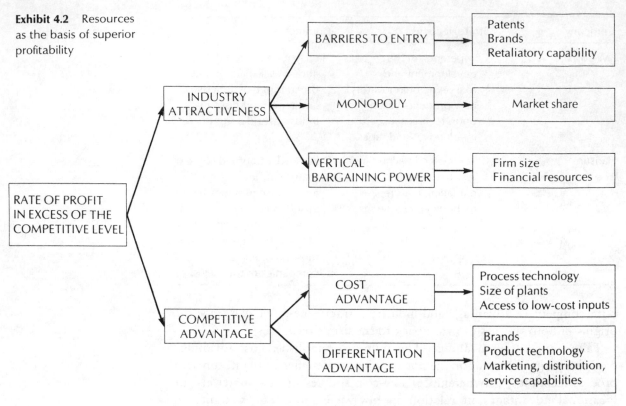

that contemporary developments in strategy have overemphasized external analysis to the near exclusion of internal analysis, but also that resources are the fount from which the firm's profits flow. The remainder of this chapter outlines a resource-based approach to strategy formulation. The essence of the approach is that the firm should seek self-knowledge in terms of a thorough and profound understanding of its resources and capabilities. Such a resource-based approach to strategy comprises three key elements.

- Selecting a strategy that exploits a company's principal resources and competencies: Companies that have been successful over the long term, such as IBM, Black and Decker, Marks & Spencer (the British retailer), Siemens (the German electrical engineering giant) are those that have restricted their range of activities and their business strategies within these activities to those consistent with their resources and capabilities. Companies whose strategies have strayed beyond close linkage with their resource base (such as Chrysler and ITT during the 1970s, and Exxon during the early 1980s), suffered loss of direction and deteriorating profitability.
- Ensuring that the firm's resources are fully employed and their profit potential is exploited to the limit: Walt Disney's remarkable turnaround between 1984 and 1987 involved very little change in basic strategy. The key feature was that Disney's wealth of assets and skills were being mobilized to produce profit (see Case Note 4.1).

Case Note 4.1 The power of resource analysis: The revival of Walt Disney

When Michael Eisner arrived at Walt Disney Productions in 1984 to take over as president, the company was heading for its fourth consecutive year of decline in net income and its share price had fallen to a level that was attracting a variety of predators. Between 1984 and 1988, Disney's sales revenue increased from $1.66 billion to $3.75 billion, net income from $98 million to $570 million, and the stock market's valuation of the company from $1.8 billion to $10.3 billion. Yet during Eisner's first three years at Disney, initially as president, then as chairman, there was no obvious shift of strategy. All Disney's major strategic initiatives of the 1980s – the Epcot Center, Tokyo Disneyland, Touchstone Films, the Disney Channel, and the acquisition of Arvida – were the initiatives of the previous management.

So what happened? The essence of the Disney turnaround was the mobilization of Disney's considerable resource base.

Disney's 28,000 acres of land in Florida were put to better use. With the help of the Arvida Corporation, a land-development company acquired in 1984, Disney began hotel, resort, and residential development of its Florida landholding. The huge Disney film library was exploited, not just through the highly profitable cinema re-releases of the Disney classics, but also through videocassette sales of Disney movies and the licensing of packages of movies to TV networks. A single package of films licensed to a European TV network raised $21 million. The huge investments in the Disney theme parks were more effectively exploited through heavier marketing effort and increased admission charges. Encouraged by the success of Tokyo Disneyland, Disney embarked upon further international duplication of its US theme parks with a planned Eurodisneyland.

The most ambitious feature of the turnaround was Disney's regeneration as a movie studio. As well as maintaining Disney's commitment to high-quality family movies (and cartoons in particular), Eisner began a massive expansion of Disney's Touchstone label, which had been established in 1983 with the objectives of putting Disney's film studios to fuller use and establishing Disney in the teenage and adult markets. Disney Studios were boosted by the aggressive recruiting of leading film makers, actors and scriptwriters. In 1988 Disney became America's leading studio in terms of box office receipts. Studio production was further boosted by Disney's increasing TV presence, both through the Disney Channel and programs for network TV.

Above all, the new management team was exploiting Disney's most powerful and enduring asset: the affection of millions of people of different nations and different generations for the Disney name and the Disney characters.

- Building the company's resource base: Resource analysis is not just about deploying assets, it is crucially concerned with filling current resource gaps and building the company's future resource base. The continuing dominance of IBM and Proctor and Gamble in their respective fields of business owes much to these companies' commitment to nurturing talent, augmenting technologies, and adjusting capabilities to fit emerging market trends.

But let us not run too far ahead. The starting-point for resource analysis is to identify and assess the resources and capabilities which the firm has within its control.

Taking Stock of the Firm's Resources and Capabilities

Resource analysis takes place at two levels of aggregation. The basic units of analysis are the individual resources of the firm: items of capital equipment, the skills of individual employees, patents, brand names, and so on. But to examine how the firm can create competitive advantage we must look at how groups of resources work together to create capabilities. Exhibit 4.3 shows the relationship between resources, capabilities, and competitive advantage.

Exhibit 4.3   The two levels of resource analysis: Resources and capabilities

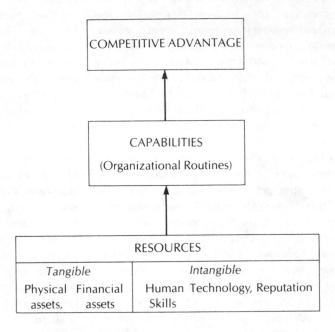

The firm's resource base

Drawing up an inventory of a firm's resources can be surprisingly difficult. No such document exists within the accounting or management information systems of most corporations. The corporate balance sheet provides a partial and distorted picture of a firm's assets. A useful starting-point is a simple classification of the principal types of resource. Hofer and Schendel have identified five types of resource: financial resources, physical resources, human resources, technological resources and organizational resources.[7] Exhibit 4.4 extends their classification of resource types, and points to the role of different types of asset both in conferring competitive advantage and constraining strategy choices.

Tangible resources   Tangible resources are the easiest to identify and to evaluate: financial resources and physical assets are identified in the firm's financial statements and are valued using standard accounting methods. At the same time, company financial statements are renowned for their propensity to obscure strategically-relevant information, and to mis-value assets. The balance sheet certainly provides a starting-point but, once financial data have been gleaned, it is important to get behind the accounting numbers and look at simple facts pertinent to evaluating the potential of the resources for creating competitive advantage. Information that Bethlehem Steel has fixed assets with a book value of $480m. is of little use in assessing the strategic value of these assets. Where are Bethlehem's

Resource	Main characteristics	Key indicators
Financial resources	The firm's borrowing capacity and its internal funds generation determine its investment capacity and its cyclical resilience.	Debt/equity ratio. Ratio of net cash to capital expenditure. Credit rating.
Physical resources	The size, location, technical sophistication, and flexibility of plant and equipment; location and alternative uses for land and buildings; reserves of raw materials constrain the firm's set of production possibilities and determine the potential for cost and quality advantage.	Resale values of fixed assets. Vintage of capital equipment. Scale of plants. Alternative uses of fixed assets.
Human resources	The training and expertise of employees determine the skills available to the firm. The adaptability of employees determines the strategic flexibility of the firm. The commitment and loyalty of employees determines the firm's ability to maintain competitive advantage.	Educational, technical and professional qualifications of employees. Pay rates relative to industry average. Record of labor disputes. Rate of employee turnover.
Technological resources	Stock of technology including proprietary technology (patents, copyrights, trade secrets) and expertise in its application of know-how. Resources for innovation: research facilities, technical and scientific employees.	Number and significance of patents. Revenue from patent licenses. R&D staff as a percentage of total employment.
Reputation	Reputation with customers through the ownership of brands, established relationships with customers, the association of the firm's products with quality, reliability, etc. The reputation of the company with the suppliers of components, finance, labor services, and other inputs.	Brand recognition. Price premium over competing brands. Percentage of repeat buying. Objective measures of product performance. Level and consistency of company performance.

Exhibit 4.4 Classifying and appraising the firm's resources

plants located; what are their capacities; what is the age and type of the equipment, and how flexible are they with regard to inputs, output variations and product varieties?

A strategic assessment of tangible resources is directed towards answering two key questions:

- What opportunities exist for economizing on the use of finance, inventories, and fixed assets?
- What are the possibilities for employing existing assets more profitably?

The first may involve using fewer tangible resources to support the same level of business, or using the existing resources to support a larger volume of business. The success of companies which have pursued growth through acquisitions within mature industries, such as ConAgra in the US and Hanson in Britain, has been managements' ability to rigorously prune the cash and assets needed to support the turnover of acquired businesses.

The returns to a company's tangible resources can be increased in several ways. Resources can be utilized more productively: Following the acquisition of Belridge Oil, Shell was able to greatly increase the output of its oil fields through the application of enhanced recovery techniques. Resources can be transferred to more profitable uses within the company: increasingly department stores are leasing floor space to specialty retailers. Finally, resources can be sold to other companies. The opportunities for breaking up asset-rich, low-profit companies encouraged many company acquisitions during the 1980s. Kravis Kohlberg Roberts & Co. is a specialist in the calculation of companies' break-up values and the use of leveraged buy-out firm, to gain control and subsequently dismember large, poorly-performing corporations. KKR's acquisitions between 1986 and 1988 of R. J. R. Nabisco (for $20.6 billion), Safeway Stores (for $6.2 billion), and Owens-Illinois (for $3.7 billion) were followed by divestment of businesses and assets to buyers capable of a much more profitable utilization of the resources involved.[8]

Intangible resources   Over time, working capital, fixed capital and other tangible assets are becoming less important to the firm, both in value and as a basis for competitive advantage. At the same time intangible resources remain invisible to accountants and auditors. On most firms' balance sheets, inclusion of intangibles is restricted to "goodwill arising on acquisition" and capitalized R & D expenditure. Hence, accounting evaluations of net worth increasingly bear little or no relationship to the true value of a firm's resources. The most valuable assets owned by consumer goods firms are likely to be their brand names; yet these either receive no valuation in a company's balance sheet or are valued only when they are acquired. When Nestlé acquired the British chocolate manufacturer Rowntree in 1988, the bid price exceeded the book value of Rowntree's assets by over

500 percent: An indication of the value of Rowntree's brand names such as Kit Kat and Quality Street.[9]

To identify and appraise intangible resources it is useful to distinguish between human and nonhuman intangibles. While people are clearly tangible, the resources which they offer to the firm are their skills, knowledge, and reasoning and decision-making abilities. In economist's terminology the productive capability of human beings is referred to as "human capital". Identifying and appraising the stock of human capital within a firm is complex and difficult. Individuals' skills and capabilities can be assessed from their job performance, from their experience, and from their qualifications. However, these are only indicators of an individual's potential. The problems of recognizing an individual's capabilities are exacerbated by the fact that people work together in terms where it is difficult to observe directly the contribution of the individual to overall corporate performance. The tendency for firms to resort to indirect approaches to assessing performance – hours spent at the office, enthusiasm, "professional" appearance, and attitudes – points to the difficulty of appraising individuals within the confines of their own jobs, let alone any broader-based assessment of an individual's capabilities. If a company is to develop, to adjust to changing environmental conditions, and to exploit new opportunities, it must have knowledge, not only of how its employees perform in their present and past jobs, but of their repertoire of skills and abilities.[10] Dave Ulrich of the University of Michigan points to the role of a human resource information system as a valuable tool for sustaining a company's competitive advantage.[11]

The tendency to overlook, misunderstand, and undervalue intangible resources is equally true for non-human intangibles. Xerox Corporation's failure to recognize and exploit the advances in personal computer technology from its PARC facility is a classic example of a company squandering its critical resources. Conversely, some of the most consistently profitable companies are those which have established and safeguarded core intangible resources. The building and protection of brand reputation is central to the success of American Express, Coca Cola Corporation, Philip Morris, and Proctor and Gamble. Competitive advantage in the US airline industry depends critically upon ownership of gate slots at hub airports. The importance of intangible resources as the basis for competitive advantage is indicated by a survey conducted by David Aaker (see Exhibit 4.5).

While intangible resources receive scant recognition from accountants, their values are being increasingly recognized by the stock market. Exhibit 4.6 lists the members of top 100 US companies (ranked by stock market valuation) with the highest ratio of stock price to book value. Two types of company dominate the list: those with valuable technological resources (notably pharmaceutical companies, an industry where patents are particularly effective), and companies with very strong brand names (especially in non-durable consumer goods). An alternative explanation of the high

Exhibit 4.5 The sustainable competitive advantage of 248 Californian businesses

	Percentage of businesses identifying particular factors			
	Hi-tech	Service	Other	Total
Reputation for quality	38	44	43	42
Customer service/product support	34	35	22	31
Name recognition/high profile	12	37	31	29
Retain good management and engineering staff	25	38	7	26
Low-cost production	25	13	31	21
Financial resources	16	23	21	21
Customer orientation/market research	19	23	13	19
Product line breadth	16	22	25	19
Technical superiority	44	6	13	19
Installed base of satisfied customers	28	19	6	18
Segmentation/focus	10	19	24	18
Continuing product innovation	22	18	15	18
Product characteristics/differentiation	18	13	15	15
Market share	18	12	13	15
Size and location of distribution	15	11	19	14
Low price/high value offering	9	18	9	13
Knowledge of business	3	22	6	13
Pioneer/early entrant	16	10	9	11
Efficient, flexible production/operations adaptable to customers	6	15	6	10
Effective sales force	15	8	6	9

The table lists the 20 factors which were mentioned most frequently by the respondent companies.

Source: David A. Aaker, "Managing assets and skills: the key to a sustainable competitive advantage", *California Management Review*, Winter 1989, p. 94.

valuation ratios of these companies might be the stock market's assessment of their potential for high growth of profits. This explanation is unappealing, however, since many of these companies are located in slowly growing markets.

From Resources to Capabilities

Identifying capabilities: value chain analysis

Most resources have no intrinsic value. Their value derives from what they can contribute to production. But identifying the contribution of individual resources to the final output of the firm is exceedingly difficult. Resources typically work together in complementary groups where their individual

Company	Ratio
Ralston Purina	13.50
Merck	9.88
Coca Cola	9.62
General Mills	8.33
Microsoft	7.91
Wal Mart Stores	7.33
Warner-Lambert	7.13
Walt Disney	6.14
Waste Management	5.91
Abbot Laboratories	5.75
Colgate Palmolive	5.64
Kellogg	5.46
SmithKline Beckman	5.36
Johnson & Johnson	5.18
Eli Lilly	5.15
American Home Products	4.82
H. J. Heinz	4.71
Pepsi Cola	4.57
Bristol Myers Squibb	4.31
Apple Computers	4.00
AT&T	3.67
Philip Morris	3.59
Campbell Soups	3.57
Dun & Bradstreet	3.50

Exhibit 4.6 Major US companies with ratio of stock price to book value in excess of 3.50 at the end of 1989

Source: Business Week, December 25, 1989.

contributions are not readily observable. Hence, to appraise the potential for competitive advantage we need to examine the ways in which resources collaborate in particular productive activities. The focus of our concern here is not describing or evaluating the resources of the firm directly, but analyzing what capabilities these resources confer upon the firm. Since our objective is to establish competitive advantage for the firm, we need to identify capabilities relative to other firms: What can the firm do *better* than its competitors? These are what are known as the "distinctive competencies"[12] or "strategic capabilities"[13] of the firm.

To examine the firm's capabilities, some classification of the firm's activities is needed. Exhibit 4.7 shows a simple classification of a firm's principal functions and a set of questions for guiding inquiry into the firm's distinctive competencies. In appraising capabilities we are concerned not only with current competencies in existing activities, but with the potential of the firm: how can the capabilities of the firm be expanded, developed, and redeployed?

An alternative framework for classifying the activities of the firm and analyzing the capabilities (and the resources) of a firm is the *value chain*. Most goods and services are produced by a vertical chain of firms. The

Exhibit 4.7 Identifying a company's capabilities: sources and examples

Functional area	Capability	Example
Corporate head office	Effective financial control systems.	Hanson Mars
	Expertise in strategic control of diversified corporation.	General Electric
	Effectiveness in motivating and coordinating divisional and business unit management.	IBM
	Management of acquisitions.	ConAgra, BTR
	Values-driven, in-touch corporate leadership.	Wal Mart Stores Federal Express
Management information	Comprehensive and effective MIS network, with strong central coordination.	American Airlines Ryder Systems
Research and development	Capability in basic research.	IBM, AT&T Sony
	Ability to develop innovative new products.	
	Speed of new product development.	Canon
Manufacturing	Efficiency in volume manufacturing.	Briggs and Stratton
	Capacity for continual improvements in production processes.	Toyota
	Flexibility and speed of response.	Benetton Worthington Industries
Product design	Design capability.	Pinifarini Apple
Marketing	Brand management and brand promotion.	Proctor and Gamble PepsiCola
	Promoting and exploiting reputation for quality.	American Express
	Understanding of and responsiveness to market trends.	The Limited Campbell Soup
Sales and distribution	Effectiveness in promoting and executing sales.	IBM Glaxo
	Efficiency and speed of distribution.	Federal Express The Limited
	Quality and effectiveness of customer service.	Walt Disney Marks & Spencer

supply of bread, for example, involves a chain comprising the farmer, the miller, the baker, and the retailer. The value created in a loaf of bread may be allocated between the companies involved. In a similar way, the individual firm can be viewed as a chain of related activities. The resources and capabilities required at each stage depend upon the nature of the activity being undertaken. The simplest representation of the firm's value chain is McKinsey and Company's *business system* which views the firm as a series of closely-linked groups of activities (see Exhibit 4.8).

TECHNOLOGY	PRODUCT DESIGN	MANUFACTURING	MARKETING	DISTRIBUTION	SERVICE
Source	Function	Integration	Prices	Channels	Warranty
Sophistication	Physical	Raw materials	Advertising/promotion	Integration	Speed
Patents	characteristics	Capacity	Sales force	Inventory	Captive/independent
Product/Process	Aesthetics	Location	Package	Warehousing	Prices
choices	Quality	Procurement	Brand	Transport	
		Parts production			
		Assembly			

Exhibit 4.8 The McKinsey business system

Michael Porter advocates the use of the value chain as the primary tool for diagnosing competitive advantage. He proposes a rather more complex version of the value chain which distinguishes between front-line operations ("*primary activities*") and "*support activities*". Porter's "generic value chain" identifies five "primary activities":

- "inbound logistics" (receiving inputs, storing them, and materials handling);
- operations (production activities);
- "outbound logistics" (warehousing and physical distribution);
- marketing and sales;
- service.

Exhibit 4.9 shows a typical value chain.

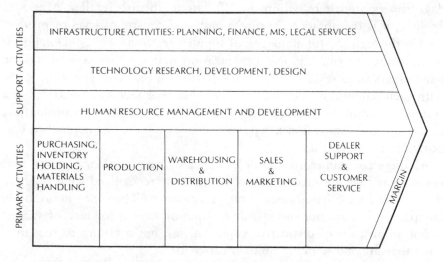

Exhibit 4.9 A typical value chain for a manufacturing company

An important problem is objectivity. In assessing their own competencies, organizations frequently fall victim to past glories, hopes for the future, and their own wishful thinking. Among the failed industrial companies of both the US and Britain are many which believed themselves world leaders with superior products and customer loyalty:

- Sheffield, England, once supplied cutlery and silverware to the world. Its belief in its superior production skills and product quality was one of the principal reasons for its near extinction in the face of foreign competition.[14]
- Lack of competition between domestic producers and easy access to sources of coal and iron ore encouraged a stubborn belief among leading US steelmakers in the superior quality of American steel and the technological lead of their industry. This was a major factor in their reluctance to adopt new process technology and customer-orientated marketing, and ultimately their failure to respond to increasing international competition during the 1970s.[15]
- During the late 1970s and early 1980s, BankAmerica's steady increase in revenues and profits and its position as the world's largest bank, diverted its attention from the underlying reality of the deteriorating quality of its top and middle management, its technological backwardness, and the declining quality of its loan portfolio.[16]

Similarly, firms may be unaware of the competencies they possess. In the mid-1950s Richard and Maurice McDonald owned a single hamburger restaurant in San Bernardino, California. It was Ray Kroc, then a milkshake salesman, who recognized the merits of the McDonald's approach to fast food and the potential for replicating the McDonald's system.[17]

To identify and appraise a company's capabilities, managers must look broadly, look deeply, and look from different perspectives. Every organization has some activity where it excels or has the potential to excel. For Federal Express it is the ability to operate a system that guarantees next-day delivery anywhere within the US. For the British retailer, Marks & Spencer, it is the ability to ensure a high and consistent level of product quality through careful managing of supplier relations. For McDonald's it is the ability to run a global organization that supplies several million hamburgers from several thousand outlets in all four corners of the globe with each hamburger identical to any other. For General Electric it is a system of corporate management that reconciles control, coordination, flexibility, and innovation in one of the largest and most diversified corporations in the world.

All these companies are examples of highly successful enterprises. One reason why they are successful is that they have recognized what they can do well and have based their strategies upon it. There are many other companies that are not successful. A common reason for lack of success is not an absence of distinctive competencies, but a failure to recognize what they are and to put them to effective use.

For example, the failure of EMI in the medical electronics industry was unrelated to the brilliance of its X-ray scanner or the competence of the

R&D team which developed it. The problem was that EMI did not possess the manufacturing capabilities to produce it in sufficient volume or at low enough cost, it did not have the distribution and service capability within the US to build upon its initial lead, and its top management had no experience of a business of this type.

Salomon's slumping profitability between 1986 and 1988 was primarily due to its expansion into areas of business beyond its core competencies. Salomon's success had been built upon its capabilities in trading and underwriting bonds. By expanding globally, and into stocks, junk bonds, and mergers and acquisitions, not only was Salomon extending its business beyond its primary area of expertise, but it did not possess the general management capability to effectively manage a much larger and more diversified corporation.[18]

Organizational routines: the basis of a company's capabilities

Strategic capabilities or distinctive competencies are activities that the firm can perform better than competitors, but what is their basis and their nature? We have observed that capability is the consequence of different resources working together in a complementary team. But what is the nature of the interrelationships and interactions which these resources have? What determines the ability of resources to work together to perform complex activities within the organization? And how does a firm go about creating capability in a particular activity?

In one of the most profound and insightful inquiries into the nature of firm capabilities to date, Richard Nelson and Sidney Winter of Yale University have developed the concept of "organizational routines."[19] Organizational routines are regular and predictable patterns of activity which are made up of a sequence of coordinated actions by individuals. The behavior of the organization may be viewed as huge networks of routines. At the manufacturing level a series of routines governs the passage of raw materials and components through the production process to the factory gate. Sales, ordering, distribution, and customer service activities are similarly organized through a number of standardized, complementary routines. Even top management activity comprises a number of routines. There are routines for monitoring business unit performance, routines for capital budgeting, routines for employee appraisal and promotion. The strategy of the corporation may be viewed as a routine: It is a set of guidelines which precondition the firm's responses to events.

Thus, the concept of the organizational routine is a particularly powerful basis for comprehending the capabilities of the firm. The characteristics of routines that we have examined explain why it is difficult to replicate a firm's activities, and why firms find it difficult to respond to new situations. Nelson and Winter also argue that routines fulfill other functions within the firm. They represent a truce between the conflicting interests of different members of the organization. They provide a means through which management can control the activities of the organization: establishing routines for performing particular tasks within the organization facilitates the management of the organization. In particular, it establishes standards for the smooth functioning of the organization, despite the fact that resources (people especially) are so heterogeneous.

The concept of organizational routines offers illuminating insights into the relationships between resources, capabilities, and competitive advantage.

The relationship between resources and capabilities   An important implication of organizational routines is that the firm's competencies are not simply a consequence of the collection of individual resources which the firm controls. The types, the amounts, and the qualities of the resources available to the firm have an important bearing on what the firm can do since they place constraints upon the range of organizational routines that can be performed and the standard to which they are performed. However, resources do not exclusively determine what the firm can do and how well it can do it. A key ingredient in the relationship between resources and capabilities is management's ability to achieve the cooperation and coordination between resources required for the development of organizational routines. The ability of the firm to motivate and socialize its members in order to gain their cooperation and commitment depends upon the organization's style, culture, leadership, and systems of control, reward and communication. Peters and Waterman stress the importance of "shared values" in promoting cooperation and commitment.[20] All these influences we can regard as types of corporate resource which are common ingredients of the whole range of a company's routines.[21]

The tradeoff between efficiency and flexibility.   Routines are to the organization what skills are to the individual. Just as the individual's skills are carried out semi-automatically, without conscious coordination, so organizational routines involve a large component of tacit knowledge, which implies limits on the extent to which the organization's capabilities can be articulated. Just as individual skills become rusty when not exercised, so it is difficult for organizations to retain coordinated responses to contingencies that arise only rarely. Hence there may be a tradeoff between efficiency and flexibility. A limited repertoire of routines can be performed highly efficiently with near-perfect coordination – all in the absence of significant intervention by top management. The same organization may find it extremely difficult to respond to novel situations.[22]

Economies of experience   Just as individual skills are acquired through practice over time, so an organization's capabilities are developed and sustained only through experience. The advantage of an established firm over a newcomer is primarily in the organizational routines that it has been perfecting over time. The Boston Consulting Group's "experience curve" is a naive and mechanistic representation of this relationship of experience to performance. By investigating the characteristics and evolution of the underlying organizational routines a more insightful and predictively-valid understanding of the relationship is possible. For instance, in industries where technological change is rapid, new firms may possess an advantage over established firms through their potential for faster learning of new routines because they are less committed to old routines.

The complexity of capabilities Some capabilities derive directly from individual resources. The appeal of the Old Course Hotel in St Andrews, Scotland, derives from its unique location adjacent to the world's oldest golf course. The reputation of Harley-Davidson is primarily a consequence of its status as the sole surviving remnant of the US motorcycle industry. In other cases, a capability may require complex interaction between heterogeneous resources, or may involve an integrated set of routines. For example, Federal Express's nationwide, next-day delivery service involves a meticulously-coordinated set of routines relating to customer ordering, collection, transportation, sorting, tracking, and delivery. Each routine typically requires a number of resources, such as operating skills, customer service skills, communication skills, transportation equipment, and communication and data-processing equipment. IBM's legendary customer service capability is similarly complex. It requires commitment, coordination, and responsiveness within its service departments, and close links between the service function, manufacturing, product design and development, and marketing; effective employee training programs; management information systems; and a deeply-entrenched set of values that have been nurtured over decades. As we shall see, the complexity of capabilities in terms of the interrelationships between resources and routines is critical to a firm's ability to sustain a competitive advantage and to reap profits from a competitive advantage.

Appraising the Rent-earning Capacity of Resources and Capabilities

By identifying the firm's resources and capabilities and establishing areas of strength relative to competitors, the firm can adjust its strategy to ensure that the firm's strengths are fully utilized and its weaknesses are protected. The discussion of Walt Disney in Case Note 4.1 shows that the benefits of adjusting strategy to achieve a closer fit with resources, can be substantial. In addition, our analysis of the firm's resources and capabilities can go further and evaluate their capacity for generating profits for the firm.

In appraising the capacity of the firm's resources and capability to yield profits over the long term, we need to evaluate them; first, in relation to the firm's ability to appropriate returns from its resources, and, secondly, in relation to the sustainability of the competitive advantage. I shall deal with this second issue of sustainability only briefly, since chapter 5 explores it more thoroughly. Exhibit 4.10 summarizes the relationships to be discussed, according to four key criteria:

- appropriability;
- durability;
- transferability;
- replicability.

Exhibit 4.10

Appraising the rent-generating capacity of resources and capabilities: The four key criteria

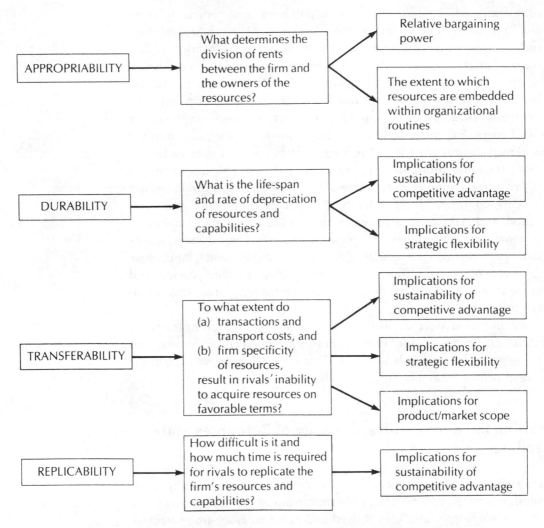

Appropriability

In drawing up an inventory of the firm's resources, an immediate problem was the determination of the boundaries of the firm's resource base. The company balance sheet, we noted, shows the principal categories of tangible resources owned by the firm and their values. Yet for most firms, plant, machinery, and other tangible assets represent a minority of the total resource base. Intangibles such as reputation, information, and know-how have greater monetary value, and they provide the most important sources of competitive advantage.

Once we go beyond financial and physical assets, ownership becomes less clear. The firm can establish property rights in certain intangible assets: Patents, copyrights, and brand names, for example. Typically, however, only a fraction of a firm's reputation and knowledge is protected by legally-enforceable ownership. The primary basis for the capabilities of a firm are the skills of its employees: Companies in the service sector have long recognized this truth and manufacturing companies are increasingly recognizing the same fact. The problem for the firm is that employees' skills are the property of the individuals not of the firm, and employment contracts and employment law offer the firm only limited access to these skills and limited control over employees. The consequences for the firm are twofold: first, the employee is mobile between firms so that the firm cannot reliably base a strategy upon the specific skills of individuals; secondly, the employee is in a good position to ensure that his or her full contribution to the prosperity of the enterprise is reflected in the salary and benefits received.

But the capabilities of the firm, we have observed, are located within groups of individuals and supported by other resources such as reputation, corporate management systems, and the systems of values that mesh together the employees of departments and companies. To what extent are the capabilities that reside in IBM's advanced semi-conductors research teams, or in Citibank's foreign exchange dealing department owned by the firm rather than by the individuals within them? From the point of view of the firm, the key issue is the degree of control which the firm can exercise and the extent to which the capability can be maintained even when individual employees leave. A firm's dependence upon skills possessed by highly-trained and highly-mobile key employees is particularly important in the case of professional service companies where the main resources are human expertise. Acquisitions of such "human capital intensive" companies have given rise to contention over attempts to distinguish the assets of the firm from the skills and experience of individual employees (see Case Note 4.2).

Similar issues have arisen in relation to high-technology start-up companies which have been such a prominent feature of the evolution of the US electronics sector. Typically, these companies are founded by technologists and managers which leave large, established electronics companies in order to develop and exploit ideas and products which they conceived of at their former employers. Charles Ferguson has claimed that these start-ups involve the individual exploitation of technical knowledge which rightfully belongs to the former employers of these new entrepreneurs. The tendency for large, US, technology-based companies to spin-off numerous entrepreneurial start-ups, rather than being a tribute to the dynamism of American business enterprise, represents a failure of leading US microelectronics companies to maintain ownership and control over the technologies that they develop internally.[23]

Faced with ambiguity over property rights in key resources, an important

---

Case Note 4.2   Our assets just walked out on us!

In the summer of 1987, Martin Sorrell, CEO of WPP Group PLC, bought Lord, Geller, Fredrico, Einstein (LGFE), one of New York's most respected advertising agencies, best known for its Charlie Chaplin advertisements for IBM. The acquisition followed WPP's purchase of J. Walter Thompson and a string of other agencies which had established WPP as one of the world's largest advertising agencies.

Friction between LGFE and its British parent, WPP, over issues of business and creative independence of LGFE, reached a climax in March 1988. The chairman, president and four top executives from LGFE left to establish a new agency, Lord, Einstein, O'Neill & Partners. They were joined on March 22 by over a dozen other key employees. The exit of employees was followed by the defection of clients. One client, the president of the *New Yorker* magazine explained: "If you're used to working with someone who is generating ideas and helping you, you stay with them. This is a matter of personal loyalties." Meanwhile, the parent company, WPP was busy taking legal action against the new agency contending that the former LGFE employees had conspired to take away Lord

Geller's business, while at the same time trying to quash rumors that Lord Geller was about to close.

WPP obtained a temporary injunction against Richard Lord and Arthur Einstein Jr from soliciting or accepting business from any of LGFE's clients. The new firm also took to the courts charging Martin Sorrell and WPP with libel and slander.

By the end of 1988, WPP's LGFE subsidiary was in a sorry state. Despite loyalty from a few clients – Schieffelin and Somerset decided to keep its $8 million advertising account for Hennessey cognac with LGFE – many of LGFE's largest clients switched to other agencies. IBM put its $120 million account up for competition and awarded part of it to the new agency Lord, Einstein, O'Neill & Partners. Sears Roebuck and Pan Am also withdrew their business from LGFE. Following this loss of business, LGFE was forced to lay off one-third of its employees. In the meantime the defectors made quick progress: a $30 million advertising account was won from Saab Scania North America, and the court injunction against Lord and Einstein was lifted.

Source: Wall Street Journal, March 23, 1988, pp. 1 & 21, and subsequent issues.

---

strategic issue for the firm is the means by which it can secure its control over such resources, and ensure that it obtains an adequate share of the returns from these assets. The issue of the firm's control over its resources is clearly critical to the firm's ability to use its resources as a secure base for formulating and implementing strategy. But ambiguity over ownership and control is also important from another perspective: The firm's ability to appropriate the returns to its resources. An implication of a resource-based concept of the firm is that the profits of the firm are returns to resources owned by the firm. Even monopoly profits may be regarded as being returns to the resources upon which the monopoly and its perpetuation are based. A critical consequence of ambiguity over ownership and control of a resource is indeterminacy over the allocation of the returns to the resource. For example:

- When the municipal bond dealing department at Prudential Bache earns a gross trading income of over $100 million a year, what part of this accrues as profit to the firm?
- When individuals at 3M pioneer the development of commercially successful products such as reflective traffic signs and Post-it notes, to what extent does 3M profit?

The division of rents between the firm and its employees depends upon relative bargaining power. If the individual employee's contribution to productivity is clearly identifiable, if the employee is mobile, and if he could offer similar productivity to other firms, then he or she is in a strong position to expropriate a substantial proportion of the contribution in salary or bonus or commission. To the extent that Wayne Gretsky can convince the owners of the Los Angeles Kings ice hockey team that the club's increased revenues can be attributed to Gretsky's drawing power, then he will be in a strong position to appropriate the greater part of the increased margin in his next contract with the club.

Conversely, the less easy it is to identify individuals' contributions and the more firm-specific are the skills being applied, the greater is the proportion of the return which accrues to the firm. The tendency for professional service firms to be organized as partnerships rather than corporations partly reflects the superiority of a partnership in avoiding bargaining conflict between owners and employees in enterprises where the capital stock is primarily human skills. A recent trend among investment banking firms has been to reduce the image and reputation of individual stars and gurus and increase the identity and reputation of the firm and the team. The attempt by the firms to restore control over their investment banking skills and reputations resulted in conflicts with senior employees at Citibank, Salomon Brothers, Merrill Lynch, and First Boston.[24] In effect what these companies are doing is to ensure that their reputations are identified with the company through the skills of teams of employees rather than associated with individual superstars. As a result the returns from reputation accrue to the firm rather than to the individual.

Durability

Some resources are more durable than others and, hence, are a securer basis for competitive advantage. The increasing pace of technological change is shortening the useful life-span of most capital assets, to the extent that five-year periods of depreciation no longer represent accounting conservatism for many industries. Across the whole manufacturing sector, firms are writing down or writing off the value of fixed assets well before they are fully depreciated. Intangible assets vary substantially in durability. While the value of patents is increasingly being curtailed by technological leapfrogging, consumer brand names show remarkable durability. Brands such as Heinz sauces, Kelloggs' cereals, Campbell's soups, Hoover's vacuum cleaners, and Singer's sewing machines were market leaders for periods of almost a century. Corporate reputation is similarly long-living: the reputations of General Electric, IBM, DuPont, and Proctor and Gamble as well-managed, socially-responsible, financially-sound companies, producing reliable products, and taking good care of their employees are decades long and continue to give these companies credibility and attention in every field of business which they enter.

Transferability

The firm's ability to sustain its competitive advantage over time depends upon the speed with which rivals can acquire the resources and capabilities needed to imitate the success of the initiating firm. The primary means to acquire the resources and capabilities needed to compete is to purchase and hire the required inputs. The ability to do this depends upon the transferability of the resources and capabilities. Some resources, such as raw materials, components, machines performing standard operation, and certain types of employee, are transferable between firms and can be bought and sold with little difficulty. Some resources are not easily transferable. Fixed plant and large machines are not easily transportable. Other resources, such as technical knowledge and brand names, may be firm-specific in the sense that their value declines on transfer to another firm. Other resources, such as the reputation of a firm, may be completely firm specific and, although valuable to the firm itself, may have no market value. Where resources are highly differentiated and information on their quality is poor (e.g. managers), hiring from the market can be highly risky.

Transfer of capabilities is particularly difficult where a firm's capability is the consequence of resources working together as a team. To acquire that capability requires transfer of the team. The defection of 16 of First Boston's mergers and acquisitions staff to Wasserstein, Perella, and Company indicates, however, that such transfer can occur.[25]

The implication is that firms whose capabilities are deeply embedded within complex teams of resources run less risk of having their capabilities acquired by competitors than firms whose capabilities are dependent on individual, transferable resources. Resources that are easily transferable between firms are relatively unimportant as far as strategy is concerned. If they can be acquired and disposed of on the open market, a firm's access to them is limited only by its financial resources. Firm-specific assets, on the other hand, play a key role in establishing the identity of the firm, and securing competitive advantage over sustained periods.

If resources and capabilities are highly differentiated and are not easily transferable (i.e. they are "firm-specific") other consequences for strategy follow. If a firm cannot readily dispose of particular resources, it is obliged either to use them or to let them waste. As a result, such resources play an important role both in limiting the flexibility of the firm in changing its strategy and in providing an important incentive to diversification in order to more fully exploit any underutilized resources and skills.

Replicability

The firm specificity of a resource or routine limits the ability of a firm to acquire it simply by purchase on the market. The second route by which a firm can acquire a resource or capability is by creating it itself through investment. Some capabilities can be easily imitated through replication. The advantage gained by one retailer extending his store's opening hours or a newspaper's use of color printing can be copied without great difficulty. If legal barriers exist to replication, as in the case of patented products and processes, then replication can be more difficult. Probably the least replicable capabilities are those which are based upon the exercise of highly complex organizational routines. How does IBM motivate its people? How does Nucor, the steel manufacturer, maintain such a remarkable combination of efficiency and flexibility? The answer lies in the nature of the organizational routines upon which these capabilities are based. The complex nature of these routines and the fact that they are based upon tacit rather than codified knowledge, means that diagnosing and recreating them is exceedingly difficult. Indeed, very often the top management of the company itself does not fully understand how their company is able to perform the way it does.

Even when codified, it still may be very difficult to imitate a competitor's superior performance. It is widely accepted that McDonald's success in the world fast-food industry is based upon a highly sophisticated and detailed operating system which regulates the operation of every McDonald's outlet from employee behavior and dress, to cleaning procedures, to the placing of the pickle on the burger. These procedures are detailed in the manuals of every McDonald's manager. Yet the system itself is only one aspect, equally important is ensuring its implementation through management information, incentives, and controls.

Similar difficulties of imitation have applied to Western firms' adoption of successful Japanese industrial practices. Two of the simplest and best-known Japanese manufacturing practices are just-in-time inventory systems and quality circles. Both are simple ideas which require neither sophisticated knowledge nor complex operating systems. Yet the successful operation of both requires a degree of cooperation and a set of attitudes such that few American or European firms have been successful in introducing with the same degree of success as Japanese companies.

If relatively simple practices such as these are difficult to imitate, it becomes easy to see how firms which successfully execute highly complex skills can maintain their competitive advantage over very long periods of time. IBM's commitment to customer service and 3M Corporation's approach to the development of new products are distinctive competencies which are located not in any particular department or unit, but permeate the whole corporation and are built into the fabric and culture of the organization. Moreover, because these routines are broadly-based and are not particular to any particular product or production technology, they are not as constraining or as subject to obsolescence as more specific routines.

Identifying Resource Gaps and Developing the Resource Base

Our analysis so far has been in terms of appraising and exploiting the firm's existing pool of resources and competencies. A resource-based approach to strategy must be concerned not only with deploying existing resources but in investing in the resources that will secure the long-term future for the firm. Such investment is concerned not just with the maintenance of resources but with augmenting the firm's resources so that positions of competitive advantage can be strengthened and the firm's strategic opportunity set broadened.

Hence a key feature of resource analysis is that, once a strategy has been formulated based upon a matching of the firm's capabilities with the opportunities available in the external environment, the firm must reconsider the implications of the strategy for the firm's resource needs. In other words, what resource gaps need to be filled?

The turnaround of Walt Disney between 1985 and 1987, we have observed (Case Note 4.1), involved no substantially new strategic directions. The major element in boosting performance was a fuller utilization of Disney's existing assets, and a regenerating creativity. One of the implications of the adjustments to Disney's strategy was that, in order to exploit more fully the Disney resources of theme parks, movie studios, land reserves, and the power of the Disney name, additional resources were required. In particular, revitalization of movie making was achieved through heavy investment in creative talent in the form of directors, actors, scriptwriters, and cartoonists. The acquisition of the Arvida Corporation provided the real estate development skills necessary for better utilizing Disney's large land holdings. The building a new marketing team was instrumental in boosting attendance at Disneyland and Disney World.

General Motors' strategy for regeneration automation and quality enhancement has similarly placed great emphasis on identifying and filling the resource deficiencies which the strategy caused. GM's need for electronic technology was the principal stimulus for its acquisition of Electronic Data Systems. Likewise its quest for improved product quality encouraged its joint ventures with Toyota.

The implications of the firm's strategy for its resources are not only in terms of the emergence of resource gaps. The pursuit of a particular strategy not only utilizes a firm's resources, it also augments resources through the creation of skills and knowledge which are the products of experience. Hiroyuki Itami has introduced the concept of *dynamic resource fit*: "Effective strategy in the present builds invisible assets, and the expanded stock enables the firm to plan its future strategy to be carried out. And the future strategy must make effective use of the resources that have been amassed."[26] Matsushita's multinational expansion has closely followed this principle of parallel and sequential development of strategy and resources. In developing production in a foreign country, Matsushita has typically begun with the production of batteries then moved on to the production of products requiring greater manufacturing and marketing sophistication. Arataroh Takahashi explained the strategy:

In every country batteries are a necessity, so they sell well. As long as we bring a few advanced automated pieces of equipment for the process vital to final product quality, even unskilled labor can produce good products. As they work on this rather simple product, the workers get trained, and this increased skill level then permits us to gradually expand production to items with increasingly higher technology level, first radios, then televisions.[27]

This dynamic resource fit may also provide a strong basis for a firm's diversification. Sequential product addition as expertise and knowledge is acquired is a prominent feature of the strategies of Honda in extending its product range from motorcycles, to cars, to lawn mowers, and boat engines, and of 3M in expanding from abrasives, to adhesives, to computer disks, video- and audiotape, and a broad range of consumer and producer goods.

Summary

In this chapter we shifted the focus of our attention from the external to the internal environment of the firm. This internal environment comprises many features of the firm, including its resources; its organizational structure; its systems of information, communication, reward, and control; its style of management; its values and its traditions. Our focus is on what the firm can *do*. This directs us towards the resources of the firm and the way that resources work together in organizational routines. This is not to say that the structure and systems of the organization are not important; they are critical to the effectiveness with which strategy is implemented. However, since firms possess a considerable measure of flexibility in their choices of organizational structure and management systems, we can regard these features of the internal environment primarily as consequences rather than determinants of strategy choice.

The approach of this chapter has been to emphasize a number of conceptual aspects of the firm's resources and routines in order to convey understanding of the nature of the firm's capabilities, and to explore in some depth the relationships between the firm's resource base, its competitive advantage, and its profit potential. At the same time the approach is highly practical and applicable. To assist application to specific company cases, Exhibit 4.11 summarizes the principal stages of resource analysis in a flow diagram.

Exhibit 4.11 A framework for resource analysis

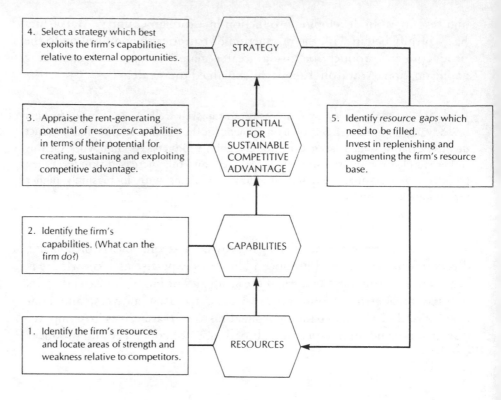

Notes

1. Analysis of the internal environment of the firm has also been given prominence by researchers who have investigated the *process,* of strategy formulation. Researchers who have approached strategy formulation from a behavioral science perspective view strategy formulation, not as rational optimizing decisions made with objective information, but either as an evolving pattern of decisions and actions (see Henry Mintzberg "Crafting strategy," *Harvard Business Review,* July–August 1987, pp. 66–75) or as a political process within the firm (see Andrew M. Pettigrew, "Strategy formulation as a political process," *International Studies of Management and Organization* 7, (2), (1977), pp. 78–87.

2. B. H. Liddell Hart, *Strategy* (Praeger, New York, 1954), p. 365.

3. Theodore Levitt, "Marketing myopia," *Harvard Business Review,* July–August 1960, pp. 24–47.

4. Economists describe returns to durable resources over and above the costs of these resources as "economic rents" or, to the extent that these resources eventually depreciate and the returns associated with them also decline, "quasi-rents."

5. See W. J. Baumol, J. C. Panzer, and R. D. Willig, *Contestable Markets and the Theory of Industrial Structure* (Harcourt Brace Jovanovich, New York, 1982).

6. These jointly-owned resources have the characteristics of "public goods," i.e. their benefits can be extended to additional firms at negligible marginal cost and without depreciating the value of the resource.

7. Charles W. Hofer and Dan Schendel, *Strategy Formulation: Analytical Concepts* (West, St Paul, 1978), pp. 145–8.
8. "King Henry," *Business Week*, November 14, 1988, pp. 125–7.
9. "No accounting for taste," *Economist*, June 25, 1988, p. 83.
10. In their seminal essay on the role of information within the firm, Armen Alchian and Harold Demsetz, "Production, information costs, and economic organization," *American Economic Review*, 62 (1972), pp. 777–95, regard the monitoring of input productivity as the fundamental task of management.
11. Dave Ulrich, "Human resources: the competitive road not taken," *Information Strategy: The Executive's Journal*, Summer 1988, pp. 4–11.
12. P. Selznick, *Leadership in Administration* (Harper and Row, New York, 1957).
13. R. T. Lenz, "Strategic capability: A concept and framework for analysis," *Academy of Management Review* 5 (2), (1980), pp. 225–34.
14. R. M. Grant, "Business strategy and strategy change in a hostile environment: failure and success among British cutlery producers," in Andrew Pettigrew (ed.), *The Management of Strategic Change* (Blackwell, Oxford, 1987).
15. Paul R. Lawrence and Davis Dyer, *Renewing American Industry* (Free Press, New York, 1983), pp. 60–83.
16. "The most beleaguered banker," *Fortune*, January 5, 1987, p. 86.
17. *Forbes*, January 15, 1973.
18. "What's behind the profit squeeze at Salomon," *Business Week*, April 20, 1987, p. 72.
19. R. R. Nelson and S. G. Winter, *An Evolutionary Theory of Economic Change* (Belknap, Cambridge, Mass., 1982).
20. Tom Peters and Robert Waterman, *In Search of Excellence* (Harper and Row, New York, 1982).
21. See Jay B. Barney, "Organizational culture: can it be a source of competitive advantage?" *Academy of Management Review* 11 (1986), pp. 656–65.
22. This observation is supported by John Freeman and Michael Hannan, "Niche width and the dynamics of organizational populations," *American Journal of Sociology*, 88 (1984), pp. 1116–45. They observe that, in the restaurant industry, specialists survived better than generalists, except where the environment was highly variable, in which case generalists displayed greater adaptability.
23. Charles Ferguson, *International Competition, Strategic Behavior, and Government Policy in Information Technology Industries*, PhD Thesis, MIT, 1987. For a summary and critique see George Gilder, "The revitalization of everything: The law of the microcosm," *Harvard Business Review*, March–April 1988, pp. 49–61. For a reply see Charles Ferguson, "From the people who brought you voodoo economics," *Harvard Business Review*, May–June 1988.
24. "The decline of the superstar," *Business Week*, August 17, 1987, pp. 90–6.
25. "Catch a falling star," *Economist*, April 23, 1988, pp. 88–90.
26. H. Itami, *Mobilizing Invisible Assets* (Harvard University Press, Boston, 1987), p. 125.
27. A. Takahashi, *What I learned from Konosuke Matsushita*, Jitsugyo no Nihonsha, Tokyo, 1980 (In Japanese). Quoted by Itami, ibid., p. 25.

FIVE

The Nature and Sources of Competitive Advantage

One Saturday afternoon in downtown Chicago, Milton Friedman, the famous free-market economist, was shopping with his wife.

"Look Milton!" exclaimed Mrs. Friedman, "There's a $20 bill on the sidewalk!"

"Don't be foolish, my dear," replied the Nobel laureate, "If that was a $20 bill, someone would have picked it up by now."

Economist's anecdote of doubtful authenticity

Introduction

A firm can earn a rate of profit in excess of the "normal" or "competitive" rate, either by locating in an attractive industry, or by establishing a competitive advantage over its rivals. Of the two sources of superior profitability, competitive advantage is of increasing importance. The reasons are not difficult to discern. Since the 1970–80s the pressure of competition has increased across the whole business sector. In industries producing traded goods, the rising tide of international trade has opened previously sheltered domestic markets to vigorous import competition. In industries where profitability was once protected by substantial barriers to entry, new entry has been encouraged by deregulation, diversification by domestic companies, and multinational expansion by overseas companies.

These trends have had dire consequences for corporate profitability. In both the US and Western Europe, corporate profitability since the mid-1960s, despite a revival during the latter 1980s, has been on a downward trend. At the same time, the interindustry dispersion of profitability has narrowed. Most of the industries which were once as safe havens for comfortable profits, such as oil, computers, investment banking, health care services, and aerospace, have suffered increasing competitive pressures. Hence, the primary goal for strategy must be the establishment of a position of competitive advantage for the firm. Over the longer term this is as vital for firms in seemingly-attractive industries as for firms operating in intensely-competitive environments. Just as during the 1980s, the oil companies and investment banks discovered that prosperity was not assured simply by inclusion within the industry fold, so in today's glamour industries such as pharmaceuticals, medical equipment, and pollution control, companies will need to adjust to a time when survival will depend upon their ability to establish competitive advantage.

The primary purpose of this chapter is to explore the nature and the sources of competitive advantage. Chapters 2 and 3 provided an introductory analysis of the *external* sources of competitive advantage: The conditions which must be met to satisfy customers and to survive the pressures of competition establish the prerequisites for competitive advantage ("key success factors") in an industry or industry segment. Chapter 4 examined the *internal* sources of competitive advantage: the potential offered by the firm's resources and capabilities. In this chapter and the next two chapters, we draw together external and internal sources of competitive advantage. The central theme of this chapter is the competitive process. Competition provides the incentive for establishing advantage and the means by which advantage is eroded. By understanding the nature of competition in an industry we can identify the potential for establishing and sustaining competitive advantage.

The Emergence, Erosion, and Sustainability of Competitive Advantage

As a foundation for our analysis, consider how competitive advantage emerges and how it is sustained. A starting-point is a definition of competitive advantage:

When two firms compete (i.e. when they locate within the same market and are capable of supplying the same customers), one firm possesses a competitive advantage over the other when it earns a higher rate of profit, or has the potential to earn a higher rate of profit.

Competitive advantage, then, is the ability to outperform rivals on what we assume to be firms' primary performance goal: Profitability. Note that competitive advantage may not be revealed in higher profitability: a firm may wish to trade profit for market share gain, which may ultimately involve the destruction of a rival. Alternatively, a firm may wish to forego profits in the interests of philanthropy, rewarding employees, or indulging in corporate status symbols.

For profit differences to emerge between competing firms, *change* must take place. Change may be external to the industry (an *exogenous* disturbance) or it may be initiated within the industry (an *endogenous* disturbance). An exogenous disturbance can take the form of any change in the industry's external environment: new customer preferences, regulatory changes, changing relative prices of inputs, or advances in scientific knowledge. For such disturbances to result in profit differences between firms requires either that the effects are asymmetric between firms, for example, because the firms have chosen different market segments or different production technologies, or that the firms have different capabilities to respond to the opportunities that external changes present. Both passive and active consequences of exogenous disturbance are determined by differences between firms in their stock of resources (defined broadly to include information, reputation with customers, and market positions).

Emergence

Endogenous disturbances typically arise from innovation within the industry in the form of new products, new processes, new management techniques, or new approaches to marketing. The extent to which profit differentials arise from endogenous disturbance also depend upon differences between firms' resources: innovative capability depends upon insightful environmental scanning, creativity, entrepreneurship, and managements' ability to coordinate across functions.

Hence, differences in the profitability of firms competing in the same industry are likely to depend upon the extent of change and the extent of differences in firms' resource bases. The more turbulent is an industry's environment, the greater the number of sources of change, and the greater the propensity of firms to innovate then the greater the opportunities for competitive advantage and associated profit differences. Industries such as tobacco, brewing, and flour milling have comparatively stable environments where profit differentials between firms are comparatively small. The toy industry, on the other hand, experiences rapid changes in demand, technology, and fashion. The quest for novelty and the success of some companies in creating the next craze ensures a wide dispersion of interfirm profitability.

Once established, competitive advantage is subject to erosion by competition. The essence of the competitive process is the imitation by rivals of the competitive advantage established by any one firm. For competitive advantage to be sustained over time requires the existence of barriers to imitation. Rumelt uses the term "isolating mechanisms" to describe "barriers which limit the ex post equilibrium of rents among individual firms."[1] Isolating mechanisms are of two main types.

Erosion through competition

The first is information. If companies are unaware of the superior performance of a competitor or if they have difficulties in diagnosing the sources of the competitor's success they will not be able to challenge the advantaged firm. Secondly, if companies cannot acquire on equal terms the resources needed to challenge the advantaged competitor, again they will be unable to successfully imitate. The easier it is for rivals to understand the "secrets of success" of the advantaged firm and the easier it is to acquire resources necessary for imitation, the faster the competitive advantage will be eliminated.

The tendency for the profit differentials associated with competitive advantage to erode over time is supported by other factors. Disadvantaged firms decline and are eventually eliminated by bankruptcy or acquisition. At the same time the superior returns earned by some firms become capitalized into the values of the resources, while, in the long run, these resources wear out. However, this convergence of firms' profitability can be a slow process. Empirical studies show considerable dispersion between the profits earned by different firms even in mature industries. Even over periods of a decade and more, interfirm profit differentials tend to erode only slowly, while a large proportion of firms maintain rates of profit almost permanently above or below the averages for their industries.[2]

Competitive advantage in trading markets

To understand how different market characteristics and resource characteristics determine the sources and sustainability of competitive advantage, it is useful to distinguish between *trading markets* where firms buy and sell, but do not engage in significant production activities, and *first-hand markets* for goods and services where firms are engaged in the physical transformation of inputs into goods and services. As a point of reference, let us first consider perfectly competitive trading markets, known in the finance literature as "efficient" markets.

Perfect competition exists where there are many buyers and sellers, an homogenous product, no barriers to entry and exit, and free flow of information. Equilibrium is established where all firms earn "normal" profits. The closest real-world example of perfect competition is found in financial markets (the markets for securities, credit, foreign exchange, and commodity futures). In these markets the concept of *efficiency* is used to describe the performance associated with perfectly competitive market operation. An "efficient" market is one where prices reflect all available information. Since prices adjust instantaneously to newly-available information, no market trader can expect to earn more than any other. Any differences in ex post returns reflect either different levels of risk selected by different traders, or purely random factors such as luck. Since all available information is reflected in current prices, no trading rules based upon historical price data or any other available information can offer excess returns: it is not possible to "beat the market" on any consistent basis. In other words, competitive advantage is absent.

The conditions of competition and the absence of competitive advantage in efficient markets are a direct consequence of the types of resources required by participants in these markets and the mobility of these resources. There are only two primary resources required in financial markets: finance and information. If both are equally available to all participants, then there is no basis for one to gain competitive advantage over another.

In order for competitive advantage to exist, imperfections (or "inefficiencies") must be introduced into the perfectly competitive model. Let us consider different sources of imperfection of competition, showing how these imperfections depend upon the conditions of resource availability, and the implications which follow for competitive advantage.

Imperfect availability of information   A key departure in most financial markets from the conditions for efficiency results from imperfect availability of information. In all financial markets the problem of "insider information" arises from the privileged access of some market participants to information. At the same time, the competitive advantage arising from insider information may be of very short duration. Once a market participant begins acting on the basis of insider information, then other operators are alerted to the existence of the information. Even though they may not know the content of the information, they are able to imitate the behavior of the market leader. A commonly followed strategy in stock markets is to detect and follow insider transactions by senior company executives. Attempts by insider traders to obscure their identities are motivated by the desire to avoid triggering imitative behavior as well as to avoid detection by market regulators and legal authorities.

Transactions costs   If markets correspond to the conditions of efficiency except for the presence of transactions costs, then competitive advantage accrues to those traders who are able to minimize their transaction costs. In trading markets, transactions costs as a proportion of turnover are likely to depend upon the efficiency of the traders' information and transactions processing systems, and the total volume of transaction. In stock markets, low transactions costs are also attainable by traders who economize on research and market analysis and minimize the transactions required to attain their portfolio objectives. Studies of mutual fund performance show:

Net of all management fees, the average managed investment fund performed worse than a completely unmanaged buy-and-hold strategy on a risk-adjusted basis ... Further, the amount by which the funds fell short of the unmanaged strategy was, on average, about the same as the management cost of the funds.[3]

The observation that competitive advantage is attained through minimizing transaction costs is further supported by evidence that, over the long term, "market-index funds" outperform managed funds.

Systematic behavioral trends   If the current prices of securities fully reflect all available information, then future returns are independent of past returns and securities prices move in a random walk.[4] Suppose that price movements are not determined exclusively by the arrival of new information, then there is scope for a strategy which uses understanding of how prices really do move. Some stock market "anomalies" are well documented, notably, the "small firm effect", "January effect", and "weekend effect."[5] More generally, it is widely believed by professional traders in financial markets that prices move in systematic patterns which are the result of "market psychology", the trends and turning points of which can be established from past market movements. Chart analysis uses hypotheses concerning relationship between past and future price movements as a forecasting tool. Even if chart-based strategies are capable of yielding superior returns (and most empirical evidence is doubtful), the ability to profit from such strategies again depends upon restricted availability of information. Once the determinants of price movements are well understood and a sufficient number of traders take advantage of the predictions generated, then market behavior changes and the predicted pattern of price movements breaks down.

Overshooting   Inefficiencies can also arise in trading markets from the propensity of market participants to overreact to new information with the result that prices overshoot. The implication is that securities which have benefited from positive news will be overbought, and those which have been depressed by bad news will be underbought. It follows that advantage may be gained through a *contrarian strategy*: selling securities which have gained in price, buying securities which have fallen in price. Evidence on the success of contrarian strategies in the stock market is presented by De Bondt and Thaler.[6] Contrarian strategies can offer competitive advantage in any markets where competitors tend towards strongly imitative behavior. In many industries profit cycles are a consequence of closely correlated investment behavior among competitors, which then offers opportunity for contracyclical investment. T. Boone Pickens built Mesa Petroleum into a highly profitable oil company through buying offshore oil leases during the early 1970s, when most of the industry was competing for onshore leases, then selling many of its oil properties during the boom in upstream investment in 1979–80. Warren Buffett, the billionaire chairman of Berkshire Hathaway is another committed contrarian: "The best time to buy assets may be when it is hardest to raise money," he observed.[7]

Competitive advantage in first-hand markets

The role of resource idiosyncracy   The transitory nature of competitive advantage in trading markets is a result of the characteristics of the resources required to compete: finance and information. Because finance is a relatively homogeneous resource, it yields competitive advantage in trading markets only in the event of unusually large transactions (e.g. the acquisition of R. J. R. Nabisco). Information is highly differentiated and offers greater potential for competitive advantage. However, since it, like finance, is easily transferable, the competitive advantage it offers tends to be fleeting.

The markets for first-hand goods and services are quite different. The suppliers to these markets must produce and production requires complex combinations of resources. Many of these resources are idiosyncratic, that is, each resource possesses unique characteristics. As a result each producer possesses a unique combination of resources. A consequence of interfirm differences in resources is that changes in the external environment result in the emergence of competitive advantages. In the aftermath of the oil shocks of 1974 and 1979, European and Japanese car manufacturers whose know-how and production facilities were geared to the manufacture of small, fuel-efficient automobiles were put at an advantage to the Big Three US producers. When oil prices fell rapidly after 1982, Ford and Chrysler, which had maintained their capacity for building large, rear-wheel drive cars, gained an advantage over General Motors which had invested heavily in smaller, front-wheel drive cars.

A second consequence of the complexity and the idiosyncrasies of the resources required for producing goods and services is that competitive advantages are more readily sustained over time. We have noted that sustaining competitive advantages depends upon their protection by "isolating mechanisms", which arise, first, from imperfect transparency of the linkages between resources, strategies and competitive advantage and, secondly, from barriers to the acquisition of the resources required for imitation. We shall discuss each in turn.

Causal ambiguity leading to uncertain imitability   In order to imitate the strategy of a successful rival, a firm must first diagnose the source of its rival's competitive advantage. In most industries there is a serious identification problem in linking superior performance, first to the characteristics of the strategy which generates that performance, and second to the resources upon which that strategy is based. Lippman and Rumelt refer to this problem as "uncertain imitability" arising from "causal ambiguity."[8] Consider IBM's superior performance in the computer industry during the past quarter century. Is it a result of IBM's commitment to customer service; its fast-follower approach to product innovation; its emphasis on efficient, high quality manufacturing? And what are the key resources which support that strategy: are they IBM's financial resources; its extensive, finely-tuned sales and customer support network; the commitment of IBM's employees to common goals? In Lippman and Rumelt's analysis, uncertain imitability is introduced as a random variable in the cost functions of would-be imitators. In practice, the level of the uncertainty in imitators' diagnoses of the competitive advantage of successful rivals depends upon the complexity of the competitive advantage (in terms of the range of performance variables over which advantage is established) and the complexity of the resources and capabilities upon which the competitive advantage is based.

Impediments to resource acquisition: imperfect transferability and barriers to replication Having diagnosed the sources of a rival's competitive advantage, the imitator must then succeed in replicating that competitive advantage. This requires the acquisition of the resources upon which the strategy is based. A firm may augment its resource base in two ways:

- it can purchase resources from external factor markets
- it may create them through internal investment.

Sustaining a competitive advantage over time depends critically upon the lags involved in rivals' acquisition of the resources required to mount a competitive challenge. This depends upon the characteristics of the resources themselves.

The ability to acquire resources externally is dependent upon the inter-firm transferability of the resources. The transferability of resources is limited by transactions costs and impediments to mobility. The markets for most factors of production are hindered by search costs, contracting costs, and contract enforcement costs. Transaction costs are greater for idiosyncratic resources than for nonspecific resources.[9] Particular problems of transferability arise in the case of resources which are not only unique, but are specific to particular firms. Resources are *firm specific* to the extent that their value declines upon transfer between firms. Chapter 4 looked at how brand names, technological know-how, and reputation may lose value in transfer to another firm. Similarly, senior managers may be less productive in a new company than in the companies where they developed their skills and interpersonal relationships. In general, any capabilities which reside in the coordinated efforts of a team of organizational members, what Nelson and Winter refer to as "organizational routines" are difficult to transfer.[10]

The alternative to the external acquisition of resources is to create them internally. In the case of team-based skills or organizational routines, only the individuals can be hired; the team skills must be developed internally through design and practice. Even where process technology is acquired through the purchase of new equipment, it takes time to develop the complementary skills required to operate the technology: "I have myself watched in Hungary a new imported machine for blowing electric lamp bulbs, the exact counterpart of which was operating successfully in Germany, failing for a whole year to produce a single flawless bulb," observed Polanyi.[11] Businesses that require the integration of a number of complex, organizational routines may take years to reach the standards set by industry leaders. At GM's Van Nuys plant, the shift from traditional assembly-line operation to Toyota-style, team-based production required considerable learning and adjustment. After two years the new production arrangements had been only partially implemented and productivity and quality remained well below target.[12] The highly-tuned network of complementary skills required by newspapers and broadcasting organizations represent particularly formidable problems of replication. Fox Broadcasting needed three years of experimentation, learning and adjustment in order to establish its television network as a viable competitor to ABC, CBS, and NBC.[13]

The relationships we have discussed between the nature of competition, the sources of imperfection in competition and the opportunities for establishing and sustaining competitive advantage are summarized in Exhibit 5.1.

Assumptions about the characteristics of markets and resources	Imperfections of competition	Strategy for establishing advantage
Efficient market where finance and information available to all traders on equal terms.	None	No basis for competitive advantage.
Costs incurred in trading (e.g. information search, administration, order processing).	Transaction costs	Minimize transaction costs.
Psychological characteristics of traders results in regularities in market behavior.	Predictable patterns of behavior	Analyze past behavior to determine the future (e.g. chart analysis).
Imitative responses to new information.	Overshooting	Pursue contrarian strategies.
Idiosyncratic resources and imperfect transparency of resource-performance linkages.	Causal ambiguity	Build advantages which require complex combinations of resources and skills.
Firm specific resources and transaction costs in the markets for resources and capabilities.	Imperfect resource transferability	Base strategies upon imperfectly transferable resources and capabilities.
Long development periods for some resources and capabilities.	Imperfect resource replicability	Base strategies upon resources and capabilities which require a long time to replicate.

Exhibit 5.1 Market characteristics, imperfections of competition, and strategies to secure competitive advantage

Sustaining competitive advantage through deterrence

Thus far, our analysis of the sustainability of competitive advantage has dealt with rivals' abilities to replicate the competitive advantage of the incumbent firm. But the period over which competitive advantage is sustained also depends upon the rivals' *incentive* to imitate another firm's competitive advantage. The profitability which a rival anticipates from imitating the competitive advantage of an apparently successful company depends, to a great extent, upon the ability of the incumbent firm to influence those expectations. Game theoretic modeling of competitive behavior has made valuable advances in the analysis of interactions between incumbent firms and would-be challengers. A central element in an incumbent's deterrence of challengers is influencing the information available to potential challengers. Drawing upon the discussion of signalling and deterrence in chapter 3, we can identify three principal methods in which a firm can sustain a competitive advantage through discouraging competitors:

- obscuring superior performance;
- threats;
- preemption.

Obscuring superior performance   The information problem facing the would-be imitator of the competitive advantage of a successful rival has been viewed so far as the problem of diagnosing the sources of superior performance. However, before a rival can consider imitation, it must first be alerted to the existence of that competitive advantage. In other words, it must be able to identify higher profits being earned by a competing firm. In any gold rush where mineral rights are imperfectly defined, the sustainability of competitive advantage depends critically upon the successful prospectors keeping their find secret.[14] In order to discourage would-be competitors, firms may choose to forego short-term profits through "limit pricing."[15] Recent contributions to the analysis of limit pricing view it as a means by which incumbents signal to other firms that they are low-cost producers.[16] A recent survey of the effectiveness of alternative means of protecting innovation found that, for process innovations, secrecy was more effective than patents.[17]

Threats   A threat is a promise to retaliate against a competitor which encroaches upon a firm's competitive position. For a threat to be effective in deterring a competitive challenge, it must be credible. Since carrying out a threat is usually costly to both the aggressor and the victim, it needs to be supported by commitment. As was noted in chapter 3, investments in deterrence can include excess capacity, excess inventories, and reputations for aggressive behavior. The problem of these investments in credible threats is that, not only are they costly, they also limit the strategic options available to the threatening player.

Preemption   Finally, incumbents can limit the opportunities available to would-be challengers by preemption of the investment opportunities open to rivals. Preemption may involve brand proliferation, patent proliferation, market saturation through additions to capacity, and building geographically-extensive distribution networks.

Finally, even if a rival's successful strategy can be imitated, it does not necessarily imply that it will confer equivalent success to the follower firm. A firm's ability to sustain a position of competitive advantage against imitators may be reinforced by the cumulative and self-sustaining characteristics of some types of competitive advantage. The old adage that "success breeds success" is confirmed by the presence of several sources of first-mover advantage:

First-mover advantage

- investment funds from initial competitive advantage;
- experience;
- the availability of inputs on favorable terms.

Initial competitive advantage offers a profit flow which permits the firm to invest at a faster rate than competitors, to avoid the costs of raising external finance, and to use its higher valuation ratio to acquire rival firms. Thus, initial advantage can be used to generate further advantages. Even if the initial advantage has a limited lifespan, it can be used to facilitate investment in other sources of competitive advantage. Pilkington's revolutionary float glass process was a competitive advantage whose life was limited to the term of the patent. However, Pilkington used its profits and income from patent licenses to invest heavily in new plant, expand multinationally by acquiring overseas competitors, and finance R&D into fiber optics and other new uses of glass.

The second source of first-mover advantage is experience. A firm that initially gains sales can use the experience it acquires as the basis for subsequent cost reduction. Thus, cost advantages can become cumulative. We shall explore economies of experience more fully in the next chapter.

Finally, firms which experience initial success may subsequently attract inputs on more favorable terms. This is most obvious in the case of human resources. It is much easier for IBM, Proctor and Gamble, and Walt Disney to attract highly capable graduates and junior managers than poorly-performing companies such as Sears Roebuck, Chrysler, or Goodyear. Similar tendencies are apparent in other inputs. Credit terms from suppliers are typically better for profitable than unprofitable firms.

Creating Competitive Advantage through Responsiveness and Innovation

The preceding analysis has viewed competitive advantage as accruing to firms which possess superior resources and capabilities, and subsequently being eroded through imitation by competitors. In practice, we can expect firms to be more proactive in both creating and overturning competitive advantage. To establish competitive advantage firms must be opportunistic and creative. Similarly, in order to successfully challenge industry leaders, finding new ways of competing may be more effective than imitating the current leaders. In analyzing these dynamic approaches to competitive advantage we can distinguish between strategies which anticipate and respond to external change, and strategies which create change through innovation.

Competitive advantage through responsiveness to change

The success of Campbell's Soup and Frito Lay in food processing and The Limited, The Gap, and Benetton in clothes retailing, lies in the responsiveness of these companies to changes in the market. As fashion cycles become compressed and customer preferences become increasingly fragmented, so competitive advantage increasingly depends upon the ability to respond flexibly and quickly to emerging market trends. In the oil industry, efficiency in refining was dependent upon scale-efficient refineries, long-term planning of capacity additions, and operational planning of product flow from wellhead to retail outlets. As turbulence and competition in the oil market have increased, cost efficiency is increasingly dependent upon flexibility in purchasing to take advantage of price differentials in the market for crude oil, flexibility in the ability to refine different types of crude, and flexibility in changing the composition of refined products to match changes in demand.

Responsiveness also involves anticipating changes in the basis of competitive advantage over time. As an industry moves through its life-cycle, as the identity of competitors changes, and as resources depreciate or become replicated by competitors, so firms must identify emerging sources of competitive advantage and invest in the required resources and capabilities ahead of time. Entering the 1990s, several companies had improved their competitive positions through responsiveness to increasing concerns over the environment. An advertising claim by AEG, the German appliance manufacturer, that its dishwashers were kinder to freshwater newts contributed to a 30 percent boost in sales.[18] Monsanto's subsidiary, G. D. Seale, has shown notable foresight in building a competitive position which it hopes will outlive the expiration in 1992 of the patents on its outstandingly-successful artificial sweetener, NutraSweet. Searle initially based its competitive advantage upon worldwide patenting which was extended through special legislation for a further five years beyond the normal 17-year patent term. However, in anticipation of patent expiration Searle has invested heavily in further barriers to competition. It has strongly promoted the

NutraSweet brand name with its distinctive "swirl" logo, and it has invested in a $160 million, scale-efficient production facility in Georgia for NutraSweet. Trade secrets will be used to the maximum to protect its production know-how.[19]

Responsiveness to the opportunities for competitive advantage provided by change in the external environment requires two key capabilities:

- environmental scanning to identify change:
- the flexibility to redeploy resources.

Environmental scanning to identify and anticipate change does not necessarily involve the traditional methods of amassing and analyzing vast quantities of market research and economic data. As we shall examine in chapter 7, contemporary approaches to market intelligence are moving away from formal analysis of market statistics towards direct communication with customers.

A company's own sales data is also valuable in tracking market trends. Benetton's information network which relays sales data from the cash registers in its retail outlets back to its corporate headquarters in Polanzo, Italy, is a critical component of Benetton's responsiveness to market trends. Analysis of market trends in terms of style and color preferences permits information to be fed back to Benetton's agents and retailers, so that they can then adjust their orders.

Responsiveness requires that firms have the flexibility to redeploy resources to meet changes in external conditions. While advanced manufacturing technology such as flexible manufacturing systems and computer integration can promote flexibility, flexibility is primarily a function of organization structure, systems of decision making, and attitudes. Flexibility requires fewer levels of hierarchy, greater decentralization of decision making, and informal patterns of cooperation and coordination. Benetton's responsiveness to market trends is achieved through a highly flexible network. At the retail level Benetton operates through a system of country and regional agents who coordinate the retail outlets within their territories. At the production level, Benetton's own production facilities are supported by over 200 subcontractors. A remarkable feature of this vertically-integrated network is an absence of formal contracts. In order to maximize speed of response to changes in customer color preferences, Benetton dyes most of its garments after manufacture in contrast to the usual industry practice of dying the thread prior to manufacturing the garment.[20] For effective response to external change, speed is of the essence. George Stalk Jr argues that the key source of competitive advantage of leading Japanese companies such as Honda, Matsushita, and Toyota is speed: These companies compete through time-based manufacturing, time-based sales and distribution, and time-based innovation.[21]

Competitive advantage through innovation: identifying "new game" strategies

Dynamic competitive advantage is not just a matter of responding to external change; it involves creating change through innovation. Schumpeter's view of the competitive process as "a gale of creative destruction" was one of market leadership being eroded not by imitation, but by innovation. The management of technology will be addressed in chapter 9. But innovation does not relate only to technological innovation, it includes all new ways of performing business activities. Many firms which have achieved startling success in mature industries – Nucor and Chaparral Steel in the steel industry, The Limited in retailing, Frank Purdue in broiler chickens, McDonald's in fast food – have done so not by innovation in the technical sense, but innovation in the strategic sense: they have adopted novel approaches to competing in their respective industries.

Innovation typically requires imagination, intuition, and creativity rather than deductive analysis. However, there are frameworks and approaches that can be useful in identifying new ways of competing. By mapping the activities which the firm performs and the linkages between activities, the value chain provides a representation of the firm that can then be manipulated to suggest new ways of competing. On this basis, McKinsey and Company distinguish between "Same Game" and "New Game" strategies. New game strategies typically take the form of new configurations of the chain of activities which are performed in the industry. The ways in which firms do business in an industry and the range of activities which they encompass are often the result of convention. By reconstructing and rearranging the value chain a company can change the "rules of the game" so as to:

● capitalize on its distinctive competencies;
● catch competitors off guard;
● erect barriers to protect the advantage created.

McKinsey quotes Savin in the North American market for plain-paper copiers as an example of the potency of new game strategies in challenging an established firm with a seemingly-impregnable competitive position, and an illustration of the application of the value chain in formulating new game strategies (see Case Note 5.1).

The key element in the formulation of new game strategies is to identify the activities in which a firm has the potential for advantage and then to devise a strategy which achieves the maximum leverage of these advantages. Among airlines, several companies have competed successfully through redefining and reconfiguring the activities they perform. Laker and People's Express achieved remarkable, if temporary, success in budget air travel by radically pruning the number of activities which they performed and so achieving substantially lower operating costs than those incurred by established airlines. American Airlines, on the other hand, established a substantial differentiation advantage over other airlines by extending the range of its activities into a national sales and distribution network through

Case Note 5.1 Using the Value Chain to Help Formulate New Game Strategies: Savin and Xerox

For most of the 1970s, Xerox possessed a near monopoly position in the North American market for plain-paper copiers. Xerox's dominance rested, first, upon the wall of patents which the company had built over several decades and, second, on the scale economies and reputation which its market dominance conferred. The first company to compete effectively with Xerox during the late 1970s was Savin. The basis of Savin's challenge was an approach which sought, not to imitate Xerox's success, but to compete in an entirely different manner.

Savin developed and patented a new low-cost technology. Its product design permitted the use of standardized parts that could be sourced in volume from Japan. Assembly was also undertaken in Japan. The result was a product whose cost was about half that of Xerox's. To avoid the costs of leasing and the need for a costly direct sales force, Savin distributed through existing office equipment dealers.

The principal differences between the approach of Savin and that of Xerox can be seen by comparing the main activities of the companies:

	XEROX	SAVIN
Technology and design	Dry xerography High copy speed Many features	Liquid toner Low copy speed Few features and options
Manufacture	Most manufacturing (including components) in house	Machines sourced from Ricoh in Japan
Product range	Wide range of machines	Narrow range of machines for different volumes and uses
Marketing	Machines leased to customers	Machines sold to customers
Distribution	Direct sales force	Distribution through dealers
Service	Directly operated service organization	Service by dealers and independent service engineers

Source: Roberto Buaron, "New-game strategies," *McKinsey Staff Paper*, March 1980.

its Sabre ticketing system. Nike and Reebok are companies which adopted a new configuration of the value chain in shoe manufacture in order to exploit international comparative advantages. Their R&D and design is located in the US; shoe components are manufactured in the newly-industrializing companies of Taiwan, Hong Kong, and South Korea; while manufacturing is increasingly undertaken by subcontractors and joint-venture partners mainly in the developing countries such as Thailand, China, and the Philippines. Across a wide range of US manufacturing industries, especially consumer electronics, toys, bicycles, and apparel, companies are withdrawing from manufacturing activities and concentrating upon those activities where they can secure a competitive advantage.

Types of Competitive Advantage

A firm can achieve a higher rate of profit (or potential profit) over a rival in one of two ways: either it can supply an identical product or service at a lower cost, or it can supply a product or service which is differentiated in such a way that the customer is willing to pay a price premium which exceeds the additional cost of the differentiation. In the former case the firm possesses a *cost advantage*, in the latter a *differentiation advantage*. In pursuing cost advantage, the goal of the firm is to become the cost leader in its industry or industry segment. Cost leadership is a unique position in the industry which requires that the firm "must find and exploit all sources of cost advantage ... [and] sell a standard, no-frills product."[22] Differentiation by a firm from its competitors is achieved "when it provides something unique that is valuable to buyers beyond simply offering a low price"[23] (see Exhibit 5.2).

Exhibit 5.2 The sources of competitive advantage

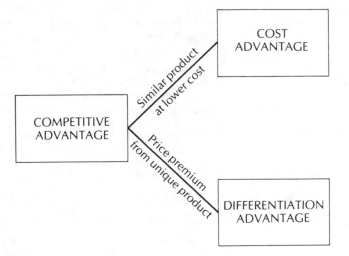

These two sources of competitive advantage define two basic approaches to business strategy. A firm that is competing on the basis of low cost is clearly distinguishable from a firm which competes through differentiation in terms of its market positioning and its resource and organizational requirements. Exhibit 5.3 outlines some of the principal features of cost leadership and differentiation strategies. By combining the two sources of competitive advantage with the firm's choice of *scope*, that is, whether to compete across the market or within a particular segment, Michael Porter has defined three generic strategies: cost leadership, differentiation, and focus (see Exhibit 5.4).

Porter views cost leadership and differentiation as mutually exclusive strategies. A firm which attempts to pursue both is "stuck in the middle":

The firm stuck in the middle is almost guaranteed low profitability. It either loses the high volume customers who demand low prices or must bid away its profits to get this business from the low-cost firms. Yet it also loses high-margin business –

Generic strategy	Key strategy elements	Resource and organizational requirements
Cost leadership	Investment in scale efficient plant; design of products for ease of manufacture; control of overheads, R&D; avoidance of marginal customer accounts.	Access to capital; process engineering skills; frequent reports; tight cost control; structured organization and responsibilities; incentives related to quantitative targets.
Differentiation	Emphasis on branding and brand advertising, design, service, and quality.	Marketing abilities; product engineering skills; creativity; capability in basic research; subjective rather than quantitative measurement and incentives; strong interfunctional coordination.

Exhibit 5.3 Some general features of cost leadership and differentiation strategies

the cream – to the firms who are focussed on high margin targets or have achieved differentiation overall. The firm which is stuck in the middle also probably suffers from a blurred corporate culture and a conflicting set of organizational arrangements and motivation system.[24]

In practice, few firms are faced by such stark alternatives. Differentiation is not simply an issue of "to differentiate or not to differentiate". All firms must make decisions about where to position their product or service in the market. Adopting a low-price, low-cost strategy generally implies a market positioning based upon a single-line, limited-feature, standardized offering. However, such a positioning does not necessarily imply that the product or service is a commodity. In the case of IKEA furniture, McDonald's hamburgers, and Rent-A-Wreck car hire, a low-price, no-frills offering

		SOURCE OF COMPETITIVE ADVANTAGE	
		Low cost	Differentiation
	Industry wide	COST LEADERSHIP	DIFFERENTIATION
COMPETITIVE SCOPE	Single segment	FOCUS	

Exhibit 5.4 Porter's generic strategies

Note: A "focus" strategy is defined by its emphasis on a single industry segment. However, within that segment a focus strategy may be orientated either towards low cost or differentiation.

is also associated with a clear market positioning and a unique brand image. Similarly, firms which aim towards positions of differentiation advantage cannot be oblivious to cost. In most industries, the market share leader is a firm which achieves a position of modest differentiation at an acceptable cost. Few market leaders are also the lowest cost producers in their industries. The lowest cost producers are likely to be small or fringe suppliers with exceptionally low overheads. In the US automobile market, General Motors and Ford combine high differentiation with strong emphasis on cost efficiency; the cost leaders are typically importers such as Yugo and Hyundai. In international air transport, despite the existence of economies of scale, the cost leaders are not the major airlines but are charter airlines which operate aging aircraft at near full-capacity, with non-union labor, and very low overheads.

The reconciliation of high differentiation with low cost is one of the greatest strategic challenges facing firms in the current economic environment. Japanese manufacturers of consumer durables such as Honda, Toyota, Sony, and Matsushita, are masters in reconciling good design, high quality, and strong marketing and distribution with world-beating manufacturing efficiency. One of the most important findings of recent empirical research into manufacturing performances has been to explode the myth of the quality/cost tradeoff. A host of studies show that current innovations in manufacturing technology and manufacturing management result in simultaneous increases in productivity and quality.[25] Achieving higher quality in terms of fewer defects and greater product reliability frequently involves simpler product design, fewer component suppliers which are more closely monitored, and fewer service calls and product recalls. All of these save cost. Tom Peters observes an interesting asymmetry:

Cost reduction campaigns do not often lead to improved quality; and, except for those that involve large reductions in personnel, they don't usually result in long-term lower costs either. On the other hand, effective quality programs yield not only improved quality but lasting cost reductions as well.[26]

Differentiation and cost reduction can be complementary in other ways. High levels of advertising and promotional expenditure can increase market share which then permits the exploitation of scale economies across a wide range of functions. Moreover, the existence of scale economies in advertising and other differentiation activities means that a market share leader can improve its relative cost position by forcing rivals to compete on product differentiation. The heavy advertising campaign with which Apple launched its Macintosh computer in 1984, was partly motivated by the desire to "up the stakes" for smaller manufacturers of personal computers which did not possess a sales base sufficient for large-scale advertising. Similarly, Honda's product strategy of annual model changes increased the pressure on other motorcycle manufacturers who did not have the sales volume to justify the heavy fixed costs of annual model changes.[27]

In the next two chapters we shall develop and operationalize these concepts of cost and differentiation advantage by presenting frameworks for diagnosing the sources of cost and differentiation advantage and formulating strategies which exploit these sources of advantage.

Summary

This chapter has examined the interaction between industry conditions and firms' resources in determining the potential for competitive advantage. Opportunities for competitive advantage emerge whenever change occurs. But competition causes the erosion of superior profitability. Sustainability of competitive advantage depends upon the existence of *isolating mechanisms*: barriers to rivals' imitation of successful strategies. Important isolating mechanisms include *causal ambiguity* concerning the determinants of success, and *barriers to the acquisition and replication of key skills and resources.*

In the next two chapters we shall analyze the two primary sources of competitive advantage: cost advantage and differentiation advantage. In both these areas it will be useful to disaggregate the firm into a series of separate but interlinked activities. For this purpose we shall use the *value chain* as a central organizing framework. This chapter has shown how the value chain can assist in identifying new approaches to competing within an industry. The value chain provides a powerful and versatile framework for understanding the sources of competitive advantage in an industry, for assessing the competitive position of a particular firm, and for recommending strategies to enhance a firm's competitiveness.

Notes

1. Richard P. Rumelt, "Towards a strategic theory of the firm," in R. Lamb (ed) *Competitive Strategic Management* (Prentice-Hall, Englewood Cliffs, NJ, 1984), pp. 556–70.
2. See John Cubbin and Paul Geroski, "The convergence of profits in the long run: Inter-firm and inter-industry comparisons," *Journal of Industrial Economics*, 35 (1987), pp. 427–42; Robert Jacobsen, "The persistence of abnormal returns," *Strategic Management Journal* 9 (1988), pp. 415–30; and Dennis C. Mueller, "Persistent profits among large corporations," in Lacy Glenn Thomas (ed.) *The Economics of Strategic Planning* (Lexington Books, Lexington, Mass., 1986), pp. 31–61.
3. Frank J. Finn, *Evaluation of the Internal Processes of Managed Investment Funds*, Contemporary Studies in Economic and Financial Analysis, vol. 44 (JAI Press, Greenwich, Conn., 1984), p. 6.
4. Eugene F. Fama, "Efficient capital markets: a review of theory and empirical work," *Journal of Business* 35 (1970), pp. 383–417.

5. Simon Keane, "The efficient market hypothesis on trial," *Financial Analysts Journal*, March/April 1986, pp. 58–63.

6. Werner De Bondt and Richard Thaler, "Does the stock market overreact?" *Journal of Finance* 42 (1985), pp. 793–805.

7. *Fortune*, October 23, 1989, p. 24.

8. S. A. Lippman and R. P. Rumelt, "Uncertain imitability: An analysis of interfirm differences in efficiency under competition," *Bell Journal of Economics*, 13 (1982), pp. 418–38.

9. Oliver E. Williamson, "Transaction cost economics: The governance of contractual relations," *Journal of Law and Economics*, 19 (1979), pp. 153–6.

10. R. R. Nelson and S. G. Winter, *An Evolutionary Theory of Economic Change* (Belknap Press, Cambridge, Mass., 1982), Chapter 5.

11. Michael Polanyi, *Personal Knowledge: Towards a Post-Critical Philosophy*, 2nd ed. (Harper & Row, New York, 1962), p. 52.

12. Clair Brown and Michael Reich, "When does union–management cooperation work? A look at NUMMI and GM-Van Nuys," *California Management Review* Summer 1989, pp. 26–44.

13. "Lights, action, O.K. Mr Murdoch, you're on," *Business Week*, October 13, 1986, pp. 136–9.

14. See, for example, B. Traven, *The Treasure of the Sierra Madre* (Knopf, New York, 1947).

15. Joe S. Bain, "A note on pricing in monopoly and oligopoly," *American Economic Review* 39 (1949), pp. 448–64.

16. P. Milgrom and J. Roberts, "Limit pricing and entry under incomplete information," *Econometrica* 50 (1982), pp. 443–60.

17. R. C. Levin, A. K. Klevorick, R. R. Nelson, and S. G. Winter, "Appropriating the returns from industrial research and development," *Brooking Papers on Economic Activity* 3 (1987), pp. 793–6. See also chapter 9 in this book.

18. "The perils of greening business," *The Economist*, October 14, 1989, p. 75.

19. David J. Teece, "Profiting from technological innovation: Implications for integration, collaboration, licensing, and public policy," in David J. Teece (ed.), *The Competitive Challenge: Strategies for Industrial Innovation and Renewal* (Ballinger, Cambridge, Mass., 1987), pp. 137–158.

20. "Benetton (A)" and "Benetton (B)" in William H. Davidson and Jose de la Torre, *Managing the Global Corporation* (McGraw-Hill, New York, 1989).

21. George Stalk Jr, "Time – the next source of competitive advantage," *Harvard Business Review*, July–August 1988, pp. 41–51.

22. Michael E. Porter, *Competitive Advantage* (Free Press, New York, 1985), p. 13.

23. Ibid., p. 120.

24. Michael E. Porter, *Competitive Strategy* (Free Press, New York, 1980), p. 42.

25. See, for example, Jack R. Meredith, "Strategic advantages of the factory of the future," *California Management Review*, Winter 1989, pp. 129–45.

26. Tom Peters, *Thriving on Chaos* (Knopf, New York, 1987), p. 80.

27. The potential for differentiation to assist the attainment of cost leadership is analyzed by Charles Hill, "Differentiation versus low cost of differentiation and low cost: a contingency framework," *Academy of Management Review* 13 (1988), pp. 401–12.

SIX

Competitive Advantage: Analyzing Cost Advantage

SEARS MOTOR BUGGY: $395

For car complete with rubber tires, Timken roller bearing axles, top, storm front, three oil-burning lamps, horn, and one gallon of lubricating oil. We found there was a maker of automobile frames that was making 75 per cent of all the frames used in automobile construction in the United States. We found on account of the volume of business that this concern could make frames cheaper for automobile manufacturers than the manufacturers could make them themselves. We went to this frame maker and asked him to make frames for the Sears Motor Buggy and then to name us prices for those frames in large quantities. And so on throughout the whole construction of the Sears Motor Buggy. You will find every piece and every part has been given the most careful study; you will find that the Sears Motor Buggy is made of the best possible material; it is constructed to take the place of the top buggy; it is built in our own factory, under the direct supervision of our own expert, a man who has had fifteen years of automobile experience, a man who has for the past three years worked with us to develop exactly the right car for the people at a price within the reach of all.

Extract from the Sears Roebuck Catalogue, 1909, p. 1150.

Outline

Introduction
The Experience Curve
    Plotting an experience curve
    Strategy implications
    The dubious case for market share
    Dangers of using the experience curve as basis for strategy
    Appraising the experience curve
The Sources of Cost Advantage
    Economies of scale
    Economies of learning
    Process technology
    Product design
    Input costs
    Capacity utilization
    Operational efficiency and organizational slack
Using the Value Chain to Analyze Costs
Producer Cost versus User Cost
Dynamic versus Static Approaches to Manufacturing
Summary

Introduction

Historically, business strategy analysis has emphasized cost advantage as the primary basis for competitive advantage in an industry. This focus on cost advantage partly reflects economists' preoccupation with price as the principal medium of competition between firms. The ability to compete on price is ultimately dependent upon cost efficiency. It also reflects large industrial corporations' preoccupation with the quest for scale economies through investment in mass production and mass distribution during the period 1950–74.

For some industries cost advantage may be the sole basis for competitive advantage: If a product or service is a commodity, then the opportunities for competing on dimensions other than cost are extremely limited. Even in industries where the principal dimensions of competition are differentiation, as competition intensifies over time, so cost efficiency becomes a prerequisite for survival and success. In industries such as pharmaceuticals, investment banking, airlines, car rental, and brokerage services, firms are increasingly competing on price as well as service, innovation, and reputation. As a result extensive corporate restructuring has taken place in these sectors.

We shall examine the sources of cost advantage and develop a framework for assessing a firm's cost position and for formulating cost reduction strategies. The analysis is in three principal steps:

- how to identify the basic sources of cost advantage in an industry;
- how to appraise the cost position of a firm within its industry through disaggregating the firm into its separate activities;
- how to use the analysis of costs and relative cost position as a basis for recommending strategies for enhancing cost competitiveness.

The Experience Curve

We begin our analysis of costs with an exposition and assessment of the role of the *experience curve* in strategy formulation. The experience curve is interesting for three reasons: because of its pervasive influence on strategic thinking during the 1970s and early 1980s; because it provides a suitable introduction into the sources of cost advantage; and because it demonstrates how analysis of the determinants of relative cost can yield clear strategy prescriptions.

During the decade which followed the publication by the Boston Consulting Group of *Perspectives in Experience* in 1968, the experience curve exercised a powerful influence, not only on the analysis of costs, but on strategy analysis as a whole.[1] It is one of the best known and most influential concepts in the history of strategic management. Its basis is the systematic reduction that was observed in the time taken to build airplanes during the late 1930s and Liberty ships during the Second World War with subsequent units of production.[2] This concept of *economies of learning* was generalized by BCG to encompass the behavior of all added costs as cumulative production volume increased. In a series of studies from bottle caps and refrigerators to long distance calls and insurance policies, BCG observed a remarkable regularity in reductions in costs and prices which accompanied increases in cumulative production. As cumulative production was doubled, so unit costs and prices typically fell by between 20 and 30 percent. BCG summarized its observations in *The Law of Experience*: *The unit cost of value added to a standard product declines by a constant percentage (typically between 20 and 30 per cent), each time cumulative output doubles.*

"Unit cost of value added" is total cost per unit of production *less* the cost per unit of production of bought-in components and materials. If suppliers of components and materials are subject to similar cost reductions as volume increases, then "unit cost" may be substituted for "unit cost of value added" in the above definition. The Law of Experience may be expressed more precisely in algebraic form:

$$C_n = C_1 n^{-a}$$

where
C_1 is the cost of the first unit of production;
C_n is the cost of the nth unit of production;
n is the cumulative volume of production;
a is the elasticity of cost with regard to output.

Graphically, the experience curve is characterized by a progressively declining gradient, which, when translated into logarithms, is linear (see Exhibit 6.1). The size of the experience effect is measured by the proportion by which costs are reduced with subsequent doublings of aggregate production.

Experience curves may be drawn for the output of a product either by a firm or by industry, and may use either cost or price data. Using prices rather than costs assumes that margins are constant. Exhibit 6.2 shows examples of experience curves estimated by the BCG.

Constructing an experience curve is a simple matter once the data are available. The data required are cost per unit of production (or, more precisely, cost per unit of production *less* the cost of bought-in materials and components) and data on production volume over time. The cost data must be expressed in constant price terms to eliminate the effects of inflation. Unit costs can be expressed either in monetary units or as an index.

Plotting an experience curve

The greatest single problem with drawing an experience curve is that cost and production data must relate to a standard product. In practice, few products remain the same over extended periods of time. As a result, unit costs must be adjusted for increases in quality over time and other changes in product features and design.

Exhibit 6.1 The
experience curve

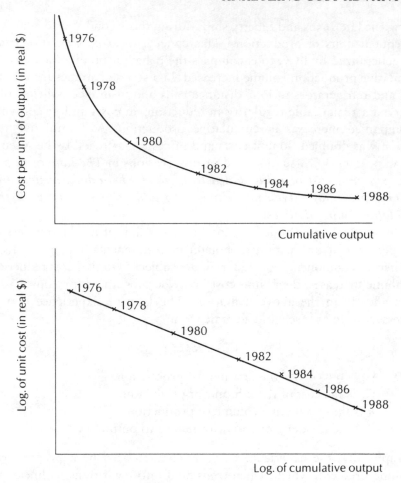

When constructing an experience curve for an industry, these difficulties of changing product characteristics make it preferable to use price rather than cost data. Official indices of wholesale prices are normally adjusted to take account of changes in quality and other major distortions. The ready availability of wholesale price data and output data for most manufacturing industries make the construction of industry-level price-experience curves easy and almost costless.

Firm-level experience curves pose more complex data problems. Obtaining a run of cost data over a sufficient period of time is difficult because of changes in accounting conventions, problems of allocating costs within a multiproduct firm, and difficulties in adjusting for changes in product characteristics. In general, the experience curve for a firm will differ in slope from the industry experience curve because of the ability of firms to *transfer* experience, that is, to learn from one another.

Strategy implications

The significance of the experience curve lies in its implications for business strategy. If costs decline with cumulative output in some systematic fashion, then a firm's costs relative to its competitors depend upon its cumulative

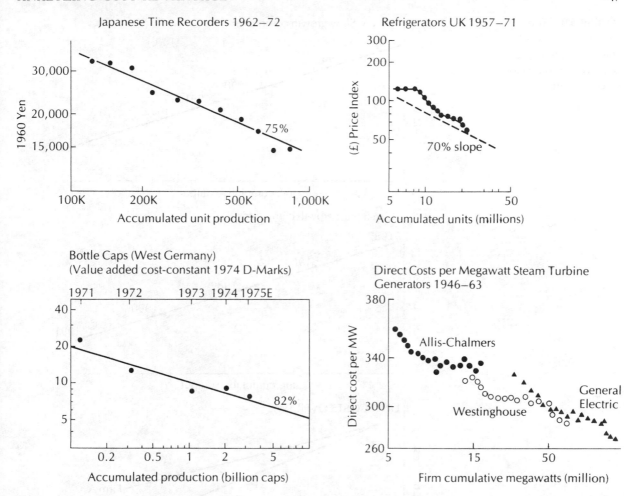

Exhibit 6.2 Examples of experience curves

output relative to competitors. If a firm can expand its output at a greater rate than its competitors, it is able to move down the experience curve more rapidly than its rivals, and in doing so can open up a widening cost differential. Exhibit 6.3 shows that, when two firms start at the same position and face identical experience curves, the firm with the faster output growth establishes a growing cost advantage over time. If the faster growing firm reduces prices in line with costs, then the rival suffers a rapidly eroding profit margin and will eventually be forced out of the industry.

The quest for experience-based cost economies further implies that a firm's primary strategic goal should be market share. If two firms enter an industry at about the same time and hold steady market shares, then their cumulative production volumes are proportional to their market shares. Assuming that the firms move down identical experience curves, their relative costs are also proportional to their relative market shares. If their prices are the same, it follows that their profitability is also proportional to market share.[3]

The dubious case for market share

Exhibit 6.3 The experience curve offers a widening cost advantage to a fast-growing firm

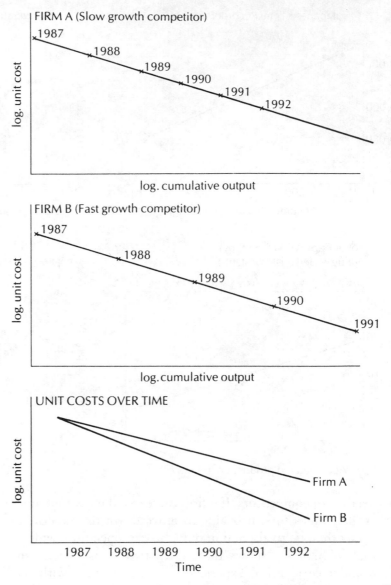

In 1987 Firms A and B start at the same point on identical experience curves. Firm B expands its output at twice the rate of Firm A. In each subsequent year, Firm B enjoys a widening cost advantage over the more slowly growing firm. If the faster growing firm lowers price in line with its cost reductions, then Firm A will eventually be forced out of business.

The inference that BCG made was that market share should be the primary strategic goal of the firm. How is a firm to gain market share leadership? The key is pricing policy. The firm should price its products not on the basis of current unit cost, but on the basis of anticipated unit cost.[4] BCG, in its study of the British motorcycle industry, observed that British motorcycle manufacturers adopted cost-plus pricing. Honda, on the other hand, priced to meet market share objectives, on the assumption that, once sufficient sales volume had been achieved, costs would fall to a level that offered a satisfactory profit margin.[5]

The goal of cost leadership through output expansion also points to the advantages of offering a broad rather than a narrow product range and expanding internationally rather than restricting sales to the domestic market.[6]

A number of empirical studies, most notably those undertaken by the PIMS program, have confirmed the positive relationship between profitability and market share.[7] The PIMS findings are summarized in Exhibit 6.4. Both PIMS and BCG found that the critical variable determining ROI was not market share itself, but *relative* market share, that is, a firm's market share relative to that of its largest competitor. Thus, if Ford has 12 percent of the Western European car market and its largest competitor, Fiat, has 16 percent, Ford's relative market share in Europe is 0.75. The sources of the relationship between profitability and market share are indicated in Exhibit 6.5. Large share businesses tend to benefit from lower costs as a result of the more productive use of resources. In addition, market share leaders possess a differentiation advantage which arises from customer perception that the market leader supplies higher quality products.

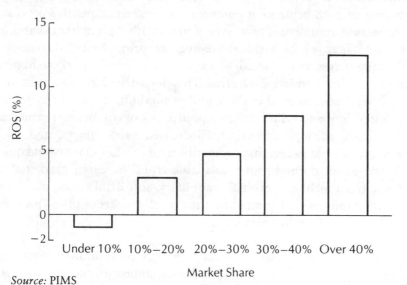

Exhibit 6.4 The relationship between market share and pretax return on sales

Source: PIMS

Despite the incontrovertible evidence linking market share to profitability, no consensus exists as to the interpretation of the relationship. The view of PIMS and BCG that market share confers superior profitability and their recommendation that increasing market share should be the primary strategy goal for companies has come under increasing attack on a number of grounds. First, there is doubt as to causation. Association is not the same as causation and it is not clear whether market share confers superior profit, whether profitable firms use their profit earnings to buy market share, or whether both high profits and high market share are consequences

Exhibit 6.5 The relationship between market position, cost advantage, price advantage, and profitability

	Market share rank				
	#1	#2	#3	#4	#5 or below
Investment/sales	46.3	52.1	52.5	51.4	54.9
Receivables/sales	14.7	14.7	14.71	4.8	15.3
Inventory/sales	18.5	19.6	20.5	20.6	22.3
Purchases/sales	41.8	43.4	45.8	48.8	51.3
Marketing/sales	8.9	9.5	9.5	9.3	9.2
R&D/sales	2.1	2.3	1.9	1.8	1.9
Relative quality (%)	69.0	51.0	47.0	45.0	43.0
Relative price (%)	105.7	103.8	103.4	103.2	103.0
Pretax profit/sales	12.7	9.1	7.1	5.5	4.5

Source: R. D. Buzzell and B. T. Gale, *The PIMS Principles* (Free Press, New York, 1987), p. 75.

of some third variable. For example, both may be rewards to efficiency, innovation, or successful differentiation. A study by Rumelt and Wensley using the PIMS data concluded that the positive relationship between market share and profitability was not the result of market share generating profit, but of both being joint outcomes of a risky competitive process.[8]

The second argument is that, even if firms with high market shares have cost advantages which yield above-average profitability, this does not imply that investments aimed at increasing a firm's market share will necessarily offer attractive returns. This is particularly the case if the relationship between market share and profitability is well known within an industry. Since all firms have the opportunity of competing for increased market share through advertising, increased sales efforts, and adding capacity, we would expect that competition for market share would quickly erode any super-normal profits available from increased market share.[9] Evidence from airlines, personal computers, soft drinks, and many other industries confirms that competition for market share leads to price wars which lower profitability for all firms.

Dangers of using the experience curve as a basis for strategy

The fallacy of composition Honda's strategy of volume manufacturing backed by aggressive pricing and marketing aimed at market share goals was successful against European and American competitors such as Norton-Villiers-Triumph and Harley-Davidson because the latter pursued cost-plus pricing directed towards short-term profit targets.[10] The fundamental fallacy of BCG's doctrine of experience economies through pricing-for-market-share is that, while it may be successful for the individual firm, it can be fatal when attempted by a number of firms. During the 1970s, US and European producers of steel, petrochemicals, ships, and automobiles followed the lead of their Japanese competitors by investing heavily in new, scale efficient plants while cutting margins in anticipation of lower costs. The results were disastrous: overinvestment combined with the oil crises of 1974 and 1979 resulted in chronic excess capacity and intense price competition. In shipbuilding, steel, oil refining, synthetic fibers, and bulk petrochemicals, industry-wide losses were sustained.

Economies of experience are earned not given A further fallacy induced by the experience curve is the notion of automaticity in the relationship between volume increase and cost reduction. Cost reductions do not just happen. For learning to take place there must be a desire to learn through observation, reflection, and the will to improve. A critical ingredient of experience economies is the quest for better ways of performing particular tasks; costs must be managed down. The ability of Japanese firms to achieve continuing cost reductions with increased production owes much to the persistence with which firms such as Honda, Toyota, and Matsushita have sought constant, incremental improvement across all aspects of their operations.

But if economies of experience really comprise a stream of incremental improvements in dexterity, organization, product design, materials handling, and process innovation, why should the production of vast numbers of units be a prerequisite for conceiving and implementing such improvements? Experience economies can be "short-circuited" in several ways.

- acquiring experience from others;
- transferring experience between the divisions of the company;
- innovating in order to leapfrog down the experience curve.

By observation, espionage, reverse engineering, and poaching employees from other firms, a company can assimilate many of the benefits of their competitors' experience. A major element of Xerox's reversal of its market share losses in the world copier industry was a thorough analysis of competitors' lower costs. This involved detailed studies of the design of competitors' machines, their manufacturing methods, and their systems of sales and distribution.[11]

The experience which Honda gained as the world's leading manufacturer of motorcycles was of tremendous benefit to Honda when it entered the markets for cars, generators, and lawnmowers. Similarly, multinationals such as General Motors, Sony, and Proctor and Gamble transfer the experience gained in their home markets to their overseas subsidiaries.

Experience can perfect existing technology. It can also constrain innovation. In the US steel industry, the lowest cost producers are not the long-established steel giants such as USX (formerly US Steel) and Bethlehem but innovative recent entrants such as Nucor and Chaparral. The tendency for experience to act as constraint as well as a source of efficiency, means that fundamental process innovations are often introduced by newcomers or by smaller firms in the industry.

Appraising the experience curve

The experience curve is simply a generalization of empirical observations. It cannot be assumed that increasing accumulated production will inevitably lead to cost reductions of some predetermined proportion, nor can it be assumed that growth of accumulated output is a prerequisite for cost competitiveness. Even if the relationship is strong both at industry and firm levels, it is not appropriate to imply that firms must pursue market share as their primary strategic goal.

The value of the experience curve is not in the mechanistic application of naive strategy rules, but in the recognition of the potential for cost reduction in all production processes. Economists and engineers tend to view a firm's level of unit cost as determined by some predetermined *cost function*: Unit costs are a function of input/output coefficients, scale of operation, and input prices. In practice, the efficiency with which firms convert inputs into output depends upon internal factors as well, in particular from learning through experimentation and practice, from innovation, and from a host of incremental improvements implemented by employees. Appreciation of the role of experience points to the complexity of the everyday operations of most firms and the scale of the task which firms face in entering an unfamiliar industry.

The experience curve also points to the fact that experience-based cost reductions are available even in long-established industries. In these mature industries, technical change may be slow, but attention to cost reduction, particularly through minor process innovations, improved organization, and product redesign, is frequently the key factor which distinguishes successful from unsuccessful firms.

The Sources of Cost Advantage

To make further progress with our analysis of costs we need to look beyond mechanistic approaches such as the experience curve and seek to understand cost competitiveness by identifying the factors which determine a firm's cost position. Experience-based cost reductions are a combination of four separate factors:

- learning by doing (the pure learning effect);
- economies of scale (as volume of output expands);
- process innovation;
- improved product design.

To these we can add three further factors which influence the cost position of a firm relative to its competitors:

- the cost of inputs;
- capacity utilization;
- residual differences in operating efficiency.

Exhibit 6.6 lists the primary sources of intercompany cost differences.

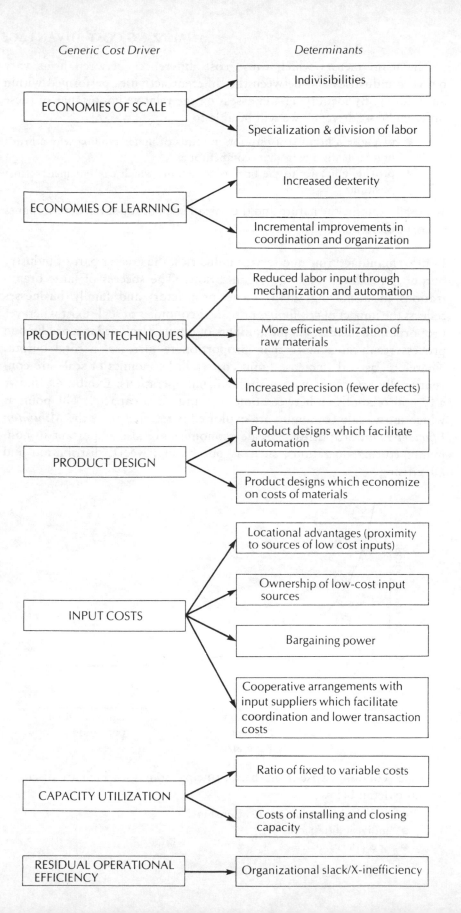

Generic Cost Driver	Determinants

ECONOMIES OF SCALE
- Indivisibilities
- Specialization & division of labor

ECONOMIES OF LEARNING
- Increased dexterity
- Incremental improvements in coordination and organization

PRODUCTION TECHNIQUES
- Reduced labor input through mechanization and automation
- More efficient utilization of raw materials
- Increased precision (fewer defects)

PRODUCT DESIGN
- Product designs which facilitate automation
- Product designs which economize on costs of materials

INPUT COSTS
- Locational advantages (proximity to sources of low cost inputs)
- Ownership of low-cost input sources
- Bargaining power
- Cooperative arrangements with input suppliers which facilitate coordination and lower transaction costs

CAPACITY UTILIZATION
- Ratio of fixed to variable costs
- Costs of installing and closing capacity

RESIDUAL OPERATIONAL EFFICIENCY
- Organizational slack/X-inefficiency

Exhibit 6.6
Determinants of differences in unit costs between competitors

The main factors which cause cost differences between firms vary between industries and between the different activities performed within an industry. By identifying and assessing the relative importance of these different "cost drivers," we will be able to:

- diagnose a firm's cost position in terms of understanding why a firm's unit costs diverge from its competitors;
- provide guidance to the firm as to actions which can enhance its cost position.

We shall examine the nature and the role of each of the seven determinants of cost differentials.

Economies of scale

In most manufacturing and service industries, the greater part of industry output is produced by large organizations. The success of large organizations in displacing small, owner-proprietor, and family businesses reflects the impact of *economies of scale*. Economies of scale exist wherever proportionate increases in the amounts of inputs employed in a production process result in a more than proportionate increase in total output. Therefore, as scale increases, unit costs fall. Economies of scale are conventionally associated with manufacturing operations: Exhibit 6.7 shows a typical relationship between unit cost and plant capacity. The point at which most scale economies are exploited is referred to as the *Minimum Efficient Plant Size* (MEPS). Scale economies are also important in non-manufacturing operations, such as purchasing, R&D, distribution and advertising.

Exhibit 6.7   A typical long-run average cost curve for a plant

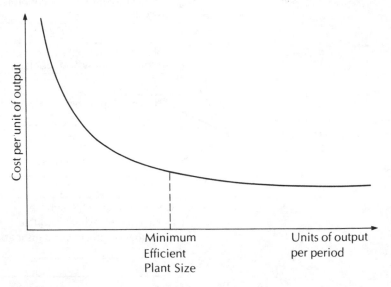

Scale economies arise from three principal sources, which are discussed in more detail below:

- technical input–output relationships;
- indivisibilities;
- specialization.

Technical input–output relationships   In some activities, increases in output do not require proportionate increases in input. Thus in production or distribution activities involving the construction or use of large containers, economies of scale arise from the fact that material costs are related to surface area which increases at the square of average dimensions, while output is related to volume which increases at the cube of average dimensions. A similar relationship exists in inventory requirements: as sales or output increase, inventories do not need to be increased proportionately.

Indivisibilities   Many inputs are "lumpy": they are simply unavailable in small sizes. Hence, they offer economies of scale as firms are able to amortize the costs of these items over larger volumes of output. Most units of capital equipment are indivisible below a certain size. Indivisibilities also arise in particular employees (a plant needs just one gatekeeper and medical officer) and in specialist units. There is a minimum feasible size to an effective R&D department in terms of the specialist scientific and engineering skills required and the equipment needed for development and testing. In many industries, the more-or-less fixed costs of new product development are the principal reason for the advantage of large over small enterprises. In automobiles, the costs of developing a new model from drawing board to production line is typically around $1.25 billion.[12] Small nationally-based automobile manufacturers such as American Motors, Rover, Saab, and Lancia have found new product development costs prohibitive and were forced to seek larger partners. In aerospace, huge development costs had caused the industry to concentrate around three main aircraft producers (Boeing, Airbus Industrie, and McDonnell Douglas) and three jet engine manufacturers (GE, Pratt and Whitney, and Rolls Royce). Large, indivisible costs are also a feature of advertising. An effective advertising campaign using national media requires a large minimum budget to have a measurable impact. The ability to spread advertising costs over a large market share is a substantial advantage over smaller rivals. Exhibit 6.8 shows how high market share is associated with low unit costs of advertising for US brands of soft drinks.

Specialization   Larger volumes of output require the employment of more inputs which permits increased specialization of the tasks of individual inputs. Specialization by labor ("division of labor") is particularly import-ant in this respect. The production process can be disaggregated into a series of separate tasks which can be performed by specialist workers using specialist equipment. Specialization by labor results in increased dex-terity, avoids loss of time from workers switching between jobs, and assists mechanization and automation. Economies of scale from special-ization are traditionally associated with economies of mass production in assembly-type manufacturing processes. However, the benefits of spe-cialization of labor are also evident in information and skill-based indus-tries where tasks and knowledge are highly specialized. In investment

Exhibit 6.8 Scale economies in advertising: US soft drinks in 1974

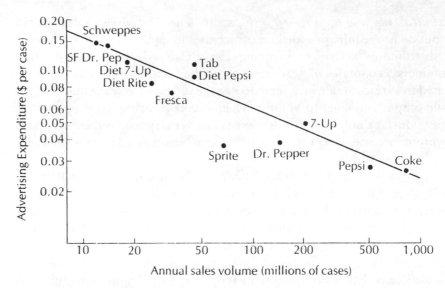

Source: prepared by the Boston Consulting Group for the UK Department of Industry

banking, management consulting, and software development, firms with a large, international spread of sales are able to provide a full range of specialist expertise at a lower cost than smaller firms.

Scale economies and concentration   The scale economies are the single most important determinant of an industry's level of seller concentration. The extent of scale economies is indicated by Minimum Efficient Plant Size as a proportion of industry size. Exhibit 6.9 shows comparisons for US industries. However, MEPS relates only to scale economies in production. In many industries high concentration reflects scale economies in other activities. High seller concentration in cigarettes, household detergents and disposable diapers can be related primarily to scale economies in advertising and promotion; concentration in personal computers, pharmaceuticals, and telecommunications equipment is mainly due to scale economies in R&D.

Current trends in the importance and extent of scale economies   In a static world with undifferentiated products and compliant employees, it is likely that, in most industries, scale economies would continue up to very high levels of output implying a predominance of very large plant and firm sizes. In practice, the exploitation of scale economies is constrained by several factors:

- product differentiation;
- dynamic factors;
- problems of motivation and coordination.

	Minimum efficient plant size as % of US output	Increase in unit cost at half MEPS (%)	Four-firm concentration ratio (%)
Flour mills	0.7	3.0	18.0
Bread baking	0.3	7.5	12.0
Printing paper	4.4	9.0	23.0
Sulfuric acid	3.7	1.0	32.0
Synthetic fibers	11.1	7.0	41.0
Auto tires	3.8	5.0	56.0
Bricks	0.3	25.0	16.0
Detergents	2.4	2.5	48.0
Turbogenerators	23.0	n.a	55.0
Diesel engines	21–30.0	4–28.0	42.0
Computers	15.0	8.0	65.0
Automobiles	11.0	6.0	85.0
Commercial aircraft	10.0	20.0	89.0

Exhibit 6.9 Scale economies and seller concentration in US industries

Sources: F. M. Scherer, *Industrial Market Structure and Economic Performance,* 2nd edn, (Rand McNally, Chicago, 1980; US Department of Commerce).

Where *preferences are differentiated*, customers are willing to trade lower prices for products with differentiated features. In clothing, cosmetics, automobiles, and a whole range of other consumer products, customers' demands for variety and individuality result in firms and plants remaining far below the sizes consistent with the full exploitation of scale economies.

A major problem with scale-efficient production facilities is their *specificity and inflexibility*. In a static environment this poses few problems, but in a dynamic environment, very large plants and firms have greater difficulties than smaller units in adjusting to fluctuations in demand, in input availability, in changes in product specifications, and in changes in technology.[13] As the business environment becomes increasingly turbulent, so firms' emphasis shifts from static efficiency towards flexibility.

A key constraint on the pursuit of scale economies in many manufacturing industries is the increased difficulties of managing very large plants. Many of these problems, such as strained labor relations, increased supervision costs, and increased wastage, arise from the lower levels of motivation that accompany the more impersonal, bureaucratic environments of large organizations. As firms become more participative, less hierarchical organizations, so motivation and coordination become increasingly important for effectiveness and efficiency.

Current trends in plant size are being driven by technology. Increased automation has resulted in smaller plants in terms of size and employment, though frequently their capacities are the same or even greater since automation permits greater productivity and encourages multiple shift, or even continuous, operation.

Economies of learning

The principal source of experience-based cost reduction is learning by organization members. Repetition reduces costs by decreasing the time required for particular jobs, reducing wastage and defects and improving coordination between jobs. Some of the most interesting evidence on such learning derives from the observation of very long runs of major items of capital equipment produced during World War II.[14] For example, in 1943 it took 40,000 labor-hours to build a Convair B-24 bomber. By 1945 it took only 8,000 hours.[15] Economies of learning tend to increase as the complexity of the operation increases. Thus, learning effects have a dominant influence on cost economies in aircraft manufacture, shipbuilding, civil engineering, and process plant construction. Boeing's efficiency in the production of large jet airliners owes much to learning economies on very long runs of each plane type. In contrast, the prohibitively high costs of the Concorde supersonic jet were a result, not only of the huge development costs but of the high costs of building just 14 planes at two separate locations.

Learning effects are the result of the establishment and refinement of *organizational routines* within the firm (see chapter 4). All production processes are the result of a coordinated network of many hundreds of individual routines. Efficiency depends critically upon the quality of coordination between the people within each routine and between the various routines. The start up of a new company involves a huge input of conscious planning and management to achieve the coordination needed for output to occur at all. With constant repetition, the need for planning and management supervision is steadily reduced to the point where the organization, when in "standard mode" can operate almost automatically.

Process technology

In the manufacture of most goods and services a number of alternative production technologies exist. A particular production method is technically superior to another where, for each unit of output, it uses less of one input without using more of any other input. Where a production method uses more of some inputs but less of others, the relative cost efficiency of the alternative techniques depends upon the relative prices of the inputs. Thus, the lowest cost assembly of consumer electronic goods can occur in Brazil, Philippines, and Thailand using simple, labor-intensive production techniques, or in Japan using fully-automated assembly techniques.

The development or adoption of a new production technique can be an important source of cost advantage. Pilkington's development of the float glass process (the manufacture of flat glass through the revolutionary process of floating molten glass on a bath of molten tin) gave it an unassailable cost advantage in glass production for a sustained period of time. The early adoption by Matsushita and Sony of automated insertion of components, gave them a substantial cost advantage over RCA and Zenith in the US market for televisions.

Increasingly, process innovations are quickly adopted by competitors and maintaining cost leadership through technological progressiveness requires constant technological advance through incremental process innovations. Diffusion of process innovation is assisted by the embodiment of process technology in the latest capital equipment. As a result, firms which are expanding most rapidly, and hence have the highest rates of net investment, find it easier to attain technological leadership than firms experiencing slower growth. This is one reason for the closing gap in productivity between the rapidly-expanding, newly-industrializing countries of the Far East and the more slow-growing advanced countries of North America and Western Europe. At the same time, we must be careful not to minimize the difficulties associated with the adoption of new process technology.

As was observed in chapter 4, new production methods require complex new organizational routines to be developed. The adoption of flexible manufacturing systems (FMS) and computer-integrated manufacture (CIM) is not simply a matter of installing new plant and equipment. Exploiting the productivity benefits depends critically upon the redesign of products, restructuring of organizations, and changes in human resource management.[16] Jaikumar found that the superior performance yielded by FMS systems in Japan compared to those in America could be attributed to the failure of American companies to adjust their management methods to the requirements of the new technology.[17] Between 1979 and 1986, General Motors spent $40 billion on new technology, new plants, and redesigned models with a view to becoming the world's most efficient volume manufacturer of automobiles. A plethora of difficulties and misfortunes have resulted in this huge investment offering only meager returns. For example, the $400 million refurbishment of GM's Buick City complex at Flint, Michigan encountered several years of teething problems which encouraged plant management to replace some of the new automated lines by traditional manual methods. Meanwhile, GM's much-publicized Saturn project launched in 1982 to build a new car model on a greenfield site using state-of-the-art production technology had failed to begin production by mid-1990.[18]

By contrast, other US companies have made great improvements in productivity, and in other measures of manufacturing performance, through changing the organization and management of production without substantial investment in advanced capital equipment. The productivity gains at the joint GM/Toyota NUMMI plant at Fremont, California are a sharp contrast to the disappointing performance at some of GM's highly automated plants. The fascinating feature of the Fremont experience is that it made heavy use of Toyota's management methods, yet capital investment was modest.[19] At Northern Telecom's Santa Clara plant, substantial cost reductions were achieved in the manufacture of PBXs through a reorganization of production and the implementation of just-in-time scheduling but with little investment in automated equipment.[20]

Product design

Exploiting the productivity benefits of new manufacturing technology is critically dependent upon the redesign of products.

For example, automated insertion of components into TV sets required a radical redesign of the TV set involving all solid-state components and modular subassemblies. The redesign of TVs by US and European manufacturers which accompanied their adoption of automated production methods during the mid-1970s resulted in a reduction in the number of components in a TV receiver of up to 50 percent.

BCG's motorcycle study identified Honda's "design-for-manufacture" as opposed to the British "pure engineering" approach as a major factor in the huge cost differential between the two.

IBM's "Proprinter" exemplifies how close attention to manufacturability in the design process can lead to outstanding cost efficiency (see Case Note 6.1).

Redesign of products has also been a major method by which manufacturers have sought to reconcile scale economies with product differentiation. In order to exploit scale economies in design, development, and component production, Ford and GM have reduced their model ranges, introduced common models throughout the world, and standardized engines and major components between different model ranges. At the same time they have sought to offer highly differentiated ranges by offering models featuring differences in styling, differences in trim, and a wide range of customer choices with regard to color, accessories, and optional features. Ford estimated that, on basis of the options available to customers with regard to color, trim, and accessories, it would be possible to run its US plants at capacity for a full day without producing two identical cars.

Input costs

Where the firms within an industry purchase their inputs in the same competitive input markets, we can expect every firm to pay the same price for identical inputs. In most industries, however, differences in the costs incurred by different firms for similar inputs can be an important source of overall cost advantage. Common sources of lower input costs include:

- locational differences in input prices;
- ownership of low-cost sources of supply;
- bargaining power;
- cooperative relationships with suppliers.

Locational differences in input prices   Most important here are differences in wage rates between different countries. In labor-intensive industries such as clothing, footwear, hand tools, and toys, the wide disparity in wage rates between developed and developing countries gives an almost unassailable cost advantage to producers in the latter. The survival of these

---

Case Note 6.1 Cost reduction through design for manufacturability: the IBM Proprinter

When IBM introduced its first personal computer in 1983, the most inexpensive printer it supplied cost $5,000. Hence, the new PC was supplied with a Japanese-made printer. Facing up to the challenge of introducing an inexpensive printer for use with its PC, IBM assembled a small technical team comprising designers, manufacturing engineers, and automation specialists, at Charlotte, North Carolina. The emphasis which IBM placed upon a quality machine which could be manufactured at low cost encouraged designers and manufacturing engineers to work closely together.

Their emphasis in designing the printer was to reduce the number of parts from 150, found in the typical PC printer, to 60. For ease of assembly, the printer was designed in layers so that robots could build it from the bottom up. All screws, springs, pulleys, and other fasteners which required human insertion and adjustment were eliminated. The elimination of fasteners was facilitated by the use of molded plastic components which clipped together.

Ralph Gomory, former senior vice-president of science and technology at IBM reported that:

the Proprinter came out essentially as planned. It was made from only 62 parts. It printed faster and had more features than the competition – and the team developed it in half the usual time. The product was so well-designed for automated manufacture that it turned out to be easy and inexpensive to assemble by hand – so easy in fact that IBM eventually shifted a good deal of Proprinter production from the automated plant in Charlotte to a manual plant in Lexington, Kentucky. An additional benefit was that the Proprinter proved unusually reliable in the field. Fewer parts meant fewer assembly errors, fewer adjustments, and fewer opportunities for things to go wrong later.

The smaller number of parts and ease of manufacture – the printer could be manually assembled in three and a half minutes – established IBM as a cost leader in PC printers. Only five months after its launch, the Proprinter was the best-selling printer on the market.

A similar approach was adopted by IBM in designing its LaserPrinter which was launched in Spring 1990. A team of design and manufacturing engineers, supported by a fully integrated CAD/CAM system, resulted in a printer which was made up of far fewer parts than Hewlett-Packard's comparable LaserJet III and where almost all screws were replaced by snap-on fasteners. As with the Proprinter, the LaserPrinter was designed for automated assembly, yet it was found that simplicity of design resulted in hand assembly proving to be cheaper and simpler.

Sources: Ralph E. Gomory, "From the ladder of science to the product development cycle", *Harvard Business Review*, Nov.–Dec. 1989, p. 103; MIT Commission on Industrial Productivity, *Made in America: Regaining the Productive Edge* (MIT Press, Cambridge, Mass., 1989), pp. 69–70; "IBM discovers a simple pleasure", *Fortune*, May 21, 1990, p. 64.

---

industries in Western Europe and North America requires competing on the basis of differentiation, shifting production to low-cost offshore locations, or successful lobbying for import restrictions.[21] Other locational differences in input costs arise from the transport costs of raw materials and international differences in energy costs. For example, in pulp and paper, Canadian and Scandinavian producers have benefited from their access to forest and hydroelectric power. But cost advantages arising from differences in wage rates and raw material prices tend to be unstable due to the volatility of exchange rates. The experience of the 1980s demonstrated that exchange rates cannot be relied upon to offset differences in inflation rates between countries, to balance trade, or to otherwise level the playing field of international competition.

Ownership of low-cost sources of supply In industries where raw materials are a significant input, some firms are likely to achieve a cost advantage by possession of low-cost sources of the raw material. Before the first oil crisis, US oil companies which owned Middle East oil reserves (notably the members of Aramco) had a significant cost advantage over companies which were mainly dependent on domestic sources of crude. During the later 1970s, the so called "Aramco advantage" reappeared as a result of the Saudi government's pricing policy for crude. Similarly, in the British Columbia forest products industry, firms which held leases over the best tracts of Crown lands had significantly lower log costs than less well-endowed firms.

Bargaining power   Where bought-in products form a major proportion of costs and where these bought-in inputs are supplied by oligopolistic producers, differences in buying power between the firms in an industry can be an important source of cost advantage. In retail trade, the dominance by national and regional chains of packaged groceries, electrical appliances and, to an increasing extent, clothing, is more a reflection of the ability of chain retailers to obtain preferential discounts from their suppliers than of their efficiency advantages over independent retailers.[22]

Cooperative relationships with suppliers   While in the past, aggressive use of bargaining power was viewed as the most effective means by which manufacturers could ensure low costs in their supplies of raw materials and components, recent developments in technology and organization are forcing companies to redefine their relationships with suppliers. Automobile manufacturers used to prefer arms-length relationships with suppliers with discipline exercised by maintaining two or more suppliers for each component. However, as a result of quality upgrading, the introduction of just-in-time scheduling, and the need for technical cooperation, the major automobile assemblers have drastically reduced their number of component suppliers and now treat them as close, long-term partners who share technology, production plans, and cost data. Cooperation has also been encouraged by suppliers becoming responsible for an increasing proportion of the manufacturing process. In the automobile industry suppliers are increasingly supplying modular subassemblies rather than individual components to the car manufacturers.[23] At Northern Telecom's Santa Clara plant, closer cooperation with a smaller number of suppliers (70 percent fewer) cut warehouse space and inventories by half and improved the quality of incoming material by 65 percent. Similar experiences are found right across manufacturing industry from Cadillac[24] to Apple[25] and AT&T.[26]

Capacity utilization

Our discussion of scale economies implied that variations in output are through variations in the scale of plants. This is true only in the long run. In the short and medium term, plant capacity is more or less fixed and variations in output are associated with variations in the extent of plant utilization. During periods of low demand, plant capacity is underutilized; during periods of peak demand, output may be pushed beyond the normal full-capacity operation with overtime working, additional shifts, faster machine operation, and cut-backs in maintenance time. Such departures from normal capacity operation are associated with higher unit costs. When there is excess capacity, fixed costs must be spread over a smaller volume of output. If fixed costs form a large proportion of total costs (which is typically the case in capital-intensive industries and industries where workers receive a guaranteed minimum wage), excess capacity can raise unit costs substantially. Operation beyond the limits of normal capacity also raises unit costs through overtime premiums, increased costs of machine breakdowns, and increased costs of quality control.

In declining industries and industries subject to sharp fluctuations in demand, the ability to speedily adjust capacity to the current level of demand can be a major source of cost advantage. During the years 1985–7 Exxon's ability to increase profits despite the depressed state of the world's oil markets owed much to the speedy and drastic surgery which it performed on excess capacity in transportation, refining, and distribution. Similarly, as the automobile industry enters the 1990s with a massive overhang of excess capacity, a critical determinant of the companies' relative costs will be the flexibility and speed which they show in bringing capacity into line with output.

Operational efficiency and organizational slack

In many industries, the basic cost drivers, such as scale, technology, design, input costs and capacity utilization, explain only part of the differences in the levels of unit costs of competing firms. After taking account of these factors there is typically still a margin of unexplained cost differential between firms producing similar products which can be traced to residual differences in operational efficiency and in administrative overhead. This residual inefficiency has been termed "organizational slack"[27] or "X-inefficiency."[28] Its principal source is simply the desire of employees, both at managerial and shopfloor levels to maintain some margin of inefficiency in preference to the strains of operating at maximum efficiency.

A revealing source of evidence of the extent of residual inefficiency is provided by observations of company turnarounds. When a firm's future is threatened by financial crisis, the first stage of a turnaround strategy is a shedding of unnecessary costs. Chrysler's fight for survival between 1979 and 1980 included inventory reduction, plant closure, and a reduction of white-collar workers by over 40 percent. The result was a reduction in Chrysler's breakeven level of capacity utilization from 80 to 55 percent.

Further evidence of hidden inefficiencies is given by studies of cost and productivity at different plants of the same company. Comparisons between costs and productivity at British and Continental European assembly plants of multinational automobile companies show that, despite similar product lines, technology and capital equipment, productivity was substantially higher on the Continent as a result of fewer strikes, lower levels of manning of equipment, fewer restrictive working practices, and lower inventories.[29]

Using the Value Chain to Analyze Costs

The costs of the firm are the aggregate of the costs of a number of different activities. Different activities tend to have different cost structures determined by different cost drivers. For example, in bicycle manufacture the two main activities are component production and assembly. The primary cost drivers in each activity are different. In component production the cost efficiency of one manufacturer relative to another depends mainly upon scale of production and the technology utilized. At the assembly level, wage rates are likely to be the key determinant of relative costs. Hence, for analyzing a company's cost competitiveness, the value chain is a useful framework for disaggregating the firm into a number of separate activities in order to identify:

- the factors which determine the costs of performing different activities, and their relative importance;
- why the firm has different costs from its competitors;
- which activities the firm performs efficiently, and which inefficiently;
- how costs in one activity influence costs in another;
- which activities should be undertaken within the firm and which activities should be contracted out.

The principal stages of using the value chain to analyze costs are to:

- disaggregate the firm into separate activities;
- establish the relative importance of different activities in the total cost of the product;
- identify cost drivers;
- identify links;
- examine the scope for reducing costs.

Disaggregating the firm into separate activities   Deciding the appropriate disaggregation of the firm into value chain activities is a matter of judgement. Very often the firm's own divisional and departmental structure is a useful guide. The principal considerations are:

- the separateness of an activity from other activities;
- the importance of an activity;
- the dissimilarity of activities in terms of the factors determining cost behavior;
- the extent to which there are differences in the way that competitors perform the particular activity.

Establishing the relative importance of different activities in the total cost of the product   Porter suggests the assigning of operating costs and assets to each value activity. Even with access to management and cost accounting data, this can be a major exercise. The size and cost of some of the assignments undertaken by Porter's consulting company, Monitor, point to the heavy data requirements of detailed value chain analyses. However, if the purpose of the study is to identify likely areas for improving cost performance, it may be sufficient as a preliminary examination to assign some approximate estimates of magnitude. A second reason for starting with an initially approximate cost allocation is that in the course of a priori analysis of activities and their cost drivers, the classification of the firm into value activities may be adjusted and the analysis will identify more precisely which are the key areas in which detailed cost information is required.

Identifying cost drivers   For each activity, what factors determine the level of cost of the firm relative to other firms? Management accounting systems can tell a firm the total costs of the business; they may also be able to break down costs between activities in a meaningful way. Their key weakness for decision-making purposes is that they offer little guidance as to what factors determine costs.[30] In order to reduce costs, a firm must know the principal factors which determine the costs incurred. Through analysis of cost drivers, many firms have found that conventional sources of cost advantage – scale economies, wage costs, and number of models produced – are less important in determining cost differences between manufacturers than product design, and the organization of production activities. For example, Xerox discovered that its high service costs relative to competitors reflected the complexity of its copiers which required 30 different interrelated adjustments.[31]

Identifying linkages   How can the firm's activities be adjusted or recon-figured, so that actions in one activity reduce costs in other activities? Davidson Rubber, a division of Ex-Cello-O Corporation, sought to lower costs of flexible car bumpers by automating their painting. However, this automation painting necessitated manual smoothing of surface imper-fections prior to painting. By developing, in cooperation with Dow Chemi-cal, a new material for the bumpers, Davidson was able to automate painting without the need for smoothing, and achieved cost savings of over $8 million a year.[32] Similarly, many firms have achieved several sharply reduced costs of quality control and after sales service not by adjusting these activities, but by imposing more stringent quality standards upon their component suppliers.

Examining the scope for reducing costs   Having identified the activities responsible for the major portions of overall costs and established the cost drivers for each activity, the firm is positioned to identify the potential for cost reduction in three main areas.

First, for activities where scale economies are important, can volume be increased? One feature of Caterpillar's ambitious cost reduction strategy of the 1980s was to spread the costs of major indivisibilities such as R&D, component manufacturing plants, and dealer support over a larger volume of sales through introducing additional new models, entering the supply of forklift trucks, and expanding its sales of diesel engines to other customers.

Secondly, where wage costs are important, can wages be reduced either directly or by relocating production? Several airlines, notably Continental, American, and United, have sought competitiveness in the deregulated US air transport market by forcing wage cuts on employees. The US TV manufacturers sought to survive Far Eastern competition with the establishment of assembly plants in Mexico, Taiwan, and Korea.

Finally, if a certain activity cannot be performed efficiently within the firm, can the activity be contracted out, or the component or service be bought in? In the drive by New York banks to cut costs, Bankers Trust has been in the forefront through its policy of transferring support services and administrative operations to outside suppliers. In 1988 it transferred its accounts payable, employee records, and payroll departments (including 125 of its employees) to Xerox.[33]

Case Note 6.2 demonstrates the application of the value chain to the analysis of cost advantage for a hypothetical automobile manufacturer.

Producer Cost Versus User Cost

Our analysis of cost efficiency as a source of competitive advantage assumes that low-cost production can be translated into prices which undercut those of competitors, and that value-conscious customers will purchase from the lowest-priced supplier. This equivalency between low-cost production and low cost for the customer breaks down when products are differentiated and when the product is consumed jointly with other goods and services. In such instances, it may be difficult to determine which firm in an industry is the cost leader, and the identity of the cost leader may be contingent upon market circumstances and the characteristics of the customer.

Consider the US automobile market. The lowest-cost suppliers during the late 1980s, judging by selling prices, were probably Yugo and Hyundai. Yet neither firm was particularly successful in so far as each company lost market share between 1987 and 1990. This partly reflects the fact that both companies faced disadvantages with regard to differentiation. However, this is not the whole story, for although both companies appeared to be cost leaders, they were not necessarily low cost from customers' point of view. To the customer the price of a car is just one element in a complex equation which determines the cost of motoring. This equation may not

Case Note 6.2   Applying the value chain to cost analysis: an automobile manufacturer

1 IDENTIFY ACTIVITIES
Establish the basic framework of the value chain by identifying the principal activities of the firm.

2 ALLOCATE TOTAL COSTS (APPROXIMATELY)
For a first stage analysis a rough estimate of the breakdown of total product cost by activity is sufficient. The important consideration is to identify which activities are important in terms of their contribution to total cost, and which therefore offer most scope for cost reductions.

3 IDENTIFY COST DRIVERS (– See diagram)

4 IDENTIFY LINKAGES
Examples include:
1. Consolidation of orders into larger, less frequent orders to increase quantity discounts on components and materials increases inventories of these items.
2. Higher quality components reduce costs in assembly and quality control.
3. Fewer defects in manufacturing reduce warranty costs incurred in the service & dealer support.
4. Design of car models with common components exploits scale economies in components.

5 MAKE RECOMMENDATIONS FOR COST REDUCTION
Purchasing: Concentrate purchases on fewer suppliers in order to increase bargaining power and facilitate cooperation. Increase frequency of deliveries by suppliers to permit just-in-time component supply.

R&D/Design/Engineering: Reduce frequency of model changes. Reduce number of different models (e.g. single range of models for all countries in the world. Design to facilitate automation of assembly. Design for interchangability of components.

Component manufacture: Exploit economies of scale through concentrating production of each component type on single plant. Contract out production of all components where scale of production or run lengths are suboptimal, or where independent suppliers have technology advantages. For components where labor costs are important (e.g. seats, dash-

---

Value chain activities:

SUPPLIES OF COMPONENTS AND MATERIALS

PURCHASING

INVENTORY HOLDING

R&D/DESIGN/ ENGINEERING

COMPONENT MANUFACTURE

ASSEMBLY

TESTING/ QUALITY CONTROL

INVENTORIES OF FINAL GOODS

SALES & MARKETING

DISTRIBUTION

SERVICE/ DEALER SUPPORT

Cost drivers:

Prices of bought-in components depend on: Order sizes
Total value of purchases over time per supplier
Location of suppliers
Relative bargaining power
Extent of cooperation

Size of R&D commitment
Productivity of R&D/design
Number & frequency of new models
Sales per model

Scale of plant for each type of component
Vintage of the process technology used
Location of plants
Run length per component
Level of capacity utilization

Scale of plants
No. of models per plant
Degree of automation
Level of wages
Employee commitment & flexibility
Level of capacity utilization

Level of quality targets
Frequency of defects

Cyclicality and unpredictability of sales
Flexibility and responsiveness of production
Customers' willingness to wait

Number of dealers. Sales per dealer
Desired level of dealer support
Frequency and seriousness of defects requiring warranty repairs/recalls

(Case Note 6.2 cont.)

boards, trim) seek to relocate production in low wage countries. Improve capacity utilization through plant rationalization or supplying components to other manufacturers.

Assembly: Increase labor productivity through automation. Improve capacity utilization through improved sales forecasting and bigger promotions during seasonal downturns. To lower costs of quality control and warranties, reduce defects through improved employee morale and increase employee involvement.

even include the purchase price of the car – the key elements are likely to be depreciation cost, interest costs, fuel costs, repairs, and insurance. Hence, in terms of overall user cost, the Yugo with its high rates of depreciation and high repair costs may represent a high-cost option in comparison to, say, a Toyota or Honda. Similar issues arise for the suppliers of components. Low production costs do not necessarily convert into low user costs. Costs to the user are likely to depend not just upon the price of the component, but also upon the reliability of delivery and the consistency of the quality of the component. Differences between the producer cost and user cost of a product or service raise some interesting strategic issues.

First, if the product in question is consumed jointly with other products and services, the effectiveness of cost reduction in establishing a competitive advantage depends upon the proportion of overall system cost which the product accounts for. Since the cost of a safety helmet accounts for a very small cost of the overall cost of cycling, customers are likely to be less sensitive to the cost of the safety helmets than to the cost of bicycles. Hence, a cost leadership strategy may be more attractive to a bicycle manufacturer than to a safety helmet manufacturer. Similarly, since electricity meters represent only a small fraction of electricity utilities' costs of supplying electricity, a differentiation is likely to be more attractive means by which a meter manufacturer can establish competitive advantage than cost reduction.

Secondly, differences in the structure of user costs between different market segments may mean that a supplier's competitive position varies between segments which, in turn, may imply different strategies for different segments. For example, how might Yugo revive its flagging US market position? Given its low selling price combined with high initial depreciation and low durability, it could begin by identifying customers for which the Yugo offers low overall user cost: For example, customers with high cost of borrowing, who keep their cars for a comparatively long time, who do not use their cars intensively, and are able to undertake minor repairs themselves. In the market for Owens-Corning's fiberglass roofing materials, an analysis of user cost by type of roofing application revealed the applications where Owens-Corning has a clear cost advantage, applications where Owens-Corning had a clear cost disadvantage, and applications where competitors were closely matched. The analysis pointed to a marketing strategy which was differentiated by market segment.[34]

Dynamic versus Static Approaches to Manufacturing

The sources of cost advantage can be divided into *static* and *dynamic* sources: scale economies, input prices, capacity utilization, and residual operating efficiencies are static in nature; learning and innovation are dynamic. Robert Hayes, Steven Wheelwright, and Kim Clark of Harvard Business School identify overemphasis on static efficiency at the expense of dynamic efficiency as a key determinant of America's industrial decline.[35] The rise of American manufacturing during the early decades of the twentieth century and the startling production achievements of World War II were the result of a dynamic approach to manufacturing which represented a marriage between the values and commitment of the artisan, the principles of scientific management, and the potential of technological progress.

In the post-war period, argue Hayes, Wheelwright, and Clark, this dynamic approach to manufacturing transferred from American to Japanese companies. US managers turned their attention from manufacturing to marketing, finance, corporate planning, and government relations. Research and development increasingly moved away from production processes and entered a new research-driven environment located in corporate R&D departments and focussed on new products rather than on continuous process improvements. As companies lost touch with their manufacturing operations and became increasingly reliant upon financial data, quantitative targets, and scientific approaches to production management, the result was a shift from a culture of striving for improvement to one of static optimization.

Regeneration of US industry requires a readoption of the dynamic approach to manufacturing. It requires a focus on the product rather than financial performance as the raison d'etre of the firm, commitment to quality, reestablishing production workers as artisans rather than machine-hands, and the quest for constant improvement of products and processes. Exhibit 6.10 contrasts dynamic with static approaches.

Examples of the potential of dynamic approaches to manufacturing are legion. In the ruins of the British cutlery industry, an industry decimated by competition from South Korea, one company has broken away from the stubborn commitment to established production methods, established machinery, and established product standards and designs. While most companies were reconciling themselves to retrenchment and decline, one firm, Richardson Sheffield, succeeded in establishing itself as the world's largest manufacturer of kitchen knives through the steadfast and unremitting pursuit of product improvement, continuous incremental improvements in process technology, and rigorous cost-consciousness.[36]

Exhibit 6.10
Characteristics of
dynamic and static
approaches to
manufacturing

Dynamic	Static
The Production System Artisan mode of production involving: ● problem solving; ● creation of knowledge by production workers; ● workers' control over the product; ● orientation towards the product and the customer.	*The Production System* Production dominated by the imperatives of Scientific Management: ● quest for the "one best way"; ● people matched to tasks; ● supervise, reward, and punish to ensure conformity of individual efforts and company objectives; ● use staff to plan and control.
Management of Technology Emphasis upon: ● continual improvement in small steps; ● commercial needs establish the R&D agenda (technology pulled in by practical demands); ● product and process innovation intimately related; ● teamwork and cross-functional collaboration.	*Management of Technology* ● science driven; research findings seeking commercial applications; ● concentrated in corporate R&D departments; ● emphasis on product innovation and on large-scale projects.

Source: Based upon the ideas and concepts in Kim Clark and Robert H. Hayes, "Recapturing America's manufacturing heritage", *California Management Review*, Summer 1988, pp. 9–33.

Concern over American business's neglect of manufacturing and products has been a persistent theme in the recent debate over the competitiveness of US industry. Since Hayes and Abernathy's attack on several of the assumptions and approaches which have characterized American management practice,[37] there has been a stream of contributions on the need to move manufacturing strategy into the forefront of companies' competitive strategies.[38] We shall return to the role of manufacturing technology and manufacturing strategy in the next chapter.

Summary

Cost efficiency may no longer be a guarantee of security and profitability in today's fast-changing markets, but in almost all industries it is a prerequisite for success. In industries where competition has always been primarily price-based – steel, food products, textiles, and mortgage loans – increasing intensity of competition is requiring more intensive and radical approaches to cost reduction. In industries where price competition was once muted – airlines, investment banking, and computers – firms are for the first time being forced to reconcile the pursuit of innovation, differentiation, and service quality with vigorous cost reduction.

The approaches used by managers and strategy consultants to analyze costs and formulate strategies for cost efficiency have changed substantially in recent years. In general, the approaches and techniques used today are more detailed, more complex, and more down-to-earth than those of the past. Cost advantage was once focussed on the key role of a single key variable: experience or scale economies. The disappointing results achieved by firms which sought sustained cost leadership through building scale-efficient plants and in seeking experience curve benefits through aggressive buying of market share, attests to the conceptual naivety and empirical frailty of these approaches.

The foundations for a strategy of cost reduction must be an understanding of the determinants of a company's costs. The principal message of this chapter is the need to look behind cost-accounting data and beyond simplistic theories of experience curves and scale effects, and to analyze the individual activities of the firms and their cost drivers.

The voluminous evidence on the effectiveness of cost reduction across a wide range of firms yields two principal findings: the sources of cost advantage are numerous, and generalization is difficult. There are no short cuts to cost analysis. The primary requirements are a detailed breakdown of the firm into separate activities, identification of the underlying factors which determine the level of costs the firm sustains in each activity, and assessment of the firm's cost position in each activity relative to competitors.

The implications of this type of analysis are likely to be detailed and far reaching. Some avenues for cost reduction may be major strategic reorientations: new, scale-efficient plant; more advanced process technology; relocating production operations offshore; or organizational changes involving the removal of several layers of management. However, the evidence from companies which have been most successful in achieving substantial and sustained reductions in total cost is that the cost reduction is most likely to be an accumulation of many hundreds of small, individual changes in equipment, design, operating, and administrative procedures throughout the whole company. Effectiveness in such cost reduction depends less on the quality of the strategic analysis and more on the motivation, alertness, and responsiveness of employees throughout the company.

Notes

1. Boston Consulting Group, *Perspectives on Experience* (Boston Consulting Group, Boston, 1968). See also Boston Consulting Group, *History of the Experience Curve*, Perspective No. 125 (Boston Consulting Group, Boston, 1973).

2. Louis E. Yelle, "The learning curve: historical review and comprehensive survey," *Decision Sciences* 10 (1979), pp. 302–28.

3. A rigorous analysis of the profit gains to market share leadership under differently sloped experience curves and different competitive conditions is developed by David Ross, "Learning to dominate," *Journal of Industrial Economics* 34 (1986), pp. 337–53.

4. This is sometimes referred to as "penetration" pricing, as opposed to "full-cost" pricing, or "skimming."

5. Boston Consulting Group, *Strategy Alternatives for the British Motorcycle Industry* (HMSO, London, 1975).

6. For a discussion of the policy implications of the experience curve, see Charles Baden Fuller, "The implications of the learning curve for firm strategy and public policy," *Applied Economics* 15 (1983), pp. 541–51.

7. Robert Buzzell, Bradley Gale, and Ralph Sultan, "Market share – a key to profitability," *Harvard Business Review,* January–February 1975; Robert Buzzell and Fredrick Wiersema, "Successful share-building strategies," *Harvard Business Review,* January–February 1981; Robert Jacobsen and David Aaker, "Is market share all that it's cracked up to be?," *Journal of Marketing* 49 (1985), pp. 11–22.

8. Richard Rumelt and Robin Wensley, *In Search of the Market Share Effect* (Paper MGL-63, Graduate School of Management, UCLA, 1981).

9. See Robin Wensley, "PIMS and BCG: new horizons or false dawn?," *Strategic Management Journal* 3 (1982), pp. 147–58.

10. Boston Consulting Group, *Strategy Alternatives for the British Motorcycle Industry* (HMSO, London, 1975).

11. "Cutting costs without killing the business," *Fortune,* October 13, 1986, p. 71.

12. "The world car restarts," *Economist,* June 11, 1988, p. 70.

13. This argument was first made by David Schwartzman, "Uncertainty and the size of the firm," *Economica,* August 1963.

14. Leonard Rapping, "Learning and World War II production functions," *Review of Economics and Statistics,* February 1965, pp. 81–6.

15. Kim B. Clark and Robert H. Hayes, "Recapturing America's manufacturing heritage," *California Management Review,* Summer 1988, p. 25.

16. Robert H. Hayes and Ramchandran Jaikumar, "Manufacturing's crisis: new technologies, obsolete organizations," *Harvard Business Review,* September–October 1988, p. 85.

17. Ramchandran Jaikumar, "Postindustrial manufacturing," *Harvard Business Review,* November–December 1986, pp. 69–76.

18. "General Motors: What went wrong," *Business Week,* March 16, 1987, pp. 102–10; "Shrinking giant," *Wall Street Journal,* June 6, 1988, pp. 1 & 14.

19. Clair Brown and Michael Reich, "When does union–management cooperation work? A look at NUMMI and GM-Van Nuys," *California Management Review,* Summer 1989, pp. 28–9.

20. R. M. Grant, R. Krishnan, and A. B. Shani, "Appropriate technology and the relative roles of hardware and software in the quest for manufacturing excellence," (Discussion Paper, School of Business, Cal Poly, November 1989).

21. For a fuller discussion, see Robert M. Grant, "Business strategies for adjusting to low-cost international competition in mature industries," in J. McGee and H. Thomas (eds), *Strategic Management Research: A European Perspective* (John Wiley, Chichester and New York, 1986) pp. 195–218.

22. R. M. Grant, "Manufacturer-retailer relations: the shifting balance of power," in G. Johnson (ed.) *Retailing and Business Strategy* (John Wiley, 1987), pp. 43–58.

23. "The arrival of haute courtier," *The Economist,* July 29, 1989, pp. 53–4.

24. "U.S parts makers just won't say uncle," *Business Week,* August 10, 1987, pp. 76–7.

25. John Sculley, *Odyssey* (Fitzhenry and Whiteside, Toronto, 1987), p. 309.

26. "Cutting costs without killing the business," *Fortune,* October 13, 1986, p. 72.

27. R. M. Cyert and J. G. March, *A Behavioral Theory of the Firm* (Prentice-Hall, Englewood Cliffs, NJ, 1963).

28. H. Leibenstein, "Allocative efficiency versus X-efficiency," *American Economic Review,* June 1966.

29. Central Policy Review Staff, *The Car Industry* (HMSO, London, 1979).

30. The failure of firm's accounting systems to adjust to change is indicated by the large number of companies which continue to allocate overhead costs on the basis of direct labor costs, even though direct labor is likely to represent only a small proportion of total costs. See "Uncovering a company's costs," *Economist,* June 11, 1988, pp. 71–2.

31. "Cutting costs without killing the business," *Fortune,* October 13, 1986, p. 72.

32. Ibid., pp. 75–6.

33. "Bankers Trust transfers departments to Xerox in bid to cut costs and staff," *Wall Street Journal,* June 17, 1988, p. 3.

34. *Owens-Corning Fiberglass Corporation Commercial Roofing Division (A).* Case No. 1–383–040 (Harvard Business School, Boston, 1982).

35. Robert H. Hayes, Steven C. Wheelwright, and Kim B. Clark, *Dynamic Manufacturing: Creating the Learning Organization* (Free Press, New York, 1988).

36. C. Baden-Fuller, R. M. Grant, and C. Hampden-Turner, "How Richardson Sheffield has achieved a cutting edge," *Financial Times,* February 15, 1988.

37. Robert Hayes and William Abernathy, "Managing our way to economic decline," *Harvard Business Review,* July–August 1980, pp. 67–77.

38. See, for example, Robert Hayes and Steven Wheelwright, *Restoring our Competitive Edge: Competing through Manufacturing* (John Wiley, New York, 1984); Bela Gold, "Computerization in domestic and international manufacturing," *California Management Review,* Winter 1989, pp. 130–43; M. L. Dertouzos, R. K. Lester, R. M. Solow, and the MIT Commission on Industrial Productivity, *Made in America: Regaining the Productivity Edge* (MIT Press, Cambridge, Mass., 1989).

SEVEN

Competitive Advantage: The Analysis of Differentiation Advantage

"What's so special about your company?"
"How are you *different* from your competitors?"
"Ex-act-ly how?"
"What is your *uniqueness* in the *marketplace*?"
          Mike Kami, strategy consultant, quoted by Tom Peters, *Thriving on Chaos*.

Introduction

A firm differentiates itself from its competitors "when it provides something unique that is valuable to buyers beyond simply offering a low price."[1] *Differentiation advantage* occurs when a firm is able to obtain from its differentiation a price premium in the market which exceeds the cost of providing the differentiation.

Any firm can differentiate its offering to customers in a limitless number of ways. At the same time every firm faces a different range of differentiation opportunities. The potential for differentiation is determined, in part, by the technical features of a product and the characteristics of its market. Complex consumer durables, such as automobiles and cameras, offer greater opportunities for differentiation than standardized industrial products, such as aluminum ingots or random-access memory chips. Yet, even commodity products offer potential for differentiation: "Anything can be turned into a value-added product or service for a well-defined or newly-created market," claims Tom Peters.[2] Peters gives the example of Milliken & Company's success in the market for the lowly "shop towel" – towels and cloths for factories, hospitals, and other institutions. Milliken's customers are industrial launderers who rent the towels to the final users. Milliken supplies its customers not just with towels but with sales training, promotional materials, audio-visual sales aids, seminars, and market research data. It maximizes customer responsiveness by computer-based order entry and fast, low-cost distribution. Milliken achieved a rate of sales growth several times that of its competitors and a return on investment of over 50 percent for most of the 1980s.

Differentiation extends beyond the addition of sophisticated product features (Mercedes automobiles), developing an upmarket image (American Express), or dominating customer awareness through brand advertising (Pepsi Cola). Differentiation goes beyond the product or service and encompasses all aspects of the way in which a company does business and relates to its customers. McDonald's position in the fast-food industry is determined less by the features and quality of its hamburgers as by its speed of service, reputation for cleanliness, and approach to children. The most successful companies at establishing differentiation advantage are those which build differentiation into their identity, style, and values. Ultimately differentiation is all about a firm's responsiveness to customer requirements. Tom Peters calls for "total customer responsiveness":

Every action, no matter how small, and no matter how far from the firing line a department may be, must be processed through the customer's eyes. Will this make it easier for the customer? Faster? Better? Less expensive? ... Long-term profit equals revenue from continuously happy customer relationships minus cost.[3]

Because differentiation is about uniqueness, it is not amenable to analysis using standardized conceptual and technical tools. The keys to successful differentiation are:

- understanding of customer needs and preferences;
- commitment to customers;
- knowledge of the company's capabilities;
- innovation.

However, to the extent that successful differentiation necessitates an intimate knowledge both of customers and of the company's own business, it is possible to apply analytic approaches which can guide and stimulate intuition and innovation, which provide frameworks for evaluating alternative differentiation strategies, and which establish an arena for discussion and the interchange of ideas. In this chapter we shall:

- examine what differentiation is;
- analyze the sources of differentiation in terms of customers' preferences and characteristics, and the firm's capacity for supplying differentiation;
- utilize the value chain to link the firm's differentiation capability to customers' demand for differentiation.

In providing a systematic framework for the analysis of differentiation, we shall be well placed to understand why differentiation has provided some firms with so strong and durable a source of competitive advantage and formulate differentiation strategies which are appropriate to particular industries and particular firms.

The Nature of Differentiation and Differentiation Advantage

The potential for differentiating a product or service, we have seen, is only partly determined by its physical characteristics. For a product which is technically simple (a pair of socks or a brick), which satisfies uncomplicated needs (a corkscrew or a nail), or which must meet specific technical standards (a spark plug or a thermometer), differentiation opportunities are constrained by technical or market factors. Products which are complex (an airplane), satisfy complex needs (an automobile or a vacation), or which do not need to conform to stringent technical standards (wine, toys) offer much greater scope for differentiation.

Differentiation variables

Beyond these constraints the potential in any product or service for differentiation is limited only by the boundaries of the human imagination. In the case of simple products such as shampoo, toilet paper, and cigarettes, the proliferation of brands on any supermarket's shelves is a testimony to both the ingenuity of firms and the complexity of customer preferences.

In analyzing differentiation we shall be focussing primarily upon observable characteristics of a product or service which are relevant to the preferences and choice processes of customers. These include characteristics of the product or service such as size, shape, color, weight, design, material, and technology. Clearly relevant is the performance of the product or service in terms of reliability, consistency, taste, speed, durability, and safety. The products and services which complement the product in question are also important in relation to differentiation potential. These include presales services, after-sales services, accessories, availability and speed of delivery, credit, and the ability to upgrade the product in the future. For consumer products these performance variables directly determine the utility which consumers gain from the product. For producer goods these performance variables are concerned with customer firms' ability to make money in their own businesses; hence these performance variables are valuable sources of differentiation if they lower customers firms' costs or increase their ability to differentiate their own products.

However, by focussing on these observable and tangible differentiation features, it is important that we do not overlook the role of *intangibles*. The value which a buyer perceives in a supplier's offerings may not correspond precisely to the measurable benefits of the product or service. There are few products where customer choice is determined solely by objective performance criteria. Social, emotional, psychological, and aesthetic considerations are present in choices over all products and services. The desire for status, exclusivity, individuality, and security are extremely powerful motivational forces in choices relating to most consumer goods. The power of these intangible characteristics in driving customer choice is all the greater when the performance of the product or service is difficult to ascertain, as with cosmetics, medical services, or education. Later in the chapter we shall explore customers' motivation and the role of image differentiation in greater depth.

Differentiation and segmentation

Conventional strategy analysis treats differentiation and segmentation as separate strategy variables. Differentiation is concerned with *how* the firm competes; in what ways the firm can offer uniqueness to its customers. Segmentation is concerned with *where* the firm competes; issues of product-market scope. While segmentation choices are concerned with selecting particular geographical, product, or customer segments; differentiation decisions are concerned with selecting the sources of uniqueness which the firm will use to distinguish its offerings from those of its competitors. These might include *consistency* (McDonald's hamburgers), *reliability* (Federal Express's next-day delivery), conferring *status* (American Express), *quality* (Marks & Spencer), and *innovation* (Philips).

While segmentation is a feature of market structure, differentiation is a strategic choice by a firm. A segmented market is one in which demand can be divided into segments with distinct demand functions. Differentiation is concerned with a firm's positioning within a market or a segment in relation to the various product characteristics which influence customer choice.[4] Simply by locating within a segment, a firm does not necessarily differentiate itself from its competitors within the same segment.

The distinction between differentiation and segmentation can also be seen from the fact that a firm may be committed to a differentiation strategy, and yet position itself within the mass market. IBM, General Motors, and Burger King all aim at well-defined positions of differentiation within their markets, while aiming at market share leadership. In many instances, however, it is not possible to unambiguously separate decisions concerning differentiation from the choice of which segments in which to compete. By offering uniqueness in its product or service offerings, the firm must inevitably appeal more to the preferences of some customer groups than to others. Hence, decisions about differentiation have implications for which industry segments the firm is focussing upon. By selecting performance, engineering, and style as the basis on which BMW competes in the automobile industry, it inevitably addresses itself to different market segments from Volvo or Chrysler. The same is true even for broadly-targeted firms: in the personal computer market, IBM's commitment to customer service focusses it upon the business computer rather than home computer segment and, within the business computer segment, on users requiring a high level of support, rather than those seeking either low-priced student computers or technologically-advanced, high-performance computers.

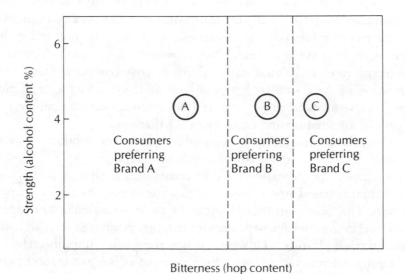

Exhibit 7.1 Brand positioning and market shares in the beer industry

One way of depicting market segmentation and differentiation is by mapping preferences and product positioning in relation to product attributes. Suppose consumers' preferences for beer are determined by two main attributes; alcoholic content (determined by original specific gravity) and bitterness (determined by the input of hops). If customer preferences are evenly distributed along both attributes, then consumers' ideal points will also be evenly distributed over the characteristics space shown in Exhibit 7.1. If firms A, B, and C select the same alcohol contents for their beers but choose different degrees of bitterness, we would expect the market to be divided between the three brands as shown in the diagram.

However, if preferences are not evenly distributed across the attributes but fall into three main clusters, then we can regard the market as being segmented. Products can be defined both in terms of the segments into which they fall and in terms of their positioning within each segment. However, such simple positioning is unlikely to describe differentiation in most markets. In practice, differentiation is achieved only partially by basic preference positioning; equally important is presentation, advertising, distribution channel, and a whole range of intangible characteristics.

The sustainability of differentiation advantage

Although strategy analysis has traditionally emphasized cost advantage as the primary basis for establishing a competitive advantage over rivals, in many respects, low cost is a far less secure basis for sustainable competitive advantage than differentiation. The growth of international trade has been particularly important in revealing the fragility of seemingly well-established positions of domestic cost leadership. During the 1960s, RCA, by virtue of its scale and manufacturing efficiency, was probably the lowest cost supplier of TVs to the US market. The invasion of the US market, first by the Japanese, then by the Taiwanese and South Koreans, devastated RCA's competitive position within a few years. More generally, there are few manufacturing industries where North American and European firms have maintained a position of cost leadership over low-wage competitors from the newly-industrializing countries. Moreover, in internationally-competing industries, cost leadership is seldom clear cut: Movements in exchange rates can cause rapid shifts in cost competitiveness. The appreciation of the US dollar between 1982 and 1985 offset all of Caterpillar's achievements in improving its international cost competitiveness by means of automation and capacity rationalization.

Even in relation to domestic competition, low-cost production is an increasingly vulnerable source of competitive advantage.

For example, the increasing pace of technological change means that cost advantages based upon scale and experience may be undercut by a competitor's process innovation. During the 1970s several major European and US steel companies invested heavily in large, integrated iron and steel plants at coastal locations. However, it was the small minimill steel firms using a quite different technology which emerged as the cost leaders in the industry.

Also, where cost advantage is built upon technical capabilities, the embodiment of new technology in new equipment and the increased intercompany mobility of personnel speeds the transfer of technology and experience between firms.

The superiority of differentiation advantage over cost advantage is indicated by the strategies pursued by US companies which have been consistently successful over the long term. Exhibit 7.2 lists companies among the 100 largest US industrial corporations with the highest return to stockholders. The success of most of these companies has been based upon differentiation rather than cost leadership.

The increased emphasis on differentiation advantage by American, European, and Japanese firms during the past decade has focussed on three principal areas:

- quality;
- brand loyalty;
- innovation.

Quality If the primary strategic goal of business firms during the 1960s and 70s was efficiency, during the 1980s it was quality. Some industries,

Company	Average annual return 1977–87 (%)
Triangle Industries	35.2
Conagra	33.4
Anheuser Busch	29.6
James River Corporation	27.1
Quaker Oats	26.6
H. J. Heinz	26.1
Sara Lee	25.4
I. C. Industries	24.7
Martin Marietta	24.3
Abbot Laboratories	24.1
Westinghouse Electric	24.0
Philip Morris	23.4
American Brands	23.4
NCR	23.3
Borden	23.3
PPG Industries	23.0
Rockwell International	22.7

Exhibit 7.2 Companies among the 100 largest US industrial corporations by sales with the highest return to stockholders, 1977–87

Source: "The Fortune 500", *Fortune*, April 25, 1988, pp. D11–D14.

notably automobiles, have become so traumatized by the issue of quality that quality management has permeated virtually all aspects of company operations.

Brand loyalty Emphasis on customer brand loyalty is apparent from the huge acquisition premiums paid for brand-rich companies. The clamor for established brands was apparent in a number of the mega-takeovers of 1989 including: Philip Morris's $13 billion purchase of Kraft (book value $2 billion); Kohlberg Kravis Roberts' $24.5 billion purchase of RJR Nabisco (book value $6 billion); Grand Metropolitan's $5 billion takeover of Pillsbury (book value $1.8 billion).

Innovation Increasingly industrial corporations in America, Europe, and Japan are recognizing innovation as their primary basis for sustainable competitive advantage in global markets. Innovation is no longer the preserve of the R&D department, but is the responsibility of every function of the firm.

Analyzing Differentiation: The Demand Side

Successful differentiation involves a matching of customers' demand for differentiation with the firms' capacity to supply differentiation. Let us begin with the demand side. Analyzing customer demand enables us to determine the potential for differentiation in a market, the willingness of customers to pay for differentiation, and the most promising positioning for a firm in relation to differentiation variables.

Customer needs and product attributes

Analyzing demand begins with understanding why customers buy a product or service. What needs and requirements are to be satisfied by a household's purchase of a personal computer, or a firm's commissioning of an advertising agency? Asking simple, direct questions about the purpose of a product and its performance attributes can offer striking insights into the potential for differentiation. Kenichi Ohmae recounts a striking example (see Case Note 7.1).

Case Note 7.1 Understanding what a product is about

Getting back to strategy means getting back to a deep understanding of what a product is about. Some time back, for example, a Japanese home appliance company was trying to develop a coffee percolator. Should it be a General Electric-type percolator, executives wondered? Should it be the same drip-type that Philips makes? Larger? Smaller? I urged them to ask a different kind of question: Why do people drink coffee? What are they looking for when they do? If your objective is to serve the customer better, then shouldn't you understand why that customer drinks coffee in the first place? Then you would know what kind of percolator to make.

The answer came back: good taste. Then I asked the company's engineers what they were doing to help the consumer enjoy good taste in a cup of coffee. They said they were trying to design a good percolator. I asked them what influences the taste in a cup of coffee. No one knew. That became the next question we had to answer. It turns out that lots of things can affect taste – the beans, the temperature, the water. We did our homework and discovered all the things that affect taste.

Of all the factors, water quality, we learned, made the greatest difference. The percolator in design at the time, however, didn't take water quality into account at all ... We discovered next that grain distribution and the time between grinding the beans and pouring in the water were crucial. As a result we began to think about the product and its necessary features in a new way. It *had* to have a built-in dechlorinating function. It *had* to have a built-in grinder. All the customer should have to do is pour in water and beans ...

To start you have to ask the right questions and set the right kinds of strategic goals. If your only concern is that General Electric has just brought out a percolator that brews coffee in ten minutes, you will get your engineers to design one that brews it in seven minutes. And if you stick to that logic, market research will tell you that instant coffee is the way to go ... Conventional marketing approaches won't solve the problem. If you ask people whether they want their coffee in ten minutes or seven, they will say seven, of course. But it's still the wrong question. And you end up back where you started, trying to beat the competition at its own game. If your primary focus is on the competition, you will never step back and ask what the customers' inherent needs are, and what the product really is about.

Virtually all products and services serve multiple needs. In order to understand more precisely the weighting of different needs and the performance criteria which customers use to evaluate a product or service, it is instructive to examine how customers choose between competing suppliers. A key element in the turnaround of Apple Computer between 1985 and 1987 was developing an intimate understanding of companies' computing needs and the reasons for IBM's success in the business sector. By understanding the performance criteria which were important to business, Apple was able to reposition its Macintosh computer within the market, refocus its marketing strategy, and restructure its distribution and service operations.

Market research has developed numerous techniques for analyzing customer preferences and product attributes in order to guide the positioning of new products and repositioning of existing products within the market. Techniques include:

- multidimensional scaling;
- conjoint analysis;
- hedonic price analysis.

Multidimensional scaling permits customers' perceptions of competing products' similarities and dissimilarities to be represented graphically and for the dimensions to be interpreted in terms of key product attributes.[5] For example, a pharmaceutical company's survey of consumer ratings of competing pain relievers resulted in the mapping shown in Exhibit 7.3.

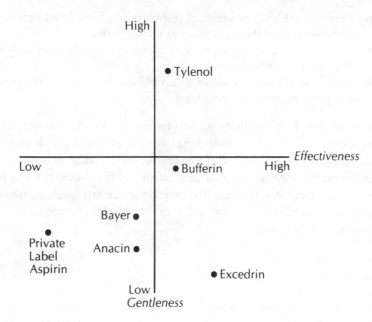

Exhibit 7.3 Customer perceptions of competing pain relievers mapped by multidimensional scaling

Source: Glen L. Urban and John R. Hauser, *Design and Marketing of New Products* (Prentice-Hall, Englewood Cliffs, NJ, 1980), p. 221. Reprinted in Alan Rowe, Richard Mason, Karl Dickel, and Neil Snyder, *Strategic Management: A Methodological Approach* (Addison-Wesley, Reading, Mass., 1989), p. 125.

Conjoint analysis is a powerful means of analyzing the strength of customer preferences for different product attributes. The technique requires, first, an identification of the underlying attributes of a product and, secondly, asking consumers to rank hypothetical products which comprise alternative bundles of attributes. On the basis of this data, tradeoffs can be analyzed and the simulations can be run to determine the proportion of customers who would prefer a hypothetical new product to competing products already available in the market.[6] Rowe et al.[7] describe conjoint analysis undertaken by BCG of potential personal computer buyers. The analysis identified price, manufacturer's reputation, portability, processing capability, memory capacity, word-processing capability, and styling as critical attributes. The data gathered on customer preferences and tradeoffs were used to predict the share of customer preferences which the forth-coming Apple Macintosh and IBM PC Junior would obtain, and to simulate the effects of changing the design features and prices of the new products on customer preferences.

Hedonic price analysis   Lancaster's characteristics analysis of demand views the demand for a product as comprising customers' demand for the underlying attributes which the product provides.[8] A wristwatch may combine three principal attributes: accuracy in recording time, ease of reading the time, and aesthetic appeal. For a new watch to be competitive in the market, it must:

- offer a watch with an identical combination of attributes that is already being offered on the market but at a lower price;
- offer a watch at the same price as competing watches but with more of at least one attribute; *or*
- offer a watch with a different combination of attributes than those currently available to the market.

The price at which a product can sell in the market is the aggregate for the prices charged for all the individual attributes of the product. Hedonic price analysis observes price differences for competing products, relates these differences to the different combinations of attributes offered by each product, and calculates the implicit market price for each attribute. For example, it is possible to relate price differences for automatic washing machines to differences in:

- capacity;
- spin speed;
- energy consumption;
- features (e.g. number of programs, electronic control);
- reliability (as indicated by consumer organizations' data).

By estimating (using multiple regression analysis) the implicit price for each attribute, it is possible to determine the price premium that can be charged for additional units of a particular attribute. In Britain, it was estimated that a machine which spins at 1,000 rpm sells at about a $200 price premium to one which spins at 800 rpm.[9] If the cost of adding the faster spin is only $50, it is profitable to differentiate by means of faster spin.

A key element of all differentiation decisions is an estimate of the price advantage which differentiation will support. The essence of all approaches to evaluating the incentive for differentiation is estimating the *value which differentiation creates for the buyer*. In the case of producer goods, creating value for the buyer means increasing his or her profit. This means lowering the buyer's cost or increasing his or her own differentiation. Analysis of the cost-reducing benefits of differentiation is relatively easy. For example, the increase in value to the buyer of a copier which collates and staples is equivalent to the savings in labor costs from undertaking their activities by separate means. Quantifying the impact of one firm's differentiation on another firm's differentiation is more difficult. In the case of consumer goods, creating value for customers is through increasing their satisfaction which, of course, is likely to be the result of a myriad of factors.

The problem with analyzing product differentiation in terms of measurable performance attributes is that it does not delve very far into the underlying motivations for buying decisions. Very few goods or services are acquired to satisfy basic needs for survival: most buying reflects social goals and values in terms of the desire to find community with others, to establish one's own identity, and to make sense of what is happening in the world. Some purchases serve as information: they signal self-image, rank, and values. Some mark social events and bond social relationships as, for instance, with the giving of presents at birthdays and weddings. Others, such as houses and insurance policies, confer security. The symbolic role of personal possessions is deep-seated, powerful, and extends back to the earliest human societies.

The role of social and psychological factors

Social and psychological influences are not restricted to consumer goods: purchases of producer goods are seldom based exclusively upon objective performance criteria. A company's choice of suppliers may reflect a company's need for identity and security, and also the social and organizational aspirations of individual purchasing officers.

To understand customer demand and identify potential profitable avenues to differentiation therefore requires that we analyze not only the product and its characteristics, but the customer and his or her characteristics. If purchase decisions are driven by the need to identify with others, to establish individuality, and to proclaim aspirations, it is vital to look behind the product and investigate the life-style, personality, and social grouping of the customer. Such analysis can be both systematic and quantitative in terms of establishing demographic (age, sex, race, location), socioeconomic (income, education), and psychographic (life-style, personality type) factors which correlate to patterns of buying behavior.

Despite the statistical rigor of formal market research techniques, the key to effective differentiation is to develop *understanding* of what customers want and how they behave. The answer, claims Tom Peters, is very simple: business people need to *listen to their customers*. "Good listeners," says Peters, "get out from behind their desks to where the customers are ... Further, good listeners construct settings so as to maximize 'naive' listening, the undistorted sort ... Finally, good listeners provide quick feedback and act on what they hear."[10] It is important however that "naive listening" is not confused with naive understanding of customer needs. To really understand customer needs and preferences, listening is insufficient. Companies must observe and analyze customers' use of the product. We shall return to this issue when we examine the value chain in relation to differentiation analysis.

Exhibit 7.4 Identifying the potential for differentiation on the demand side

Exhibit 7.4 outlines some of the questions which need to be addressed in analyzing the potential for differentiation within a market.

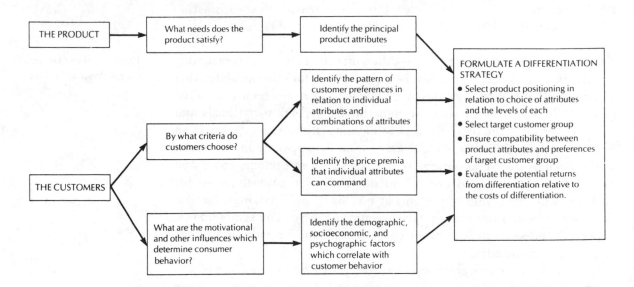

Broad-based versus focussed differentiation

Differentiation, we have observed, may be consistent with a broad market appeal or with focussing upon a specific market segment. The choice of market scope has important implications for the orientation of demand analysis. A firm which wishes to establish a broad-based position of differentiation advantage in an industry is primarily concerned with the *general* features of market demand: What general needs are being satisfied by the product? What do customers have in common in terms of their motivations and choice criteria? The firm needs to focus not on the factors which distinguish customer groups and which segment their demand, but on the requirements and the aspirations which they have in common. To establish a position of uniqueness while still appealing to a broad market is no easy task:

- McDonald's has extended its appeal across age groups, social groups and national boundaries by emphasizing a few qualities with universal appeal: speed, consistency, value, hygiene, and family life-styles.
- The British retailer Marks & Spencer has been similarly successful in establishing a reputation for product quality and fair dealing that extends across the class divisions which segment British markets.

- Honda and Toyota have positioned themselves within the US market to achieve a broad-based market appeal in contrast to the more targeting position of most American and European brands within age groups and socioeconomic segments.

Establishing a differentiated niche position in a market necessitates more specific analysis: What are the differences between customers' needs and between the customer groups? What groups of customers are not being adequately served by the existing range of offerings? The emphasis is on the factors which distinguish one group from another and one set of needs from another. In principle, a focussed approach to differentiation should displace a broad-based approach. If customers are presented with a wide range of highly targeted product offerings they should be able to find a targeted product that meets their preferences more closely than a product that is designed for the market as a whole. Certainly the strategy of offering a wide product range to appeal to a number of distinct product segments was successful for General Motors in displacing Ford as market leader during the 1920s and 30s.

At the same time, segment-focussed approaches to differentiation run particular risks. Apart from the higher costs which are incurred in supplying a narrow rather than a broad market, there are dangers that market segments can change over time, or that a firm had adopted an inappropriate segmentation in the first place. To the extent that a segmented approach is based upon existing differences in customers and their demand, it is inherently conservative. A problem with General Motors segmented approach to the US automobile market was that many consumers within the segments which GM had targeted no longer wanted to be identified with the segment which GM had defined for them

The danger with all analysis is that, instead of being a guide to understanding, it distorts through oversimplification. Nowhere is this more evident than in the application of predetermined market segmentations and customer classification to the analysis of customer demand. By focussing upon demographic and life-style differences between groups of customers, upon different purchase occasions and patterns of use, and the particular requirements of different distribution channels, it is possible to overlook customers' real needs and preferences. GM's concern over the positioning of each of its model ranges in relation to market segments first identified by Alfred Sloan Jr encouraged it to overlook customers' increasing concern with economy, safety, and reliability. If differentiation is really about creating "total customer responsiveness" then analysis should bring us closer to customers and not obscure them.

Analyzing Differentiation: The Supply Side

**The drivers of
uniqueness**

While demand analysis identifies the customers' demands for differentiation and their willingness to pay for it, creating a differentiation advantage is crucially dependent upon a firm's ability to supply differentiation and to supply it at a cost below the price premium which it creates. Identification of the firm's potential to supply differentiation necessitates examining the activities of the firm and the resources which the firm has access to. Differentiation, I have noted, is concerned with the provision of *uniqueness*. A firm's opportunities for creating uniqueness in its offerings to customers are not located within a particular function or activity but can arise in virtually everything that the firm does. Porter identifies a number of *drivers of uniqueness* over which the firm exercises control:[11]

- product features and the performance which the product offers;
- the services which the firm provides (e.g. credit, delivery, repair);
- the intensity of particular marketing activities (e.g. rate of advertising spending);
- content of activities (e.g. type of pre- and after-sales services provided);
- the technology employed in performing an activity (e.g. the precision with which products are manufactured, computerized order processing);
- the quality of inputs procured for an activity;
- procedures governing the conduct of particular activities (e.g. frequency of quality control inspections, service procedures, frequency of sales visits to a customer);
- the skill and experience of employees in activities;
- the control procedures used in different activities;
- location (e.g. with retail stores);
- the degree of vertical integration (which influences a firm's ability to control inputs and intermediate processes).

**Differentiation of
hardware and
software**[12]

In analyzing a firm's potential for creating uniqueness in the market it is useful to distinguish between differentiation of products and differentiation of services. Shiv Mathur observes that most transactions do not involve a single product or a single service, but are a combination of products and services.[13] In analyzing the potential for differentiation, Mathur distinguishes between differentiation of the product ("hardware") and differentiation of ancillary services ("software"). On this basis, four transactions categories can be identified (Exhibit 7.5).

Exhibit 7.5 The
transactions matrix

		SOFTWARE	
		Differentiated	Undifferentiated
HARDWARE	Differentiated	SYSTEM	PRODUCT
	Undifferentiated	SERVICE	COMMODITY

Source: Shiv Mathur, "Competitive Industrial Marketing Strategies," *Long Range Planning* 17 (4) (1984).

Selecting one of these generic transactions categories is basic to the firm's choice of differentiation strategy. Since economies of scale are usually more important in the production of goods than of services, some industries have tended to mass-produce relatively undifferentiated hardware, and to differentiate through complementary services.

- In household appliances, increasing standardization of the products has been accompanied by differentiation through warranties and quality-of-repair services.
- As gasoline has become a standardized product, so oil companies and retailers have sought to differentiate through retail service, the attractiveness of filling stations, and retailing a wider range of consumer goods.

Differentiation choices are also influenced by the stage of maturity of the product and its industry. Mathur identifies a *transactions cycle* over which the extent and basis of differentiation shift (Exhibit 7.6). The cycle runs through four phases:

1   In the early stages of development firms are obliged to provide a high level of customer support and firms typically supply *systems* which comprise differentiated products and differentiated support services.

2   As the market grows specialist suppliers of particular types of hardware and software emerge. Hence, there is a process of *unbundling* as some firms specialize in either products or services.

3   As the market matures, a process of *commoditization* occurs as differentiation within products and services gives way to increased standardization aimed at reducing costs and prices.

4   Faced by strong price competition among commodity offerings, firms seek new approaches to differentiation through *augmenting* products and developing new systems of products and services orientated towards the needs of particular customer groups. Such trends are evident in retail stores: the high degree of differentiation of independent stores gave way to standardized chains many of which specialize in the supply of goods, while separate specialist stores offer repair, service, and information. The commoditization of retailing has been followed by the emergence of *concept retailers* which have recombined goods and services to establish lifestyle-orientated differentiation. Service stations have followed a similar pattern of development. The emergence of specialist gas stations has been followed by a return to more complex transactional forms. Increasing numbers of service stations offer not only gas, oil, and repair services, but are evolving into convenience stores offering food, drink, leisure items, and video rentals.[14]

This cycle is apparent in the evolution of the personal computer industry. The early entrants, Apple, Commodore, Tandy, and then IBM, supplied systems comprising hardware (computers, monitors, printers) and software (computer programs, training, presales and after-sales service). Subsequent entrants included specialist hardware companies and specialist software companies. During the mid-1980s, standardization around IBM compatibility caused personal computers to become an increasingly

Exhibit 7.6 The
transactions cycle

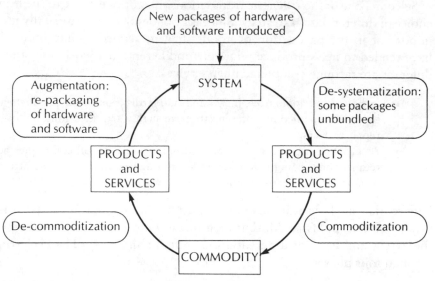

Source: Shiv Mathur, "Competitive Industrial Marketing Strategies," *Long Range Planning*
17 (4) (1984).

commodity-like product. However, during the later 1980s differentiation
reemerged through the repackaging of hardware and software into systems,
such as desktop publishing systems, office data-processing and communication networks, and engineering workstations.

**Tangible
differentiation,
intangible
differentiation, and
the role of signalling**

For any firm the range of differentiation opportunities is wide and the firm
must decide which forms of differentiation are likely to be most successful
in distinguishing the firm in the market and which are most valued by
customers. In establishing a coherent and effective position of differentiation in a market, a firm needs to assemble a complementary package
of differentiation measures. If Beck's beer wishes to differentiate itself on
the basis of the quality of its ingredients, then it must adopt production
methods that are consistent with quality ingredients, and packaging, advertising, and a distribution system which are appropriate to a quality product
at a premium price.

For differentiation to be effective requires that it is communicated to
the customer. Hence tangible differentiation needs to be *signalled* to the
customer through intangible differentiation. These signals include advertising, brand name, the reputation of the supplier, the retail environment
in which the product is sold, and the association of the supplier with sports
and cultural events through sponsorship. The role of these intangibles is
to signal to the customer the true worth and performance of the product.
Signalling is also achieved through tangible aspects of differentiation:
Packaging is a particularly powerful vehicle for the creation of an image.

The need for signalling variables to complement performance variables
in differentiation depends upon the ease with which performance can be
assessed by the potential buyer. A perfume can be sampled before purchase

and its smell assessed, but the perfume's ability to augment the identity of the wearer and its impact upon social relationships are uncertain. Hence, the key role of the brand name, the manufacturer's name, packaging, advertising, and lavish promotional events in establishing an identity for the perfume in terms of the implied personality, life-style, and aspirations of the user.

Signalling is similarly vital for financial service companies. The customer cannot identify by simple observation the integrity, financial security, and competence of a broker, fund manager, or insurance company. Hence, the emphasis which financial service companies accord to symbols of security, stability, and competence: large, well-located head offices; conservative and tasteful office decor; smartly dressed and courteous employees; historical associations; and perceptions of size.

Even where the performance attributes of a product are observable by the customer before purchase, signalling by means of branding is important in identifying a product with a particular supplier and in saving on search costs for the customer. Unless the customer can identify a product with a particular supplier, then the incentive for differentiation is greatly reduced since there is no *reputation effect*.

Strategies for reputation building have been the subject of rigorous theoretical analysis.[15] Some of the propositions arising from this research are:

- quality signalling is primarily important for products whose quality can only be ascertained after purchase ("experience goods");
- expenditure on advertising is an effective means of signalling superior quality since suppliers of low quality products will not expect repeat buying, hence it will not be profitable for them to spend money on advertising;
- a combination of premium pricing and advertising is likely to be a superior in signalling quality than either price or advertising alone;
- the higher are the sunk-costs required for entry into a market, and the greater the total investment of the firm, the greater are the incentives for the firm not to cheat customers through providing low quality at high cost.

The costs of differentiation

Differentiation adds cost. The direct costs of differentiation include such elements as the costs of higher-quality inputs; the costs of larger inventories in order to guarantee speedy filling of orders; the costs of heavy advertising to sustain brand strength. In addition there are indirect costs of differentiation which arise through the interaction of differentiation variables with cost variables. To the extent that differentiation narrows the product-market scope of a firm, it also limits the potential for exploiting scale economies. To the extent that differentiation requires product innovation and the introduction of new models, it hampers the exploitation of experience curve economies.

However, a strategy of differentiation does not inevitably mean increasing vulnerability to low-cost competition. Probably the single most significant differentiation variable is quality. There exists a large body of empirical evidence which shows that quality either is costless or that its costs are small relative to its benefits. The PIMS program has identified quality and market share as the two most important determinants of a business unit's profitability. Exhibit 7.7 shows that quality adds a significant premium to price while having little or no effect on cost. As a result quality is strongly associated with superior profitability.

Exhibit 7.7 The impact of relative quality and relative market share on price, cost, and profitability

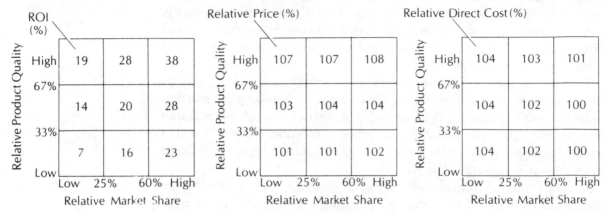

Source: Robert Luchs, "Successful businesses compete on quality not cost," *Long Range Planning* 19 (1986), pp. 12–24

The costs of differentiation can also be offset by any tendencies for differentiation to expand the market share of a firm and hence permit exploitation of scale economies. The tendency for many firms to increase their advertising budgets during recessions reflects their desire to spread fixed costs over an expanded sales base. In some instances a differentiation strategy can improve a firm's cost position through shifting the basis of competition in an industry. In chapter 5 we noted how Honda's annual model changes and Apple's decision to support its new Macintosh computer with heavy TV advertising had the effect of putting smaller companies under substantial cost pressure.

One means of reconciling differentiation with cost efficiency is to *postpone differentiation* to later stages of the firm's value chain. Economies of scale and the cost advantages of standardization are frequently greatest in the manufacture of basic components. By utilizing a modular design with common components, economies of large-scale production can be achieved, while targeting a broad range of products upon the specific requirements of particular customer groups. The automobile industry has taken a leading role in this process. The introduction of "world cars" by GM and Ford has permitted substantial cost savings in R&D, design, testing, tooling, and component production. At the same time the companies offer distinct national features and a wide range of customer choices over color, accessories, and trim.

The effect of new manufacturing technology is causing traditional trade-offs between efficiency and variety to break down. The introduction of computer-aided manufacture, just-in-time scheduling, and computer-integrated manufacturing have made the objective of an "economic order quantity of one" realistic while simultaneously cutting unit costs. In the manufacture of household appliances, consumer electronic products, and a variety of other producer and consumer products, a number of different models are manufactured on the same assembly line with close to zero changeover time. At Kawasaki Motors' motorcycle plant at Lincoln, Nebraska, production was switched to mixed-model production on January 1, 1983. Previously, manufacture had been in lots of at least 200 of each model. Yet, mainly through reorganizing the production process, adopting just-in-time scheduling, and adapting some machinery, the plant reduced changeover time in frame production from half a day to less than ten minutes.[16]

Bringing it all Together: The Value Chain in Differentiation Analysis

There is little point in identifying the attributes which customers value most if the firm is incapable of supplying those attributes. Similarly there is little purpose in identifying a firm's unique abilities to supply certain elements of uniqueness, if those attributes are not valued by customers. The key to successful differentiation is in matching the firm's capacity for creating differentiation with customers' potential demand for it. For this purpose the value chain provides a particularly useful framework. There are four principal steps in the analysis:

- construct a value chain for the firm and the customer;
- identify the drivers of uniqueness in each activity;
- select the most promising differentiation variables for the firm;
- locate links between the value chain of the firm and that of the buyer.

Constructing a value chain for the firm and the customer   On the basis of the importance of different activities, the separateness of different activities, and the differences between activities in their capacity for creating differentiation, draw a value chain for the firm and its customer. If the customer is not the final customer it is useful to draw a value chain for firms at later stages in the value chain as well. If the firm supplies different types of customer – for example if a steel company supplies steel strip to automobile manufacturers and domestic appliance manufacturers – draw separate value chains for each of the main categories of customer.

Identifying the drivers of uniqueness in each activity   Assess the firm's potential for differentiating its product by examining each activity in the firm's value chain and identifying the variables and actions through which the firm can achieve uniqueness in relation to competitors' offerings. Exhibit 7.8 identifies sources of differentiation within Porter's generic value chain.

Exhibit 7.8 Identifying the potential for differentiation in the supply side: Sources of differentiation in Porter's generic value chain

Selecting the most promising differentiation variables for the firm   Among the numerous drivers of uniqueness which we can identify within the firm, which should be selected as the primary basis for the firm's differentiation strategy? On the supply side there are three important considerations.

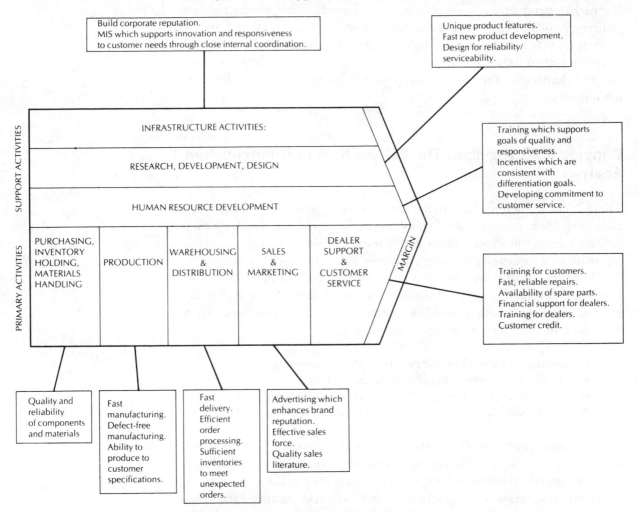

First, we must establish where the firm has greater potential for differentiating, or can differentiate at lower cost than rivals. Our concern is with *competitive advantage*, hence differentiation must be based upon the firm's internal strengths in terms of resources and skills.

Secondly, in order to determine which activities should have priority as the sources of differentiation, we need to *identify links between activities*.   For example, product reliability is likely to be the outcome of several linked activities: monitoring of purchases of inputs from suppliers, the skill and motivation of production workers, the stringency of quality control, and product testing. If a particular level of product reliability is sought, the firm must determine the least-cost means of achieving that reliability and the coordination between activities which is required.

Thirdly, the ease with which different types of uniqueness can be sustained must be considered. The more differentiation is based upon resources which are specific to the firm or skills which involve the complex coordination of a large number of individuals, the more difficult will it be for a competitor to imitate the particular source of differentiation. Thus, offering business class passengers wider seats and more leg room is an easily imitated source of differentiation. Achieving high levels of punctuality represents a more sustainable source of differentiation.

Locating links between the value chain of the firm and that of the buyer
The objective of differentiation is to yield a price premium for the firm. This requires that the firm's differentiation must create value for the customer. Creating value for the customer involves one of two activities:

- either the firm lowers the costs to the customer;
- or the firm assists product differentiation by the customer.

For example, Hotpoint lowers retailer's costs by offering a speedy delivery service which enables retailers to hold lower stocks, while enhancing retailers' differentiation by appointing them as exclusive dealers within particular localities. To identify the means by which a firm can create value for its customers it must locate the links between differentiation of its own activities and cost reduction and differentiation within the customer's activities.

Locating these links is also useful for evaluating the potential profitability of differentiation. The value which differentiation creates for the customer represents the maximum price premium which the customer will pay. If the provision of just-in-time delivery by a component supplier costs an additional $1,000 a month but saves an automobile company $6,000 a month in reduced inventory, warehousing, and handling costs, then it should be possible for the component manufacturer to obtain a price premium that easily exceeds the costs of the differentiation.

As an example of the application of the value chain to the analysis of differentiation advantage, Case Note 7.2 considers Crown, Cork and Seal Inc., a metal container company which during the 1970s and early 1980s achieved the highest profitability within its industry through simultaneously pursuing a strategy of cost leadership and differentiation advantage.

Value chain analysis for consumer goods   Value chain analysis of the type outlined above is most readily applicable to producer goods where the

Case Note 7.2 Analyzing Crown, Cork and Seal's potential for differentiation advantage in the US metal container industry

The metal container industry is a highly-competitive, low growth, low profit industry. The products lack much potential for differentiation and buyers (especially beverage and food canning companies) are very powerful. Clearly cost efficiency is essential but are there also opportunities for superior profitability through differentiation?

STAGE 1: Construct value chain for firm and customers. The principal activities of the can manufacturer and its customers (canners) are shown in the diagram.

STAGE 2: Identify the drivers of uniqueness. For each of the can making activities it is possible to suggest several possible differentiation variables. Examples are shown on the diagram.

STAGE 3: Select key variables. To select the most promising differentiation variables, the resource strengths of CC&S must be considered. The strong technical skills of CC&S point to the design and manufacture of products to meet particular technical and design specifications, and the provision of sophisticated technical services to customers. The strong customer orientation of CC&S also suggests customer services (technical support, flexible and speedy delivery, fast order processing) are also likely to be prom-

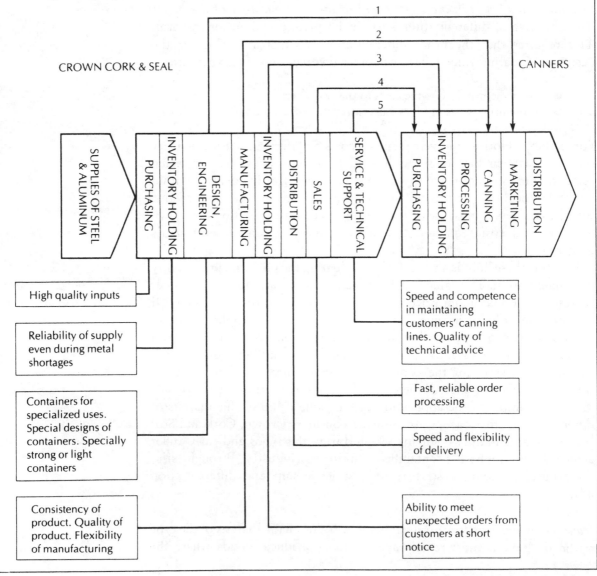

---

ising variables. Note that some differentiation activities may be linked – for example, the capability to meet unexpected demands from customers can be achieved by stockholding, by keeping a margin of spare capacity on hand, or by flexible production scheduling.

STAGE 4: Identify linkages. To determine differentiation likely to create value for the customer, linkages are made between CC&S's potential for differentiation and the potential for reducing cost or adding differentiation in any of the customers' activities. Five examples are shown in diagram:

1 Designing distinctive cans for customers may assist their own marketing activities.
2 Consistent quality of can lowers customers' canning costs by avoiding breakdowns and hold-ups on their canning lines.
3 By maintaining high stocks and offering speedy delivery, customers can economize on their own stockholding (they may even be able to move to a just-in-time system of can supply).
4 Efficient order processing can reduce customers' ordering costs.
5 Capable and fast technical support can reduce the costs of breakdowns on canning lines.

Source: Information is drawn from "Crown Cork and Seal Company, Inc.", in C. R. Christensen et al., Business Policy: Text and Cases, 5th edn. (Irwin, Homewood, Illinois, 1982).

---

customer is also a company with an easily-definable value chain and where linkages between the supplier's and the customer's value chains are readily apparent. However, the same analysis can be applied to consumer goods with very little modification. Few consumer goods are consumed directly; in most cases consumers are involved in a chain of activities before the total consumption of the product.

This is particularly evident for consumer durables. A washing machine is consumed over several years in the process of home laundry. The process begins with search activity prior to purchase. In the home laundry process, the machine is used together with water, detergent, and electricity, to wash clothes, which are later dried and, possibly, ironed. Continued use of the washing machine requires service and repair. We have a complex value chain for the customer with many links between the value chains of manufacturer, retailer, and consumer.

Even non-durables are seldom consumed directly without the consumer engaging in prior productive activity. A frozen TV dinner must be purchased, taken home, removed from the package, and heated before consumption. After eating the consumer must clean any crockery, cutlery, or other utensils employed. Again we have a chain of activities where the manufacturer has opportunities to create value for the consumer by eliminating or facilitating any of these activities. Takahiro Fujimoto has emphasized the need for companies to integrate their design process with the consumption process of the product.[17] For example, as the differentiation advantages of Japanese automobile companies in terms of reliability and fuel efficiency are increasingly replicated by US and European producers, so the companies are seeking new sources of differentiation. Toyota has undertaken detailed analysis of the wide range of activities that consumers engage in when using an automobile, and the features associated with consumer satisfaction from each activity. The research has revealed characteristics, such as the sound which the doors make when they are closed and the tone of the engine noise when the automobile is being driven, as important to customers in their perceptions of quality.

Summary

The attraction of differentiation over low cost as a basis for competitive advantage is, first, that it is less vulnerable to being overturned by turbulence in the external environment, and, secondly, that it is more difficult to replicate.

The potential for differentiation is near limitless for any business: it may involve physical differentiation of the product, it may be through the services which accompany a product, it may be tangible or intangible.

The essence of differentiation advantage is to increase the perceived value of the offering to the customer either more effectively or at lower cost than do competitors. This requires that the firm matches the requirements and preferences of customers with its own capacity for creating uniqueness.

The value chain provides a useful framework for analyzing differentiation advantage. By analyzing how value is created for customers and by systematically appraising the scope of each of the firm's activities for achieving differentiation, the value chain permits a matching of demand-side and supply-side sources of differentiation.

Successful differentiation requires a combination of astute analysis and creative imagination. The two are not antithetical. A systematic framework for the analysis of differentiation can act as a stimulus to creative ideas.

Notes

1. Michael E. Porter, *Competitive Advantage* (Free Press, New York, 1985), p. 120.
2. Tom Peters, *Thriving on Chaos* (Knopf, New York, 1987), p. 56.
3. Ibid., p. 185.
4. These distinctions are developed in more detail by Peter R. Dickson and James L. Ginter, "Market segmentation, product differentiation and marketing strategy," *Journal of Marketing* 51 (1987), pp. 1–10.
5. See S. S. Schiffman, M. L. Reynolds and F. W. Young *Introduction to Multidimensional Scaling: Theory, Methods, and Applications* (Academic Press, New York, 1981).
6. See P. Cattin and D. R. Wittink, "Commercial use of conjoint analysis: a survey," *Journal of Marketing*, Summer 1982, pp. 44–53.
7. Alan Rowe, Richard Mason, Karl Dickel, and Neil Snyder, *Strategic Management: A Methodological Approach* (Addison Wesley, Reading, Mass., 1989), pp. 127–8.
8. Kelvin Lancaster, *Consumer Demand: A New Approach* (Columbia University Press, New York, 1971).

9. Phedon Nicolaides and Charles Baden Fuller, *Price Discrimination and Product Differentiation in the European Domestic Appliance Market* (Centre for Business Strategy, London Business School, 1987).

10. Tom Peters, *Thriving on Chaos* (Knopf, New York, 1987), p. 149.

11. Michael E. Porter, *Competitive Advantage* (Free Press, New York, 1985), pp. 124–5.

12. This section draws heavily upon Shiv Mathur, "Competitive industrial marketing strategies," *Long Range Planning* 17 (4) (1984).

13. Ibid., pp. 102–9.

14. Ibid.

15. For a survey see Keith Weigelt and Colin Camerer, "Reputation and corporate strategy: a review of recent theory and applications," *Strategic Management Journal* 9 (1988), pp. 443–54.

16. Richard J. Schonberger, *World Class Manufacturing Casebook: Implementing JIT and TQC* (Free Press, New York, 1987), pp. 120–3.

17. Takahiro Fujimoto, "Managing effective development projects." Presentation to Strategic Management Society Conference, San Francisco, October 1989.

EIGHT

Competitive Advantage and Strategy Formulation in Different Industry Environments: Classifying Industries

No company ever stops changing ... Each new generation must meet changes – in the automotive market, in the general administration of the enterprise, and in the involvement of the corporation in a changing world. The work of creating goes on.

Alfred P. Sloan, President of General Motors 1923–37, Chairman 1937–56, in *My Years with General Motors*

Outline
Introduction
The Life-cycle Model
   Demand growth
   Creation and diffusion of knowledge
   Industry structure and competition
The Dynamics of Competition as a Basis for Classification
   Local monopoly markets
   Traditional industrial markets
   Schumpeterian markets
BCG's Strategic Environments Matrix
   Volume businesses
   Stalemate businesses
   Fragmented businesses
   Specialization businesses
Summary

Introduction

While every industry is unique in terms of its characteristics and the identities of its member firms, competition in any industry is a function of common structural variables. In chapter 2 we showed how a common framework of industry analysis can be used to predict the characteristics of competition and the likely profitability of an industry. We can go further. On the basis of types of structural features and the sources of competitive advantage we can classify industries into a limited number of industry types. For each industry type, certain patterns of competition are typical and certain strategies are likely to be more effective than others.

Grouping industries in this way is useful for several analytic purposes. The ability to identify an industry with a group of similar industries can help us understand the nature of competition and the sources of competitive advantage in an industry. Such grouping can assist the transfer of ideas and strategies from one industry to another. The success which Philip Morris has experienced in brewing and food processing stems from its ability to identify similarities between these industries and the tobacco industry, and to transfer strategies and marketing policies which have been successful in its core tobacco business to its Miller and Kraft/General Foods subsidiaries.

Hence, industry classification is more than just a short-cut to strategy analysis. The process of classification is a valuable tool for revealing similarities between industries and for highlighting crucial differences. As such, industry classification is a valuable heuristic for strategy analysis. It provides a powerful tool for understanding the underlying dynamics of an industry, and a useful procedure for generating insights into the appropriate strategies to adopt.

The Life-Cycle Model

The principal basis for classifying industries used in this book is maturity. The key assumption is that industries follow a life-cycle which comprises a number of evolutionary characteristics common to different industries. The industry life-cycle is the industry-level equivalent of the product life-cycle, a well-known marketing concept.[1] To the extent that an industry produces a range and a sequence of products, then the duration of an industry life-cycle is likely to be longer than that of a single product. "Teenage Mutant Ninja Turtles" are likely to have a life cycle of a few years; the life-cycle of the toy industry is much longer. Four stages are typically defined:

- introduction;
- growth;
- maturity;
- decline.

An industry's evolution is driven by two underlying factors: demand growth and the production and diffusion of knowledge.

Demand growth   The life-cycle and the stages within it are defined by changes in an industry's growth rate over time. The characteristic profile is that of an S-shaped growth curve. In the introduction stage the industry's products are little-known, there are a few pioneering firms, and a few pioneering customers – market penetration is initially slow. During the growth stage diffusion of information about the products causes accelerating market penetration, and the rate of demand growth increases. In the maturity stage the market approaches saturation, demand shifts from new customers to replacement demand, and the rate of growth of industry sales slows. Finally, as the industry becomes challenged by new industries which produce technologically-superior substitute products, so the industry enters its decline stage.

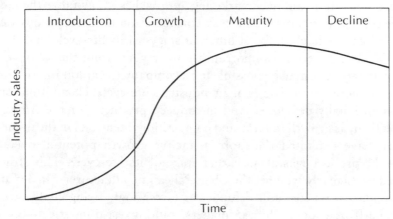

Exhibit 8.1 The growth curve and stages in the industry life-cycle

The duration of the various phases of the life-cycle varies considerably from industry to industry. The life-cycle of the railroad industry extended for about 100 years from 1840 before entering its declining phase. In the case of the US automobile industry, the introduction stage lasted about 25 years: from the final decade of the nineteenth century until industry growth took off in 1914–15. The growth phase lasted about 40 years: maturity of the industry in terms of slackening of the growth rate dates from the mid-1950s. In other industries, the cycle has been much shorter. The first Apple personal computers were assembled by Steve Jobs and Steve Wozniak in 1976. By 1978 the industry was in its growth phase with a flood of new and established firms entering the industry. Towards the end of 1984, the first signs of maturity appeared: growth stalled, excess capacity emerged, and the industry began to consolidate around a few companies.

In general, industry life-cycles are shortening. Improved dissemination of information increases the rate of product diffusion. New production technology has increased the speed with which firms can design and establish manufacturing capability for new products. Accelerating technical change hastens the onset of obsolescence. Compact disks are a product which passed almost immediately from introduction to growth phase. By 1988 compact disks outsold conventional record albums in the US and by 1990, only six years since their introduction, the market displays signs of maturity.

The pattern of evolution is also far from uniform. Some industries may never enter a declining phase. Industries supplying basic necessities such as residential construction, food processing, and clothing are likely to remain mature but are unlikely to enter prolonged decline. Some industries may experience a rejuvenation of their life-cycle. In the 1960s, the world motorcycle industry, previously regarded as mature, entered a decade-long spurt of growth as the recreational use of motorcycles developed. The TV receiver industry has experienced several revivals: the first caused by color TV; the second by the demand for multiple TV receivers within a household; the third by the demand for videos and computers. The advent of high-definition television promises a further cycle. The potential for product innovation and new marketing approaches to revitalize the industry life cycle is an important strategy consideration in mature industries.

An industry is likely to be at different stages of its life-cycle in different countries. Hence, even if opportunities for regenerating the whole cycle are not apparent, it may be possible for a company to exploit international differences between the stages of an industry's life-cycle. US multinationals have traditionally developed and introduced products for the American market then, as growth faltered and competition intensified in the domestic market, have exploited the more attractive growth potential overseas, where the product was at an earlier stage of its life-cycle. This strategy worked particularly well for the US metal can manufacturers. In a mature US can market where canned food was increasingly being challenged by fresh and frozen foods, the can makers could invest domestically in new equipment while shipping their older lines to the still-growing overseas markets.[2]

Creation and diffusion of knowledge

The second critical factor driving the industry life-cycle is the creation and diffusion of knowledge. New knowledge in the form of product innovation is responsible for an industry coming into being and the further development and diffusion of knowledge is a major driving force of competition.

On the producer side, the typical development pattern is as follows. In the introduction stage product technology advances rapidly, there is no dominant product technology and rival technologies compete for attention. In the growth stage, competition based upon performance, reliability and suitability for large-scale manufacture results in some technologies being eliminated as a dominant technical standard and design configuration emerges. In the maturity phase, product technology diffuses and the emphasis of knowledge development shifts to the quest for cost efficiency through process innovation. In the course of maturity, the pace of technological advance, both in product and process innovation slows considerably.

On the customer side, the principal factor in the development of knowledge is the diffusion of experience-based information. In the early stages of the life-cycle, customers are first-time buyers and there is limited information available regarding the performance attributes of competing products. As an industry enters its maturity phase, replacement demand predominates. Most customers are knowledgeable and experienced, and they are influenced by manufacturers' reputations and independent sources of objective information.

Industry characteristic	Introduction	Growth	Maturity	Decline	**Exhibit 8.2** The evolution of industry structure and competition over the life-cycle
Demand	High income buyers. Buyers need convincing and educating.	Rapidly increasing market penetration.	Mass market, replacement/repeat buying.	Customers knowledgeable.	
Technology	Not standard technology.	Some technologies eliminated.	Well-diffused technical know-how; quest for technological improvements.		
Products	Poor quality. Wide variety. Frequent design changes.	Design and quality improves. Reliability of key importance.	Standardization lessens differentiation. Minor model changes predominate.	Product differentiation lessens.	
Manufacture & Distribution	Short production runs. High skilled labor content. Specialised distribution channels.	Capacity shortages. Mass production. Competition for distribution.	Emergence of overcapacity. Deskilling of production. Long production runs. Reduced no. of lines carried by distributors.	Heavy overcapacity. Re-emergence of speciality channels.	
Trade	Shift of manufacture from advanced countries to poorer countries.				
Competition	Few companies.	Entry with many mergers and failures.	Shake out. Price competition increases.	Price wars, exits.	
Key success factors	Product innovation. Support services. Establishing credible image of firm and product.	Design to allow large scale manufacture. Access to distribution. Establishing strong brand.	Cost-efficiency scale, process innovation, buyer selection.	Reduce overheads. Signal commitment. Rationalize capacity.	

Exhibit 8.2 summarizes the principal features of each stage of the industry life cycle. The driving forces of demand growth and an accumulating stock of knowledge give rise to changes in industry structure and competitive behavior over the industry life-cycle.

Industry structure and competition

Product differentiation Emerging industries are characterized by a wide variety of product types which reflect the diversity of technologies and designs, lack of consensus over customer requirements, and a range of distribution channels. Technical standardization increases product uniformity and the emphasis of differentiation shifts to marketing variables, ancillary services such as credit and after-sales service, and product features in the form of "optional extras". In the course of maturity, increasing consumer knowledge is likely to hasten the elimination of inferior varieties and designs, and frivolous differentiation. As a result the product may evolve towards commodity status unless producers are effective in developing new dimensions for differentiation.[3]

The structure of manufacturing and distribution Market growth and technological change are the primary determinants of the structural evolution of manufacturing and distribution. The introduction phase is marked by short production runs, underdeveloped process technology, and high-cost production involving a heavy input of skilled labor. Before Henry Ford, cars were craftsman-built on an individual basis in small workshops. This "garage-stage" of both development and production was also apparent in the personal computer industry. During the growth phase, the pressure on capacity provides the main impetus for process innovation and the replacement of small-scale batch production by large-scale continuous production (or at least, large batches). Distribution channels also develop as small-scale, specialized distribution channels give way to larger-scale, more generalized channels. Maturity is normally associated with mass-production of a limited product range and the quest for cost efficiency. As the rate of productivity increase exceeds the rate of market growth, so excess capacity emerges and pressures for efficiency, consolidation, and rationalization intensify. During maturity distribution may segment with the mass-market served by a few large-scale, limited-line, distributors, and market niches served by specialist distributors.

Location and international trade Vernon's life-cycle theory of international trade predicts that the industry life cycle is associated with important changes in the international location of industry and with the pattern of trade.[4] The theory is based upon two assumptions. First, that the demand for new products emerges first in the richer, developed countries (especially the United States), and then diffuses internationally. Secondly, that new products require substantial inputs of technology and sophisticated skills, the intensity of which declines with maturity. The result is the following development pattern.

- New industries initiate in high income countries (notably the US) where there are ample technical and scientific resources and the affluent demand for novel goods and services. As demand grows in overseas markets (initially Western Europe) these are served by exports.
- Continued growth of overseas markets and reduced need for inputs of technology and sophisticated labor skills make production attractive in some overseas markets. As lower cost production expands in these markets, either by subsidiaries of a US multinational or by domestically-owned firms, the US begins to import.
- Continued maturity resulting in further deskilling of production, reduced product differentiation, and fewer opportunities for innovation result in

the growing comparative advantage of low-wage countries: Initially, the newly-industrializing countries of the Far East, Southern Europe and Latin America; later the developing countries. Production shifts away from Western Europe, North America, and Japan who become wholly dependent upon imports from low-wage countries.

The basis of competition Because of the diversity of evolutionary patterns across industries, there are few generalizations that can safely be made about the development of competition. Industries which begin with patent-protected new products are likely to start out as near-monopolies, then become increasingly competitive (plain-paper copiers). Others begin with many rivals and become increasingly concentrated (commercial aircraft). In some industries entry barriers rise in the course of the life-cycle (automobiles); in others entry barriers fall (local newspapers). While structural trends differ, some general patterns in the evolution of competitive behavior can be discerned.

Probably the most important trend is the shift from non-price competition to price competition. In the introduction stage, competition revolves around technical progressiveness and product performance. In the growth phase reliability, brand reputation, and securing channels of distribution emerge as major dimensions of competition. Increased customer knowledge and greater product standardization, shifts the focus of competition towards price. The onset stage of price competition can be traumatic. An unexpected slowdown in demand or the emergence of a firm with a clear cost advantage can precipitate an industry shake-out involving the elimination of weaker companies and consolidation of the industry around a few leaders.

In the course of maturity, price competition usually intensifies. Increasing cost efficiency of manufacture, the emergence of excess capacity, and the growth of international competition (particularly from low-wage countries) are powerful stimuli for aggressive pricing. Once the industry enters its decline phase then, depending upon the height of exit barriers and the strength of international competition, price competition may degenerate into destructive price wars.

Key success factors at different phases of the life-cycle From the changes in the nature of market demand and the changes in competitive conditions during the life-cycle, one can predict how the basis for competitive advantage is likely to shift during the different phases of the cycle.

During the introductory phase innovation is the basis for competitive success. But innovation alone is not enough. The firm needs to design and develop the product, to manufacture it, and to deliver it to customers. Hence, in an emerging industry firms need to support their innovation by a broad array of vertically-integrated capabilities. At the same time, potential customers need convincing and they need support. Success during the introduction phase also requires firms to establish a credible image for itself and its product and to establish the means to market the product and provide after-sales service.

The key challenge of the growth phase is scaling up. As the market expands, so the firm needs to adapt its product design and its manufacturing capability to large-scale production. To utilize increased manufacturing capability access to distribution becomes critical. At the same time the tensions which organizational growth imposes creates the need for internal administrative and strategic skills.

Maturity shifts the emphasis of competitive advantage to cost efficiency. Key determinants of cost efficiency are likely to be scale-efficient plants, process innovation, and location. As competition increases in the buying industry and in distribution channels, so the selection of customers and distributors with good growth potential becomes important.

Once decline begins, cost efficiency depends upon maintaining a balance between capacity and demand. Adjusting capacity to sales and encouraging the exit of competitors becomes the key to maintaining adequate profitability.

Exhibit 8.3 presents empirical evidence on performance and strategic differences between firms in the growth and mature stages of the cycle.

The life-cycle is the most common method of industry classification used in strategy analysis. However, numerous other approaches to classification are possible: industries can be classified by type of customer, e.g. into producer-good and consumer-good industries; by the primary resources used to compete, e.g. into technology-based, marketing-based, or professional-skill based industries; or by the geographic scope of the industry, whether local, national, or global. The critical issue in evaluating the usefulness of any means of classification is whether it can offer insights into the similarities and differences between industries for the purposes of formulating winning strategies. In the following sections I outline two further approaches to industry classification which I have found useful for understanding competition and issues of strategy formulation. The first is Jeffrey Williams' dynamic approach to classifying strategic environments. Williams' classification recognizes that industries follow different development paths, in particular, some industry environments are fairly stable over time, others exhibit high rates of change. The second approach, that of the Boston Consulting Group, uses the sources and nature of competitive advantage as the basis for classification. BCG's *Strategic Environments Matrix* offers insight into different sources of competitive advantage and is an illuminating example of the value of 2×2 classification matrices to generate strategy prescriptions.

Variables	Growth	Mature	Decline
Efficiency			
ROI	.005	.008	− .233*
Capacity utilization	− .100*	.061*	.107
Employee productivity	.308*	.127	− .087
Value added/revenue	.155	.063	− .428*
Industry & product			
Technological change	.580*	− .159*	− .044
Customization	.185	.151	.035
Relative product breadth	− .055	.032*	− .341*
Relative price	.018	− .049	− .047
Market share	.030	.062	− .064
R&D			
Sales from new products/total sales	.499*	− .179*	− .383*
Product R&D/revenue	.537*	.042*	− .365*
Process R&D/revenue	.484*	− .029*	.003
Production and investment			
Total inventory/revenue	.045	.107	.081
Newness of plant and equipment	.323*	− .211*	− .676*
Investment/revenue	.305*	.028*	− .052*
Backward vertical integration	.026	− .043	.001
Forward vertical integration	− .030	.029	− .023
Marketing			
Sales force/revenue	.278*	− .049*	− .279*
Advertising and promotion/revenue	− .250*	− .328*	− .384*

Exhibit 8.3 Strategy and performance differences between businesses at different stages of the life-cycle

The table shows the standardized means of each variable for businesses at each stage of the life cycle. Category means which are significantly different from the average for all categories at the 0.05 probability level are indicated by an asterisk.

The data were obtained from 1,234 industrial products manufacturing businesses included in the PIMS data base during the period 1970–80.

Source: Carl Anderson and Carl Zeithaml, "Stage of the product life cycle, business strategy and business performance", *Academy of Management Journal* 27 (1984), pp. 5–24.

The Dynamics of Competition as a Basis for Classification

As we have already observed, the business environment is being transformed by accelerating technological change and the global expansion of markets. These trends, argues Jeffrey Williams,[5] are reshaping the corporate landscape, and in the process are causing new types of market environment to emerge. The central theme of Williams' analysis of industry types is competitive dynamics. The key feature of an industry environment is its *rate of change* as indicated by the rate of new product introduction, the duration of product life-cycles, and the rate of decline of unit costs. These dynamic characteristics of industries are not exogenously determined. Unlike traditional strategy analysis where the underlying structure of the industry is given and the firm's task is to formulate a strategy which is appropriate to industry conditions, Williams views the structure and evolution of industries as heavily dependent upon the strategies which the member firms pursue. On the basis of market breadth, rate of technological change, and stability of supplier–customer relations, Williams identifies three market types:

- local monopolies;
- traditional industrial markets;
- dynamic, Schumpeterian markets.

Exhibit 8.4 summarizes the key characteristics of these three categories.[6]

Exhibit 8.4 Williams' classification of market types

	Local monopoly	Traditional industrial	Schumpeterian
Economies of experience	Small.	Moderate.	Substantial.
Customer relations	Stable and long term. Based upon close personal contact.	Moderately stable. Brand loyalty vital. Emphasis on defending market share.	Unstable with volatile market shares.
Market scope	Narrow. Firms' markets are local or a few customers.	Markets defined broadly: national or global mass-markets.	Typically broad geographically but often segmented by product/customer type.
Competition	Sheltered markets; competition weak.	Market share battles; competition on price and advertising.	Intense rivalry in product and process innovation.
Key success factors	Dominate local market and build barriers through close customer ties.	Exploit economies of scale and mass marketing. Market share key.	Fast product innovation. Move quickly down the experience curve. Adopt novel strategies.

Source: Jeffrey R. Williams, "*I don't think we're in Kansas any more ... A perspective on our expanding markets*," Graduate School of Industrial Administration, Carnegie-Mellon University, Working Paper 20–86–87, January 1988.

Local monopoly markets

Local monopoly markets are at one extreme in terms of the intensity of competition. These markets sell specialized products to relatively few customers. Williams describes these as "the 20th century equivalent of the early craftsmen's guild ... regional businesses with negligible focus on productivity and little direct price competition. Each monopolized its immediate geographical area and hand-produced whatever goods the local population needed, maintaining personal contact with the customer."[7] In present times, "shielded markets" are typically those where firms use their idiosyncratic resources and capabilities to meet highly-specific customer requirements. Examples include high-technology defence contractors such as North American Rockwell (a leading contractor on the space shuttle) and Grumman Aerospace (builder of the F-14 fighter plane); professional service companies which rely upon close client contact such as corporate law firms and private bankers; and more traditional local monopolists such as the Baby Bells and airlines which dominate gate slots at regional hubs. Product differentiation in these markets tends to be high: customers are resistant to standardization and elasticity of demand is low, reflecting the fact that customers prefer a higher-priced specialty product (such as designer clothing or Rolls Royce cars) to a lower-priced mass-produced product. Governments also display strong preferences for differentiated products, such as military and telecommunications equipment. Since quality is usually not readily observable, price is often regarded as a signal of quality which provides a further disincentive for price competition.

Important features of these shielded monopolists are the effort they give to maintaining close customer relations, often supported by a strong emphasis on product and service quality. High-quality, low-volume production with lack of competition encourages craft-based production which is vertically-integrated, makes intensive use of highly skilled labor, and places little emphasis on attaining economies of scale or experience. Typically the experience curve for these industries is shallow and in the absence of volume gains and process innovation, annual reduction in real unit costs is typically less than 2 percent.

Traditional industrial markets

Traditional industries are those where market size is large and not heavily segmented, and where the rate of product innovation is modest. Competition in these markets is dominated by the quest for the benefits of size: economies of scale from standardized production and the reputation benefits of brand leadership. Market domination, though sought, is seldom achieved; products are close substitutes in these markets and market shares respond both to price and advertising. The stategy of cost-leadership/brand awareness/product variety is exemplified by McDonald's, Sears, and General Motors. For these strategies to be effective, companies must build organizations which emphasize efficiency through control, competence through experience and specialization, and perfection through the elimination of problems and defects. Despite the fact that many of these industries are highly mature (automobiles, glass, appliances, tires), the quest for cost advantage through scale efficiency, process technology, and product design improvement typically results in continuous cost reduction over time in the order of 2–8 percent a year.

Schumpeterian markets

Schumpeterian markets are those driven by a "gale of creative destruction" in the form of a stream of innovation. Established products are constantly being displaced by new products which, if successful, show rapid rates of growth. Industries where product innovation is the dominant form of competition include semiconductors, telecommunications, computers, consumer electronics, financial services, recorded music, entertainment, and certain fashion goods. At the same time innovations are quickly imitated, and speed in exploiting new products is essential. Hence, success in these industries does not depend exclusively upon product innovation; manufacturing and marketing capabilities play a key role in exploiting commercial opportunities for innovation and moving down the experience curve ahead of competitors. Williams points to annual average reductions in real unit costs in excess of 8 percent being typical for these products. Exhibit 8.5 shows the rapid rate of price reduction for several products within this category. Successful firms in Schumpeterian markets are innovators which can establish first mover advantage (e.g. Hewlett Packard in calculators, Intel in microprocessors, and Sony in consumer electronics) but also those firms which are fast-followers and can achieve cost reduction through process innovation (e.g. Texas Instruments and Motorola in semiconductors, and Matsushita in consumer electronics).

The implications of these fast-moving Schumpeterian markets for companies' organizational structures and management systems are far-reaching. The large-scale, scale efficiency-orientated, hierarchical organizations appropriate to traditional industrial markets are quite inappropriate for Schumpeterian markets (as Exxon found to its cost when it tried to establish Exxon Office Systems as a major player in the market for office computer systems and printers). The key requirements for success in these industries are organizations which can nurture innovation and use *speed* to respond to market changes and outmaneuver competitors.

It is important to recognize that industries may move from one class to another. Over time, technology and the opening of the "mass market" has caused many industries to move from craft-based local monopolies to scale-orientated industrial markets. Saville Row, the center for bespoke tailoring in London, is one outpost of "local monopoly" in a now-industrialized market. In other industries, such as local telephone services, trucking, and banking, deregulation has been instrumental in the shift from local monopoly market to traditional industrial market. In other industries, corporate restructuring is driven by the need to adjust to a transition from traditional industrial to Schumpeterian market structures. Shoes and toys are both traditional industries where product innovation and compression of product life-cycles have transformed competitive conditions.

The use of the industry categories in formulating a strategy is complicated by the fact that some industries may be hybrids; that is, they may combine the productivity characteristics of more than one market category. Williams observes that in personal computers, the production of basic

Industry	Period	Average annual real change in producer price index (%)
Local monopoly industries		
Surgical, orthopedic, and prostatic appliances	1983–9	+ 4.9
Boat repair	1981–8	+ 2.8
General job printing	1982–9	+ 2.6
Musical instruments	1985–9	+ 2.6
Map, atlas and globe cover printing	1982–9	+ 2.3
Entertainment	1980–7	+ 1.8
Highway construction	1970–8	+ 1.7
Burial caskets	1982–9	+ 1.7
Residential construction	1970–8	+ 1.6
Traditional manufacturing industries		
Passenger cars	1982–9	+ 0.3
Wheeled tractors	1982–9	0.0
Metal cans	1981–9	− 0.1
Electric lamps	1983–9	− 0.7
Gasoline engines (under 11 hp)	1982–9	− 0.8
Household refrigerators	1981–9	− 0.9
Dynamic, Schumpeterian industries		
Home electronic equipment	1982–9	− 3.6
Microprocessors	1981–9	− 4.6
Microwave cookers	1982–9	− 4.6
Analog integrated circuits	1981–9	− 4.8
Digital PBXs	1985–9	− 4.9
Color TVs (more than 17-inch screens)	1980–9	− 6.0
Memory integrated circuits	1981–9	− 6.0
Digital computers	1988–9	− 10.3

Exhibit 8.5
Productivity growth in different types of industry (as indicated by real annual rate of change of price indices)

Source: US Bureau of Labor Statistics.

components such as keyboards, cabinets, and power supplies are traditional, high-volume industries; components such as microprocessors and disk drives are dynamic, Schumpeterian industries; while applications software and customer support are craft-based, sheltered industries. Similarly in telecommunications equipment, electronics and fiberoptics provide Schumpeterian competition on the technological front; manufacturing of switching equipment is subject to important scale economies; while the presence of government-owned national telephone companies provides close customer contact typical of local monopoly markets. The differences between competition and competitive advantage between different activities within the personal computer and telecommunications industries pose considerable difficulties for strategy and organization. In particular, it may make it desirable for the firm to specialize in activities which are located within a single industry category. For a firm to span activities which fall into different categories, it may be desirable to carry these out within separate operating units.

BCG's Strategic Environments Matrix

In the life-cycle model of the industry, the stage of maturity of an industry determines its key structural characteristics which, in turn, determine the nature of competitive advantage within it. BCG's Strategic Environment Matrix reverses this direction of causation: it is the nature of competitive advantage in an industry which determines the strategies which are viable in an industry, which in turn determine the structure of the industry.

The BCG classification relies upon two variables to classify industries:

- the number of viable strategy approaches available within the industry;
- the size of the competitive advantage which is available to the industry leader.

The number of strategy approaches depends upon the complexity of the industry in terms of the diversity of sources of competitive advantage. Thus, in commodity products where there is no opportunity for differentiation, competitive advantage must be achieved through cost leadership. Furthermore, if all firms face identical input costs and technologies, then scale is a dominant strategic variable. If an industry's products and customers' requirements are complex, as with the case of automobiles, fashion clothing, and restaurants, the sources of competitive advantage are several and the number of viable strategy types may be several.

The second variable, the potential magnitude of competitive advantage, depends primarily upon the cost and demand characteristics of the industry. Where substantial economies of scale are available (either through production efficiencies, or through the ability to spread large indivisible costs of R&D or advertising over increasing sales volume) substantial cost advantage may accrue to the market leader. In other industries, such as computers or soft drinks, substantial differentiation advantages may accrue to firms with the leading brand positions.

On the basis of high and low values of each of these two variables, four industry categories can be established (see Exhibit 8.6).

Volume businesses

Businesses with few sources of advantage but where the size of the available competitive advantage is large are termed "volume businesses." Competition is cost based and scale economies are typically of key importance. Classic examples are jet engines (where the size of experience-based cost reduction and economies from spreading development costs have reduced the number of global players to three (GE, Pratt and Whitney, and Rolls

	Small	Big
Many	**FRAGMENTED** apparel, housebuilding, jewelry retailing, sawmills	**SPECIALIZATION** pharmaceuticals, luxury cars, chocolate confectionery
Few	**STALEMATE** basic chemicals, volume grade paper, ship-owning (VLCCs), wholesale banking	**VOLUME** jet engines, food supermarkets, motorcycles, standard microprocessors

SOURCES OF ADVANTAGE

SIZE OF ADVANTAGE

Royce), and food supermarkets where size determines both cost (primarily through buying power) and differentiation advantage through variety and advertising potential.

The key success factor in a volume business is market share. Market share confers economies of scale; the firm which achieves the largest market share and greatest growth in market share will also achieve the greatest cost reduction through economies of experience. Hence, profitability is likely to be closely correlated with market share.

The implications for strategy are quite straightforward. Strategy must be orientated toward exploiting economies of scale and experience. The firm must aim for the largest market possible by operating nationally or even internationally, so achieving the widest possible distribution. Pricing must be orientated toward market share rather than profit objectives and must anticipate future cost reductions. Production must be concentrated upon scale-efficient plants which embody the most cost-efficient process technology. If differentiation of products is necessary to broaden the market appeal, then differentiation should be *postponed*; that is, left to the final stages of production and distribution so that it does not compromise the quest for scale efficiency.

Stalemate businesses

"Stalemate businesses" are those where the sources of advantage are few and the size of potential advantage is small. As a result the environment is highly competitive: Firms compete with similar strategies but none is able to obtain significant advantage over another. The consequence is low profitability all round. Industries in this category include those producing commodity products where firms have similar input costs, similar technologies and limited opportunity for scale advantage. Examples include wholesale banking, bulk marine transportation, and newsprint. Volume businesses tend to evolve into stalemate businesses as growth slackens, technology becomes diffused, and firms' cost advantages become eroded.

Since stalemate industries are inherently unattractive, the key strategy recommendation is to avoid this type of business. For firms on the outside, spotting a stalemate industry is fairly easy. For firms on the inside, the key issue is to perceive the emergence of stalemate early on so that a timely exit can be executed. Once embroiled in a stalemate industry, survival and profitability is crucially dependent upon a high level of operational efficiency, low administrative overheads, and a corporate management that is ruthlessly cost conscious. As demonstrated by Crown Cork and Seal in metal containers and ConAgra in poultry and meat packing, such a strategy can offer attractive returns even in unpromising industry environments.

An alternative is to change industry conditions through some form of innovatory approach to competing (a "new game" strategy). For example, in the US steel industry Chaparral and Nucor have adopted new technologies, new forms of employee involvement, new organization structures, new approaches to customer interaction. Compared to US Steel, Bethlehem, and the other rusting giants, the "mini-mills" were remarkably profitable during the 1980s.

Another avenue is differentiation, even for the apparently most undifferentiable products. "The more the world perceives the product to be a commodity, the greater the opportunity to differentiate and create new and unexpected niches through the unending accumulation of small advantages," claims Tom Peters who cites as examples, Frank Purdue Farms in poultry, and Elgin Corrugated Box Company in paper containers.[8]

Fragmented businesses

Fragmented businesses are those where the sources of competitive advantage are many, but the potential size of the advantage is small. Typically fragmented industries supply differentiated products in markets where brand loyalty is low, technology is well-diffused, and minimum efficient plant size (MEPS) is small relative to total market size. Fashion clothing, restaurants, and video rental stores are examples of such industries.

Success factors in such industries include cost efficiency through a high level of operational efficiency, the choice of market segments which are comparatively attractive, creativity to achieve novel forms of product differentiation, and rapid response to change.

Large companies tend to be at a disadvantage to small companies in a fragmented industry. For a large firm to succeed, it must organize like a small firm through decentralization and through an entrepreneurial approach backed by appropriate incentives based upon business unit performance. One successful approach to competing in a fragmented business is by franchising.

An alternative approach for the large or for the aggressively-growing smaller firm is to attempt to transform the business into a specialized or volume business. The chain-store movement of the 1920s and '30s transformed retailing from a fragmented into a volume business. McDonald's transformed the fast-food industry from a fragmented into a volume business.

Specialized businesses are those where the sources of advantage are many and size of the potential advantage is substantial. The characteristics of a typical specialization business include:

- varied customer needs;
- the presence of first-mover advantages, brand loyalty, and scale economies which create barriers against competitors seeking to serve the same need;
- there are large specific costs associated with serving each market niche and shared costs are few, hence there are no major advantages to firms with a broad market or product scope.

The key feature of specialization businesses is differentiation. Each firm does something different and as a result competition is indirect rather than direct. The focus of competitive activity is product design, innovation, and brand promotion rather than price. Specialized businesses include pharmaceuticals, luxury cars, perfumes, and management consulting.

The strategies which are appropriate to specialization businesses depend upon the competitive character of these businesses. BCG regards two variables as critically important in determining the strategies and management skills appropriate to different specialization businesses: the degree of *environmental stability* and the *ability to systematize* customer and competitor behavior. On the basis of these two variables, Exhibit 8.7 defines four types of business and four approaches to strategic management:

- analytical;
- experimental;
- perceptive;
- creative

Where the market environment is stable and market behavior is sufficiently regular to permit systematization, then an analytic approach to strategy formulation is possible. In luxury cars concepts of style and quality change slowly. Success depends upon the careful analysis of customer requirements and competitors' positioning.

An environment which is stable, but where customers' and competitors' behavior cannot be systematized is conducive to experimental approaches to new product introduction and strategy adjustment. The food industry is stable, but it is difficult to predict the market's acceptance of new products. In developing and marketing new convenience food products a meticulous experimental approach is called for.

Where the environment is variable but where behavior is systematic, perceptive skills are the key to competitive advantage. Hence, in hi-tech environments the key is to perceive how new technological opportunities can better serve existing customer needs.

Environmental variability combined with inability to systematize requires *creativity* in order to establish competitive advantage. In fashion clothing, not only do markets change quickly, but fashion trends and cycles are not amenable to techniques of market analysis. Success in fashion clothing accrues to companies which, through creativity and style, become trendsetters.

Exhibit 8.7
Specialization businesses: strategic characteristics and general management skills

		CREATIVE	EXPERIMENTAL
	low	fashion general publishing	toiletries magazines food products
ABILITY TO SYSTEMATIZE		PERCEPTIVE	ANALYTICAL
	high	high-tech	luxury cars confectionery paper towels
		high	low

ENVIRONMENTAL VARIABILITY

Summary

Classifying industries according to their competitive characteristics fulfills two useful purposes. First, it acts as a short-cut in strategy analysis. Categorizing industries and applying generalizations concerning the type of competition likely to emerge and the kinds of strategy likely to be effective provides a quick and useful first-cut analysis for the purposes of strategy formulation. Secondly, classifying an industry requires comparison with other industries. Such comparisons, by highlighting similarities and differences with other industries, can form the basis of a deeper understanding of the industry's structure, competitive character, and sources of advantage.

There is no right or even best way to classify industries. Indeed, to gain insight and understanding, there is merit in applying alternative classifications. The next three chapters draw from different bases of classification to discuss strategy formulation and strategy implementation in three different industry types. The first two, emerging industries and mature industries, are defined principally in terms of the life-cycle model. The merits of this approach are, first, that most industries appear to be subject to common evolutionary forces (notably the pattern of demand growth and the development and diffusion of technology), and, secondly, that a focus upon evolution over time can help the firm in anticipating and planning for change in its environment. At the same time, our analysis recognizes that some industries retain the dynamic, technology-based character of emerging industries and do not reach a state of maturity. Hence, Williams' concept of "dynamic Schumpeterian" markets will be useful in understanding these industries. The third industry category, global industries, focusses upon the distinctive environmental features and strategic and organizational issues associated with industries subject to international competition.

Notes

1. The concept of the product life-cycle is associated with the work of Everett M. Rogers, *The Diffusion of Innovations* (Free Press, New York, 1962) and Theodore Levitt, "Exploit the product life cycle," *Harvard Business Review*, November–December 1965, pp. 81–94. For a contemporary discussion, see Philip Kotler, *Marketing Management: Analysis, Planning, and Control*, 5th edn (Prentice-Hall, Englewood Cliffs, NJ, 1984), ch. 11.
2. "Crown Cork and Seal Company, Inc." in C. R. Christensen, K. R. Andrews, J. L. Bower, R. G. Hamermesh, and M. E. Porter, *Business Policy: Text and Cases*, 5th edn (Irwin, Homewood, Illinois, 1982).
3. In Mathur's *"transaction cycle"* differentiation reemerges as products and services are recombined into new systems (see chapter 7).
4. R. Vernon, "International investment and international trade in the product cycle," *Quarterly Journal of Economics* 80 (1966), pp. 190–207.
5. This section draws upon the pioneering research of Jeffrey R. Williams which is contained in several papers: Jeffrey R. Williams, *The Productivity Base of Industries*, Working Paper 19–83–84, Carnegie-Mellon University, Graduate School of Industrial Administration, May 1984; Jeffrey R. Williams, *"I don't think we're in Kansas any more ..." A perspective on our expanding markets*, Graduate School of Industrial Administration, Carnegie-Mellon University, Working Paper 20–86–87, 1988; and Jeffrey R. Williams and Robert S. Novak, "Aligning CIM strategies to different markets," *Long Range Planning*, 19, February 1990, pp. 126–35.
6. Jeffrey R. Williams, *"I don't think we're in Kansas any more ..."*, pp. 15–16.
7. Ibid., pp. 23–6.
8. Tom Peters, *Thriving on Chaos* (Knopf, New York, 1987), pp. 56 and 60.

NINE

Strategy Formulation and Implementation in Emerging and Technology-based Industries

> The best way to predict the future is to invent it.
>
> John Scully, Chairman, Apple Computers

Outline

Introduction

New products and services and new industries which produce them are emerging all the time. New markets are created through the development of new technology (biotechnology, fiberoptics); through the application of existing technology to new products (personal computers); through the emergence of new personal needs (health farms, sex-change clinics, stress-management counselling); through environment problems (pollution control and waste management); and through new instruments for investment and risk management (traded options, interest, and currency swaps).

Some industries have undergone periods of rejuvenation that have given them the characteristics of new industries; most notably rapid growth and the entry of new producers. Resurgent industries include motorcycles during the late 1960s and early 1970s, dance studios during the late 1970s, and bottled mineral water during the 1980s.

From the point of view of strategy formulation, the primary feature of emerging industries is the central role of innovation. Innovation is responsible for the creation of new industries and, because it is the primary source of both cost and differentiation advantage, innovation is the driving force of competition.

While maturity is generally associated with a slowing of the rate of technological change, some industries demonstrate a capacity for continual innovation. In pharmaceuticals, biotechnology, communications, and electronics, product innovation continues to be the driving force of competition. These industries retain many of the features of emerging industries. Innovation also plays a continuing role in other industries which are clearly mature: In food processing, fashion goods, and automobiles, constant new product development, market changes, and technological change in related industries provides important innovative opportunities.

The purposes of this chapter are:

- to develop insight into competition in emerging and technology-based industries;
- to introduce concepts and tools of analysis which can help in locating sources of competitive advantage and formulating appropriate strategies in emerging and technology-based industries;
- to understand the process and the determinants of innovation in order to guide companies' management of technology and, in particular, to identify organizational and managerial factors conducive to the effective strategy implementation in emerging and technology-based industries.

First, we consider the principal structural characteristics of emerging industries in order to understand and predict the nature and intensity of competitive behavior in these types of environment. Secondly, we examine the sources of competitive advantage in emerging industries, focussing primarily upon the role of innovation as a basis for competitive advantage. Thirdly, we consider the problems of strategy implementation in emerging and technology-based industries, with emphasis upon the establishment of conditions which are conducive to innovation. Finally, we explore some of the particular problems of reconciling innovation with operational efficiency in mature companies.

Structural Characteristics of Emerging Industries

Emerging industries are as those which are in the introductory and growth phases of their life cycles. For practical purposes it is useful to include within this category industries where product innovation continues to be the principal dimension of competitive activity.

The primary feature of emerging industries is technological change. Abernathy and Utterback have identified patterns of technological change which correspond closely to the industry life-cycle (see Exhibit 9.1).[1] Initially innovation takes the form of a fundamental product innovation with a clear discontinuity with the past. This breakthrough is followed by a spate of further product innovations which take the form of refinements to the original innovation and the development of competitive products. The lack of a dominant technology or product configuration during this early stage is reflected in rivalry between different technologies, designs and production and distribution systems.

To offer a few examples, between 1890 and 1920, the automobile industry featured a wide diversity of engine configurations and transmission designs, not to mention body designs and steering and braking systems. Not until the 1920s did a dominant type of car emerge with regard to technology and design. By the 1960s, the technology and design of the mass-produced, family car varied little between competing manufacturers: Volkswagen maintained its rear-engined, air-cooled engine, the Dutch manufacturer DAF featured a unique transmission, American cars remained substantially larger than those elsewhere in the world. By the 1980s, even these distinctive features had disappeared.

Similarly, the development of the video cassette recorder (VCR) featured competition between five companies and a number of different technologies. The American company Ampex pioneered video-tape recording for commercial use and in 1970 developed its "Instavideo" video recorder/camera. RCA during the early 1970s worked on both a VCR product and its video-disc system. Sony developed several video-tape technologies before launching, first its U-Matic VCR, and then Betamax in 1975. The Victor Company of Japan, together with its parent company Matsushita, also adopted the U-Matic standard before introducing its VHS system in 1976. Not until 1987 when Sony finally switched to the rival VHS system did a single standard emerge.[2]

Uncertainty over which technology and product design will ultimately emerge as the industry standard is exacerbated by the fact that different approaches offer different advantages and disadvantages and, even if one approach is clearly superior, this does not guarantee its acceptance. In the mid-nineteenth century, the 3ft 6in. railway gauge was accepted as the standard for British railways, despite the technical superiority of Brunel's 6ft gauge. In VCRs, the displaced Betamax system offered a higher quality of reproduction than the ultimately-dominant VHS system. In typewriter keyboards the QWERTY arrangement of keys is dominant despite the

Technology

Exhibit 9.1 The
pattern of innovation
over time

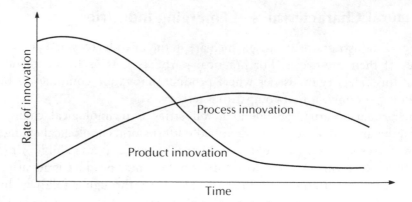

Source: William J. Abernathy and James M. Utterback, "Dynamic model of process and product development", Omega 3 (6) (1975)

inconvenience of this layout compared to DSK (the Dvorak Simplified Keyboard).[3]

One consequence of the uncertain outcome of competition between rival technologies is that technological forecasting, always a hazardous game, is especially difficult in new industries. The implications of technological uncertainty for business risk is made more serious by the fact that establishing a particular approach as the industry standard requires heavy investment in development, production facilities, and marketing. These investments may prove to be worthless for the runner-up.

Once product technology becomes more standardized, product innovation tends towards incremental improvement and the priority for technological development shifts towards the goal of reducing production cost through process innovation. Process innovation follows product innovation, since it is not until a product's technology and design becomes stable that large-scale production becomes feasible. Thus, before developing the Model-T, Henry Ford developed and produced five different engines ranging from two to six cylinders in a craft-based job shop. It was not until he finalized the design of the Model-T that the shift towards assembly line mass-production became economical.[4]

This development pattern of innovation results in unit costs which are initially very high reflecting heavy development costs and inefficiently-small production runs, but which fall rapidly once the process innovation commences, and the industry moves down the experience curve. The ballpoint pen, invented by a Hungarian, Ladislao Biro, in 1940 is a classic example. In the 1945 Christmas season, Gimbel's New York store was selling the pens for $12.50. By the early 1950s the price had fallen to 15 cents.[5] Rapid cost reduction is a feature of many products which feature low differentiation, high demand elasticity, and limited service content (see chapter 8). Moreover, significant cost reduction may continue for many years, led by process innovation and design modification. For example, over the 17-year period 1965–82, the prices of black and white televisions fell by an average of 4.32 percent per annum.[6]

Emerging industries are characterized by high rates of demand growth. Two phases of growth are apparent. The first stage, the introduction phase, growth of demand is constrained by the novelty of the product or service, high manufacturing cost, lack of reliability, and customer ignorance. In the case of consumer goods, customers are likely to be technological enthusiasts among the upper income brackets. As technology, and with it product reliability, advances, as product distribution expands, and customer awareness increases, so market penetration increases and exponential demand growth ensues.

However, the successful transition from the introduction phase to the growth phase is far from certain. When Xerox introduced its first plain-paper copier in 1959 and when Steve Jobs and Steve Wozniak introduced their first personal computer in 1977, the success of the companies, or of the industries that they spawned, was far from certain. Technological achievement and a successful introduction of the new product do not guarantee commercial viability.

For example, Concorde was a technically-superb aircraft, but airlines' doubts over their ability to operate it profitably were such that the only sales made were to the British and French state-owned airlines. Du Pont's "Corfam" was a technical break-through: the first synthetic leather substitute that could "breathe" like leather. But the product failed to gain acceptance either from the shoe manufacturers or their customers and after running up losses of almost $100 million, Du Pont ceased production of Corfam in 1971.[7] What we observe is that the *technological uncertainty* that characterizes product development and introduction is superseded by *market uncertainty* as to the future growth and size of the market. Conventional market forecasting techniques are of limited help. During the late 1950s, Eastman Kodak was considering whether to purchase patents for the new xerography process. A study commissioned from Arthur D. Little estimated the potential US market for plain-paper copiers at less than a few hundred.

A further feature of demand during the early phases of an industry's life-cycle is buyers' lack of knowledge about the product or service. Customer ignorance has two effects: it makes them cautious and it makes them dependent upon the manufacturer for presales and after-sales service. Hence, faced by an absence of established distribution channels and service facilities, early entrants into an industry typically find it necessary to be highly-integrated downstream. The manufacturer needs to invest heavily in customer education, the provision of after-sales services, and, frequently, distribution. Early entrants into the home computer industry faced the problems of finding distribution outlets (several chose mail order), instructing customers in the products' use, and providing repair services and software support. Similarly, the early involvement of the oil companies in establishing filling stations was a consequence of the apparent inability of the existing retail sector to provide gasoline service to a rapidly expanding market.

Entry barriers

The role of technology as the basis for competitive activity during the early stages of an industry's growth also results in technology creating entry barriers to emerging industries. Once an innovation has occurred, subsequent entry depends primarily upon the incumbent's ability to protect the innovation, either by patents or by safeguarding the know-how. If the product is patent-protected, entry depends upon obtaining a license or innovating around the patents. If not, successful entry depends upon the ability to imitate the innovation. Either way, entry requires certain technological resources; the most important being employees with the requisite skills and training. In most new industries the limited pool of technically-trained labor – biochemists, electronic engineers, metallurgists, software writers, and the like – represents a key barrier to entry.

Risk may also provide an important barrier to entry. To the extent that new industries are perceived by financial markets as high risk and investments in research and development are poor colateral for loans, firms in emerging industries are likely to experience a high cost and limited availability of capital. The development of California's Silicon Valley owed much to the presence of a small number of venture capitalists who were willing to invest in high-tech, high-risk start-ups.

It is also true, however, that new industries lack many of the barriers which restrict entry into more mature industries. In the early stages of an industry's life, established firms are unlikely to have built substantial advantages over potential entrants. Brand loyalty is not well entrenched, distribution channels are still developing, capital requirements are comparatively modest, and all firms are close to the top of the experience curve. Industry development is typically accompanied by rising entry barriers as the scale of production increases and firms establish clear market positions.

Key Issues for Strategy Formulation

Forecasting

The decision to enter an emerging industry and the formulation of a strategy which will establish competitive advantage in an emerging industry must be based, first and foremost, upon a view of how the industry will develop. Essential elements of such a forward look are ideas as to the potential size and growth rate of the market, the technology and design which are likely to dominate the industry, the most likely distribution channels, the likely entrants, and the most powerful competitors which will emerge.

Most conventional techniques for forecasting the environment are of limited value in emerging industries for two reasons. First, most conventional forecasting techniques (econometric forecasting for example) are based upon the extrapolation of current trends into the future. In the case of new technologies and new industries few data are available, and those which do are of limited value in predicting the future. Hence, to forecast technological changes and the future development patterns of emerging industries, qualitative analysis which draws upon imagination and expert opinion tends to be superior to quantitative forecasts based upon data analysis. Among useful forecasting techniques are:

- scenario building;
- the Delphi technique.

Over the past decade, *scenarios*, pioneered by Herman Kahn's Hudson Institute, have gained increasing popularity as a tool of strategy formulation.[8] A scenario is an internally consistent view of what the future may turn out to be. The value of scenarios is in being able to combine the interrelated impacts of a wide range of economic, technological, and social factors into a number of distinct alternative pictures of the future. Scenarios are conducive to the exercise of the imagination and have been shown to be valuable in identifying possible threats and opportunities, generating flexibility of thinking by managers, and developing highly practical approaches to the management of risk. Industry scenarios can be used to develop alternative views of how the market and industry structure may develop and what the implications for competition and competitive advantage might be. The Royal Dutch/Shell Group of Companies has pioneered the use of scenarios as a basis for long-term strategic planning in an industry subject to rapid and discontinuous change.[9]

The Delphi technique, developed at the Rand Corporation, draws upon the coordinated views of a panel of experts to reach agreed forecasts about future developments. While the technique is a powerful method for synthesizing and probing the knowledge and experience of leading experts within a field, there is always a risk that group processes will result in an irrational judgement.[10] Delphi techniques have been used extensively by computer, electronics, and pharmaceutical companies.[11]

A second reason for the failure of conventional forecasting techniques in the area of technological change is their emphasis on predicting the future values of external variables: Levels of market demand, the costs of raw materials, exchange rates, government policy interventions, and so on. In an emerging industry, the future is determined by the firms which develop the industry. If a company is to be an industry leader, strategy must be developed, not in response to industry changes, but in order to shape industry changes.

Predicting the shape of technological change in fast-moving industries must be concerned more with perception than with technique. The critical management requirement is to recognize the potential which emerging technologies offer for meeting customers' real needs. There is ample evidence that established firms' vested interests in current technologies can prevent the objective appraisal of competing technologies. As a result, industry leaders become incapable of anticipating change and they are overtaken by competitors. In tire cords, the shift from cotton to rayon to nylon to polyester was associated with a shift of industry leadership first to the American Viscose Company (rayon), then to Du Pont (nylon), and then to Celanese Corp (polyester). In electronic components, Sylvania, a leader in vacuum tubes, continued to invest in vacuum-tube technology and discounted the advantages of the emerging solid-state technology. Richard Foster refers to this phenomenon as "technological myopia" and points to the need for top management to be alert to: (1) the role of new technologies in redefining served markets; (2) the cultural factors which encourage a company to defend its established technological expertise; and (3) evidence of decay in the company's technological position.[12]

The profitability of innovation

The attraction of industries characterized by high rates of technological change is, first, that they typically display high rates of market growth and that the technological potential of these industries offers opportunities for highly profitable innovation. As Emerson observed: "If a man ... make a better mousetrap than his neighbor, though he build his house in the woods, the world will make a beaten path to his door." Yet, how profitable are firms' investments in innovation?

The empirical evidence is far from clear. The PIMS data shows a negative relationship between R&D expenditure as a percentage of sales and both ROI and ROS. New product introductions also depress profitability.[13] However, since there are substantial lags between investment in R&D and new product introduction and return, little is revealed by current relationships. Research on the determinants of long-run profitability by Dennis Mueller failed to establish clear-cut results. The data showed that the combination of large market share with high levels of industry-level patent-intensity was conducive to high profitability, but firms with high patent-to-sales ratios relative to their industry average did not earn significantly higher rates of return.[14] The absence of any positive relationship between firms' patent activity and their profitability was surprising given that accounting rates of return for R&D-intensive firms are overstated by the tendency for book values to undervalue investments in R&D.

The finding that innovation is only conducive to profitability when combined with large market share is consistent with Joseph Schumpeter's view of competition. Innovation, as we have noted is the primary vehicle for the process of "creative destruction", hence to derive profitability from innovation requires some measure of market control. The empirical results also give rise to the question: "What determines the profitability of innovation?"

For innovation to contribute to social welfare requires that it yields benefits in excess of the amount invested. The issue then arises as to how these benefits are distributed. If the innovator has a monopoly over the innovation then most of the value created by the innovation can be appropriated by the innovator in profits. If the innovation is imitated, then imitators also gain profits from the innovation. As an innovation is imitated, so the profits from innovation are eroded through competition and the benefits of the innovation accrue largely to customers.

The ability of the innovator to appropriate the value of an innovation therefore depends on his or her ability to create barriers to imitation. Four principal barriers may be identified:

- patents (and other property rights such as copyrights and legally-protected trade secrets);
- secrecy;
- lead time;
- learning-curve advantages;
- complementary resources.

The protection which patents offer depends critically upon the type of innovation. Not all inventions are patentable: ideas are not normally patentable, and in new areas of technology such as biotechnology and computer software, patent law is not clearly defined. Once granted, the effectiveness of a patent depends upon the ease with which a patent can be circumvented. Patents have failed to offer protection for some new drugs because of the ease with which rivals have formulated slightly different compounds which have similar properties.

As a result, secrecy may provide more effective protection than patents (this is particularly the case for process innovations – see Exhibit 9.2). Indeed, patents and secrecy are likely to be mutually exclusive means of protection: if an innovation is to be protected by secrecy then patenting is undesirable since it makes public information about the innovation which may assist rivals in circumventing the patent.

When the period between research and market launch is long, lead time can provide a vital barrier to imitation. In pharmaceuticals the FDA approval procedure typically imposes a five-year delay upon would-be imitators. In financial services, on the other hand, innovations such as brokerage cash management accounts, money-market checking accounts, interest rate swaps, stripped bonds, and country-specific equity funds have been imitated within periods of a few months. Research shows that patents have the effect of raising the costs of imitation, while in some industries patents actually reduce the time lag for imitation.[15] Lead time may be effective, not only in giving the innovator breathing space, but also in permitting the innovator to build a cost advantage by moving down the product's learning curve ahead of imitators.

If a patent fails to provide effective protection for an innovation, then it is unlikely that patent licenses will permit the innovator to appropriate the full value of his invention. Lack of effective patent protection encourages innovators to commercialize their innovations themselves. If commercialization requires complementary resources such as sophisticated production know-how; inputs whose supplies are limited; or a specialized service network, then the limited availability of these complementary resources will provide a barrier to imitation. Exhibit 9.2 shows that one category of complementary resources, sales and service networks, are particularly important as a means of protecting product innovation. If investment in complementary resources is required in order to appropriate the value of an innovation, complex issues of strategy formulation arise. For small firms and new business ventures the need to invest substantial sums in manufacturing and distribution may be well beyond the resources of the company. There are also important implications for risk. If investment in complementary resources is the primary means of protecting against imitation, then innovators must commit themselves to heavy investment very early on – possibly before the direction of technological development of the industry or the existence of a substantial market for the product are apparent.[16] These issues of appropriability and risk have important implications for the relative merits of first mover and follower strategies.

Exhibit 9.2 The effectiveness of alternative means of protecting the competitive advantages of new or improved processes and products

Method of Appropriation	Overall sample means	
	Processes	Products
Patents to prevent duplication	3.52	4.33
Patents to secure royalty income	3.31	3.75
Secrecy	4.31	3.57
Lead time	5.11	5.41
Moving quickly down the learning curve	5.02	5.09
Sales or service efforts	4.55	5.59

The means show responses from 650 individuals across 130 lines of business. The range was from 1 (= not at all effective) to 7 (= very effective).
Source: R. C. Levin, A. K. Klevorick, R. R. Nelson, and S. G. Winter, "Appropriating the returns from industrial research and development", *Brookings Papers on Economic Activity* 3 (1987), p. 794.

The timing of entry and innovation: to lead or to follow?

Timing represents probably the most critical and the most difficult issue in strategy formulation in emerging and technologically-based industries. The central issue is the choice of leadership or followership. The leader in entry and innovation can be first to grab the prize. However, the leader also bears the highest risks and the costs of pioneering. Optimal timing of entry into an emerging industry and the introduction of new technology is a complex issue. Casual observation of the comparative success of leaders and followers for a sample of innovations reveals no clear pattern (see Exhibit 9.3).

The distribution of profit between an innovator and a follower is dependent on many of the same factors which determine the profitability of innovation. David Teece[17] points to three sets of factors as particularly important in determining the relative advantages of innovators and followers:

- appropriability;
- complementary resources;
- influence over industry standards.

Appropriability The ability of innovators to appropriate the value created by their innovations has been discussed in the previous section. Critical in determining the distribution of profit between pioneers and followers is the effectiveness of legal instruments of protection. Innovations differ in terms of whether or not legal protection is available and the effectiveness of the protection in erecting a barrier to imitation. The two examples of winning pioneers in Exhibit 9.3 had the benefit of effective patent protection. Appropriation by pioneers of the benefits of their innovation is also dependent upon the characteristics of the technology. If patents or copyrights do not offer effective protection the speed of diffusion depends critically upon the ability to communicate the innovation. Codified knowledge, such as the recipe for Coca Cola, or the basic design of Chrysler's popular passenger vans, can be easily communicated and imitated. Tacit information such as Shell's techniques for deep-water drilling or Toyota's manufacturing systems, is less easy to transmit.

Complementary resources The more important are complementary resources for the successful commercialization of an innovation, then the greater are the costs and risks assumed by the pioneer. If complementary resources are specialized, then it is likely that the pioneer must not only undertake investment in the innovation, the pioneer must also undertake the investment in complementary resources required for commercializing the innovation. By delaying entry until the industry's infrastructure is better developed, a company can reduce its costs of entry through relying upon cooperative relationships with firms which already possess the necessary

Product	Innovator	Follower	The winner
Jet airliners	De Havilland (Comet)	Boeing	Follower
Float glass	Pilkington	Corning	Leader
X-ray scanner	EMI	General Electric	Follower
Office PC	Xerox	IBM	Follower
VCRs	Ampex/Sony	Matsushita	Follower
Diet Cola	R.C. Cola	Coca Cola	Follower
Instant cameras	Polaroid	Kodak	Leader
Pocket calculator	Bowmar	Texas Instruments	Follower
Microwave oven	Raytheon	Samsung	Follower
Plain-paper copier	Xerox	Canon	Not clear
Fiber-optic cable	Corning	Many companies	Leader

Exhibit 9.3 Leaders, followers and success in emerging industries

Source: Based in part upon David Teece, *The Competitive Challenge: Strategies for Industrial Innovation and Renewal* (Ballinger, Cambridge, Mass., 1987), pp. 186–8.

complementary resources. The failure of the Wankel rotary engine to offer substantial returns either to its inventor or to the many auto manufacturers which took out licenses on it may be attributed to the car's need for specialist service and repair expertise which limited its market acceptance. The failure of Sir Clive Sinclair's Sinclair Electronics to establish a strong position in the British home computer industry in the early 1980s was largely due to Sinclair's dependence on inexperienced sub-contractors and component suppliers, and underdeveloped distribution channels. By delaying its entry into the computer market until 1983, Amstrad was able to establish itself during 1986–8 as a market leader in European personal computers relying upon highly-efficient Asian manu-facturers and well-developed independent distributors.

When complementary resources are essential for successfully commercial-izing an innovation, companies which are well-endowed in such resources may be able to defer their entry and so avoid the risks of pioneering. Even though IBM in personal computers and GE in X-ray scanners were late entrants their strengths in manufacturing, sales and service allowed them to displace the pioneers (Apple and EMI) as market leaders.

Identifying and influencing industry standards A feature of industry evolution is the convergence of technology and design around a single dominant approach. In relation to the optimal timing of entry, a key issue is the tradeoff between the risk of early entry with the possibility of backing the wrong technological horse and the risk of being too late to influence, or establish a strong early position in, the dominant technological approach. In the personal computer industry, 1981 was probably the optimal time for the entry of IBM. The pioneers had developed a market for personal computers, but technical standards were still fluid. By 1986 IBM had established de facto standards for the industry which virtually every firm in the industry with the exception of Apple felt obliged to follow.

The size of the risk of entering early when several technologies and designs are competing for supremacy depends upon the costs of switching technologies later on. If switching imposes heavy costs in terms of product development, capital investment, and loss of customer goodwill, this enhances the attractions of a follower strategy. Against this must be set the potential gains of leadership in terms of being able to set, or at least influence, the industry standard. Telefunken's technical leadership in the German color television industry, resulted in its being well placed to press for the adoption of its PAL system as the color broadcasting standard for most of Western Europe. The benefits were, first, the royalties it received from other manufacturers for the use of its patents and, secondly, power to restrict imports into its domestic market.[18]

Managing risks

The presence of technological and market uncertainties, the difficulties of forecasting, the high rate of entry by new competitors, and the need for heavy investment in R&D (the returns from which are likely to be long term) imply high risks in emerging industries. Two indicators of the riskiness of emerging industries are the high cost of capital to firms and projects in new industries and the frequency of company failure. Hence, effective management of risk is a vital ingredient of survival and success in emerging industries.

The issue of risk has been discussed in relation to the timing of entry and the choice of being a pioneer or a follower in innovation. Once such basic issues have been dealt with, there are numerous other strategic choices that have important implications for the amount of risk that the firm bears. Risk cannot be avoided, but it can be managed. Three methods of coping with risk have been suggested:

- cooperating with lead users;
- limiting risk exposure;
- flexibility.

Cooperating with lead users   During the early phases of industry development, careful monitoring and response to market trends and customer requirements is essential to avoid major errors in technology, design and performance. Von Hippel argues that lead users provide a vital source of market data for developing new products.[19] Hence, identifying users whose present strong needs will become general market trends in the future, and developing close ties with such customers can be vital in maintaining technological progressiveness. Cooperation with lead users yields three major benefits:

- an "early warning system" for emerging needs and technological trends;
- assistance in the conception and development of new products and processes – in electronic instruments, customers' ideas initiated most of the successful new products introduced by manufacturers;[20] similarly, in aluminum refining, fabricators have been the source of the majority of innovations;[21]
- by targeting early adopters, the firm can achieve an early cash flow to contribute to further development expenditures.

In industrial products, the most innovative and technologically-conscious customers are easy to identify, and their own decisions may also have an important influence on the technological choices of other firms. In consumer products, early adopters are frequently young, educated, affluent consumers in urban areas; although this is not always the case. A key element in Nike's recapturing of market leadership from Reebok in the US market for sports shoes was Nike's market research and new product testing with inner-city street gangs which Nike identified as fashion trendsetters in sneakers. In electronics and aerospace, governments, and the military in particular, play a crucial role as early adopters. In the US, Britain, and France, government contracts are major sources of finance for R&D into innovative, sophisticated products. However, the extent to which security and R&D support from defense contracts confers advantage in commercial markets is debatable. Recent evidence suggests that dependence on defense contracts has made US and European companies unwilling to withstand the rigors of international competition and unresponsive to customer requirements.

Limiting risk exposure   The high level of risk in emerging industries also requires that firms minimize their exposure to the effects of risk and uncertainty by appropriate financial policies. Uncertainties over development costs and the timing and amount of future cash flows require a strong balance sheet with limited debt financing.

For example, Apple's ability to survive a severe revenue slump in 1984–5 and the ensuing industry shake-out owed much to its strong cash position and lack of debt. Hewlett Packard's commitment to financing all expansion out of retained profits has been an important source of strength for the company in navigating a course through technological change and economic turbulence.

The vulnerability of even very large companies to the risks imposed by huge development costs is illustrated by Rolls Royce's bankruptcy in 1971, a consequence of the soaring costs of its RB211 engine. Similarly, the cost of developing a second generation of X-ray scanners combined with an unexpected fall in revenue was sufficient to bring down the diversified music and electronic company EMI. EMI's scanner business was acquired by GE, the remainder of EMI was taken over by Thorn.

One reason for EMI's financial vulnerability was its decision to set up its own manufacturing, marketing, and servicing facilities to develop its scanner innovation. Innovators can reduce their exposure to risk by relying upon the investments of other companies. This might include the leasing of capital equipment, buying in major components, and contracting out wherever possible. The computer industry offers many examples of cooperative arrangements between firms in order to reduce investment requirements and pool capabilities. Many companies reduced the cost of entry into personal computers by such reliance upon outside suppliers. Even IBM was heavily dependent upon external suppliers of components, sub-assemblies, and software for its initial range of personal computers.

Flexibility   Finally, the high level of uncertainty in emerging industries makes flexibility critical to long-term survival and success. Since technological and market changes are difficult to forecast, it is essential that top management closely monitors the environment and that the organization responds quickly and effectively to demand fluctuations, changing preferences regarding technology and design, changing patterns of distribution, and the emergence of new customer segments. According to Tom Peters,[22] a vital element in flexibility is recognizing and responding to failures. Peters quotes Soichiro Honda, the founder of Honda Motor Company: "Many people dream of success. To me success can only be achieved through repeated failure and introspection. In fact, success represents the 1 per cent of your work which comes only from the 99 per cent that is called failure."

An example is Honda's responsiveness to the disappointments which accompanied its entry into the US motorcycle market. Although motorcycles were hardly a new product, Honda's US venture shares many of the pioneering characteristics of innovation. Mr Kawashima, one of Honda's initial two-man team to the US recounted the experience:

By the first week of April 1960, reports were coming in that our machines were leaking oil and encountering clutch failure. This was our lowest moment. Honda's fragile reputation was being destroyed before it could be established. As it turned out, motorcycles in the U.S. are driven much farther and much faster than in Japan. We dug deeply into our precious cash reserves to air freight our motorcycles to the Honda testing lab in Japan. . . . Our lab worked 24-hour days bench testing the bikes to replicate the failure. Within a month, a redesigned head gasket and clutch spring solved the problem. But in the meantime events had taken a surprising turn. Throughout our first eight months we had not attempted to move the 50cc Supercubs. While they were a smash success in Japan, they seemed wholly unsuitable for the U.S. market where everything was bigger and more luxurious. . . . We used the Honda 50s ourselves to ride around Los Angeles on errands. They attracted a lot of attention. One day we had a call from a Sears buyer. While persisting in our refusal to sell through an intermediary, we took note of Sears' interest . . . When the larger bikes started breaking, we had no choice. We let the 50cc bikes move. And surprisingly, the retailers who wanted to sell them weren't motorcycle dealers, they were sporting goods stores. The excitement created by the Honda Supercub began to gain momentum. . . .[23]

A similar responsiveness to customer requirements and market opportunities is apparent in the success of Apple's Macintosh computer. The original Macintosh launched in 1984 was a technologically brilliant product in search of a market. During 1985 and 1986, Apple initiated a host of strategic initiatives including cooperation with Microsoft on business applications software, opening the Mac to third-party developers, increasing memory, and targeting the desktop publishing market. The result was a transformation in the Macintosh's market positioning and appeal.[24]

Our discussion of patterns of innovation, entry barriers, complementary assets, and risk management has suggested a number of implications for the resources required for success in emerging and technology-based industries. Let us draw together several of these themes.

A critical issue is the different resources required by different types of innovation and different stages of the innovation process. A useful starting-point is the distinction between invention and innovation. Invention is concerned with creating the idea; innovation is putting the idea into commercial practice. Christopher Freeman defines innovation as "an idea, a sketch or a model for a new or improved device, product, process or system" and states that "an innovation in the economic sense is only

The resources for innovation

accomplished with the first commercial transaction involving the new product, system or device."[25] This distinction is vital in terms of the resource requirements of the different stages of the innovation process.

Invention is dependent upon creativity. A stream of empirical research has shown that many of the most important and radical innovations of this century have their origins in the creative brilliance of individuals, often without significant institutional support. A survey of a sample of the major innovations of the twentieth century by Jewkes et al.[26] revealed that a surprisingly large proportion were contributed by individual inventors, frequently working in their garage or garden shed. A study of 27 important inventions during the post-war period found that only seven emerged from the R&D departments of established corporations.[27] Not only are individuals and small firms able to compete on more or less equal terms with researchers in large corporations, they are likely to be less hampered by organizational constraints and commitment to the status quo.

These factors also go a long way to explaining the types of companies which predominate in new industries. Most new industries contain a large proportion of start-ups. Even when innovation takes place within established firms, very often it is first exploited by new companies which spin off from the corporation. Such spinoffs may occur because the established company is disinterested in developing the technology, or because the innovators seek to exploit the technology for their own gains, or it may be a strategic decision by the parent company to obtain external equity financing while providing the autonomy needed for development. Among the large number of start-up companies in California's Silicon Valley are many which were set up by engineers from Hewlett Packard, Xerox's Palo Alto Research Center, Stanford University, and UC Berkeley.

Later stages of the innovation process involving the development of inventions into manufacturable, marketable products require more varied combinations of resources. These may include development and test engineers, manufacturing engineers, market research and marketing expertise, and manufacturing and distribution facilities. The resources and capabilities required by the commercialization phases of innovation are what have been referred to earlier as "complementary assets". In general, these later phases of the innovation process are likely to require far higher investment expenditures than the earlier research and conceptualization phases.

The different resource requirements of the different stages of the innovation process have implications for the types of companies which are likely to excel at each stage. While small, start-up companies may possess some advantages in harnessing the expertise and enthusiasm that are key ingredients in the early creative phase, larger, established companies are likely to possess the finance, development skills, marketing knowledge, and manufacturing capability necessary for successfully taking the innovation to market. Specialization by companies according to their comparative advantages implies that large companies whose strengths are in the commercialization stages of innovation should not seek to be self-sufficient in innovation. In consumer electronics, the success of Matsushita, Samsung, and several other Japanese and Korean companies, reflects their willingness to license technology from all over the world and then to develop, integrate, and commercialize that technology internally. By contrast, one source of the poorer performance of Philips, RCA in the same markets may reflect their propensity to look internally for new product innovation. The apparent unwillingness of US companies to exploit technologies developed by other companies has been termed the "Not-Invented-Here" syndrome which is the consequence of well-established, tightly-knit project groups to believe that they have a monopoly of relevant knowledge in their field.[28] In addition, large, established firms have the option of entry through the acquisition of innovative and pioneering start-up companies: IBM, 3M, and Exxon have all used such toehold acquisitions as means of entering new areas of business.

Strategy Implementation in Emerging Industries: Creating the Conditions for Innovation

So far we have noted the importance and characteristics of technical change in emerging industries, identified the structural features of emerging industries, and explored some issues of timing, risk, and resources. However, if the primary source of competitive advantage in emerging and technology-based industries is innovation, what can we say about its fostering and management? The answer is: not very much. And the reason lies in the nature of innovation. Because innovation is based upon the production and application of new ideas. The sources of innovation are not as readily subject to diagnosis as, say, the sources of cost advantage. The essence of innovation is creativity, and one of the key features of creativity is its resistance to planning, particularly to hierarchical planning.

This is not to say that strategies in emerging industries cannot be formulated on a rational, analytic basis or that innovation should be immune to strategic planning. Once the firm has determined that the basis for competitive advantage in an industry is product and/or process technology, it faces critical questions:

- How is a technological advantage to be achieved?
- Which are the most promising technologies to pursue?
- What resources should be allocated to R&D?
- Should we be a pioneer or a follower?

The problem is that there is a huge gulf between answering these questions and actually achieving a position of competitive advantage in an emerging industry. Given that the outcomes of innovation in terms of the features of the products and process technologies are unknown at the time when

From strategy formulation to conditions for innovation

resources are committed to R&D – and there is no predetermined relationship between investment in R&D and the output of innovations – the productivity of investments in R&D are largely dependent upon the organizational conditions which foster innovation. Hence, the most crucial challenge facing firms in emerging and technology-based industries is: How does the firm create conditions which are conducive to innovation?

To answer this question we must return to the distinction between invention and innovation. Invention is dependent upon creativity. Creativity is not simply a matter of individual brilliance, it depends upon the organizational conditions which are conducive to the generation of ideas and imagination at the individual and group levels. Similarly innovation is not just a matter of acquiring the resources necessary for commercialization, innovation is a cooperative activity which requires interaction and collaboration between technology development, manufacturing, marketing, and various other functional departments within the firm.

The conditions for creativity

Invention has two primary ingredients: knowledge and creativity. Only by understanding the determinants of creativity, then fostering it through the appropriate organizational environment can the firm hope to successfully innovate. Creativity is an individual act which establishes a relationship between concepts or objects which had not previously been linked such that a new insight is provoked. Creative ideas are frequently triggered by accidents: an apple falling on Isaac Newton's head; James Watt observing a kettle boiling. Creativity also requires personal qualities. Research shows that creative people share certain personality traits: they are curious, imaginative, adventurous, assertive, playful, self-confident, risk-taking, reflective, and uninhibited.

Motivating creativity presents a further challenge. Creatively-orientated people are typically responsive to different incentives from those which are effective in motivating other members of the organization:

They desire to work in an egalitarian culture with enough space and resources to provide the opportunity to be spontaneous, experience freedom, and have fun in the performance of a task that, they feel, makes a difference to the strategic performance of the firm. Praise, recognition and opportunities for education and professional growth are also more important than assuming managerial responsibilities.[29]

Creativity is likely to be stimulated through interaction with other people. It has been estimated that engineers and applied scientists spend between half and three-quarters of their time communicating with others. Michael Tushman's research into communication in R&D laboratories concludes that developing communication networks is one of the most important aspects of the management of R&D.[30] An important catalyst to interaction is play. According to Fry and Saxberg, play creates an environment of inquiry, liberates thought from conventional constraints, and provides the opportunity to establish new relationships by rearranging ideas and structures at a safe distance from reality.[31] John Sculley describes Apple's attempts to create such an atmosphere of playfulness:

Almost every building had its own theme, so meeting and conference rooms aren't identified by cold, impersonal numbers. Instead they are named by employees who decide upon the theme of their building. In our "Land of Oz" building, the conference rooms are named Dorothy and Toto. Our Management Information Systems Group has meeting rooms named "Greed", "Envy", "Sloth", "Lust", and the remaining deadly sins. It's not an accident that many of these are the symbols of childhood (popcorn included). William Blake believed that in growing up, people move from states of innocence to experience, and then, if they're fortunate, to "higher innocence" – the most creative state of all.[32]

These conditions for creativity have far-reaching organizational implications. In particular, they point towards an organizational structure and organizational systems which are quite different from those appropriate to an organization which is orientated towards efficiency. Exhibit 9.4 contrasts some characteristics of the two types of organization.

Although innovation is stimulated by creative thought and accident, this does not imply that creativity should be unfocussed or undirected. Even at the invention stage, creativity must be directed toward need. The incentive for creativity is frequently the desire to solve problems. Few important inventions have been the result of spontaneous creative activity by technologists, almost all have resulted from grappling with practical problems. James Watt's conceptualization of an improved steam engine was triggered by repair work on an early Newcomen steam engine owned by Glasgow University. The basic inventions behind the xerox copying process were the work of Chester Carlson, a patent attorney who became frustrated by the problems of accurately copying technical drawings. The design for the Sony "Walkman" was stimulated by a Sony engineer watching Californian youngsters on roller skates. The stimulus provided by real-world problems explains my earlier observation that customers are the most fertile sources of innovation: it is customers who use products and services and who are consequently most closely in touch with the problems of matching existing products and services to their needs. The problem of "ivory tower" R&D departments is their isolation from outside stimulation. Thus, the poor innovatory performance of large corporate R&D departments may partly reflect the stultifying influence of bureaucracy on creativity, but it may also reflect the effect of large highly-structured organizations in isolating technologists and designers from the needs and problems of customers and manufacturing operations. Monsanto goes to great lengths to guide development teams towards areas with the greatest commercial potential. Monsanto's concern is to avoid what they term "trombone oil projects" – wonderfully innovative products for which the market is tiny. "Let them know you're in the research business not for the pursuit of knowledge but for the pursuit of product" says Monsanto CEO Richard Mahoney.[33]

Exhibit 9.4 The characteristics of "operating" and "innovating" organizations

	Operating organization	Innovating organization
Structure	Bureaucratic. Specialization and division of labor. Hierarchical control.	Flat organization without hierarchical control. Task orientated project teams.
Processes	Operating units controlled and coordinated by top management which undertakes strategic planning, capital allocation and operational planning.	Processes directed towards generation, selection, funding and development of ideas. Strategic planning flexible, financial and operating controls loose.
Reward systems	Financial compensation, promotion up the hierarchy, power and status symbols.	Autonomy, recognition, equity participation in new ventures.
People	Recruitment and selection based upon the needs of the organization structure for specific skills: functional and staff specialists, general managers, and operatives.	Key need is for idea generators who combine required technical knowledge with creative personality traits. Managers must act as sponsors and orchestrators.

Source: Based upon Jay R. Galbraith and Robert K. Kazanjian, *Strategy Implementation: Structure, Systems and Processes*, 2nd edn (West, St Paul, MN, 1986).

From invention to innovation: the need for coordination and leadership

Once a company moves from invention to innovation the additional resource requirements become substantially greater and more complex: in addition to creative ideas, innovation requires a product design and production equipment which permits cost-efficient manufacture, adaptation to customer preferences, marketing strategies which ensure a successful introduction of the product, and the establishment of distribution and customer-support facilities. The complex, multifunctional character of innovation poses awkward organizational problems. If different organizational arrangements are established between different functions as with, for example, a loosely-structured R&D department, and a more bureaucratically-structured production department, a high level of differentiation may inhibit the integration which is the essence of successful innovation.

The problem of corporate R&D departments located in geographically-separate facilities isolated from the stimulus of customer and organizational need has already been mentioned. A more damaging detriment of such isolation, however, may be the barriers which it presents to the transfer of ideas from research into marketable, manufacturable new products. Xerox Corporation's Palo Alto Research Center (PARC) was one of the most successful research centers in the US electronic industry responsible for important breakthroughs in custom chips, computer-aided design, artificial intelligence, computer graphics, and laser printing. Yet,

Xerox was able to exploit commercially only a small fraction of the output of PARC. The key problems were in the lack of coordination and cooperation between PARC and the rest of Xerox. PARC tended to initiate its own projects rather than work on problems which Xerox's operating divisions were experiencing, and the innovations which emerged from PARC either competed with some of Xerox's current products or lacked the leaders to take them to market. In the mid-1970s PARC developed an innovatory *Alto* computer, some of which were test-marketed, but the product was abandoned because it competed with another computer being developed by Xerox, the 8010 workstation. Subsequently, many of the innovations pioneered by PARC's computer group appeared in Apple's Lisa and Macintosh computers.[34]

An important reason for the failure to effectively commercialize the fruits of research may be resistance to new change which is inherent in virtually all organizations. Innovation is a source of change which upsets established organizational routines, imposes adjustment costs, increases the insecurity of organizational members, interferes with the pursuit of internal efficiency, and threatens established power positions. The more stable the administrative hierarchy, the greater is the resistance to innovation. Elting Morrison's analysis of the opposition by the US naval establishment to the remarkable improvements in gunnery accuracy made possible by continuous-aim firing provides a fascinating anatomy of organizational resistance to innovation.[35] The tendency for separate, R&D laboratories to be highly productive research units which contribute little to marketable innovation has been a feature of US and British industrial performance in a number of technologically-based industries. The consequence has been a general movement towards the integration of R&D within the corporation through the establishment of cross-functional product teams responsible for taking promising ideas from their conception through to the launching of new products on to the market. The team-orientated approach to product development is represented by Ford's development of its Taurus model (Case Note 9.1).

While team-based approaches to innovation are conducive to cross-functional coordination, the role of individual leadership in the innovation process must be recognized. The contribution of individual creativity to invention has already been discussed. Equally important is the role of the individual in driving the innovation process. Typically it is the individual's desire for the development of his or her idea which provides the most powerful motivating force for the successful commercialization of that idea. A general characteristic of companies that are consistently successful in innovation is that they capture and direct individuals' drive for success through offering some kind of entrepreneurial role to these "product champions". Given the propensity of organizations to resist change, innovations need the leadership by committed enthusiasts in order to overcome the organization's vested interest in stability and the status quo. Schon's study of 15 major innovations concluded that, "the new idea either finds

Case Note 9.1   Product development at Ford: from a sequential to a team approach

The sequential approach: pre-Taurus
Designers designed a car on paper, then gave it to the engineers, who figured out how to make it. Their plans were passed on to the manufacturing and purchasing people ... The next step in the process was the production plant. Then came marketing, the legal and service departments, and finally the customers. If a glitch developed, the car was bumped back to the design stage for changes. The farther along in the sequence, however, the more difficult it was to make changes.

The team approach: the Taurus
With Taurus ... we brought all disciplines together, and did the whole process simultaneously as well as sequen-

tially. The manufacturing people worked with the design people, engineering people, sales and purchasing, legal, service and marketing.

In sales and marketing we had dealers come in and tell us what they wanted in a car to make it more user-friendly ... We had insurance companies – Allstate, State Farm, American Road tell us how to design a car so when accidents occur it would minimize the customer's expense in fixing it ... We went to all stamping plants, assembly plants and put layouts on the walls. We asked them how to make it easier to build ... It's amazing the dedication and commitment you can get from people.

Source: Taurus project leader, Veraldi. Quoted by Mary Walton, *The Deming Management Method* (Dodd, Mead, New York (1968), pp. 130–1).

a champion or dies".[36] This vital role of the product champion (or in their terminology, the "business innovator") was confirmed by the SAPPHO project's comparative analysis of 43 pairs of successful and unsuccessful innovation.[37]

A prominent example of the role of product champions in leading team efforts to develop new products in a large, mature organization is provided by 3M Corporation. Case Note 9.2 outlines 3M's approach to conceiving, developing and marketing new products.

The Management of Transition in Emerging Industries

Changes in the competitive environment

One of the most difficult aspects of strategic management in emerging industries is managing transition as the industry moves from its introduction into its growth phase. During the introduction phase the tasks of management are clearly defined: the firm must develop the product or process, it must work, and the mechanisms for supplying it to the customer must be established. Once technology and design becomes more clearly defined, once a market for its product is established and market penetration begins to accelerate, changes in competition ensue and changes in strategy are called for.

During the introductory phase, the basis of competitive advantage was innovation. Strategy formulation was concerned primarily with selection and development of technologies and the launching of new products. The key issue for strategy implementation was establishing an organizational environment conducive to innovation. During the growth stage, technological change continues to be rapid, but its character changes. Competition between divergent technologies declines as inferior approaches are eliminated and both technology and product design converge towards an

Case Note 9.2 Innovation at 3M: the role of the product champion

"Start little and build"

We don't look to the president, or the vice-president for R&D to say, all right now, Monday morning 3M is going to get into such-and-such a business. Rather, we prefer to see someone in one of our laboratories, or marketing or manufacturing, or new products bring forward a new idea that he's been thinking about. Then, when he can convince people around him, including his supervisor, that he's got something interesting, we'll make him what we call a 'project manager' with a small budget of money and talent, and let him run with it.

In short, we'd rather have the idea for a new business come from the bottom up than from the top down. Throughout all our 60 years of history here, that has been the mark of success. Did you develop a new business? The incentive? Money. Of course. But that is not the key. The key ... is becoming the general manager of a new business ... having such a hot project that management just has to become involved whether it wants to or not.

(Bob Adams, vice president for R&D, 3M Corporation)

Scotchlite

Someone asked the question, "Why didn't 3M make glass beads, because glass beads were going to find increasing use on the highways? ... I had done a little work in the mineral department on trying to color glass beads we'd imported from Czechoslovakia and had learned a little about their reflecting properties. And, as a little extra-curricular activity, I'd been trying to make luminous house numbers — and maybe luminous signs as well — by developing luminous pigments.

Well, this question and my free-time lab project combined to stimulate me to search out where glass beads were being used on the highway. We found a place where beads had been sprinkled on the highway and we saw that they did provide a more visible line at night ... From there, it was only natural for us to conclude that, since we were a coating company, and probably knew more than anyone else about putting particles onto a web than anybody, we ought to be able to coat glass beads very accurately on a piece of paper.

So, that's what we did. The first reflective tape we made was simply a double-coated tape — glass beads sprinkled on one side and an adhesive on the other. We took some out here in St Paul and, with the cooperation of the highway department, put some down. After the first frost came, and then a thaw, we found we didn't know as much about adhesives under all weather conditions as we thought ...

We looked around inside the company for skills in related areas. We tapped knowledge that existed in our sandpaper business on how to make waterproof sandpaper. We drew on the expertise of our roofing people who knew something about exposure. We reached into our adhesive and tape division to see how we could make the tape stick to the highway better.

The resulting product became known as "Scotchlite", its principal application was in reflective signs; only later did 3M develop the market for highway marking. The originator of the product, Harry Heltzer, interested the head of the New Products Division in the product, and encouraged Heltzer to go out and sell it. Scotchlite was a success and Heltzer became the general manager of the division set up to produce and market it. Heltzer later went on to become 3M's president.

Source: "The technical strategy of 3M: start more little businesses and more little businesses", *Innovation* 5 (1969).

industry standard. This places some constraints upon the scope of product innovation, while simultaneously increasing the demand for process innovation to improve manufacturing productivity and improve quality.

Development of the market also has the effect of broadening the basis of competitive advantage. As price and reliability become increasingly important purchase criteria, efficient manufacture with effective quality control becomes necessary. As markets expand, establishing a strong position in distribution channels becomes necessary. The need to invest in manufacturing capacity, distribution, and brand awareness, while continuing to innovate, greatly increases firms' resource requirements during the growth phase. Increased financial needs can be a key factor precipitating a "shake-out" in an emerging industry. Increasing concentration in the personal computer industry between 1983 and 1985 was primarily due to the pressure imposed on smaller firms by the need to establish brand awareness and distribution. Additional resource needs extend beyond financial requirements: the development of functions other than research and development require additional skills, particularly management skills.

The implications for organizational change

The need for the firm to balance innovation with efficiency, and the increasingly differentiated managerial and organizational requirements of the different functions within the firm impose heavy adjustment pressures upon the firm. During the introductory phase the firm can exist in a purely entrepreneurial form where the entrepreneur-technologist can act both as technical and the business leader, and the firm can prosper as an organic, informal group of creative and cooperative individuals. Lack of formal controls or organization structure are possible because of the shared values of organizational members, personal loyalty to the company founder, and, frequently, through equity participation in the venture.

As the firm and the industry develop, management becomes increasingly complex. There are several important issues which transition from introductory to growth phases raises for management concerning:

- the need for cost efficiency;
- organizational structure;
- the R&D agenda.

At the production level there is pressure for cost efficiency which encourages standardization of products and design, establishment of scale efficient production units, and the quest for process innovation. All are likely to result in greater formalization of production systems. Hayes and Wheelwright observe a shift from "job shop" production methods, to batch-flow production, and subsequently to assembly-line production.[38]

In terms of organizational structure, growing firm size and the increasing importance of manufacturing, marketing, and distribution functions encourages the establishment of a functional company structure. However, within the more structured organization, the close interfunctional co-operation which is a prerequisite for successful innovation must be maintained. Product development requires that problem-solving takes place at the operational level through cooperation across functional boundaries without directly involving the managerial hierarchy. Such lateral cooperation can occur through loosely defined teams and project groups, or, more formally, through a matrix structure.

The research and development agenda also changes. Once the firm has successfully established itself with an innovatory product or process, it must then maintain its position through a stream of innovations over time, where later innovations build upon the firm's technological base and strengthen the competitive position of the company within its existing markets. The R&D priorities shift from novelty and the quest for discontinuous performance leaps towards dependability, design modification, and cost efficiency. Ensuring that new product development is in the right direction and that it meets the requirements of customers and the manufacturing system requires that the innovation process is closely integrated within overall strategy formulation.

The implications for top management are daunting:

the organization enters a leadership crisis. Entrepreneurial control through informal communication is no longer adequate because of the growing number of employees, most of whom do not have an equity stake in the company. The trappings of a functional organizational structure must now be introduced which include: establishment of functional areas with specialists and professionals, accounting systems for inventory and purchasing, incentives, budgets, work standards and some form of hierarchy.[39]

Typically, the new demands on management necessitate changes in the top management team. This may mean augmenting top management with seasoned executives from other companies; it may require a chief executive with a different repertoire of skills. The replacement of Steve Jobs by John Sculley as Chairman of Apple Computer in 1984 was an example of this process.

The discussion so far has identified technology-based business strategies with young firms in emerging industries. Yet, as we observed early on, technology-based competition is also a feature of long-established industries, and, even in industries where technological development has slowed to snail's pace, innovation still has the potential to revitalize the competitive process, as with steel and textiles. Moreover, firms in mature industries frequently seek to maintain their growth momentum by diversifying into newly-emerging growth industries.

Managing innovation in the mature corporation

The management of innovation poses particular problems of differentiation and integration for such mature corporations. In certain functions and certain product areas, the firm needs to pursue efficiency through a bureaucratic structure with rigorous financial and operational controls, while, in developing new products and revitalizing established products, it needs to foster creativity. Fry and Saxeberg argue that it is corporations which attempt to innovate while simultaneously operating in mature and emerging business sectors which experience most strongly "the innovation paradox", the conflict between creativity and bureaucratic control.[40]

Different firms have established different approaches in responding to this diversity of organizational needs. The 3M Corporation represents one approach to the problem of reconciling creativity and operational efficiency within the mature organization. The essence of 3M's system is a duality which runs through the organization and through each employee's activities. The organization is orientated towards the management of 3M's existing activities, yet all employees are encouraged to look beyond their formal duties for opportunities to develop new products and new business ideas. Employees have the opportunity to "bootleg" time, equipment, and materials to pursue their own pet projects, and are encouraged to do so by the rewards which are given for successfully developing new businesses. These include career advancement, the recognition and creative satisfaction associated with initiating a new business, and attractive financial rewards.

Other established companies have sought to separate their mature businesses from those which are in their innovatory stages and apply very different organization structures and systems to each. Many large, mature industrial enterprises have created new venture divisions which become reservations where creativity and innovation can take place in an entrepreneurial context removed from the stifling influence of the corporate bureaucracy. Such new venture divisions typically have a two-way relationship with the more mature operating divisions. Innovations and ideas initiated within the mature divisions can be nurtured and developed in the new venture division, and innovations in the new venture division may have spinoffs for the more established businesses. Few major corporations have achieved significant commercial or innovative success through such new venture divisions. During the 1970s almost all the major oil companies established new venture divisions to create new business areas for the companies, but almost no sizeable, profitable new businesses have grown out of these initiatives.[41]

Summary

The central feature of emerging industries is the role of innovation as the basis for competition and as the determinant of industry evolution. For this reason this chapter groups industries which are in the early stages of their life cycles with those industries in which technology continues to be the primary basis of competition. As a result, the primary strategic issues in these industries concern the management of technology.

At a general level, strategy-making in technology-orientated industries is no different from other industries: the basic requirements are an intimate understanding of the nature of competition and the requirements for success in the industry, together with identification of the particular strengths and weaknesses of the enterprise. However, the peculiar properties of innovation in terms of the determinants of success in technology-based competition and the characteristics of technological-competence give rise to particularly complex issues.

A fundamental problem of strategy formulation in technology-based industries concerns difficulties of forecasting technological change, market conditions, and the evolution of industry structure. While certain generic trends are evident in terms of the shift from discontinuous to incremental product innovation and the transition from product and process innovation, the essence of the competitive process in these industries is one of "creative destruction" where forecasting is extremely hazardous. The inherent volatility and unpredictability of technological competition plays havoc with traditional approaches to strategic planning. In contrast to technologically-stable environments, where the ability to make realistic medium-term forecasts permits the detailed planning of resource allocation and product introduction, strategy formulation in fast-moving industries must concern itself with developing vision and imagination which can be used to establish a sense of direction of the company. The ability to combine consistency of direction with the alertness, responsiveness, and flexibility to take advantage of technological uncertainty and market turbulence are the keys to competitive advantage in emerging and technology-based industries.

At the same time long-term strategic investment decisions must be made. In some areas of technology the time horizons are long. In pharmaceuticals the time-span between initial research and product introduction is typically a decade; while at the frontiers of research, in superconductivity for example, the outcomes of research are unknown. This combination of environmental turbulence together with the need for long-term investment means that risk management lies at the heart of successful strategies in emerging and technology-based industries. One advantage of large firms is their ability to hedge their technological bets: at this level technology strategy may be viewed as the management of a portfolio of options on a number of risky technological opportunities.

Timing is critical: should a firm be a pioneer or a fast-follower? Analysis of the characteristics of the innovation in terms of the ability to appropriate the returns to innovation, the role of complementary resources, and the firm's ability to influence industry standards can guide timing.

These questions raise complex issues in terms of resource requirements. Resource requirements of the firm vary substantially between stages of the innovation process and the different types of technology. More important, however, to the ultimate success of companies in the industry environment is not the resources which a firm has access to, but its ability to integrate and motivate those resources in order to exploit their inherent potential for innovation. If innovation is the basic determinant of success in emerging and technology-based industries, the primary role of strategy is to create the conditions for innovation. Yet here lies the most daunting challenge for management: How can a company create the organizational conditions conducive to innovation while planning the course of the company's development? As John Sculley of Apple has observed: "Management and creativity might even be considered antithetical states. While management demands consensus, control, certainty, and the status quo, creativity thrives on the opposite: instinct, uncertainty, freedom, and iconoclasm."[42]

Fortunately, the experiences of companies such as Apple, 3M, Sony, Merck, and Honda point to solutions towards these dilemmas. The need for innovation to reconcile individual creativity with coordination points towards advantages of cross-functional team-based approaches rather than the isolation of research and development in a separate "creative" environment. The need to reconcile innovation with efficiency points towards the advantage of parallel organizational structures where, in addition to the "formal" structure geared to the needs of existing businesses and products, an informal structure exists which is the source of new products and businesses. The role of top management in balancing creativity with order and innovation with efficiency becomes critical. The success of Japanese and West German companies in the management of technology in several electronics and engineering-based industries compared to the propensity of many US and British companies both to invest in what later proves to be the wrong technological solution and to fail in the commercialization of technology may reflect the greater level of technological training and awareness among Japanese and German senior management than is typical in the US and Britain.

With the increasing pace of technological change and the intensification of international competition, the demands upon Western European and American companies for improved innovative performance will continue to increase. The challenge to mature industries in Europe and North America from low-cost production in the newly-industrializing parts of the world, implies that advanced industrialized nationals must increasingly rely upon their advantages in new and technology-based industries. But here the technological leadership of North American and European companies is being lost to Japanese companies, while companies in Singapore and South Korea increasingly narrow the gap. We shall explore aspects of these competitive issues in the next two chapters.

Notes

1. William J. Abernathy and James M. Utterback, "Patterns of technological innovation," *Technology Review* 80 (1978), pp. 40–7; and James M. Utterback and William J. Abernathy, "A dynamic model of product and process innovation," *Omega* 3 (1975), pp. 639–56.
2. Richard S. Rosenbloom and Michael A. Cusumano, "Technological pioneering and competitive advantage: the birth of the VCR industry," *California Management Review* 29 (4) (1987), pp. 51–76.
3. Stephen Jay Gould, "The Panda's thumb of technology," *Natural History* 96 (1) (1986), pp. 12–27.
4. William J. Abernathy and James M. Utterback, "Patterns of industrial innovation", in Michael Tushman and William Moore (eds), *Readings in the Management of Innovation*, 2nd edn (Ballinger, Cambridge, Mass., 1988), pp. 29–30.
5. "Bic and the heirs of ball-point builder are no pen pals," *Wall Street Journal*, May 27, 1988, pp. 1 and 27.
6. Jeffrey R. Williams, *The Productivity Base of Industries* (Carnegie-Mellon University, 1984), p. 19A.
7. Robert F. Hartley, *Management Mistakes*, 2nd edn (John Wiley, New York, 1986), pp. 56–66.
8. C.A.R. McNulty, "Scenario development for corporate planning," *Futures* 9, April 1977, pp. 128–38.

9. For an outline of Shell's approach see: J. P. Leemhuis (Corporate Planning Manager, Shell Netherlands), "Using scenarios to develop strategies," *Long Range Planning* 18 (1985), pp. 30–7; Pierre Wack, "Scenarios: uncharted waters ahead," *Harvard Business Review*, September–October 1985, p. 72 and "Scenarios: shooting the rapids," *Harvard Business Review*, November–December 1985, p. 139; Arie de Geus (Shell Head of Planning) "Planning as learning," *Harvard Business Review*, March–April 1988, pp. 70–4.

10. The classic example of group decisions leading to an undesirable and irrational outcome is the "Abilene paradox". See Jerry Harvey, "Managing agreement in organizations: the Abilene paradox," *Organizational Dynamics*, Summer 1974, pp. 63–80.

11. For a discussion of techniques of technological forecasting, see B. C. Twiss, *Managing Technological Innovation*, 2nd edn (Longman, New York, 1980).

12. Richard N. Foster, "Timing technological transitions," in Tushman and Moore (eds), *Readings in the Management of Innovation*, pp. 215–28.

13. Robert D. Buzzell and Bradley T. Gale, *The PIMS Principles* (Free Press, New York, 1987), p. 274.

14. Dennis C. Mueller, *Profits in the Long Run* (Cambridge University Press, Cambridge, 1986), pp. 111–42.

15. R. C. Levin, A. K. Klevorick, R. R. Nelson, and S. G. Winter, "Appropriating the returns from industrial research and development," *Brookings Papers on Economic Activity* (1987), pp. 783–820.

16. For a discussion of the role of complementary resources see David J. Teece, "Capturing the value from technological innovation: integration, strategic partnering, and licensing decisions," *Interfaces* 18 (3) (1988), pp. 46–61.

17. D. J. Teece, "Profiting from technological innovation: implications for integration, collaboration, licencing and public policy," in D. J. Teece (ed.), *The Competitive Challenge: Strategies for Industrial Innovation and Renewal* (Ballinger, Cambridge, Mass., 1987), pp. 185–219.

18. Jacques Pelkmans and Rita Beuter, "Standardization and competitiveness: private and public strategies in the EC color TV industry," in H. Landis Gabel (ed.), *Product Standardization and Competitive Strategy* (Elsevier, Amsterdam, 1987), pp. 135–52.

19. R. A. von Hippel, "Lead users: a source of novel product concepts," *Management Science* (1986), pp. 791–805.

20. E. A. von Hippel, "Users as innovators," *Technology Review* 5 (1976), pp. 212–39.

21. M. J. Peck, *Competition in the Aluminum Industry* (Harvard University Press, Cambridge, Mass., 1961).

22. Tom Peters, *Thriving on Chaos* (Knopf, New York, 1987), pp. 259–66.

23. Richard T. Pascale, *Honda (B)*, Harvard Business School, Case No. 384–050, pp. 5–6.

24. John Scully, *Odyssey* (Fitzhenry and Whiteside, Toronto, 1987), pp. 323–59.

25. C. Freeman, *The Economics of Industrial Innovation* (Penguin, Harmondsworth, 1974).

26. J. Jewkes et al., *The Sources of Invention*, 2nd edn, (Macmillan, London, 1969).

27. D. Hamberg, *Essays in the Economics of Research and Development* (Wiley, New York, 1966).

28. Ralph Katz and Thomas J. Allen, "Investigating the not-invented-here (NIH)

syndrome: a look at the performance, tenure, and communication patterns of 50 R&D project groups," *R&D Management* 12 (1) (1982), pp. 7–19.

29. Louis W. Fry and Borje O. Saxberg, "Homo Ludens: playing man and creativity in innovating organizations," (Discussion Paper, Department of Management and Organization, University of Washington, 1987).

30. Michael L. Tushman, "Managing communication networks in R&D laboratories," *Sloan Management Review*, Winter 1979, pp. 37–49.

31. Fry and Saxberg, "Homo Ludens," p. 9.

32. John Sculley, *Odyssey*, pp. 187–8.

33. "The innovators," *Fortune*, June 6, 1988, p. 52.

34. "The lab that ran away from Xerox," *Fortune*, September 5, 1983, pp. 76–83.

35. Elting Morrison, "Gunfire at sea: a case study of innovation," in Tushman and Moore *Readings in the Management of Innovation*, pp. 165–78.

36. D. A. Schon, "Champions for radical new inventions," *Harvard Business Review*, March–April 1963, p. 84.

37. R. Rothwell et al., "SAPPHO updated – project SAPPHO phase II," *Research Policy* 3 (1974), pp. 258–91.

38. Robert H. Hayes and Stephen C. Wheelwright, *Restoring our Competitive Advantage*, (John Wiley, New York, 1984), ch. 4.

39. Louis W. Fry and Borje O. Saxberg, "Homo Ludens: playing man and creativity in innovating organizations," (Discussion Paper, Department of Management and Organization, University of Washington, 1987), pp. 19–20.

40. Ibid., pp. 21–2.

41. R. M. Grant, *Strategy Adjustment to Environmental Change among the World's Largest Oil Companies, 1970–86* (Discussion paper, Cal Poly, 1988, available from the author).

42. John Sculley, *Odyssey*, p. 184.

TEN

Strategy Formulation and Implementation in Mature Industries

We are a true "penny profit" business. That means that it takes hard work and attention to detail to be financially successful – it is far from being a sure thing. Our store managers must do two things well: control costs and increase sales. Cost control cannot be done by compromising product quality, customer service, or restaurant cleanliness, but rather by consistent monitoring of the "vital signs" of the business through observation, reports, and analysis. Portion control is a critical part of our business. For example, each Filet-O-Fish sandwich receives 1 fluid ounce of tartar sauce and 0.5 ounce of cheese. Our raw materials are fabricated to exacting tolerances, and our managers check them on an ongoing basis. Our written specification for lettuce is over two typewritten pages long. Our french fries must meet standards for potato type, solid and moisture content, and distribution of strand lengths.

Edward H. Rensi, President and Chief Operating Officer, McDonald's USA[1]

Outline

Introduction

The Characteristics of Mature Industries

Competitive Advantage in Mature Industries

    Cost advantage and its sources

    Segment and customer selection

    The quest for differentiation

    The role of innovation in mature industries

Strategy Implementation in Mature Industries: Structure, Systems, and Style

    Efficiency through bureaucracy

    The bureaucratic model in decline

Special Features of Strategy Formulation in Declining Industries

    The adjustment of capacity to declining demand

    The nature of demand

    Strategy options in declining industries

Summary

Introduction

Despite the technological revolutions that have spawned new industries such as aerospace, petrochemicals, computers, and consumer electronics, the greater part of output and employment in the advanced industrialized countries continues to be located within industries which can be broadly described as mature. Exhibit 10.1 classifies US industries into two groups: those which in terms of age and low level of technological intensity can be described as "mature"; and those whose origins are more recent or which are subject to rapid technological change. At first sight, these mature industries are a heterogeneous group which appear to have little in common. Yet, from a strategy viewpoint, they present several similarities. In this chapter we shall examine the characteristics of mature industries, the strategies which are likely to be successful in establishing competitive advantage, and the implications of these strategies for resources, organizational structure and management style. We shall also investigate the potential for the regeneration of mature industries through innovation and new-game strategies.

Exhibit 10.1 The importance of mature industries in the US economy in 1986

	SHARE OF GNP		
Mature industries	(%)	Emerging and technology-based industries	(%)
Agriculture, forestry, fishing	2.3	Electrical & electronic equipment	2.0
Mining	3.1	Aerospace	1.3
Construction	4.6	Instruments	0.7
Lumber, wood products, & furniture	0.9	Chemicals & allied products	1.7
Stone, clay & glass products	0.6	Plastic & rubber products	0.6
Primary metal products	0.9	Air transportation	0.7
Fabricated metal products	1.4	Communications	2.3
Non-electrical machinery	2.4	Leisure & personal services	2.4
Motor vehicles & parts	1.3	Business & professional services	5.2
Food, drink & tobacco	2.1	Health services	4.6
Textiles, clothing, leather	0.8	Education services	0.6
Paper, printing, publishing	2.2		
Petroleum & coal products	0.8		
Land & sea transportation	2.9		
Public utilities	3.1		
Wholesale & retail trade	16.5		
Financial services	15.8		
Other services	3.3		
Government	12.1		
Total	77.1		22.1

Source: *US Bureau of Economic Analysis Survey of Current Business* (Dept of Commerce, Washington D.C., December 1987).

The Characteristics of Mature Industries

The principal features of mature industries were identified in chapter 8 in our discussion of the industry life-cycle. There are two main sources of the structural changes which occur during maturity:

- accumulation and diffusion of knowledge;
- slowing of industry growth.

Accumulation and diffusion of knowledge accompanies maturity. On the demand side, customers are experienced. They are informed as to the performance characteristics of rival manufacturers' products, they are clearer as to their preferences and requirements, they are better able to judge value for money. On the supply side, producers have acquired substantial experience, opportunities for innovation are more scarce and less dramatic, and technology is well-diffused among industry members such that no firm has an unassailable technological advantage.

Slowing of industry growth occurs as market penetration increases. As a result excess capacity frequently emerges during maturity.

The principal consequences of these changes for industry structure and competition are summarized in Exhibit 10.2. For the most part these

Exhibit 10.2 The characteristics of mature industries

BASIC CONDITIONS INDUSTRY STRUCTURE COMPETITION

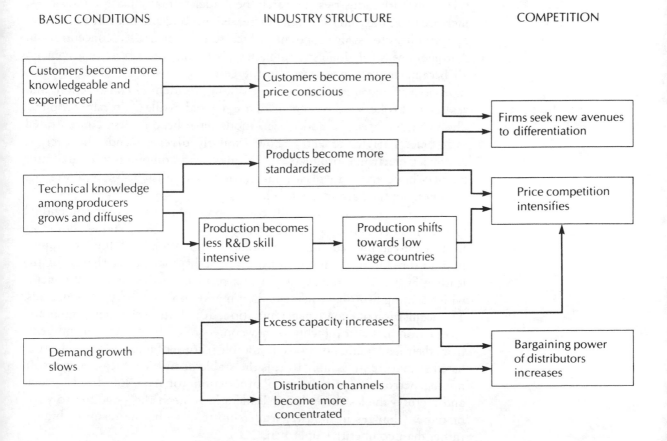

Exhibit 10.3   Average
return on invested
capital (ROI) earned by
firms over the life-
cycle and with different
growth rates

	Real rate of growth (%)		
	< 3	3–6	> 6
Growth	22.8	24.4	24.3
Maturity	21.7	22.0	24.1
Decline	16.4	22.3	

These results are for 6,600 business units on the PIMS data base over a four-year period.
Source: Robert D. Buzzell and Bradley T. Gale, *The PIMS Principles* (Free Press, New York, 1987), p. 58.

changes involve not only a difficult period of adjustment but a deterioration in industry attractiveness. Typically, mature industries are difficult environments in which to compete. Not only does the range of competitive weapons available decline as products become more standardized, but the intensity of competition increases as excess capacity, international trade, and substitution by customers increase. As a consequence profitability tends to fall during maturity. Exhibit 10.3 shows the profitability of businesses at different stages of the life-cycle and experiencing different rates of growth.

Beyond these basic commonalities, few generalizations about the structure of mature industries can safely be made. In many mature industries, increased capital intensity and increased product standardization offer opportunities for scale economies which result in increased concentration. Automobiles, steel, domestic appliances, banking, and advertising agencies all became more concentrated in the course of maturity. However, this trend is far from universal. Shoes, clothing, residential construction, and real-estate brokerage have remained fragmented, while plain-paper copiers, phonographic records, and frozen foods have become less concentrated over time. Barriers to entry show similarly diverse trends. In aircraft, consumer electronic products, soft drinks, and computer software entry barriers have risen. In plastic fabrication, specialist beers, and strategy consulting entry barriers have fallen.

Maturity in an industry usually corresponds to maturity of the individual firms. The membership of a mature industry tends to be stable with most firms long-established. Lack of radical innovation and limited opportunities for differentiation also lead to stability of market shares for the leading firms. This stability is partly a product of the heavy investments which leading firms have made in their market positions over long periods. The acquisition of experience, reputation, distribution channels, and brand recognition makes it difficult for newcomers to easily dislodge incumbents from their leadership positions. A notable feature of many of the industries listed as mature in Exhibit 10.1, is the stable positions of leading firms. In mining, petroleum, primary metal production, tobacco, soft drinks, paper, and motor vehicles the industry leaders have been the same for 50 years or more. Changes in industry leadership tend to be the result of merger rather than competitive upheaval.

Probably the most important threat to the market positions of established firms in mature industries is international competition. The US steel, automobile, construction machinery, and banking industries were comfortably-sheltered, stable oligopolies until the emergence of international competition. The entry of aggressive overseas competitors, often with substantial cost advantages has transformed competition in these industries. The existence of international trade in a product or service is probably the most important factor determining the intensity and volatility of competition within a mature industry. The lack of international trade in bricks, ice cream, hotels, newspapers, and car rental eliminates a major source of competition and instability. But even these industries are not insulated from international competition. During the 1980s all these industries experienced increasing competition as a result of the multinational expansion of US, European, and Japanese firms.

Competitive Advantage in Mature Industries

The stability of mature industries and the tendency for them to become dominated by a few large companies means that many of them correspond to what Jeffrey Williams describes as "traditional industrial markets." These are industries whose stability distinguishes them from innovation-driven "Schumpeterian markets." Strategies in these industries are strongly influenced by deeply-ingrained views on the benefits of size:

Generally, these businesses succeed through approaches to the customer which are strengthened by economies of scale. They emphasize high volume, long production runs, mass market advertising, and large-scale distribution and service. Success is often measured through a sustainable low cost position or long-lived brand loyalty.[2]

Yet, despite the apparent stability of market leaders in mature industries, closer analysis suggests that positions of competitive advantage in mature industries are vulnerable as a result of:

- increased buyer knowledge, product standardization, and limited potential for product innovation reduces opportunities for differentiation;
- diffusion of technology means that cost advantages through superior process technology or more advanced capital equipment methods are difficult to obtain and near-impossible to sustain;
- a highly-developed industry infrastructure together with the presence of powerful distributors makes it easier for new or established firms to attack firms which have highly-differentiated market positions or strong positions in particular segments;
- where products are internationally traded, cost advantage is vulnerable to adverse movements in exchange rates or the emergence of competitors located in low-wage countries.

Given these apparently unfavorable conditions for competitive advantage, let us go on to examine some of the principal means by which companies in mature industries can achieve positions of superior profitability.

Cost advantage and its sources

Because maturity has been associated with increased product standardization, conventional strategy analysis has emphasized low cost as the primary basis for competitive advantage in mature environments. Primary sources of cost advantage in mature industries are likely to include:

- experience curve effects;
- economies of scale;
- low-cost inputs;
- high levels of operational efficiency.

Experience curve effects   Research shows that experience effects occur not only in the early phases of industry evolution, but continue into maturity. In rayon fiber, denim jeans, monochrome TVs, and portable radios, substantial annual reductions in real unit costs were experienced several decades after the introduction of these products (see Exhibit 8.5). While experience curve advantages have accrued to large established firms in mature industries, to exploit economies of experience by increasing production volume is made difficult by the low growth in demand typical of mature industries. Hence, firms are obliged to seek volume growth through increased market share. In automobiles, the growth of Ford's share of both North American and European markets during the 1970s and 1980s greatly assisted its program of cost reduction.

Economies of scale   In industries which are capital intensive, or where advertising, distribution, or new product development are important elements of total cost, economies of scale are likely to be important sources of interfirm cost differences. The increased standardization that accompanies maturity greatly assists the exploitation of such scale economies. The significance of scale economies in mature industries is indicated by the fact that the association between ROI and market share is stronger in mature industries than in emerging industries.[3]

Low-cost inputs   Where small competitors are successful in undercutting the prices of market leaders in mature industries, it is frequently as a result of their access to low-cost inputs. Established firms can become locked into high-cost positions through unionization of their work forces or through inertia. The decline in the market shares of the US steel majors since the 1960s is partly the result of union agreements over wages, benefits, and working practices which guaranteed high-cost production. During the 1970s and 1980s they steadily lost ground to overseas suppliers and domestic minimills, both of which operated with substantially lower labor costs. Recent entrants into mature industries may gain cost advantages through acquiring plant and equipment at bargain-basement levels. ConAgra is adept at acquiring businesses during the troughs of their industry cycles. It purchased Armor from Greyhound in 1983 when the whole red-meat industry was in recession.[4] United States banks' acquisition of financially-troubled savings and loan institutions during 1988–90 provided a low-cost avenue to retail expansion.

High levels of operational efficiency When scale economies are relatively unimportant and technology is well-diffused, operational efficiency in terms of low overheads, closely-controlled working capital, and effective utilization of production employees is likely to be the key source of cost advantage. As was discussed in chapter 6, there is a wealth of empirical evidence that some of the most dramatic improvements in cost efficiency have little to do with capital investment or new process technology, but are the result of improved management and more highly-motivated employees. The resurgence of British Steel vividly illustrates the scale of the cost reductions which can be obtained through the pruning of overheads, capacity rationalization, and the abandonment of restrictive working practices (see Case Note 10.1). Inefficiency in mature firms can be pervasive and institutionalized. Its elimination then requires shock treatment in the form of a threat to the existence of the firm, or a change in management through acquisition. The trauma of competition which accompanied airline deregulation in the US was followed by an avalanche of cost-cutting measures. The most profitable US airlines during the late 1980s were those which had been most effective in cutting costs.[5] The British conglomerate Hanson is adept at cutting costs in its acquired businesses. At Ever Ready Batteries, Imperial Group, SCM, Kidde, and a host of other acquisitions Hanson has cut the number of employees by an average of 25 percent, slashed overheads, and adopted strict financial controls.[6]

The effectiveness of cost efficiency in improving profit performance in mature industries was supported by research into performance turnarounds among mature businesses. Hambrick and Schecter's study of US businesses which had experienced sharp improvements in ROI over a four-year period identified three successful turnaround strategies (see Exhibit 10.4). The importance of cost reduction is confirmed by Peter Grinyer's study of sharp, sustained performance improvements by a sample of British companies (most of which were long-established companies in mature industries). Apart from changes in management, the factor which most frequently distinguished the "sharpbenders" from the control group of companies was the intensive efforts by the former to reduce production costs.[7]

Case Note 10.1   Cost reduction and regeneration at British Steel

The history of the British Steel Corporation from its nationalization in 1967 up until 1980 is a case history in the failure of public enterprise. In an effort to achieve the productivity gains experienced by Japanese companies, the Corporation tried to exploit scale economies by investing in large-scale integrated iron and steel plants. Between 1970 and 1979 BSC invested more heavily in new plant than almost any other steel company in the world. The results were disappointing to say the least. Output per worker scarcely changed over the period and labor productivity in the British steel industry remained about half that of West Germany and nearly one-third that of the United States. Inefficiency and inept management characterized all levels of the organization. At senior management level, strategies were based upon wildly optimistic forecasts of the growth of world steel demand. At the operating level, inefficiency and inflexibility became institutionalized in wasteful manning agreements and a host of restrictive working practices. The power of the steel unions ensured the continued operation of a number of small, outdated, and poorly located plants. Between 1967 and 1980, public expenditure on BSC in terms of capital investment, operating losses and other forms of support totalled over $15 billion.

After the election of Mrs Thatcher's Conservative Government in 1979 and in the face of mounting financial losses, a program of capacity and cost reduction was adopted and Mr Ian McGregor was hired as BSC's new chairman from the New York investment bank Lazard Freres. Between 1980 and 1984 BSC underwent a revolution. Plant capacity was cut ruthlessly and new investment was almost halted. Working practices were reorganized with lower manning levels, increased job flexibility, and increased worker involvement in plant management and setting production targets. Heavy redundancies among managerial and support staff were implemented. The workforce was cut from 210,000 in 1976, to 81,000 in 1983, and to 53,000 in 1988. Several layers of management hierarchy were eliminated and, at the same time, decision making was devolved to plant level. Simplified, quantitative, performance targets were introduced throughout the Corporation. The results were outstanding. In the two years between mid-1980 and mid-1982 labor productivity rose 40 percent and energy consumption per ton of steel fell 13 percent. By 1987 it required five man-hours to produce a ton of steel compared to 14.5 in 1980. The turnaround in BSC's financial performance is shown below. By 1987 BSC was one of the world's most profitable steel companies. Most remarkable was the emergence of BSC as one of the lowest cost producers of steel in the world with costs per ton of steel lower than the average for firms in US, Japan, Germany, and even Korea and Brazil.

British steel's financial performance

	Pretax profit/(loss)	Sales
1980	($3,174m.)	$5,576m.
1981	($1,811m.)	$5,290m.
1982	($822m.)	$6,168m.
1983	($1,553m.)	$5,792m.
1984	($411m.)	$6,025m.
1985	($679m.)	$6,706m.
1986	$75m.	$6,706m.
1987	$317m.	$6,204m.
1988	$751m.	$7,387m.

British steel's relative costs per ton of steel

	Labor	Materials	Finance	Total ($)
BSC	110	280	25	415
US	156	274	40	470
Germany	173	295	45	513
Japan	170	190	95	555
Korea	54	265	100	419

Sources: Jonathan Aylen, *International Competitiveness and Industrial Regeneration: the Case of British Steel,* mimeo (Salford University, 1983); *Sunday Times* (of London), September 4, 1988, p. D1; *Wall Street Journal,* November 16, 1988, p. A14.

Strategy type	Principal features
Asset and cost surgery	Aggressive cost reduction through reduction of excess capacity, halting of new investment in plant and equipment, and cutbacks in R&D, marketing expenditures, receivables and inventories.
Selective product/market pruning	A refocussing upon segments that were most profitable or where the firm possessed distinctive strength. Typically this involved firms concentrating upon higher-priced, higher-quality segments. The principal benefit of the strategy was higher margins; capacity utilization did not increase.
Piecemeal productivity moves	Adjustments to current market position rather than comprehensive refocussing or reorganizing. These adjustments comprised reductions in marketing and R&D expenditures, higher capacity utilization, and increased employee productivity.

Exhibit 10.4 The characteristics of successful turnaround strategies in mature businesses

Source: Donald C. Hambrick and Steven M. Schecter, "Turnaround strategies for mature industrial-product business units," *Academy of Management Journal* 26 (2) (1983), pp. 231–48.

Segment and customer selection

In general, the profitability of mature industries is constrained by sluggish demand growth, limited scope for product differentiation, and customers' bargaining power. However, sharp differences in profit rates can arise between industry segments. Not only do growth rates of demand vary between segments, but the structure of segments with regard to concentration, buyer power, and potential for differentiation varies considerably. As a result, choice of segments is likely to be a key strategy issue in mature industries.

In the chemical industry, for example, the principal determinant of profit differences between the world's leading chemical producers during the 1980s was the extent to which they refocussed their activities from bulk chemicals to specialty chemicals. Companies which invested heavily in specialty chemicals such as Du Pont, ICI (UK), BASF (West Germany), and Ciba-Geigy (Switzerland), outperformed companies such as Shell, Union Carbide, and BP-Standard Oil which were heavily committed to bulk chemicals.[8]

In US banking, allocation of loans between regions and customer segments was the principal source of differential profit performance during the 1980s. The disastrous performance of BankAmerica during 1981–8 owed much to its heavy lending to agriculture, the oil industry, and Latin America. The geographical pattern of bank failure during 1987–90 reflected cyclical movements in regional economies: during 1989 leadership in bank failure passed from oil-based Texas to the real-estate slump states of New England and Arizona. Conversely, the more profitable larger US banks of the 1980s, such as Wells Fargo, Bank One (Columbus, Ohio), Republic New York, and PNC Financial, were those which limited exposure to Latin America and the oil patch, and concentrated upon more prosperous sectors (such as Bank One's specialization in credit card processing).[9]

The quest for differentiation

Cost leadership, we have noted, is difficult to sustain, particularly in internationally-competitive industries. Maintaining a low-cost position requires constant attention to operational efficiency and an unrelenting search for small cost reductions across the whole range of the firm's activities. Hence, attaining some insulation from the constant threat of price competition through a degree of differentiation is particularly attractive in mature industries. The problem is that the trend towards standardization narrows the scope for differentiation and reduces customer willingness to pay a substantial premium for differentiation. The creation of meaningful differentiation in mature industries therefore represents one of the greatest challenges to managers in mature industries.

Standardization of the physical attributes of a product and convergence of consumer preferences constrains but does not eliminate the potential for differentiation. Product standardization is frequently accompanied by increased differentiation of complementary services and image. In office equipment, particularly copiers, increased product standardization has encouraged firms to compete on maintenance, training services, and speed of repair. In consumer goods, maturity is often associated with the focus of differentiation shifting from physical product characteristics to image. Deeply-entrenched consumer preferences for Coke and Pepsi are a tribute to the capacity of heavy advertising over a long period to differentiate near-identical products.

Across a broad range of mature industries we can observe firms attempting to escape from the treadmill of price competition among standardized offerings through a multitude of differentiation variables. The intensely-competitive retail sector has produced some particularly interesting examples. The dismal returns on invested capital and on equity earned by many of the leading food chains (e.g. Kroger, A&P, Vons) and by old-established variety/department stores (Sears, J. C. Penney, Federated Department Stores) contrasts sharply with the sales growth and profitability of stores which have established clear differentiation through variety, style, and ambience (The Limited, Toys-R-Us, Nordstom, The Gap). Exhibit 10.5 lists large US retailers with the highest and lowest returns to investors during the 1980s. A similar pattern is evident for British retailers. During the mid-1980s, those which adopted innovative approaches to differentiation show the highest rates of sales growth and profitability, even though several of them were unable to sustain their performance into the 1990s (see Exhibit 10.6).

The role of innovation in mature industries

We have characterized mature industries as industries where the pace of technical change is low. Yet, we have also noted that the quest for

Company	Average annual total return to investors, 1978–88 (%)	Sales 1988 ($m.)
Top ten		
The Limited (Ohio)	47.2	4,071
Wal-Mart Stores (Ark.)	47.0	20,649
Giant Food (Maryland)	41.9	2,721
Toys "R" Us (N.J.)	41.8	4,000
Dillard Department Stores (Ark.)	37.1	2,558
Food Lion (N.C.)	36.5	3,815
Bruno's (Ala.)	36.2	1,982
General Cinema (Mass.)	31.1	2,324
Nordstrom (Wash.)	30.3	2,328
Marriot (Maryland)	30.2	7,370
Bottom ten		
Service Merchandise (Tenn.)	− 8.7	3,093
K Mart (Mich.)	− 13.1	27,301
Longs Drug Stores (Calif.)	− 13.1	1,925
Lowe's Cos.	− 13.7	2,517
Sears Roebuck (Illinois)	− 13.8	50,251
Winn-Dixie Stores (Florida)	− 15.4	9,008
J. C. Penny (Texas)	− 18.4	14,833
R. H. Macy (N.Y.)	− 19.7	5,729
Dayton Hudson (Minn.)	− 19.9	12,204
Tandy (Texas)	− 20.3	3,794

Exhibit 10.5 The highest and lowest performing top 50 US retailing companies in terms of return to investors

Source: Fortune, June 5, 1989, pp. 378–9.

differentiation in mature industries requires innovation: finding new approaches to uniqueness in terms of image creation, the addition of new features, or the provision of supporting services. The potential for innovation to create competitive advantage in mature industries extends beyond the differentiation of products and services. Steel, textiles, food processing, insurance, and hotel services are industries where the pace of product and process innovation is modest. In none of these industries does R&D expenditure as a percentage of sales revenue exceed 0.8 percent.[10] But it is precisely because of strong competition in these mature industries and the limited opportunities for establishing sustainable competitive advantage that creates impetus for innovation, not just in technology but also in marketing, service, and organization.

Nowhere is the powerful role of innovation in mature industries more apparent than in the oldest industry of all, agriculture. Since World War II a combination of product innovation (new varieties of plant, new breeds of animal), process innovation (mechanization, new pesticides and

Exhibit 10.6

Innovation, sales growth, and growth of ROI among British retailers, 1984–7

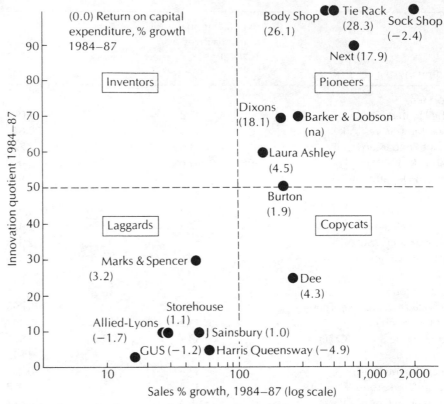

Note that innovation is measured as the proportion of sales attributable to the introduction of new products and new strategies between 1984 and 1987.
Source: Piper Trust Management Consultants and *The Economist,* July 23, 1988, p. 59.

fertilizers, new methods of planting and harvesting), and organizational change (larger farms, corporate farms, cooperative organizations, contract farming) has resulted in a rate of productivity growth which has exceeded that of the manufacturing sector.[11]

In several mature manufacturing industries, failure to innovate has caused deteriorating competitive position for leading US producers. This is particularly true in the steel and automobile industries where the maturing of the industry during the period 1930–60 was associated with emphasis on scale efficiency, increasing organizational rigidity, and a growing inability to respond to opportunities for product and process innovation. While US firms in these industries continued to lead the world in terms of output per employee, they steadily lost market share to firms which were more adaptable, more innovative, and more customer driven. In the steel industry, the major integrated steel companies lost sales to the minimills which were more technologically progressive, more flexible to market requirements, and more responsive to the interests of managers and workers. In the automobile industry, the US Big Three lost sales to the more technically-innovative, design-driven, quality-conscious, Japanese and European competitors. Not until the 1980s did the US firms initiate a broad-based response involving product redesign, new process technology, restructured working practices, drastic cut-backs in administrative staff, and cooperative arrangements with overseas automobile producers.[12] To understand this apparent conflict between, on the one hand, efficiency and, on the other, innovation and flexibility, we need to look at the structures, organizational systems, and management styles through which strategies are implemented.

Strategy Implementation in Mature Industries: Structure, Systems, and Style

To the extent that maturity is associated with environmental stability, lack of technological change, and an emphasis on efficiency as the key criterion for success, particular organizational and managerial characteristics are called for. At the beginning of the 1960s, Burns and Stalker argued that, while dynamic environments require "organic" organizational forms characterized by decentralization, loosely defined roles, and a high level of lateral communication, stable environments required a "mechanistic" organization characterized by centralization, well-defined roles, and predominantly vertical communication.[13] Henry Mintzberg describes this highly formalized type of organization dedicated to the pursuit of efficiency as the "Machine Bureaucracy".[14]

Efficiency through bureaucracy

The principal requirement for efficiency is the specialized operation of routine tasks through division of labor closely controlled by management. Such forms of organization are typically found in industries devoted to large-scale production where the basis for efficiency is the application of Frederick Taylor's principles of scientific management. Division of labor extends to management as well as operatives. The Machine Bureaucracy displays a high level of vertical and horizontal specialization. Vertical specialization is reflected in the concentration of strategy formulation at the apex of the hierarchy, while middle and junior management supervises and administers through the application of standardized rules and regulations. Horizontal specialization in the company is organized around *functional departments* rather than *product divisions*.

The Machine Bureaucracy as described by Mintzberg is a caricature of actual organizations, probably the closest approximations are found in government departments performing highly routine administrative duties. However, in most mature industries the features of bureaucracy which Mintzberg describes are familiar. Even in dynamic, fast-moving companies such as McDonald's, operating procedures are formulated into a set of precise, written rules which govern virtually every part of the business (see the quotation which introduces this chapter). The organizational characteristics of bureaucracy are clearly apparent among some of the huge industrial enterprises found in automobiles, steel, and oil. The key features of these mature organizations are summarized in Exhibit 10.7.

Exhibit 10.7 Strategy
implementation in
mature industries:
traditional features of
organization and
management

Area	Features
Strategy	Primary goal is cost advantage through economies of scale, capital-intensive production of standardized product/service. Dichotomization of strategy formulation (the preserve of top management) and strategy implementation (carried down the hierarchy).
Structure	Functional departments (eg production, marketing, customer service, distribution). Distinction between line and staff. Clearly defined job roles with strong vertical reporting/delegation relationships.
Controls	Performance targets are primarily quantitative and short term and are elaborated for all members of the organization. Performance is closely monitored by well-established, centralized management information systems and formalized reporting requirements. Financial controls through budgets and profit targets are particularly important.
Incentives	Incentives are based upon achievement of individual targets and are in the form of financial rewards and promotion up the hierarchy. Penalties exist for failure to attain quantitative targets, for failure to adhere to the rules, and lack of conformity to company norms.
Communication	Primarily vertical for the purposes of delegation and reporting. Lateral communication is limited; sometimes achieved through interdepartmental committees where needed.
Management	Primary functions of top management are control and strategic decision making. Two predominant top management styles appear to be effective: *the politician*, the organizational head who can effectively wield power through understanding of the organization and can formulate and implement strategy through consensus (eg Alfred Sloan Jr. of GM); and *the autocrat*, the CEO who leads and controls through aggressive use of decision-making authority and sheer force of personality (Lee Iacocca of Chrysler).

**The bureaucratic
model in decline**

Causes During the 1980s the Machine Bureaucracy has been on the retreat in almost all mature industries. Five factors have caused the reversal:

- increased environmental turbulence;
- increased emphasis on innovation;
- new process technology;
- alienation and conflict;
- the Japanese example.

Taking each factor in turn, bureaucracy is conducive to efficiency in stable environments. However, the centralized, structured organization cannot readily adapt to change. Achieving flexibility to respond to external change requires greater decentralization, less specialization, and looser controls.

The organizational structure, control systems, management style, and interpersonal relationships conducive to efficiency are likely to hinder innovation. As mature industries increasingly recognize the potential for innovation in the form of technological transfer from other industries (e.g. electronics, biotechnology), and new approaches to differentiation and competition, so the disadvantages of formalized, efficiency-orientated organizations have become increasingly apparent.

The efficiency advantages of bureaucratized organizations arise from the technical virtues of highly-specialized, systematized production methods. The electronics revolution has changed the conditions for efficiency. Computer-integrated manufacturing processes permit cost efficiency with greater product variety, shorter runs, and greater flexibility. As automation displaces labor-intensive, assembly-line manufacturing techniques, there is less need for elaborate division of labor and greater need for job flexibility. Simultaneously, the electronic revolution in the office is displacing the administrative bureaucracy which control and information systems once required.

Consequences of specialization, mechanistic approaches to work, and emphasis on control are alienation and the emergence of conflict between unions and management, between white collar and blue collar, between top management and middle management, and between different functional areas. Bureaucratic organizations are likely to foster conflict and provide no highly effective mechanisms for their resolution.

Across a range of mature industries from motorcycles and steel to banking and brokerage, Japanese firms have demonstrated remarkable success with organizations which feature many of the hierarchical characteristics of Western mature corporations, but fewer of the rigidities. The ability of leading Japanese firms to reconcile efficiency with innovation, and control with opportunism has been an important factor in the rethinking that is taking place in North America and Europe.

Responses In response, firms in mature industries have undergone substantial adjustment over the past decade. At Exxon, General Motors, Mobil, and Citicorp, management hierarchies have been either dismantled or radically pruned, decision-making processes have been transformed, and more participative working relationships have been encouraged. Among the most important features of change have been:

- greater decentralization of decision making;
- less emphasis on economics of large-scale production;
- increased cooperation and communication;
- profit incentives.

As well as moving operational decision making further down the line, strategy formulation has typically moved out of the top echelon of management and become more of an exercise in participation and consensus-building. Greater involvement of operational management in decision making has been encouraged by a breaking down of line-staff distinctions accompanied by pruning of head office staffs and relocation of head office functions to operational units.

There is less emphasis on economies of large-scale production and increased responsiveness to customer requirements together with greater flexibility in responding to changes in the market place.

Increased emphasis on lateral cooperation and communication has resulted from the need for increased responsiveness to customer requirements, as well as to changing market conditions which have necessitated less functional separation and increased interfunctional cooperation.

Wider use of profit incentives, both through bonuses and employee stock ownership plans (ESOPs) have been used to encourage closer identification of employees with organizational goals and to help overcome traditional conflicts between labor and capital, management and labor, and blue-collar and white-collar employees.

These trends amount to a closer convergence between the organizational and managerial characteristics of firms in mature industries and those located in the newer, more technologically-orientated industries. At the same time, the primary emphasis on cost efficiency remains. It is not that the goal of cost efficiency has been superseded, rather that the conditions for cost efficiency have changed. The most powerful force for organizational change in mature industries has been the inability of highly-structured, centralized organizations to maintain their cost efficiency within an increasingly turbulent business environment. The requirements for *dynamic efficiency* are different from the requirements for *static efficiency*. Dynamic efficiency requires the displacement of bureaucratically-controlled, highly-specialized routines by more flexible working practices. Flexibility requires higher levels of autonomy, not only to divisional and plant managers, but also to individual employees to permit them to adjust their work practices to meet changing circumstances.

Achieving dynamic efficiency through increased flexibility and autonomy does not mean less control, but a change in control mechanisms. By relying more upon cost controls and profit targets, firms can permit greater autonomy to unit managers while maintaining rigorous demands for cost efficiency. The corporate restructurings initiated by Rawl at Exxon, Iacocca at Chrysler, and Walters at British Petroleum involved a dismantling of a major part of corporate bureaucracy combined with the imposition upon business units of demanding financial targets with draconian sanctions for failure to meet targets. A key element of these sanctions is a greater willingness by the corporate headquarters of mature corporations to divest underperforming divisions and to fire senior executives associated with poor financial performance.

Special Features of Strategy Formulation in Declining Industries

Many mature industries degenerate into declining industries as a result of technological substitution, changes in consumer preferences, or demographic shifts. Shrinking market demand gives rise to strategic issues which are different from those encountered in other mature industries. Among the key features of declining industries are:

- excess capacity;
- lack of technical change which is reflected in a lack of new product introduction and stability of process technology;
- a declining number of competitors, but some entry as new firms acquire cheaply the assets of existing firms;
- high average age of both physical and human resources;
- aggressive price competition.

Yet, despite the inhospitable environment which declining industries normally offer, research by Kathryn Harrigan has uncovered several examples of declining industries where at least some participants earned surprisingly attractive rates of profits. These included electronic vacuum tubes, premium cigars, and leather tanning. However, in other industries such as prepared baby foods, rayon, and economy cigars, decline was accompanied by aggressive price competition, company failures, and instability.[15]

The consequences of decline for competition and profitability depend upon two key factors: the balance between capacity and output during decline, and the nature of demand for the product or service.

The smooth adjustment of industry capacity to declining demand is the key to stability and profitability during the decline phase. In industries where capacity exits from the industry in an orderly fashion, decline can occur without trauma. Where a substantial overhang of excess capacity persists, as has occurred in the steel industries of America and Europe and in oil tankers during 1974–84, the potential for an industry bloodbath exists. The ease with which capacity adjusts to declining demand is dependent upon:

The adjustment of capacity to declining demand

- the predictability of decline;
- barriers to exit;
- the strategies of the surviving firms.

The predictability of decline   If decline can be forecast, the more likely it is that firms can plan for it. The problems of the steel industry, oil refining, and oil transport during the late 1970s were exacerbated by the unpredictability of the oil price shock of 1974. The more cyclical and volatile is demand, then the more difficult it is for firms to perceive the trend of demand even after the onset of decline.

Barriers to exit can impede the exit of capacity from an industry. The most important sources of barriers to exit are:

- durable and specialized assets;
- costs incurred in plant closure;
- managerial commitment.

With durable and specialized assets, just as capital requirements impose a barrier to entry into an industry, those same investments also discourage exit. The longer they last and the fewer are the opportunities for using those assets in another industry, the more are companies tied to that particular industry. The intensity of price competition in steel, acetylene and rayon during the 1970s was partly a consequence of the durability and lack of alternative uses for the capital equipment employed.

Apart from the accounting costs of writing off assets, substantial cash costs may be incurred in plant closure arising from redundancy payments to employees, compensation for broken contracts with customers and suppliers, and costs incurred in dismantling and demolishing plant.

In addition to financial considerations, firms may be reluctant to close plants for a variety of emotional and moral reasons. Resistance to plant closure and divestment arises from pride in a company's traditions and reputation, managers' unwillingness to accept failure, loyalties to employees and the local community, and the desire not to offend government.

The strategies of the surviving firms Smooth exit of capacity ultimately depends upon the decisions of the industry players. The earlier that companies recognize and address the problem, the more likely it is that independent and collective action can achieve capacity reduction. In the European petrochemical industry, for example, the problem of excess capacity was partially solved by a series of bilateral exchanges of plants and divisions. Thus, ICI swapped its polyethylene plants for BP's PVC plants.[16] Stronger firms in the industry can facilitate the exit of weaker firms by offering to acquire their plants and take over their after-sales service commitments.

The nature of demand   Where a market is segmented, the general pattern of decline can obscure the existence of pockets of demand which are not only comparatively resilient, but also price inelastic. For example, despite the obsolescence of vacuum tubes after the adoption of transistors, Harrigan observed that GTE Sylvania and General Electric earned excellent profits supplying vacuum tubes to the replacement and military markets.[17] Similarly in fountain pens, companies such as Cross and Mont Blanc which continued in the quality fountain pen market have achieved steady sales and excellent profits by appealing to the price-insensitive "yuppie" market. By contrast, where the product is undifferentiated and where customer switching costs are low, the outlook is far less favorable. For commodity products, such as standard steel mill products and industrial raw materials, the prospects for earning a satisfactory margin during decline are remote.

Conventional strategy recommendations for declining industries are either to divest or to harvest; that is, to generate the maximum cash flow from existing investments without reinvesting. However, these strategies assume that declining industries are inherently unprofitable. Once we recognize that there may be considerable profit potential within a declining industry then other strategies may be attractive. Harrigan and Porter[18] identify four strategies which can be profitably pursued in declining industries either individually or sequentially:

Strategy options in declining industries

- leadership;
- niche;
- harvest;
- divest.

Leadership   By gaining leadership, a firm is well placed to outstay competitors and play a dominant role in the final stages of the industry's life-cycle. Once leadership has been attained the firm is in a good position to switch to a harvest strategy and yield a strong profit stream from its market position. Possible maneuvers in establishing leadership are:

- build market share and encourage exit by aggressive competition;
- buy market share through takeovers of competitors;
- purchase competitors' plants;
- reduce competitors' exit costs by producing spare parts and private label goods for them;
- demonstrate commitment to the industry;
- develop and disclose credible market information that reduces uncertainty about future decline of the industry and helps dispel overoptimistic hopes that some firms may cling to;
- raise the stakes: take initiatives such as product or process improvements that pressure competitors to follow and so make it costly for them to stay in the business.

Niche   Identify a segment that is likely to maintain a stable demand and other firms are unlikely to invade, then use the initiatives of a leadership strategy to establish dominance within the segment. The most attractive niches are those which offer the greatest prospects for stability and where demand is most elastic.

Harvest   A harvesting strategy is one which seeks to maximise the firm's cash flow from its existing assets, while avoiding, as far as possible, further investment. Harvesting strategies are typically orientated towards the short and medium term and seek to maximize cash flow by raising prices wherever possible, and cutting costs by rationalizing the number of models, number of channels and customers. Note, however, that a harvest strategy can be difficult to implement effectively. If competition is strong, harvesting may result in an unintended acceleration of decline, particularly if employee morale is adversely affected by a strategy which offers no development or long-term future for the business.

Divest   If the future looks unattractive, the best strategy may be to divest the business. In general, the best price for a business, or for individual plants, is obtained in the early stages of decline before a consensus has developed as to the inevitability of decline. Once industry decline is well established, finding buyers may be extremely difficult.

Choosing a strategy   Choosing the most appropriate strategy requires a careful assessment both of the profit potential of the industry and the competitive position of the firm. Harrigan and Porter pose four key questions:

- Can the structure of the industry support a hospitable, potentially profitable decline phase?
- What are the exit barriers that each significant competitor faces?
- Do your company strengths fit the remaining pockets of demand?
- What are your competitors' strengths in these pockets? How can their exit barriers be overcome?

Selecting an appropriate strategy requires matching the opportunities remaining in the industries to the company's competitive position. Exhibit 10.8 shows a simple framework for strategy choice.

Exhibit 10.8   Strategy selection in a declining industry: a simple framework

COMPANY'S COMPETITIVE POSITION

		Has strengths in remaining demand pockets	Lacks strengths in remaining demand pockets
INDUSTRY STRUCTURE	Favorable to decline	LEADERSHIP or NICHE	HARVEST or DIVEST QUICKLY
	Unfavorable to decline	NICHE or HARVEST	DIVEST QUICKLY

Source: K. R. Harrigan and M. E. Porter, "Endgame strategies for declining industries", *Harvard Business Review*, July–August 1983, p. 119.

Summary

Mature industries present challenging environments for the formulation and implementation of business strategies. Competition, and price competition in particular, is usually strong and the opportunities for building and sustaining positions of clear competitive advantage are normally limited: cost advantages are vulnerable to imitation and instability, opportunities for differentiation are limited by the tendency for maturity to be associated with standardization. Traditionally, mature industries have displayed high levels of environmental stability where the key to competitive advantage was cost efficiency through large-scale production of standardized products or services, experience curve cost advantages, and low overheads. Such conditions encouraged highly centralized, bureaucratically-organized companies directed towards maximizing the efficiency with which routine operations were performed.

Today such conditions no longer prevail. The stability of mature industries has been upset by increased international competition, increased economic turbulence, and process innovation. The consequences are twofold. First, the conditions for cost efficiency have changed. In a dynamic environment cost efficiency is no longer uniquely associated with scale, specialization, and rigid hierarchical control. The essence of dynamic is smooth, rapid adjustment to change. Secondly, in addition to being cost efficient, companies in the advanced industrialized countries have been forced to seek new sources of competitive advantage through innovation and differentiation. Reconciling the pursuit of scale economies with the need for responsiveness and flexibility, and the requirements of cost efficiency with the growing need for innovation and differentiation, is the complex challenge facing mature businesses. Many of the most successful companies in mature industries are ones which have achieved flexibility through a dismantling of bureaucratic structures and procedures, have exploited the potential which new process technology offers for combining variety and flexibility with efficiency, have encouraged high levels of employee commitment, and have rigorously imposed cost efficiency through tight financial controls.

Notes

1. Edward H. Rensi, "Computers at McDonald's," in J.F. McLimore and L. Larwood (eds) *Strategies ... Successes ... Senior Executives Speak Out* (Harper and Row, New York, 1988), pp. 159–60.

2. Jeffrey Williams, "*I don't think we're in Kansas any more....*" *A perspective on our expanding markets*," Working Paper 20-86-87, (Graduate School of Industrial Administration, Carnegie–Mellon University, 1988), p. 1.

3. Robert D. Buzzell and Bradley T. Gale, *The PIMS Principles* (Free Press, New York, 1987), p. 279.

4. "ConAgra's profits aren't chicken feed," *Fortune*, October 27, 1986, pp. 70–80.

5. "United Airlines versus American Airlines: Crying for Wolff," *Economist*, August 6, 1988, pp. 55–6.

6. See Michael Goold and Andrew Campbell, *Strategies and Style* (Blackwell, Oxford, 1987); "Hanson and Kidde: a marriage made in low tech," Business Week, August 17, 1987, pp. 36–7.

7. Peter H. Grinyer, D. G. Mayes and P. McKiernan, *Sharpbenders* (Blackwell, Oxford, 1988).

8. "European chemicals: industry profile," *Economist* July 16, 1988, pp. 68–9.

9. "The bruisers took a beating in 1987," *Business Week*, April 4, 1988, pp. 90–9.

10. "R&D scoreboard," *Business Week*, June 20, 1988, pp. 139–60.

11. Paul R. Lawrence and Davis Dyer, *Renewing American Industry* (Free Press, New York, 1983), ch. 4.

12. Ibid., chs 2 and 3.

13. T. Burns and G. M. Stalker, *The Management of Innovation* (Tavistock Institute, London, 1961).

14. Henry Mintzberg, *Structure in Fives: Designing Effective Organizations* (Prentice-Hall, Englewood Cliffs, NJ, 1983), ch. 9.

15. Kathryn R. Harrigan, *Strategies for Declining Businesses* (D. C. Heath, Lexington, 1980).

16. Joe Bower, *When Markets Quake* (Harvard Business School Press, Boston, Mass., 1986).

17. Kathryn R. Harrigan, "Strategic planning for endgame," *Long Range Planning* (1982), pp. 45–8.

18. Kathryn R. Harrigan and Michael E. Porter, "End-game strategies for declining industries," *Harvard Business Review*, July-August 1983, pp. 111–20.

ELEVEN

Strategy Formulation and Implementation in Global Industries

He knows not England who only England knows.
                                    Rudyard Kipling

Introduction

Of all the changes that have revolutionized the business environment during the period since 1960, probably the most important has been the growing internationalization of the world economy. Internationalization has involved two main developments. Foremost is the growth in world trade. The growth rate of trade has consistently outstripped that of production with the result that import penetration of most industries has increased sharply, and firms have looked increasingly to overseas markets as the primary sources of sales growth. The internationalization of the US economy is indicated by the increased penetration of the manufacturing sector by imports (Exhibit 11.1).

The second aspect of internationalization has been multinational expansion by large enterprises. In the manufacture of TV sets in the US, there was only one indigenous US manufacturer (Zenith) remaining at the end

Exhibit 11.1 Import penetration of US manufacturing industry, 1960–87 (based on OECD data)

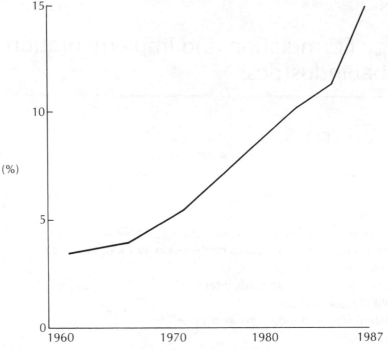

Note that import penetration is measured as:

$$\frac{\text{Value of Imports of Manufactures}}{\text{(US Manufacturers' Sales} + \text{Imports of Manufactures} - \text{Exports of Manufactures)}}$$

of 1987. All the other companies manufacturing TVs in the US were foreign owned. A similar situation was emerging in tires. By the end of 1989 most of the leading US tire makers were foreign owned: Firestone by Bridgestone of Japan, Goodrich-Uniroyal by Michelin of France, with Goodyear remaining the only US-owned producer (having narrowly escaped acquisition by the British financier, James Goldsmith). The accelerating trend towards multinationality is indicated by the growth of cross-frontier mergers. During 1987–9, 18 of the 50 largest US acquisitions were by overseas companies.[1]

Exhibit 11.2
Construction of General Motors' 1989 Pontiac Le Mans

Design: West Germany (by Opel)	Steering components: US
Steel sheet: Japan	Brake components: France, US, S. Korea
Stamping of exterior body parts: S. Korea	Tires: S. Korea
Engines: 1.6 liter – S. Korea	Windshield glass: S. Korea
2.0 liter – Australia	Battery: S. Korea
Fuel injection system: US	Electrical wiring harness: S. Korea
Fuel pump: US	Radio: Singapore
Transmission: Canada and US	Final assembly: S. Korea (by Daewoo)
Rear axle components: US and S. Korea	Major market: US and Canada

Source: General Motors Corporation; *Los Angeles Times*, Sunday February 10, 1989.

Opportunities for exploiting the benefits of international trade and overseas direct investment are revolutionizing the strategies of large companies in both manufacturing and service industries. The Big Three US automobile companies provide particularly striking examples of the extent of internationalization. Exhibit 11.2 describes the role of overseas subsidiaries, overseas suppliers, and joint-venture partners in the production of a recent General Motors model of car.

We shall examine the implications of the internationalization of the business environment for strategy analysis by focussing on two questions:

- What are the consequences of increasing international competition for business strategy formulation and, in particular, for a firm's ability to establish and sustain competitive advantage in the face of international competition?
- What opportunities do global approaches to strategy offer firms in gaining advantage over domestically-based rivals?

The first question requires that we introduce locational factors into our analysis of business strategy and competitive advantage. For example, what are the implications of a company's location within a particular country for its costs and availability of inputs, and its access to markets? The second question necessitates an evaluation of the efficiencies and strategic advantages which accrue from competing world-wide, compared to focussing upon individual countries.

Building International Competition into Strategy Analysis

Our starting-point for the analysis of strategy was to identify the sources of a company's profitability. Superior profitability, we observed (Exhibit 1.3), is a consequence either of location within an attractive industry or of achieving a competitive advantage over rivals. Up until now, our discussion of industry attractiveness has defined industries on a national basis, typically viewing imports as a source of "substitute competition." However, for many industries, national markets are simply segments within a broader global market. For industries such as aircraft, computers, telecommunications equipment, and earth-moving equipment, competition can only be understood by defining these industries on a global basis. In commercial aircraft, Boeing's principal competitor is Airbus Industrie; in copiers, Xerox's leading competitor is Canon; in color film, Kodak competes with Fuji.

Extending our analysis of competitive advantage to internationally-competing industries is somewhat more complicated. Establishing advantage requires that the firm matches its internal strengths to the key success factors of the industry. However, when firms are located in different countries, achieving cost and differentiation advantage is not simply a matter of selecting the appropriate strategies to exploit their internal strengths in relation to outside opportunities; locational factors play a critical role.

Let us proceed by extending the analysis of industry attractiveness and of competitive advantage to take account of international competition.

The implications of international competition for industry attractiveness

The first issue which arises in analyzing industries where competition extends beyond national borders is to define the geographical boundaries of the industry. Which automobile industry should Chrysler be viewed as competing within: the US industry, the North American industry, or the international industry? The criteria to be applied in determining the geographical boundaries of an industry are the same as those which were applied in chapter 2 to determine the boundaries of an industry in terms of product range.

The criteria of demand substitutability and supply substitutability can be applied equally well to determining geographical boundaries as to determining product boundaries. An industry is international in its scope, if, on the demand side, customers are willing and able to substitute imported for domestically-produced goods and, on the supply side, if producers are willing and able to shift supply from the domestic to export markets. Thus, in clothes, TVs, hand tools, and jet aircraft, customers are willing to substitute between products manufactured in the US, in Japan, West Germany, Singapore, or Brazil on the basis of changing price differentials. In these same industries, producers respond to changes in demand and exchange rates by redirecting their output between countries in search of higher profits. Conversely, industries which remain nationally bounded are those whose output cannot be readily traded. These include most services, products which are not easily transportable, such as bread, water, electricity, and building bricks, and products where government regulations and import restrictions limit trade, as with dairy products, pharmaceuticals, and nuclear-power generating plants.

The consequences of the internationalization of competition for industry attractiveness are mostly adverse. While internationalization offers increased investment and marketing opportunities to companies, it also means increased intensity of competition. Thus the growth of international trade has been accompanied by a decline in the return on invested capital in the corporate sectors of the US and most other Western nations (see Exhibit 11.3).

The impact of internationalization on competition and industry profitability can be assessed by identifying the changes in industry structure which accompany the broadening of an industry's geographical boundaries. Internationalization is likely to have a major impact on four structural variables:

- barriers to entry;
- concentration;
- diversity of competitors;
- buying power.

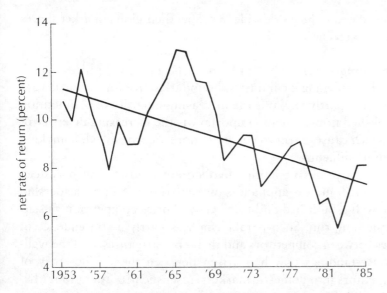

Exhibit 11.3 The rate of return on capital invested in US non-financial corporations, 1953–85

Note that the rate of return is measured as the ratio of pretax profits, net of depreciation, plus net interest, to the net stock of fixed capital plus inventories.
Source: David A. A. Aschauet, "Government spending and the falling rate of profit", *Federal Reserve Bank of Chicago Economic Perspectives* 12 (1988), p. 12

Barriers to entry   The growth of international trade has important implications for entry barriers. At the level of individual national markets, entry becomes easy for companies established in other countries. In the US automobile and consumer electronics industries, competition to established producers from domestic new entrants is unlikely; yet since the 1960s, these industries have experienced a flood of new competitors, not just from Japan and Western Europe, but from South Korea, Taiwan, Singapore, and Yugoslavia. Most of these new competitors are not new firms but overseas firms which have extended their geographical scope.

The establishment of new firms is facilitated by international trade. Firms can establish themselves in countries where entry barriers are low, then extend their operations globally. Many of the entry barriers which were effective against potential domestic entrants may be ineffective against potential entrants from overseas. For example, patent and trademark law and its enforcement may be more lax in some overseas countries. Also, the propensity of some governments to subsidize their domestic industries can negate barriers based upon large capital requirements.

Concentration   A consequence of the geographical widening of industry boundaries is that seller concentration falls. Consider the US automobile market. In 1970, GM, Ford, and Chrysler together held 84 percent of total sales; by 1987 their combined share had fallen to 67 percent. In other industries, the decline in concentration has been even more dramatic. In 1970, RCA and Zenith held 44 percent of the US market for color TVs. By 1986 their combined share of the US had fallen to 21 percent but, if the industry is considered to be worldwide in scope, their global market shares totalled a mere 4 percent.

Diversity of competitors   The fall in concentration ratios which accompanies the widening of industry boundaries from a national to a global market only partly explains the increasing intensity of competition between established firms. Equally important is the increasing diversity of competitors which causes them to compete more vigorously while making cooperation more difficult.

During the 1960s, price competition in oligopoly industries such as steel, automobiles, and domestic appliances was restrained. Price leadership patterns were well-established and firms viewed price competition as self-defeating in the long run. Such parallelism was partly a consequence of the similarities between competitors and their cost structures, and the well-developed understandings that had arisen between them. The entry of overseas competitors into domestic markets upset such coordination. Mistrust was high, different cost structures made aggressive competition more attractive for some firms, and communication was difficult. This is not to say that coordination, even collusion, is impossible on a global scale. During the 1930s, Standard Oil of New Jersey (now Exxon) and the Royal Dutch/Shell Group effectively regulated competition in the international oil industry. The world cigarette industry for much of the twentieth century was neatly divided between American Tobacco and the Imperial Tobacco Group of Britain. American Tobacco agreed not to compete within the British Empire, Imperial agreed to keep outside the Americas, while exports to other countries were handled by a jointly-owned subsidiary, British–American Tobacco (BAT).[2] However, both these industries were dominated by just two companies; once the number of players increases, the chances of "cozy coexistence" decline sharply.

Buying power   A further implication of lower barriers to national markets and an increased number of competitors is that large customers can exercise their buying power far more effectively. Automobile manufacturers increasingly look worldwide in sourcing components. Large retailers can use the threat of shifting their purchases to overseas manufacturers as a means of pressuring domestic suppliers to offer favorable terms.

The analysis of competitive advantage

Competitive advantage, we have observed, requires that a firm selects a strategy which matches its internal strengths to the opportunities for success which are available in its industry environment. If all firms in an industry face the same opportunity set, then it is a firm's resources and its deployment of these resources which determine why one firm is more successful than another. Introducing international competition complicates this analysis. When competitors reside in different countries, the success of one firm against another depends not only on the resources and strategies of rival firms, but also the advantages and disadvantages which

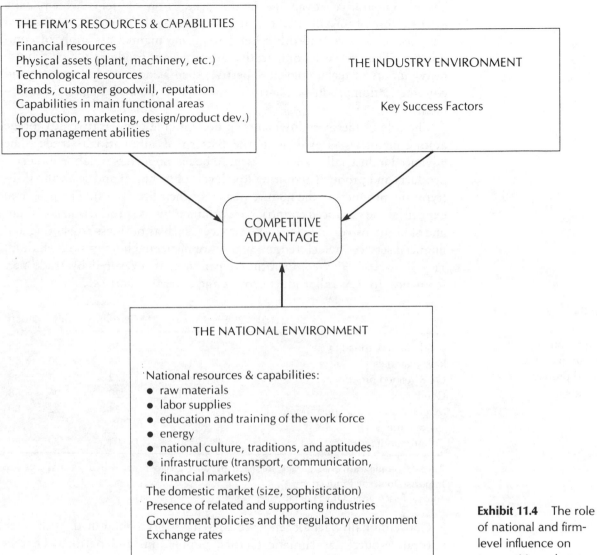

Exhibit 11.4 The role of national and firm-level influence on competitive advantage

are conferred by location. Exhibit 11.4 shows the determinants of competitive advantage in internationally-competing industries.

National influences on competitiveness – comparative advantage The role of national factors in affecting the internationally-competitive position of industries and firms is described by the *theory of comparative advantage*. The theory states that a country will have a relative competitive advantage in those products which make intensive use of those factors of products which are available in relative abundance within the country. The Philippines has an abundant supply of unskilled labor. The United States has an abundant supply of technological resources in the form of trained scientists and engineers, research facilities, and universities. The Philippines has a comparative advantage in the production of items which make intensive use of unskilled labor, such as clothing, handicrafts, mechanical and electronic toys, and other items requiring manual assembly of components. The US has a comparative advantage in products which require heavy inputs of technological expertise, such as advanced electronic and communication products, pharmaceuticals, and medical diagnostic equipment.

The role of factor endowments in determining comparative advantage among countries is evident in the pattern of international trade. The advanced industrialized nations tend to be net importers of labor-intensive products and products requiring low levels of technical and scientific skills (typically products in the mature phases of their life-cycles). The principal exports of the advanced countries are products whose production is capital- and skill-intensive, and also those services, such as business consulting and financial services, which require highly sophisticated human skills. Exhibit 11.5 shows *revealed comparative advantage*, as measured by trade performance, for several product groups and several countries.

Exhibit 11.5 Indexes of revealed comparative advantage for certain broad product categories

	US	Canada	W. Germany	Italy	Japan
Food, drink & tobacco	.31	.28	− .36	− .29	− .85
Raw materials	.43	.51	− .55	− .30	− .88
Oil & refined products	− .64	.34	− .72	− .74	− .99
Chemicals	.42	− .16	.20	− .06	− .58
Machinery and transportation equipment	.12	− .19	.34	.22	.80
Other manufactures	− .68	− .07	.01	.29	.40

Revealed comparative advantage for each product group is measured as: Exports less Imports/Domestic Production
Source: Based upon OECD data.

Conventionally, factor endowments have been identified with such natural resources as climatic factors, population, and national characteristics. Increasingly, however, it is endogenously-determined factors of production which are becoming most important as the basis of comparative advantage; namely, knowledge, skills, research facilities, management capabilities, transport and communication facilities. All of these are determined by investment at the industry and national levels. One of the central issues in the current debate over US educational policy is whether the level and the quality of public investment in education is consistent with the maintenance of America's international position as a high-wage, high-skill economy at the forefront of innovation.[3]

Government policies are also important influences on the development of comparative advantage. The success of Hong Kong in industries which require swift adjustment to change, such as finance, fashion clothing, and electronic toys, owes much to the entrepreneurial flexibility encouraged by an absence of government regulation of business. Similarly, the emergence of the Bermuda and the Cayman Islands as offshore banking centers is due to the combination of political stability, lack of regulation, and favorable taxation laws.

The size of a country's domestic market can be a vital determinant of comparative advantage in industries where the minimum efficient size of operation is large, or where demand is so segmented that a large total market is required for niches to be of a viable size.[4] A vast home market has been a major advantage for US firms in the aircraft, automobile, computer, and pharmaceutical industries. Similar scale-economy benefits are anticipated from the removal of internal barriers to trade within the European Community by 1992. Multinational corporations (MNCs) are increasingly recognizing the advantages of strong market positions within the world's largest economies. During the 1980s, European and Japanese MNCs scrambled to obtain secure US market positions. Companies such as British Petroleum, Siemens, Thomson, Sony, ICI, and Unilever all made significant US acquisitions during the 1980s, while Japanese banks and automobile companies established US subsidiaries. During the early 1990s a major strategic thrust of many US companies is to establish a strong footing within Europe. The head of McKinsey and Company's Tokyo office, Kenichi Ohmae, argues the case for "Triad Power". His thesis is that pressures of technological change, convergence of customer preferences, scale economies, and protectionism increasingly require successful world players to become true insiders within the *three* major markets of the world: the US, Europe, and Japan.[5]

Porter's analysis of national influences on international competitiveness A recent study by Michael Porter has shed further light on the role of national factors on firms' competitive advantage.[6] Porter argues that the ability of a firm's national environment to confer international advantage depends critically upon the role of the national environment in nourishing and stimulating innovation and on the quest for product improvement. Porter focusses upon four key factors in promoting international competitiveness (see Exhibit 11.6):

- factor conditions;
- demand conditions;
- strategy, structure, and rivalry;
- related and supporting industries.

A key feature of Porter's theory of international competitive performance is the emphasis it places upon *dynamic* factors. Countries which show a sustained advantage in particular sectors are those where the domestic industry is successful in upgrading and broadening the basis of its advantage as the industry develops and evolves. Japan's comparative advantage in automobiles and consumer electronics was initially based upon low-cost production; during the 1970s and 1980s it shifted to quality, particularly in

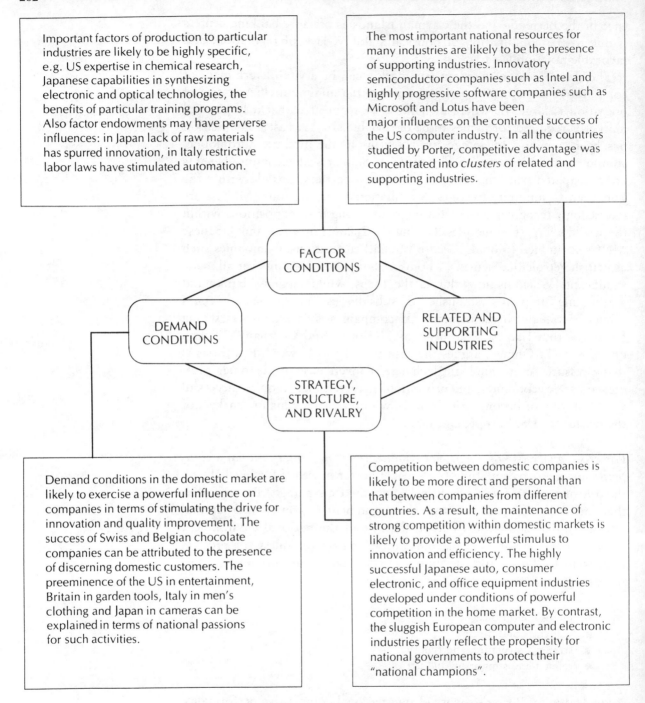

Important factors of production to particular industries are likely to be highly specific, e.g. US expertise in chemical research, Japanese capabilities in synthesizing electronic and optical technologies, the benefits of particular training programs. Also factor endowments may have perverse influences: in Japan lack of raw materials has spurred innovation, in Italy restrictive labor laws have stimulated automation.

The most important national resources for many industries are likely to be the presence of supporting industries. Innovatory semiconductor companies such as Intel and highly progressive software companies such as Microsoft and Lotus have been major influences on the continued success of the US computer industry. In all the countries studied by Porter, competitive advantage was concentrated into *clusters* of related and supporting industries.

FACTOR CONDITIONS

DEMAND CONDITIONS

RELATED AND SUPPORTING INDUSTRIES

STRATEGY, STRUCTURE, AND RIVALRY

Demand conditions in the domestic market are likely to exercise a powerful influence on companies in terms of stimulating the drive for innovation and quality improvement. The success of Swiss and Belgian chocolate companies can be attributed to the presence of discerning domestic customers. The preeminence of the US in entertainment, Britain in garden tools, Italy in men's clothing and Japan in cameras can be explained in terms of national passions for such activities.

Competition between domestic companies is likely to be more direct and personal than that between companies from different countries. As a result, the maintenance of strong competition within domestic markets is likely to provide a powerful stimulus to innovation and efficiency. The highly successful Japanese auto, consumer electronic, and office equipment industries developed under conditions of powerful competition in the home market. By contrast, the sluggish European computer and electronic industries partly reflect the propensity for national governments to protect their "national champions".

Exhibit 11.6 Porter's analysis of the determinants of international competitiveness

terms of reliability. Today, it is based primarily upon innovation and speed of product development. The key to such upgrading of competitive advantage is investment in *advanced factors of production*: sophisticated labor skills, technology, advanced management systems, and high-efficiency transportation and communications infrastructure.

Innovation plays a central role in Porter's model. Unlike the traditional theory of comparative advantage which emphasizes the availability of R&D resources as the primary determinant of innovation, Porter shifts attention to the market conditions which stimulate innovation. Two sets of factors are of critical importance. The first are demand conditions within national markets. Demanding domestic customers provide a powerful stimulus to domestic producers to be innovative and quality-orientated. The leadership of US companies in oil drilling and oilfield services reflects experience gained in demanding local conditions. German prominence in luxury cars is, in part, a consequence of German consumers' interest in well-engineered automobiles. Japanese leadership in cameras may reflect a national interest in photography. The second factor concerns the key role of strong domestic competition in providing the intense rivalry which is conducive to innovation and the quest for excellence. Nowhere is this more evident than in the Japanese copier and facsimile industries. Conversely, Porter found that few government-supported "national champions" had achieved significant international success within their respective industries.

Achieving consistency between strategy and national factors   Competing successfully in internationally-competitive markets requires that firms match their firm-level advantages to the pattern of comparative advantages within the countries where they are based. For example, hand tools such as hammers, axes, screwdrivers, and spanners require only low-level technology and limited production skills. In manufacturing hand tools, countries with abundant supplies of unskilled labor such as China and Brazil have a substantial cost advantage over high wage countries such as the United States or West Germany. To compete in the hand tool industry, there is little chance that a US firm can survive simply through a strategy of cost reduction. In order to compete, the US producer must seek to exploit whatever country-specific advantages are available to it; such as using superior technical knowledge and labor skills to innovate or to establish a quality advantage, or using proximity to the US market to meet the specific needs of US customer segments.

Similarly, in the personal computer industry, a Taiwanese manufacturer will have difficulty in establishing a competitive advantage as a supplier of state-of-the-art computers for specialized scientific usage. Taiwan does not possess the technical and research resources to facilitate such development. The Taiwanese manufacturer would be better advised to exploit Taiwan's advantages of moderate-wage, adaptable, dexterous workers by producing low-cost IBM clones.

Referring back to Exhibit 11.4, the national factors and the firm-level factors which determine competitive advantage in international markets are not separate. The resources possessed by the individual firm will reflect the conditions of resource availability within the nation as a whole. A key issue for strategy is to combine and integrate the country's comparative advantages with the firm's potential for competitive advantage.

The Multinational Strategy

International competition occurs through two mechanisms:

- international trade where nationally-based competitors sell into one another's markets;
- direct investment where firms establish operations in other countries.

So far our discussion has been concerned with the determinants of trade. Let us turn our attention to direct investment and examine the rationale behind a strategy of multinational expansion.

The determinants of direct overseas investment

Multinationals, firms with operating units in more than one country, are new. Trading companies such as the Dutch East India Company, the United Africa Company, and the Hudson's Bay Company were in the vanguard of colonial expansion during the eighteenth and nineteenth centuries. Multinational expansion of manufacturing companies did not occur on any scale until the early twentieth century and was associated primarily with the quest for raw materials by the oil companies (notably Standard Oil and Shell) and the expansion into Europe by US automobile and appliance makers such as Ford, GM, Singer, and Hoover.

For much of the twentieth century, multinational enterprise has been closely associated with US industrial supremacy. The perceived threat of expansion by US multinationals to the economic sovereignty of other countries was expressed in Jacques Servan-Schreiber's *Le Defi Americaine* ("The American Challenge") published in 1968.[7] However, since then, European and Japanese companies have been the prominent sources of overseas direct investment. These include the Japanese automobile and consumer electronics companies such as Honda, Toyota, Matsushita, and Sony; European oil companies such as British Petroleum, Elf (France), and ENI (Italy); European electrical and electronics companies such as Thompson (France) and Philips (Netherlands); and diversified MNCs such as BAT, Grand Metropolitan, and Unilever.

From these various examples of MNCs, six principal motivations for multinational expansion can be discerned:

- exploiting firm-specific assets and distinctive competencies;
- exploiting other countries' resources;
- pursuing the product life-cycle;
- exploiting superior growth and profit opportunities in overseas markets;
- risk spreading;
- overcoming trade barriers.

Exploiting firm-specific assets and distinctive competencies Prominent among MNCs are firms with strong technological capabilities, such as IBM, Xerox, Roche, and 3M, and companies with strong brand names such as Coca Cola, Nestlé, Proctor and Gamble, and Levi Strauss. Multinational growth permits them to exploit their innovations and brand differentiation overseas as well as at home.[8] A key issue which arises in relation to these resources is whether direct overseas investment is necessary to exploit these resources. If there is potential for a firm to exploit its assets in an overseas country, then why not exploit them directly by selling the use of these assets to overseas companies rather than incur the effort and risk of establishing overseas subsidiaries? For example, RCA exploited its patents in color television by licensing them to European and Japanese companies in preference to establishing overseas manufacture. Similarly, European brewers such as Löwenbrau, Heineken, and Amstel have chosen to license their brands and recipes to US brewers rather than enter the US themselves. In general, the greater the transactions costs in the markets for these assets, the greater is the incentive for a firm to exploit them directly through direct investment.[9] McDonald's decision to directly own and operate its first British restaurants, in preference to its normal policy of franchising its overseas restaurants, reflected its belief that the costs of monitoring and ensuring quality at its British restaurants and the potential risks to its own reputation of inept British management, made direct operation a more attractive alternative.

Exploiting other countries' resources Overseas direct investment does not simply involve a company seeking to exploit resources which it already possesses, a major objective of overseas expansion may be to *acquire* resources which are available overseas. Traditionally, industrial companies in Europe and North America moved overseas to exploit raw materials such as oil, bauxite, rubber, and iron ore. More recently, such overseas expansion is directed more towards the acquisition of knowledge and technical skills. European and Japanese electronics companies have established research units in California's Silicon Valley; various US manufacturing companies have established design studios in Italy.

Pursuing the product life-cycle New products tend to be developed first in the more advanced industrialized countries and directed towards more affluent consumers of these countries. Markets in less affluent countries develop later. Also, as the products enter the mature phase of their life-cycles, they become suited to manufacture in lower-wage countries. Hence, an attractive strategy is to introduce products first into the US, Japan, or West Germany, then to shift marketing and then production to newly-industrializing and developing countries.[10]

Exploiting superior growth and profit opportunities in overseas markets Even if multinationality does not confer obvious competitive advantages, where growth and profit opportunities are constrained by sluggish performance of the domestic economy, expanding into more prosperous overseas economies is clearly attractive. During the 1960s and 1970s, Britain's low rate of economic growth compared to most of Europe provided a powerful incentive for overseas investment.

Risk spreading   Multinational scope permits a diversifying of country-specific risks. The more risky the domestic economy is perceived to be, the greater the attraction of overseas over domestic expansion. Between 1985 and 1988 several major Hong Kong companies, including Hong Kong and Shanghai Bank and Swire Group, directed the major part of their expansion into North America and Europe. MNCs are much less vulnerable to exchange rate risk than domestically-based firms. For example, by switching output between its production plants in different countries, Caterpillar has gained some protection against the gyrations of the US dollar since 1981. Similarly, Honda began exporting to third country markets from its US plant in 1987–8 to take advantage of the low value of the dollar against the yen.

Overcoming trade barriers   Overseas investment can be regarded as an alternative to exporting. The greater the costs of exporting, whether from transportation or tariffs, the more attractive is overseas production. The imposition of tariff and quota restrictions on Japanese imports into Europe and North America was the principal factor encouraging Japanese automobile and consumer electronic manufacturers to establish overseas plants.

Global Strategies

So far, we have viewed international expansion, whether by exports or by direct investment, as a means by which a company can exploit its competitive advantages, not just in its home market, but in foreign markets. However, there is more to internationalization than simply extending the geographical boundaries of a company's market. International scope may also be a source of competitive advantage over nationally-based competitors. In this section we explore whether and under what conditions, firms which operate on an international basis, either by exporting or by direct investment, are able to gain a competitive advantage over nationally-focussed firms. If such "global strategies" have potential for creating competitive advantage, in what types of industry are they likely to be most effective, and how should they be used in order to maximize their potential?

The benefits of a global strategy

A global strategy is one which views the world as a single market. Theodore Levitt of Harvard Business School has argued that companies which compete on a national basis are highly vulnerable to companies that treat the world as a single global market.[11]

The basis of his thesis is, first, that national and regional preferences are disappearing in the face of the homogenizing forces of technology, communication, and travel. "Everywhere everything gets more and more like everything else as the world's preference structure is relentlessly homogenized," observes Levitt. Nor is this trend restricted to technology-based products such as computer, aircraft, and consumer electronics, it is as prevalent in branded consumer goods such as Coca Cola, Levi jeans and McDonald's hamburgers.

Secondly, firms which produce standardized products for the global market have access to scale economies in production, distribution, marketing, and management that permit them to offer a price–quality combination that nationally-based competitors cannot match. In the pharmaceutical industry, the spiralling costs of developing a new drug – now around $250 million – has forced companies to become global marketers.[12]

Levitt's argument is not that MNCs have a clear advantage over nationally-based competitors. The key issue is whether a company markets on a global basis. For instance, during the 1960s and 1970s most leading Japanese automobile and consumer electronics companies were barely multinational; their overseas subsidiaries were primarily marketing companies. Yet, companies such as Toyota, Matsushita, and Hitachi were primary exponents of global strategies. Conversely, many European and American corporations were *multidomestic* corporations rather than global corporations in the sense that each country was served by a fairly autonomous national subsidiary that managed a full range of functional activities. For example, until the late 1970s, General Motors' overseas subsidiaries, Opel in Germany, Vauxhall in Britain, and Holden in Australia, produced their own range of models, under their own brand names, for their own domestic markets. The advantage of this strategy is that it permitted flexibility in relation to local conditions, particularly in allowing differentiation on the basis of local preferences, while avoiding the administrative complexities associated with centralized control from a remote corporate head office. However, the multidomestic strategy suffers from the weakness that, in replicating the full range of operating and corporate functions in each national subsidiary, the potential for exploiting scale economies is limited by the size of each national market.

Levitt draws upon the European appliance industry to make his point. During the 1960s, Hoover sought to increase its share of the European home laundry market by more focussed and aggressive marketing in each European country. Market research told Hoover that there were distinct national preferences between countries: Italians preferred front-loading washing machines; the French preferred top-loaders; the Germans preferred a stainless steel drum, and so on. Hoover produced separate models for each national market. At the same time Italian manufacturers began expanding sales throughout Europe. They sold standardized, mass-produced, automatic washing machines which made few concessions to national preferences. The scale economies achieved by the Italians permitted them to undercut Hoover and the other European manufacturers, and by the mid-1970s to gain over 40 percent of sales in the European Community.

The message is not that all the world and its people are the same; national and regional differences exist and cannot be ignored. Underlying these differences is a commonality of goals: the alleviation of life's burdens and an expansion of leisure and spending power. When presented with a choice it is likely that customers will select the lower-priced, standardized product that meets the basic need in preference to the higher-priced, nationally-differentiated alternative.

Levitt's globalization thesis is a subject of continuing controversy. Critics have attacked both his assumptions of global homogenization of preferences and of the benefits of scale economies. Many products, culinary and skin-care products for example, are highly nationally differentiated. Also, costs of national differentiation can be surprisingly low if common basic designs and common major components are used. As manufacturing systems become increasingly flexible, costs of customizing products to meet the preferences of particular groups of customers are falling. It is notable that within the European Community, the Italian success within the appliance market proved temporary and national preferences remain strong.

Even global competitors need to make some concessions to national preferences. Honda, Sony, and American Express adjust their marketing and distribution strategies to meet local conditions, but their products are essentially globally standardized. Few companies attempt at complete standardization of products, distribution and marketing. Even Coca Cola recognizes clear national preferences. Its Hi-C Soy milk is popular mainly in Hong Kong, and its Georgia Coffee drink is consumed mainly in Japan. McDonald's also adapts to national preferences by serving beer in its German branches, wine in its French outlets, and noodles in the Philippines. Proctor and Gamble and Colgate-Palmolive, on the other hand, are leading exponents of global marketing. P&G's Pampers diapers are sold under the same slogan, "Even when they're wet, they're dry", worldwide. Colgate-Palmolive's standardization of packaging and advertising for its toothpaste makes large savings. A single commercial for Colgate tartar-control toothpaste saves around $1 million in production costs alone in each country it is shown.[13]

Global competition and strategic capability

The competitive advantage from a global approach to manufacturing, marketing, and distribution extends beyond the cost advantages from scale economies. Even in the absence of cost advantages from global scales of operation there are clear strategic advantages from an international scope. Because the global competitor faces different competitive conditions in different countries, it can use its strong position in some national markets to lever its position in countries where it is weak. Thus, although the firm pursues a global strategy in the sense that it recognizes markets as global, it also recognizes national segments in terms of competitive conditions and seeks to establish separate market objectives for each national segment. The firm can then use its positive cash flow from countries where it has a strong market position to finance competition against nationally-focussed competitors in their home markets. This practice of *cross-subsidization* does not necessarily involve aggressive price competition. To avoid triggering a price war, or anti-dumping suits, cross-subsidization will typically be used to finance heavy advertising, promotion, and dealer support which will build market share, but at the same time avoid the trauma of an all-out price war.[14]

A domestically-focussed firm is in a weak position to compete against selective competition by a global firm. Since the competitive battle affects its entire sales base, it has no overseas markets to rely upon for profit. Such was the position of the US TV manufacturers when faced by strong Japanese competition in the 1970s. The most effective response to such competition is to retaliate in the foreign MNC's own home market, since this is likely to be the primary source of its cash flow. Thus, when Kodak was attacked by Fuji in the US market – an attack that was symbolized by Fuji's capture of sponsorship of the 1984 Olympic Games in Los Angeles – Kodak's response was to attack Fuji in Japan.[15]

This global approach to competing within national markets requires a degree of central coordination of competitive strategies which conflicts with the management practices of many MNCs. Many multinationals allow a considerable degree of strategic and operating autonomy to their subsidiaries and allocate capital and management compensation on the basis of subsidiary financial performance. While this approach is well suited to achieving national differentiation, responsiveness to changing environmental conditions, and motivating managers in the subsidiaries and divisions, it makes it difficult to formulate national competitive strategies which are directed towards building an overall global market position, and it makes cross-subsidization difficult.

Operating Globally: Value-chain Analysis of Locational Decisions

For the multidomestic corporation, locational decisions pose few problems. Each national subsidiary establishes a full range of operating and corporate functions which simply replicate the parent company's domestic structure on a smaller scale. For the domestically-based global marketers locational decisions are also simple. To ensure maximum scale economies, production and corporate functions are concentrated in the home country and overseas subsidiaries simply perform export marketing and distribution. Most Japanese companies followed this approach up until the late 1970s.

However, between these two extremes, more complex locational issues arise. One source of complexity is the constraints upon the pursuit of a full global strategy. Not only are there differences in national conditions and preferences that necessitate differentiation of strategies and products to meet local conditions, but governments may use import restrictions as a means of forcing global corporations to establish manufacturing operations in export markets.

A second source of complexity is the fact that the supply of any product or service is composed of a vertical chain of activities, the characteristics of which vary considerably. If different activities within the value chain use different inputs in different proportions, the theory of comparative advantage suggests that each activity is likely to be optimally located in a different country. This phenomenon is evident from trends in the pattern of international trade. Increasingly, we observe that specialization on the basis of comparative advantage leads countries to specialize, not only in specific products, but in specific stages of the fabrication of products. For example, in electronic products such as TVs and computers, the production of components is capital and research intensive and subject to substantial scale economies; component production is concentrated in the advanced countries, notably the US and Japan. Assembly is labor intensive and is increasingly concentrated in the newly-industrialized and developing countries.

Exhibit 11.7

Comparative advantage in textiles and apparel, and in consumer electronic products by stage of processing

Industry	Country	Stage of processing	Index of revealed comparative advantage[a]
Textiles and apparel[b]	Hong Kong	1	−0.96
		2	−0.81
		3	−0.41
		4	+0.75
	Italy	1	−0.54
		2	+0.18
		3	+0.14
		4	+0.72
	Japan	1	−0.36
		2	+0.48
		3	+0.78
		4	−0.48
	U.S.A.	1	+0.96
		2	+0.64
		3	+0.22
		4	−0.73
Consumer electronic products[c]	Brazil	1	−0.62
		2	+0.55
	Hong Kong	1	−0.41
		2	+0.28
	Japan	1	+0.53
		2	+0.97
	S. Korea	1	−0.01
		2	+0.73
	U.S.A.	1	+0.02
		2	−0.65

[a] Revealed comparative advantage is measured as: (Exports − Imports/Exports + Imports).
[b] For Textiles and Apparel the stages of processing are: 1. fiber production (natural and synthetic); 2. spun yarn; 3. textiles; 4. apparel.
[c] For consumer electronics the stages of processing are: 1. components; 2. finished products.
Source: Based upon United Nations trade data.

A similar pattern is evident in the textile and clothing sector. Fiber production is concentrated in the countries with comparative advantage in agricultural production (for cotton and wool) and chemical production (for synthetic fibers). Spinning and weaving of cloth tend to be relatively capital intensive and occur both in the newly-industrialized and in the mature industrialized countries. Clothing production is labor intensive, here the developing countries have a clear comparative advantage. Exhibit 11.7 shows this pattern.

As a result, it is desirable, indeed necessary, for MNCs to examine their value chains to identify the optimal location for individual activities. This analysis involves two stages:

- determining the optimal location for each activity when viewed independently;
- consideration of linkages between activities which offer benefits from close geographical proximity of linked activities.

Exhibit 11.8 outlines a framework for considering the principal issues.

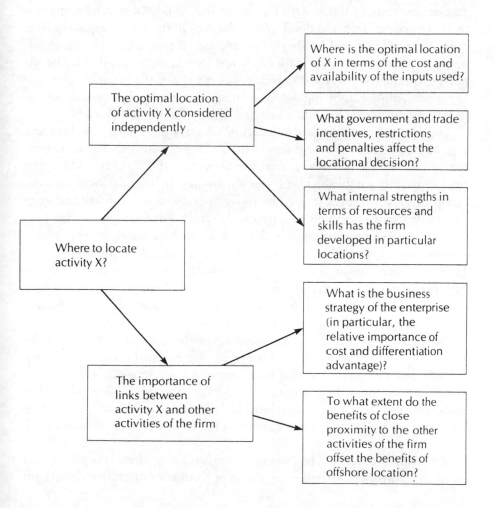

Exhibit 11.8 The international location of individual activities within the value chain: The key issues

Locating individual value-chain activities   To determine the best location
for each activity, the firm needs to identify the principal inputs to each
stage, and then to match these to the costs and availabilities of those inputs
in different countries. Consider the production of sports shoes by Nike.
There are three main stages: design, manufacture of components, and
assembly into finished shoes. The principal inputs into the design stage
are technical expertise, design and fashion expertise, and information
from marketing. These inputs are most readily available in an advanced
country which is also Nike's largest market, the US. Component production requires both skilled and unskilled labor, machinery (component
production is moderately capital intensive), and supplies of leather,
canvas, rubber, and plastics. On the basis of availability and cost, newly-
industrializing countries such as Taiwan and South Korea are the most
suitable locations. Assembly is labor intensive requiring only simple
machinery and little technical sophistication. The lowest cost locations for
assembly are developing countries with large pools of labor such as China,
India, the Philippines, and Thailand.[16]

Similar international fragmentation of the value chain is common in
among electronics MNCs. Both European and North American companies
tend to have research and development located in the US. Components are
typically manufactured in the US, Japan, and Western Europe. Assembly
may take place in Mexico, Taiwan, South Korea, or Brazil, depending, in
part, upon the technical and capital requirements of the assembly process.
Where assembly can be highly automated (as with Apple's production of
its Macintosh computer), then location within the US can be viable.

The optimal international allocation of activities for a new business
organizing green field investment in an industry is unlikely to be optimal
for a firm which is already established within the industry. Once the
firm is already established with plants running in specific locations, the
competitive advantages created by those operations will modify and even
supersede those associated with national factors. For example, a large part
of Nike's production of sports shoes is located in South Korea, where
labor costs are several times higher than in Thailand or the Philippines.
However, because of the scale of operations there, the economies of
experience that have accrued, and the high level of employee commitment
which has been established, it is still advantageous for Nike to originate a
major part of its production from Korea.

Optimal location is also dependent upon the business strategy of the
firm. For the firm which is competing on the basis of cost, the primary
consideration must be selecting locations which minimize cost. For a firm
which strives for a differentiation advantage, the availability of quality
materials and components, technical skills, and design and marketing
expertise are likely to be the major considerations in selecting location.

The role of linkages   The benefits from breaking the value chain and
locating individual activities in different countries must be traded off

against the costs of weaker links of stages in the chain. Transport costs are one consideration. In general, dispersing the value chain increases transportation cost. However, this is not always the case: shipping components to assembly plants in local markets may save on transport costs. Another cost of geographical dispersion is increased inventories. Shipping components and final products between the Far East and the United States typically takes over a month. As a result inventories and work-in-process are increased considerably. In many industries, especially automobiles, the move to just-in-time systems of component supply have greatly increased the attractions of geographically-concentrated component manufacture and assembly.

Equally important are linkages between operational and support activities for the purposes of coordination and control. Innovation we have noted requires close coordination and communication between R&D, manufacturing, and marketing. Geographical dispersion is a severe handicap to such coordination. Quality control requires coordination and swift feedback between sales activities, assembly, and component manufacture. Overall cost efficiency requires that management be able to monitor and quickly respond to cost variances anywhere within the corporation. Several US and European companies which established plants in low-wage countries subsequently discovered that the benefits of low wages were offset by the problems of low productivity; lack of coordination between supplies of materials, production, and market requirements; and poor quality control. The experiences of Nike and Jeep in China are extreme examples of the difficulties of achieving cost-efficient production in far-away places.[17]

Organization of the Multinational Corporation

Most approaches to strategy analysis regard a company's organizational structure as being contingent upon its strategy. Companies adopt a strategy which offers the best prospects for achieving competitive advantage within their particular industry, then adopt the structure which can implement that strategy most effectively. However, a company's organization structure cannot easily be adjusted over the short term and it may impose a powerful influence upon the company's strategic capability. Organizational structure is especially important for MNCs. The key strategic distinction we have made between global and multidomestic corporations is essentially a matter of the international organization of a company's activities. An MNC's structure is the major constraint upon its strategic flexibility: once an international distribution of functions, operations, and decision-making authority has been determined, reorganization can be difficult and costly, particularly when host governments become involved.

The single most important organizational issue for multinational corporations is the appropriate degree of decentralization. Which activities and functions should the company seek to retain within its home country,

The evolution of multinational structures

and to what extent should operations and decision-making authority be dispersed among overseas subsidiaries? During the development of the multinational corporation, three phases can be identified each associated with a different answer to this problem.

- the era of the European multinationals, before World War II;
- the era of the American multinationals, after World War II;
- the Japanese challenge in the 1970s and 1980s.

The era of the European multinationals, before World War II   During the early decades of the twentieth century, European multinationals – companies such as Unilever, Royal Dutch/Shell, ICI, Philips, and Courtaulds – were in the forefront of international business and played a leading role in overseas industrial development. These companies have been described by Bartlett and Ghoshal as "multinational federations": they pursued multi-domestic strategies where each national subsidiary was permitted a high degree of operational independence from the parent company undertaking its own product development, manufacturing and marketing.[18] Parent–subsidiary relations were principally organized around the appointment of senior managers to subsidiaries, authorization of major capital expenditures, and the flow of dividends from subsidiary to parent company. Such structures were an inevitable response to an era when international transport and communication were costly and unreliable, and national markets were highly differentiated. Exhibit 11.9 illustrates the allocation of activities and decision-making between parent and subsidiary companies in the European multinational.

The era of the American multinational, after World War II   The 1950s and 1960s saw the dominance of US companies across a range of manufacturing industries throughout the world. Companies such as GM, Ford, IBM, Coca Cola, Caterpillar, and Proctor and Gamble all became established as clear international leaders within their respective industries. Although the subsidiaries of US companies typically operated with a high degree of autonomy in terms of product introduction, manufacturing, and marketing, a key structural feature of the US multinationals was the dominant position of their domestic operations. Because the US was the largest and most affluent market in the world, the US base acted as the source of new products and process technology for the company as a whole. Hence the primary relationship between parent and overseas subsidiaries was technology transfer, and the primary competitive advantage of overseas national subsidiaries was their ability to utilize new products, process technology, and marketing and manufacturing know-how developed in the US.

The Japanese challenge in the 1970s and 1980s   During the 1970s and 1980s, US and European companies increasingly lost ground to Japanese

Exhibit 11.9
Centralization and decentralization in the multinational corporation

1. The European Multinationals:
   Decentralized Federations

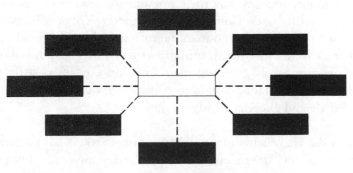

2. The American Multinationals:
   Coordinated Federations

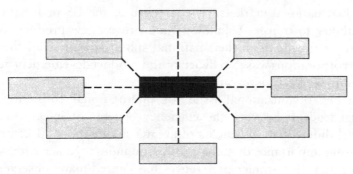

3. Japanese Global Corporations:
   Centralized Hubs

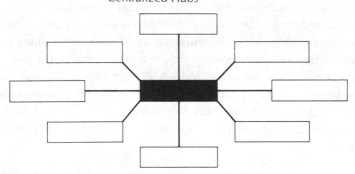

- ■ Location of primary strategic and operational decision making with the company.
- ▨ National subsidiaries possess a significant measure of strategic and operational autonomy.
- □ National subsidiaries possess little decision-making authority.

Source: Christopher Bartlett, "Building and managing the transnational: the new organizational challenge", in M. E. Porter, Competition in Global Industries (Harvard Business School Press, Boston, Mass., 1986), pp. 367–401.

companies across a range of manufacturing industries from steel and shipbuilding to electronics and automobiles. The key feature of the Japanese multinationals was their pursuit of global strategies from centralized domestic bases. Companies like Honda, Toyota, Matsushita, and NEC concentrated R&D and manufacturing within Japan, while overseas subsidiaries were established, initially at least, as sales, distribution, and service operations. By building plants of unprecedented scale to service growing world demand, Japanese companies were able to exploit substantial scale and experience advantages.

Global integration versus local adaptability

Although the victor's mantle in international markets has passed from the Europeans, to the Americans, and on to the Japanese, it is not possible to point to any particular organizational form as uniquely successful for multinational corporations. The strength of European multinationals was, and still is, their responsiveness to the conditions and requirements of individual national markets. The strength of the US multinationals was their ability to transfer technology and proven new products from their domestic strongholds to their national subsidiaries; that of the Japanese global corporations was the efficiency and product development advantages derived from global integration.

The key organizational issue for multinational corporations is the optimal tradeoff between the efficiency benefits of integration and the national differentiation benefits of greater multinational decentralization. Increasing importance of global scale economies together with worldwide convergence of customer preferences has caused many observers to proclaim the superiority of Japanese-style global integration.

Yet the evidence is not uniform. Bartlett and Ghoshal[19] point to the importance of the match between organization and the requirements of particular industries. In some industries, such as semiconductors, electronics, and motorcycles, the importance of scale economies and lack of national differences in customer requirements emphasize the benefits of global coordination. In other industries, notably processed foods, beer, and children's clothing, responsiveness to national customer preferences takes precedence over the efficiency advantages of global scale. Exhibit 11.10 summarizes Bartlett and Ghoshal's arguments and some of their evidence.

Organizing for the 1990s: the "transnational"

If national responsiveness was a key requirement for multinational success during the first half of the twentieth century, and efficiency through global integration was the foremost success factor during the past two decades, what of the future? Bartlett and Ghoshal argue that during the 1990s, companies will be forced to simultaneously achieve both efficiency and national responsiveness. While the pressure for efficiency will require a high level of global integration, increasing demands for differentiation from customers and increased pressures from governments for trade regulation and local value added will require increasing national responsiveness.

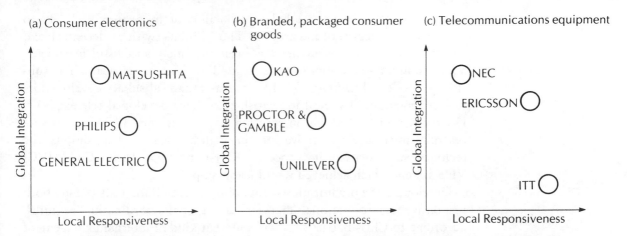

(a) Consumer electronics

(b) Branded, packaged consumer goods

(c) Telecommunications equipment

Exhibit 11.10
Organization and international success in different industries

(a) During the 1980s Matsushita was highly globally-integrated; Philips was the most multinational in terms of international spread and responsiveness of national subsidiaries to local requirements; while GE was primarily US-based and aimed at the requirements of the North American market. During the 1980s, customer preferences for consumer electronic products were highly uniform across countries, and competitive advantage was strongly determined by the ability of companies to gain access to global economies in product development and manufacture, and coordinate the global marketing of new products and new models. By the end of the 1980s, Matsushita was the clear winner, Philips was still hanging on (despite dismal profitability), while GE had left the industry.

(b) In branded, packaged, consumer goods, perpetuation of national differences during the 1980s helped Unilever, with its locally-responsive multinational spread, to remain the world leader across a number of product groups, while Proctor and Gamble was less successful with its more globally-orientated strategy. Meanwhile, Kao, the leading Japanese soaps and personal hygiene products supplier, largely failed in its attempts to penetrate international markets.

(c) Telecommunications equipment is subject both to substantial global scale economies in R&D and manufacture, and to the need for responsiveness to specific requirements of national telecom operating companies. ITT, the most international of the major players, was increasingly unable to achieve the integration necessary to lever its global position. NEC, despite its technological capabilities and dominant position in Japan, has so far failed to develop a strong position in Europe or North America. One of the most successful companies has been Ericsson, which, despite its small domestic market, has effectively combined global integration with national responsiveness.

Source: Based upon C. Bartlett and S. Ghoshal, *Managing Across Borders: The Transnational Solution*, (Harvard Business School Press, Boston, 1989).

At the same time, the pressure of international competition is placing new demands upon multinationals. Innovation is becoming increasingly important to international competitiveness. Achieving outstanding innovativeness also requires simultaneous pursuit of global integration and local responsiveness. The generation of product, process, and organizational innovations is best encouraged by a high degree of decentralization which encourages creativity and participation throughout the organization.

Conversely, the effective global introduction of innovation is likely to require a high degree of integration. Thus, Philips, with its decentralized, nationally-responsive structure has been extremely successful in encouraging company-wide innovation. In its TV business, its Canadian subsidiary developed its first color TV, its Australian subsidiary developed its first stereo-sound TV, and its British subsidiary developed teletext TVs. However, a lack of global integration has constrained its ability to successfully introduce its innovation on a global scale. Thus, despite the technical superiority of its V2000 VCR system, it was Victor Co.'s (JVC) VHS system which achieved world leadership.[20]

Developing the organizational capability to simultaneously pursue both responsiveness to national markets and global coordination requires, according to Chris Bartlett, "a very different kind of internal management process than existed in the relatively simple multinational or global organizations they may have had previously. I term this the 'transnational organization.'"[21] The distinguishing characteristic of the transnational is that it becomes an *integrated network of distributed and interdependent resources and capabilities*. The transnational corporation has several features:

- Each national unit is a source of ideas, skills, and capabilities that can be harnessed for the benefit of the total organization.
- National units achieve global scale by making them the company's world source for a particular product, component, or activity.
- The center must establish a new, highly-complex managing role which coordinates relationships between units but does so in a highly-flexible way. The key is to focus less on managing activities directly and more upon creating an organizational context which is conducive to the coordination and the resolution of differences. Creating the right organizational context involves "establishing clear corporate objectives, developing managers with broadly-based perspectives and relationships, and fostering supportive organizational norms and values."[22]

Transforming a company from either a loosely-knit multinational or a tightly-centralized global corporation into a "global network" inevitably requires substantial differentiation of subsidiary roles. Two factors are important in determining the appropriate role for a national subsidiary: the *strategic importance of the national market* and the *capabilities of the subsidiary*. On the basis of these two variables, Bartlett and Ghoshal[23] identify four generic roles (see Exhibit 11.11):

- strategic leader;
- contributor;
- implementor;
- black hole.

Strategic leader   A highly-capable subsidiary located within a key national market must play a leadership role for the company as a whole. For US multinationals, their US subsidiaries have typically occupied this role, but as other countries have closed the gap, both in affluence and technological and manufacturing capabilities, other national subsidiaries may be more appropriate leaders. For Ford's small cars, Ford of Europe has become a strategic leader.

Contributor Where a subsidiary has strong capabilities in a relatively unimportant market then it must act as contributor to the rest of the group. Ericsson's Australian subsidiary played a leading role in the development of the Swedish company's first electronic telecommunication switch. The key issue for Ericsson's headquarters management was to achieve transfer of the technology to other parts of the company.

Implementor Where market potential is limited and the country subsidiary lacks the capabilities to contribute greatly to the group as a whole, its role must be primarily to deliver the company's value added to the local market. Subsidiaries in Canada and smaller European countries typically occupy this role. They must be managed primarily for efficiency in their production, marketing, and distribution.

Black hole A difficult position for many companies is that in vital national markets they lack the capabilities to establish a strong position. Philips in Japan and Matsushita in Germany lack the local presence necessary for maintaining the companies' global positions. Joint ventures or acquisition may be necessary to fill black holes. The wave of US acquisitions by European multinationals reflects the desire of these companies to build capabilities in the key US market.

Exhibit 11.11 Roles for national subsidiaries

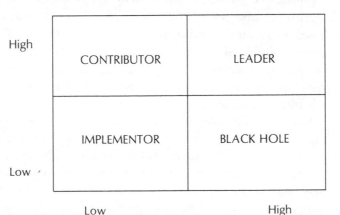

Source: Christopher Bartlett and Sumantra Ghoshal, "Tap your subsidiaries for global reach," *Harvard Business Review*, November–December 1986, p. 90.

Summary

Several critical strategic issues arise from the increasing internationalization of the business environment. Most serious for companies used to the stability of domestic markets sheltered from the full blast of international competition, is the intensification of competition which accompanies internationalization and the speed with which competitive advantage can be eroded by fast-moving, opportunistic foreign competitors. The impact of international competition in depressing profitability, increasing risk, and accelerating change underlines the need for clear-headed, soundly-based strategy analysis in globally-competitive industries. One barrier to achieving clarity of strategic direction is the spectacular leap in the amount and complexity of information and analysis necessary for the formulation and implementation of strategy in industries subject to international competition. In coming to terms with the greater complexity of international industries, an important feature of this chapter has been to show how the strategy analysis developed in this book can be extended by incorporating the features of the national environments which influence firms' competitive capabilities.

While international competition has been viewed primarily in terms of problems for companies, the internationalization of the world economy also presents unprecedented business opportunities. International markets are more competitive than nationally-sheltered markets, but they are also bigger. The ability of Asian-based companies to exploit domestic advantages of low wages and lack of regulatory constraints causes acute competitive problems for many European and American companies. At the same time, companies in the advanced industrialized countries are becoming more adept at exploiting the advantages of superior technological resources, better communication and infrastructure, and access to highly sophisticated financial markets which derive from their locations.

Also, companies are becoming less dependent upon their own home bases for resources and customers. Across a wide range of industries, from automobiles and electronics to textiles and publishing, companies are broadening their global scope through direct investment, licensing, joint ventures, and originating in order to take advantage of country-specific advantages overseas.

Some of the most interesting implications of internationalization of business are for the organization and staffing of companies. The ability to reconcile the conflicting needs for efficiency, innovation, customer responsiveness, and flexibility is giving rise to new organizational structures and new management systems. Equally important are the implications for human resource management, particularly at upper management level:

Intensifying international competition will make the home-grown chief executive obsolete, "Global, global, global," is how Noel Tichy, a professor of Michigan's graduate school of business, describes the wider-ranging chief executive of the future. "Travel overseas," Mr Danforth of Westinghouse advises future chief executives. "Meet the prime minister, the ministers of trade and commerce. Meet with the king of Spain and the chancellor of West Germany. Get yourself known." With over half of Arthur Anderson's revenue generated outside the US the company's next chief executive "will be a person with experience outside the borders of the U.S., which I have not," says Duane R. Kullberg, the head of the big accounting and consulting company. "If you go back 20 years, you could be pretty insular and still survive. Today that's not possible."[24]

Notes

1. The acquisitions included: British Petroleum (UK) of Standard Oil (Ohio), Unilever (Anglo-Dutch) of Chesebrough-Pond, Hoechst (Germany) of Celanese, ICI (UK) of Stauffer Chemical, Campeau Corporation (Canada) of Federated Department Stores, BAT Industries (UK) of Farmers Group Insurance, Bridgestone (Japan) of Firestone, Maxwell Communication (UK) of Macmillan Publishers, Sony (Japan) of CBS Records and Columbia Pictures, Beecham (UK) of SmithKline Beckman, and Grand Metropolitan of Pillsbury. (*Sources: The 1988 Business Week Top 1,000, The 1989 Business Week Top 1,000,* and *Fortune,* January 29, 1990).

2. M. Corina, *Trust in Tobacco* (Michael Joseph, London, 1975).

3. Ibid.

4. Paul Krugman, "Increasing returns, monopolistic competition, and international trade," *Journal of International Economics* (1979), pp. 469–79.

5. Kenichi Ohmae, *Triad Power: The Coming Shape of Global Competition* (Free Press, New York, 1985).

6. Michael E. Porter, *The Competitive Advantage of Nations* (Free Press, New York, 1990).

7. J. Servan-Schrieber, *The American Challenge* (Atheneum, New York, 1968).

8. The role of firm-specific assets in multinational expansion is analyzed in Richard Caves, "International corporations: the industrial economics of foreign investment," *Economica* 38 (1971), pp. 1–27.

9. David Teece, "Transactions cost economics and multinational enterprise," *Journal of Economic Behavior and Organization* 7 (1986), pp. 21–45.

10. Raymond Vernon, "International investment and international trade in the product cycle," *Quarterly Journal of Economics,* May 1966, pp. 190–207.

11. Theodore Levitt, "The globalization of markets," *Harvard Business Review,* May–June, 1983, pp. 92–102.

12. "How to go global and why," *Fortune,* August 28, 1989, p. 70.

13. "Marketers turn sour on global sales pitch Harvard guru makes," *Wall Street Journal,* May 12, 1988, pp. 1 and 17.

14. See Gary Hamel and C. K. Prahalad, "Do you really have a global strategy?" *Harvard Business Review,* July–August 1985, pp. 139–48.

15. R. C. Christopher, *Second to None: American Companies in Japan* (Crown, New York, 1986).

16. *Nike: International Context* (HBS Case Services, Harvard Business School, Boston, 1985), Case no. 9-385-328; and *Nike in China* (HBS Case Services, Harvard Business School, Boston, 1985), Case no. 9-386-037.

17. "The China bubble bursts," *Fortune*, July 6, 1987, pp. 86–9.

18. Christopher Bartlett and Sumantra Ghoshal, *Managing Across Borders: The Transnational Solution*, (Harvard Business School Press, Boston, 1989).

19. Christopher A. Bartlett and Sumantra Ghoshal, "Managing across borders: new strategic requirements," *Sloan Management Review*, Summer 1987, pp. 7–17.

20. Christopher A. Bartlett and Sumantra Ghoshal, "Organizing for worldwide effectiveness: the transnational solution," *California Management Review*, Fall, 1988, pp. 54–74. Also: "Sony isn't mourning the death of Betamax," *Business Week*, January 25, 1988, p. 37.

21. Christopher Bartlett, "Building and managing the transnational: the new organizational challenge," in M. E. Porter (ed.), *Competition in Global Industries* (Harvard Business School Press, Boston, 1986), p. 377.

22. Ibid., p. 388.

23. Christopher A. Bartlett and Sumantra Ghoshal, "Tap your subsidiaries for global reach," *Harvard Business Review*, November–December 1986, pp. 87–94.

24. "Going global: The chief executives in year 2000 will be experienced abroad," *Wall Street Journal*, February 27, 1989, pp. A1 and A4.

TWELVE

Corporate Strategy: Diversification

... in diversification we have a package that is not at all what it seems. On the outside we see an array of rationalizations that make diversification seem irresistibly attractive, but we know that, on the whole, diversified companies have not done so well. When we closely examine the reasons for diversification they tend to disappear.

Milton Lauenstein[1]

Outline

Introduction
Diversification over Time
Motives for Diversification
    The alleged risk-spreading benefits of diversification
    Growth as a motive for diversification
    Market power
Selecting Attractive Industries for Diversification
Competitive Advantage from Diversification
    Economies of scope
    The benefits of internalizing transactions
    Information advantages of the diversified corporation
Diversification and Performance
    The findings of empirical research
    The meaning of relatedness in diversification
Summary

Introduction

Diversification decisions by firms involve two key questions:

- Is the industry to be entered offering more attractive investment opportunities than those available within the firm's existing industry?
- Can the firm establish a competitive advantage over firms already established in the industry?

Hence, no new analytic framework is needed for the appraisal of diversification options. The analysis follows the same framework that was introduced in the first chapter for examining the sources of superior profitability (see Exhibit 1.2): diversification may be justified either by the superior profit potential of the industry to be entered or by the capacity of the firm to create competitive advantage in the new industry. Thus, the two main components of our analysis of diversification decisions are already familiar: Industry analysis and the analysis of competitive advantage.

The focus of this chapter is upon the latter question: What are the conditions under which diversification can lead to a company establishing a competitive advantage in a new industry and also strengthening its competitive position within existing industries? The key difference between single-business and multiple-business firms in sources of competitive advantage is that the multiple-business firm can exploit competitive advantages arising from the relationships between its different business activities; these are known as "synergies". The potential for diversification to exploit synergy in order to create and strengthen competitive advantage is the most important issue which we shall examine here.

We begin by examining the evolutionary pattern of large firms over time which can help us understand the motives for diversification. To understand why diversification has been unsuccessful for so many corporations, it is useful to question the objectives which have promoted the quest for diversification by so many large corporations.

Diversification over Time

There is little doubt that, over time, large firms tend to broaden the scope of their business both geographically and in terms of product range. Alfred Chandler's studies[2] of the long-term development large US corporations observed a common pattern of development which follows several stages:

- firms begin as single product businesses supplying a local market;
- the availability of improved methods of transport and communication permits firms to serve wider regional, and even national, markets;
- firms grow by vertical integration, in particular, firms seeking national marketing integrate forwards into marketing and distribution systems;
- excess capacity in marketing and distribution systems causes firms to diversify their product ranges.

Empirical evidence for the United States shows that, since World War II, the trend towards diversification has been persistent and strong. Wrigley[3] and Rumelt[4] classified corporations into strategic types based upon the pattern of their diversity. Over time the number of single business companies among the ranks of the Fortune 500 have fallen steadily, while the most diversified companies, whether related business or unrelated business (i.e. conglomerates) have increased in number (see Exhibit 12.1). Similar trends are apparent among large companies in other industrialized nations (see Exhibits 12.2 and 12.3).

Type of company	1949	1954	1959	1964	1969	1974
Single-business	42.0	34.1	22.8	21.5	14.8	14.4
Vertically-integrated	12.8	12.2	12.5	14.0	12.3	12.4
Dominant-business	15.4	17.4	18.4	18.4	12.8	10.2
Related-business	25.7	31.6	38.6	37.3	44.4	42.3
Unrelated-business	4.1	4.7	7.3	8.7	18.7	20.7

Exhibit 12.1
Changes in the diversity of the Fortune 500, 1949–74 (percentages)

Single business companies have more than 95% of their sales within their main business.

Vertically-integrated companies have more than 70% of their sales in vertically-related businesses.

Dominant-business companies have between 70% and 95% of their sales within their main business.

Related-business companies have more than 70% of their sales in businesses which are related to one another.

Unrelated-business companies have less than 70% of their sales in related businesses.

Source: Richard Rumelt, "Diversification strategy and profitability," *Strategic Management Journal* 3 (1982), pp. 359–70.

Type of company	1960	1970	1975	1980
Single-business	34.2	14.5	12.5	9.5
Vertically-integrated	2.0	3.3	3.4	3.0
Dominant-business	23.5	26.0	21.6	24.7
Related-business	32.0	44.4	49.0	49.7
Unrelated-business	7.4	11.8	13.5	13.2

Exhibit 12.2
Changes in the diversity of the 305 large British manufacturing companies, 1960–80 (percentages)

Source: Azar P. Jammine, *Product Diversification, International Expansion and Performance: A Study of Strategic Risk Management in UK Manufacturing*, PhD dissertation, London Business School, 1984, p. 215.

Type of company	1958	1963	1968	1973
Single-business	26.3	24.6	19.5	16.9
Vertically-integrated	13.2	15.3	18.6	18.6
Dominant-business	21.0	16.9	18.7	17.8
Related-business	30.7	35.6	36.4	39.8
Unrelated-business	8.8	7.6	6.8	6.8

Exhibit 12.3
Diversification among 118 large Japanese industrial corporations, 1958–73 (percentages)

Source: H. Itami, T. Kagono, H. Yoshihara, and A. Sakuma, "Diversification strategies and economic performance," *Japanese Economic Studies* 11 (1) (1982), pp. 78–110.

Evidence on the 1980s is less systematic yet, despite the continuation in the large number of large diversifying acquisitions, there is fragmentary evidence that the trend towards increased diversification may have halted if not reversed. In Britain, companies which had diversified most extensively during previous years became less diversified during the late 1970s and early 1980s.[5] Among US companies, corporate divestments outnumbered acquisitions during the later 1980s, while a number of diversified companies fell prey to leveraged buyouts.

Motives for Diversification

Before we can examine the performance implications of diversification, we need first to understand its motives. Consistent with the treatment of company objectives throughout this book, our analysis of diversification has begun with the assumption that diversification is motivated by the desire to increase companies' profitability. The implication of this motivation is that a successful diversification strategy is one that takes the firm into a more attractive industry or creates competitive advantage, or achieves both. But what about other motives for diversification? Since the 1960s and 1970s, diversification has been one of the most hotly debated topics in the field of strategic management. In the course of this debate several rationales have been proposed for diversification by firms. Among these, three have attracted particular attention:

- risk spreading;
- growth maximization;
- the quest for market power.

The alleged risk-spreading benefits of diversification

To consider the alleged benefits of risk spreading through diversification we need to consider "pure diversification", otherwise referred to as "conglomerate" diversification. This is where diversification simply extends corporate ownership over several independent businesses and the change of ownership has no impact on the independent profit streams of the separate businesses. By combining businesses with profit streams that are imperfectly correlated, diversification can achieve a reduction in the variability of the firm's overall profits. Since most individuals are risk-averse, risk reduction is a positive benefit to the owners of the firm. In the case of quoted companies, if the average return remains the same, but the variability of the return is reduced, then the increased attractiveness of the firm's shares to investors should be reflected in a rise in their price.

However, all this ignores the fact that individual investors can themselves spread risk by holding diversified portfolios of securities. If investors can engage in efficient home-made diversification, why should they be willing to pay a premium for the shares of diversified companies? The answer is, they do not: There is no evidence that the price-earnings ratios or the valuation ratios of diversified companies are any higher than those of specialized companies. This fact is formalized in the *Capital Asset Pricing Model* which states that risk which is relevant to determining the price of a security is not the overall variance of the security, but that part of the risk that is correlated with economy-wide fluctuations and, hence, cannot be diversified away by portfolio diversification. This is referred to as the "systematic risk" of the security and is measured by the security's "beta coefficient."[6]

Exhibit 12.4 illustrates the prediction that risk spreading by corporate diversification yields no benefit to shareholders. Two independent businesses, A and B, have streams of returns which are unaffected by their merging within a single corporation. Because the returns of A are imperfectly correlated with those of B, merging the two businesses achieves a reduction in the overall variability of return. However, if we assume that these profit returns to the firm are the same as the returns to shareholders, then the risk which concerns shareholders is the variance of the return on their overall portfolios. The contribution of each company to overall portfolio risk, the *systematic* risk, is unaffected by merging the two companies. The coefficient of systematic risk for the two companies, the beta coefficient, is simply the weighted average of those of the two businesses. Since diversification does not achieve any risk spreading that shareholders cannot do for themselves, diversification in the form of conglomerate mergers does not increase share prices.

Exhibit 12.4 The effect of pure conglomerate diversification on risk

	Expected annual rate of return	Total risk (variance of rate of return)	Beta coefficient	Systematic risk	Unsystematic risk
Business A	0.15 (=15%)	0.12	1.0	0.04	0.08
Business B	0.15 (=15%)	0.12	1.0	0.04	0.08
Business A+B	0.15 (=15%)	0.08	1.0	0.04	0.04

Businesses A and B have streams of returns with identical expected values, variances and systematic risks. When the two businesses are merged into a single enterprise, overall risk is reduced but systematic risk is unchanged.

Empirical studies generally support the absence of shareholder benefit from diversification that simply combines independent businesses. Studies of conglomerates in the US have shown that their risk-adjusted returns to shareholders are typically no better than those offered by mutual funds or by matched portfolios of specialized companies.[7]

For pure diversification to yield shareholder benefits market imperfections must be present in the form of transactions costs in securities dealing, or restrictions on the investment opportunities available to shareholders. For example, if individuals are unable to purchase the securities of overseas companies, there may be risk-spreading benefits from multinational diversification by domestic firms.

All this has been from the standpoint of the owners of the firms. There may also be risk-spreading benefits available to other stakeholders in the firm. If cyclicality in the firm's profits are accompanied by cyclicality in employment, then, so long as employees are transferable between the separate businesses of the firm, there may be benefits to employees from diversification smoothing output fluctuations. Diversification to avoid seasonal fluctuations in labor requirements is a standard feature of agriculture: by mixing crops with different planting and harvesting times the farmer can distribute his work load more evenly.

In general, it appears that managers are more enthusiastic about the risk-spreading benefits of diversification than are shareholders. Managers' risk aversity is likely to be motivated by their desire to protect their independence and their jobs. Downturns in profit, even if only temporary, can stimulate concern among shareholders and stock analysts, may make the company temporarily dependent upon financial markets for borrowing, and may encourage takeover bids.

Special issues arise once we consider the risk of bankruptcy. For firms earning low average profits, an important advantage of diversification is to avoid cyclical fluctuations of profits that render the firm temporarily insolvent. It has been shown, however, that diversification which reduces the risk of bankruptcy is beneficial to the holders of corporate debt rather than to equity holders. The reduction in risk which bondholders derive from a diversifying merger is termed the "coinsurance effect."[8] In addition, managers and other employees are likely to have strong interests in any strategy which reduces the risk of bankruptcy.

Growth as a motive for diversification

Consideration of the interests of employees (both managers and shopfloor workers) suggests further motives for diversification. It has been observed that diversification, whether by new venture or acquisition, is frequently directed towards achieving corporate growth. Growth is typically beneficial to employees since it creates opportunities for promotion. It is especially beneficial to top management whose salaries tend to be determined more by the size of the enterprise than by its profitability and whose power and status grow with organizational size. For firms in declining industries, the desire to avoid decline may provide particularly pressing motives for diversification; as the following examples show.

The decline in cigarette consumption that followed the Surgeon General's report on the health risks of smoking in 1963 was followed by a rash of diversification by the major tobacco companies, despite the fact that the businesses that they entered were all substantially less profitable than the tobacco industry. Evidence that the tobacco company's diversification was directed towards the interests of managers rather than of shareholders is further supported by the leverage buyouts mounted at R.J.R. Nabisco and BAT Industries which aimed at undoing this profitless diversification.

The transformation of the oil industry following the first oil shock of 1973–4 from a growth industry to a declining industry stimulated diversification by all the major oil companies. Again, none of the favorite destinations for diversification – coal, metals, nuclear power, solar energy – were as profitable as the oil business. Once profit pressures mounted on the oil companies, most of these non-oil businesses were divested.

This view of diversification as being motivated by managers' growth objectives is formalized in Marris' theory of managerial capitalism.[9] Managers' growth objectives result in them investing at a greater rate than would be consistent with profit maximization. They continue to trade profits for growth to the point that the valuation ratio of the firm (the ratio between the firm's stock market value and its book value) declines to the point where the firm becomes vulnerable to acquisition. Evidence supporting the Marris model is provided by the propensity of managers to divest diversified businesses when their control of the firm is threatened directly by a takeover bid or indirectly by a fall in profitability that reduces share prices and hence attracts potential predators.[10] Further support is provided by the finding that most mergers, diversifying mergers in particular, fail to increase the profitability of the merged companies.[11]

Market power

During the 1960s and the early 1970s, the emergence of a group of acquisitive, growth-orientated, highly-diversified companies known as *conglomerates* attracted considerable concern over the potentially anti-competitive effects of diversification. It was claimed that large diversified companies could exercise market power through three mechanisms:

- predatory pricing;
- reciprocal buying;
- mutual forbearance.

Predatory pricing   Just as global corporations derive strength from their ability to finance competitive battles in individual markets, through cross-subsidization, so conglomerates can similarly use size and diversification to discipline or even drive out specialized competitors in individual product markets. The key competitive weapon is predatory pricing, the ability to cut prices below the level of rivals' costs and sustain losses over the period needed to cause the competitor to exit or sell out.

Reciprocal buying   A conglomerate can lever its market share and profitability by reciprocal buying arrangements with customers. This means giving preference in purchasing to firms which are good customers for the conglomerate's own products. For instance, General Dynamics' acquisition of Liquid Carbonic Corporation in 1957 was based on the belief that General Dynamics subcontractors were likely to shift their purchases of industrial gases to Liquid Carbonic.[12]

Mutual forbearance   Corwin Edwards has argued that:

When one large conglomerate enterprise competes with another, the two are likely to encounter each other in a considerable number of markets. The multiplicity of their contacts may blunt the edge of their competition. A prospect of advantage in one market from vigorous competition may be weighed against the danger of retaliatory forays by the competitor in other markets. Each conglomerate may adopt a live-and-let-live policy designed to stabilize the whole structure of the competitive relationship.[13]

Despite the plausibility of these arguments, evidence on anti-competitive practices of these types are sparse. Certainly common patterns of diversification among competing firms in the same industries occur, which points to an awareness of the need to build countervailing strategic positions; overt abuse of conglomerate power is rare judging by the few actions which the antitrust authorities have initiated against conglomerates.

   Hence, while risk spreading, growth and quest for market power may offer incentives for diversification among companies, if the primary objective of a company is the pursuit of profit (as reflected in the maximization of shareholder wealth), diversification will be motivated by two primary goals: relocating into a more attractive industry environment, and the establishment of competitive advantage.

Selecting Attractive Industries for Diversification

Michael Porter proposes three "essential tests" to be applied in deciding whether diversification will truly create shareholder value:

- The attractiveness test – the industries chosen for diversification must be structurally attractive or capable of being made attractive.
- The cost-of-entry test – the cost of entry must not capitalize all the future profits.
- The better-off test – either the new unit must gain competitive advantage from its link with the corporation, or vice versa.[4]

The assessment of industry attractiveness was outlined in chapter 2: An important application of industry analysis is the prediction of profitability in industries which are candidates for diversification into. However, the second test explicitly recognizes that the attractiveness of an industry to a firm already established in that industry may be different from its attractiveness to a firm seeking to enter the industry. More specifically, industries such as pharmaceuticals, defense equipment, and cigarettes may be profitable precisely because they are surrounded by high entry barriers. For firms seeking to enter these industries, the costs of surmounting these barriers and becoming established in the industry may outweigh the benefits of being in the industry. Entry by new corporate ventures must risk large investments and low returns over a long period: A study of 68 diversifying ventures by established companies found that, on average, breakeven was not attained until the seventh and eighth years of operation.[15]

   If diversification is by acquisition, barriers to entry are avoided, but if the stock market is efficient, the market price of the target company's shares will accurately reflect future profit prospects. Since the acquirer must offer a premium of between 20 and 35 percent over the market price to gain control, it is likely that any superior profit prospects in the industry will be capitalized into the cost of entry.

Competitive Advantage from Diversification

Porter's third criterion for successful diversification – the "better-off" test – addresses the following issue: If two companies producing different products are brought together under the ownership and control of a single enterprise, is there any reason why they should become any more profitable?

Economies of scope

The conventional argument concerning the benefits of diversifications focusses upon the presence of *economies of scope* in common resources. If a certain input is used in the production of two products and this input is available only in units of a certain minimum size, then a single firm producing both products will be able to spread the cost of the input over a larger volume of output and so reduce the unit costs of both products.[16] Thus economies of scope exist for similar reasons as economies of scale. The principal difference is that the cost reduction gained from economies of scope arises from the increase in production volume which is achieved through producing multiple products.

Economies of scope exist primarily in two categories of resource: tangible assets which are used in joint production and intangible assets which can be transferred at low cost between the production of different commodities. Economies of scope in tangible assets arise from the ability to eliminate the duplication of certain activities across several products or services. Consider the following examples.

Distribution and service networks tend not to be highly specialized by product. Since there tends to be a minimum fixed cost of supplying and servicing a single outlet, there are economies in spreading distribution and sales costs over a range of products. For instance, in frozen foods, the costs of cold storage and refrigerated delivery costs account for around one-third of total cost. To minimize distribution costs the major integrated suppliers of frozen foods produce a wide range of frozen foods.

Similar considerations apply to service activities. For IBM and Xerox, economies of scope in the companies' service networks provided an incentive for the companies to supply a range of office equipment.

In technology-intensive industries, economies of scope in research and development facilities have provided a similar incentive for diversification. Companies typically have a single R&D department supporting a number of product divisions. An advantage of Sony, Matsushita, and Philips over US consumer electronics companies such as RCA and Zenith is that the greater product diversity of the former allowed them to spread R&D costs over a broader product base. In aerospace and electronic equipment, the ability of leading US suppliers to spread research expenditures over both defense products and civilian applications has given these companies an advantage over overseas competitors without access to large military contracts. More generally, studies of interindustry patterns of diversification show research intensity to be strongly associated with the extent of diversity.[17]

Intangible assets which can be utilized across several businesses also provide important opportunities for exploiting economies of scope. Assets such as brand names, corporate reputation and technology can be transferred from one business area to another without necessitating any physical integration of operations. Many of these assets have the characteristics of "public goods": They can be utilized in additional employment at negligible marginal cost. Thus, when American Express diversified its range of financial services with the acquisitions of Shearson and Lehman Brothers, IDS Financial Services, and Trade Development Bank, the new subsidiaries all clearly identified their new affiliations by prominent display of the American Express blue and white corporate logo and the addition of the suffix "An American Express Company" to their company names:

> ... we are creating a new kind of enterprise – one with multiple distribution channels that target select market segments with strong brand-name products and services. One expression of our multiple marketing strategy is the new logos and names for the American Express family. Our marketing strategy for the decade ahead is to sharpen our focus on the individual brand names as well as on the multiple distribution channels and carefully targeted market segments these brand names represent. At the same time, each business will continue to draw upon the marketing power and identification of the American Express name.[18]

Some of the most important intangible assets in offering opportunities for exploiting economies of scope are functional and general management capabilities; activities which, through investment and experience, a firm is capable of performing particularly well. For example, Philip Morris's success in increasing both the profitability and the market share of Miller Brewing Company was primarily due to the application of the marketing skills developed in the cigarette market. Thus, many of the marketing ideas applied in the promotion of Miller Lite were very similar to those used in the introduction of low-tar brands of cigarettes. Honda's expertise in the efficient, high-volume manufacture of reliable gasoline engines encouraged its diversification from motorcycles into cars, lawnmowers, generators, boat engines, and chain saws.

For many companies, the capabilities that have promoted successful diversification lie deeply-embedded in the enterprise's organization, management systems, and culture. For example, 3M's remarkably successful record in new product development is partly a result of its functional strengths in product development and the marketing of new products, but it is also the consequence of an organizational climate that encourages initiative and rewards entrepreneurship. General Electric's remarkable success as America's most diversified corporation owes much to the cor-

porate systems which plan, control and integrate the 40 or so Strategic
Business Units. As one executive remarked: "When Japanese managers
come to visit us, they don't ask to see our research centers or manufacturing
facilities. All they want to know about is our management system."[19] The
effectiveness of GE's strategic planning system in guiding acquisitions and
divestitures, and in reconciling rigorous cost efficiency with innovation
and market penetration among its business units is indicated by its rapid
expansion into financial services, its establishment of global market leadership in jet engines, and its dramatic restructuring of RCA.[20]

In as widely diversified a company as GE, the individual businesses,
though seemingly unrelated in terms of common resources or markets or
technologies, are linked through their dependence upon common general
management capabilities and systems. This integrating role of management
skills and corporate systems is also apparent among other successful
conglomerates. Under Harold Geneen, ITT managed a corporate empire
that was widely diversified across both industries and countries. The core
of ITT's corporate success was its comprehensive monitoring by corporate
head office of the financial and operational performance of subsidiaries
backed by incentives and sanctions which put divisional managers under
relentless pressure to achieve performance targets.[21]

Similar factors are at work at Hanson, one of the most successful British
companies of the 1980s, whose acquisitions included SCM, Kidde, Imperial
Group, and Ever Ready. The success of the company lies in the sophisticated post-acquisition management skills and highly-effective systems
of financial control through which Hanson has been able to secure drastic
cost reductions and substantial profit enhancement from mature, seemingly
unglamorous businesses.[22]

While economies of scope provide cost savings from using the same asset
in the production of several products, a critical issue is whether such
cost savings necessitate diversification within the enterprise? Why cannot
economies of scope be exploited by selling the use of the common asset to
independent firms? In practice, economies of scope are frequently exploited
by market transactions. If proprietary technology can be exploited in the
production of several products, the firm has the option of licensing the use
of its patents to other companies. In the case of brand reputation, the
owners of well-established brand names, including Gucci, Yves St. Laurent,
Harrods, and Guinness, license the use of their names to other firms for
use with designated products. In some industries, notably fast food and
personal services, franchising provides an effective mechanism for licensing
the use of brand names, product technology, and management systems. In
retail department stores a recent trend has been to exploit economies of
scope in the use of floor-space by renting areas of the stores to independent
retailers as "shops-within-shops."

Hence, economies of scope are not a sufficient condition for diversification. For diversification to yield competitive advantage requires not

**The benefits of
internalizing
transactions**[23]

only the existence of economies of scope in common resources, but also the presence of *transactions costs* which discourage the firm from selling or renting to other firms the use of the resource. Transaction costs include all the costs involved in drafting, negotiating, and safeguarding an exchange agreement. These costs are incurred not only before the transaction but also afterwards through the need to renegotiate contracts, to resolve disputes, and to ensure that commitments are fulfilled.[24] Transactions costs are likely to be particularly important when transferring intangible resources such as brand names, patents, distribution systems, and know-how between firms. Hence, exploiting economies of scope in these assets provides a particularly important motivation for diversification.[25] Consider the three examples below.

In 1972 the British electronics and music company EMI chose to establish its own medical electronics division to manufacture and market the revolutionary X-ray scanner that it had developed within its research labs. It believed that if it simply licensed its invention to established suppliers of X-ray equipment, only a small portion of the benefits from the innovation would accrue to EMI and it would be impossible to prevent the licensees from acquiring the technical knowledge that would allow them to by-pass EMI's patents.

Licensing of the use of a brand name by other firms runs the risk that the licensee may adversely affect the reputation of the brand through poor-quality products. The exclusivity value of the brand names of some European fashion houses (Yves St. Laurent, Gucci) have been adversely affected by excessive licensing. Formulating and policing a licensing agreement that protects a brand's reputation is costly. An important element in the turnaround of Harley-Davidson during 1984–90 was rigorous policing of the use of the Harley-Davidson name and logo, and the development of a licensing policy which reflected the quality image which was being developed for Harley bikes.

In the case of know-how and organizational skills, contractual agreements are particularly unsatisfactory because property rights are not clearly defined as they are for brand names and patents. The 3M Company has unrivalled know-how in the development of adhesives and the application of bonding technology and legendary capabilities in the successful launching of new products. In principle, it would be possible for 3M to sell its technical skills and new product ideas to firms already established within these fields. However, such agreements would be exceedingly difficult to draw up and enforce and it is unlikely that, through such agreements, 3M could realize the full profit potential of its capabilities. To exploit these capabilities, 3M has diversified widely into a broad range of products: Various adhesive tapes, magnetic tape, computer disks, fasteners for surgical use and water-resistant sun-tan lotion.[26]

The presence of transactions costs in any type of common resource can encourage diversification, even where economies of scope are not present. For example, the costs incurred by firms in using financial markets (in terms of the margin between borrowing and lending rates, and the under-writing costs from new issues of securities) encourages large companies to develop internal capital markets. By transferring cash between its businesses the diversified company can achieve greater independence from financial markets. One purpose of portfolio analysis (see chapter 13) is to achieve a balance between cash-generating and cash-using businesses. Some large corporations have gone further and extended their management of internal financial flows from being not just a means of minimizing financing costs, but a source of profit. Among the companies to have established in-house banks is British Petroleum. BP Finance International, established in 1985, arranges the financing of BP's 70 operating companies, undertakes standard treasury functions, trades in foreign exchange, manages leasing, and has 24-hour trading capability in short-term instruments. BP Finance International had, in 1986, over 100 employees, offices in London, New York and Melbourne, and made over $50 million in profit.[27]

Cost savings can also arise from the internal transfer of employees, particularly managers and technical experts, between the divisions of a diversified company as compared with hiring and firing in the labor market.

An important benefit of internal transfer of employees and other inputs within the diversified firm is that a company's management has much better information on the capabilities and characteristics of each of its employees than is available for job candidates attracted through the labour market. This informational advantage exists not only for individual employees but also for groups of individuals working together as teams. As a result, when diversifying into a new activity, the established firm is at an advantage over the new firm which must assemble a team from scratch with poor information on individual capabilities and almost no information on how effective the group will be in working together. Hence, in an economy where new industries are constantly arising there are reasons to expect that diversification by established firms may be more successful in exploiting the new opportunities than entirely new ventures.[28]

Information advantages of the diversified corporation

Empirical evidence supports the observation that, while new ventures and individuals frequently play a key role in pathbreaking inventions, established firms are the most successful in the commercial development of new businesses. In personal computers, the winning companies were primarily well-established companies in the electronics industry (IBM, Hewlett Packard, Toshiba, NEC); of the newcomers only Apple and Compaq achieved lasting success within the big league. In most expanding new product areas, such as pharmaceuticals, fiberoptics, facsimile machines, laser printers, and compact disks, few successful companies were entirely new enterprises; success has typically gone to established companies which have entered these innovative new areas.

The role of information and, more specifically, the greater access to information which is available within the firm than across markets offers further reasons why diversified firms may be more successful than specialized firms. We have observed that managers tend to pursue goals of self-interest which conflict with profit maximization. As a result, an *agency problem* rises in the firm: the owners of the firm (the shareholders) do not exercise direct control; their representatives, the board of directors, control the company, but the board may either be lax in its direction of salaried managers, or it may even be dominated by salaried executives. Hence, the principal constraint upon managers' pursuit of non-profit goals is the stock market in terms of vulnerability to hostile takeover.

Imperfections in the flow of information from the firm to the stock market mean that the threat of takeover is, at best, a haphazard discipline on self-serving, lazy, or incompetent managers. By contrast, if the disciplines of the capital market can be created *within* the diversified corporation then the superior access of corporate management to information on the performance of each division can be used much more effectively to allocate funds, to threaten divestiture or to fire divisional managers.

The merits of the multidivisional ("M-form"), diversified company in economizing on transactions costs and overcoming agency problems has been effectively argued by Oliver Williamson:

... the M-form conglomerate can be thought of as substituting an administrative interface between an operating division and the stockholders where a market interface had existed previously. Subject to the condition that the conglomerate does not diversify to excess, in the sense that it cannot competently evaluate and allocate funds among the diverse activities in which it is engaged, the substitution of internal organization can have beneficial effects in goal pursuit, monitoring, staffing and resource allocation respects. The goal-pursuit advantage is that which accrues to M-form organizations in general: since the general management of an M-form conglomerate is disengaged from operating matters, a presumption that the general office favors profits over functional goals is warranted. Relatedly, the general office can be regarded as an agent of the stockholders whose purpose is to monitor the operations of the constituent parts. Monitoring benefits are realized in the degree to which internal monitors enjoy advantages over external monitors in access to information – which they arguably do. The differential ease with which the general office can change managers and reassign duties where performance failures or distortions are detected is responsible for the staffing advantage. Resource allocation benefits are realized because cash flows no longer return automatically to their origins but instead revert to the center, thereafter to be allocated among competing uses in accordance with prospective yields.[29]

Diversification and Performance

The findings of empirical research

The implications of these arguments for the impact of diversification on firm performance are as follows. First, the diversified corporation can carry out the tasks of resource allocation and the monitoring and control of operational managers more effectively than the market system; we would expect that, over the long term, diversified firms would show higher profitability and more rapid growth than specialized firms. Secondly, because of the importance of economies of scope in shared resources, diversification into *related* industries will be more profitable than diversification into *unrelated* industries.

Initially, empirical research into the impact of diversification on firm performance produced clear and consistent findings on the second hypothesis. Rumelt's initial study found that, while diversification per se showed no clear relationship with profitability, sharp differences emerged between different diversification strategies.[30] In particular, firms which diversified into businesses which were closely related to their existing activities were significantly more profitable than those which pursued unrelated diversification. Subsequent research confirmed Rumelt's findings both for the US and for other countries (notably Canada, West Germany, and Japan). At the same time, the problems associated with wide-ranging unrelated diversification were highlighted by the poor performance of such conglomerates as LTV, ITT, and Allegeny International. The apparent consistency of the evidence was such that, in 1982, Tom Peters and Robert Waterman were able to conclude: "virtually every academic study has concluded that unchannelled diversification is a losing proposition."[31] On the basis both of academic research and their own observations they coined one of their golden rules of excellence – "Stick to the Knitting":

Our principal finding is clear and simple. Organizations that do branch out but stick very close to their knitting outperform the others. The most successful are those diversified around a single skill, the coating and bonding technology at 3M for example. The second group in descending order, comprise those companies that branch out into related fields, the leap from electric power generation turbines to jet engines from GE for example. Least successful, as a general rule, are those companies which diversify into a wide variety of fields. Acquisitions especially among this group tend to wither on the vine.[32]

However, recent studies undermined the apparent consistency of these findings. Some studies have shown that the apparent superior performance of related diversifiers was, in fact, due to industry factors rather than to the type of diversification strategy,[33] while other studies have found unrelated diversification to be more profitable than related.[34] Exhibit 12.5 summarizes the findings of some of the leading studies.

On the general superiority of diversified firms to specialized firms, there is evidence, both for the US and Britain, that there may be limits to the degree of diversity which can be profitably managed by most companies. One recent study found that diversified British companies were more profitable than specialized companies up to a point, after which further increases in diversity were associated with declining profitability (see Exhibit 12.6). However, in all these studies there is ambiguity over the direction of causation. To the extent that increased diversification is associated with increased profitability, is this because increased diversification increases firm profitability, or is it because more profitable firms

Exhibit 12.5

Empirical research into the impact of diversification on performance: a summary of major research findings

Study	Sample	Main findings
Rumelt (1974)[1]	500 industrial companies, 1949–69	Companies which diversified around common skills and resources were most profitable. Vertically-integrated companies and conglomerates were the least profitable.
Berry (1975)[2]	460 industrial companies	Companies which pursued narrow-spectrum diversification (within 2-digit industry groups) grew more rapidly than firms which pursued broad-spectrum diversification (across 2-digit industries).
Biggadike (1979)[3]	68 diversifying ventures by 35 large corporations	New ventures require an average of 7 years before attaining profitability.
Christensen and Montgomery (1981)[4]	128 of Fortune 500 companies, 1972–77 (sub-sample of Rumelt, 1974)	Companies pursuing related, narrow-spectrum diversification were most profitable; vertically integrated firms least profitable. But performance differences primarily a consequence of industry factors.
Bettis (1981)[5]	80 of Fortune 500 companies, 1972–77	Related diversification more profitable than unrelated, but difference primarily due to the impact of advertising, R&D, risk, and capital intensity.
Rumelt (1982)[6]	273 of the Fortune 500 companies, 1955–74	Related diversification more profitable than unrelated even after adjusting for industry effects.
Michel and Shaked (1984)[7]	51 companies from the Fortune 500, 1975 and 1981	Unrelated diversifiers earned higher risk-adjusted equity returns than related diversifiers.
Varadarajan Ramanujam (1987)[8]	225 companies, 1980–84	Related diversifiers earned higher return on equity and capital invested than unrelated diversifiers.
Dubofsky and Varadarajan (1987)[9]	Same as Michel and Shaked (1984)	Confirmed Michel and Shaked's finding that unrelated diversifiers earn higher risk-adjusted equity returns than related diversifiers.

Study	Sample	Main findings
Non-US studies		
Itami et al. (1982)[10]	112 large Japanese companies, 1963–73	After adjusting for firm size and industry factors, narrow-spectrum, related diversification most profitable.
Lecraw (1984)[11]	200 large Canadian manufacturing companies, 1961–75	Related diversification associated with higher return on equity.
Luffman & Reed (1984)[12]	439 UK companies from the Times 1000, profits, 1970–80	Conglomerates showed highest equity returns and growth of sales and profits.
Grant et al. (1988)[13]	305 large, UK manufacturing	Product diversity positively associated with profitability, but after a point relationship turns negative.

Sources:

1 Rumelt, R. P., *Strategy, Structure and Economic Performance* (Harvard University Press, Cambridge, Mass., 1974).

2 Berry, C. H., *Corporate Growth and Diversification* (Princeton University Press, Princeton, NJ, 1975).

3 Biggadike, R., "The risky business of diversification," *Harvard Business Review* 60 (1979), pp. 103–11.

4 Christensen, H. K. and Montgomery, C. A., "Corporate economic performance: Diversification strategy versus market structure," *Strategic Management Journal* 2 (1981), pp. 327–43.

5 Bettis, R. A., "Performance differences in related and unrelated diversified firms," *Strategic Management Journal* 2 (1981), pp. 379–83.

6 Rumelt, R. P., "Diversification strategy and profitability," *Strategic Management Journal* 3 (1982), pp. 359–70.

7 Michel, A. and Shaked, I., "Does business diversification affect performance?" *Financial Management* 13 (4) (1984), pp. 18–24.

8 Varadarajan, P. R. and Ramanujam, V., "Diversification and performance: A reexamination using a new two-dimensional conceptualization of diversity in firms," *Academy of Management Journal*, 30 (1987), pp. 369–80.

9 Dubofsky, P. and Varadarajan, P. R., "Diversification and measures of performance: Additional empirical evidence," *Academy of Management Journal* 30 (1987), pp. 597–608.

10 Itami, H., Kagono, T., Yoshihara, H., and Sakuma, A., "Diversification strategies and economic performance," *Japanese Economic Studies* 11 (1) (1982), pp. 78–110.

11 Lecraw, D. J., "Diversification strategy and performance," *Journal of Industrial Economics* 33 (1984), pp. 179–98.

12 Luffman, G. A. and Reed, R., *The Strategy and Performance of British Industry, 1970–80* (Macmillan, London, 1984).

13 Grant, R. M., Jammine, A. P., Thomas, H., "Diversity, diversification and profitability among British manufacturing companies," *Academy of Management Journal* 31 (1988).

Exhibit 12.6   The relationship between diversity and profitability among 304 British manufacturing companies, 1972–84

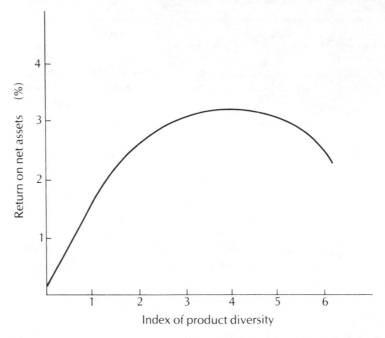

Source: R.M. Grant, A.P. Jammine and H. Thomas, "Diversity, diversification and profitability among British manufacturing companies," *Academy of Management Journal* 31, December 1988.

are using their profits to grow through diversification? Observation of profitable companies such as the tobacco companies and oil companies during the 1970s and early 1980s suggests a preference of top management to channel profit earnings into diversification rather than distribute them to shareholders.

The finding by several recent studies that unrelated diversification is more profitable than related diversification or that relatedness has no significant impact on the profitability of diversification, is surprising. Since the primary rationale for diversification is to exploit economies in common inputs and to transfer skills between businesses, what possible reasons might explain the failure of empirical research to find the consistent superiority of related over unrelated diversification? Two factors may be important. First, related diversification appears to pose particularly difficult management problems for companies; secondly, there is confusion and disagreement about what "related" diversification means and which types of relationships between businesses are the most important.

The first of these factors, the problems of managing related diversification, is a large and complex issue. It goes right to the heart of the issues surrounding the implementation of diversification strategies and the management of diversified corporations. For this reason we shall defer its discussion to the next chapter. Suffice to say at this juncture that, if there are potential economies from exploiting the links between businesses within the diversified company, then these links must be managed. As with any management activity, it is not costless.

Our discussion of economies of scope identified two major types of related-ness offering synergistic benefits from diversification: The use of common physical resources between businesses such as a common distribution system or R&D department, and the transfer of skills and reputation between businesses. Distinguishing the potential for exploiting economies of scope between businesses is no easy matter and researchers have used simple criteria for determining whether or not businesses are related. Typical criteria are similar technologies and similar markets. Under the first criterion, missile guidance systems and personal computers are related by their common utilization of electronic technology. Under the second criterion canned vegetables and frozen desserts are related because they are sold to the same customers through the same retail outlets.

However, similarities in technology and markets refer primarily to relatedness at the *operational* level, in activities such as product develop-ment, manufacturing and marketing. Relatedness may also exist at the *strategic* level through the application of common management skills to different businesses. Hence, in determining whether an acquisition or a new venture will "fit" with a company's existing range of activities, the most important factor is likely to be the ability of corporate management to apply similar strategies, resource allocation procedures, and control systems as are applied to the company's present businesses. Exhibit 12.7 lists some of the strategic factors which determine whether similarities exist between businesses in relation to corporate management activities.[35]

The meaning of relatedness in diversification

Corporate management tasks	Determinants of strategic similarity
Resource allocation	Similar sizes of capital investment projects. Similar time spans of investment projects. Similar sources of risk. Similar general management skills required for business unit managers.
Strategy formulation	Similar key success factors. Similar stages of the industry life-cycle. Similar competitive positions occupied by each business within its industry.
Monitoring and control of business unit	Goals defined in terms of similar performance variables.
Performance	Similar time horizons for performance targets.

Exhibit 12.7 The determinants of strategic relatedness between businesses

Unlike operational relatedness, where the benefits of exploiting econ-omies of scope in joint inputs are comparatively easy to forecast, and even to quantify, relatedness at the strategic level may be much more difficult to appraise. There are numerous examples of companies which identified potential synergies between businesses which in practice proved either elusive or non-existent. A classic example is the creation and rapid demise of the Allegis Corporation (see Case Note 12.1).

Case Note 12.1   The rise and fall of Allegis

On May 1, 1987, Richard J. Ferris, Chief Executive of UAL Inc., inaugurated a new era in the company's history under the new name of "Allegis Corporation." The name change symbolized the metamorphosis of UAL from an airline into a diversified travel company. Ferris explained the company's mission as follows:

Allegis is United, the airline industry leader. It is Hertz, the top car-rental company. It is Westin, a luxury hotel group. Allegis is Covia whose Apollo product is a multinational computer reservations network. It is MPI, a full-service direct marketing agency. It is United Vacations, a wholesale travel tour operator. And Allegis will soon be Hilton International, when we complete our purchase of that leading company with 88 luxury hotels in 42 countries.

Allegis Corporation ... caring for travellers worldwide ... a distinctive partnership of companies ... where people are pledged to service and quality.

Allegis will be the world's premier travel-related corporation – recognized by customers, employees, and investors as the source of superior quality and value.

Allegis customers will prefer the services of its worldwide operating partnership because they represent the best in dependability, comfort and convenience ... and because they are delivered by people whose attention to detail enhances every aspect of the travel experience ...

Allegis will also be unwavering in its dedication to bring quality and care back into the total travel experience. So we pledge to you, our customers, value, convenience, dependability, security, comfort – in sum, ease of travel that no other single corporation can match.

On June 9, only six weeks after formally adopting the Allegis name, Ferris was ousted by the board. The car rental and hotel subsidiaries were sold, and the company reverted to its name of United Airlines Inc.

What had gone wrong? Allegis broke two out of three of Porter's "essential tests" of a diversification strategy. First, its cost of entry, in terms of the prices it paid for companies during its two-year, $2.3 billion acquisition binge, was too high. Secondly, in terms of the "better-off" test, it appeared that Ferris had greatly overestimated the synergies to be exploited in bringing together airlines, hotels, and car rental under a common ownership. Indeed, it was not apparent that the chief benefit, providing one-stop shopping for the business traveler through an integrated reservations system, could not be achieved equally well by collaboration among independent companies.

While market-relatedness provided the principal benefits, the key stumbling block for the company were the strategic dissimilarities between the different businesses. While Allegis's up-market hotel chains competed on the basis of service and reputation, the principal requirement for success in the deregulated airline industry was rigorous cost cutting and the maintenance of high load factors through quick-footed operational management. Allegis's focus on servicing the needs of the business traveler deflected its attention from its critical need: Reducing costs and increasing efficiency at United Airlines.

Sources: Richard J. Ferris, "From now on," *Vis-à-Vis*, March 1987, p. 13; "Allegis: is a name change enough for UAL?", *Business Week*, March 2, 1987, pp. 54–8; "The unravelling of an idea," *Business Week*, June 22, 1987, pp. 42–3.

Summary

Diversification is a corporate minefield. In no other area of corporate strategy have so many companies made such disastrous investments. Ever since the 1960s, academics and business commentators have pointed to the dismal record of diversification by large companies; particularly those which have diversified by acquisition. Yet the diversification trend continues. Among the world's largest companies, major diversification initiatives have been undertaken by General Motors (into electronics and aerospace with the acquisition of EDS and Hughes Aircraft), Exxon (into electric motors, and office automation), Ford Motor (into financial services), Sony (into entertainment through the acquisition of RCA Records and Columbia Pictures), General Electric (into financial services), and AT&T (into computers). Consistent with the overall track record, few of these diversifications have so far been successful, and several have already been divested. Why does diversification seem to have such an irresistible attraction for companies, and what recommendations can be offered to improve the outcomes of diversification?

Much depends upon the driving forces behind diversification. In a turbulent world where technology and customer requirements are constantly changing, firms must inevitably reexamine and redefine their product scope. The complementary moves of AT&T into computers and IBM into telecommunications, the changing product mix of Hewlett Packard, and Walt Disney's moves from cartoon movies into theme parks, cable TV, and adult-audience movies can all be viewed as responses to external changes. On the other hand, diversification may be the result of escapist tendencies which result from the unwillingness of top management to come to terms with difficult competitive circumstances in their core businesses. Diversification may then be a diversion.

Behind many of the most ambitious and spectacular diversification initiatives is the worry that these investments may be motivated more by managerial than shareholder interests. The empirical evidence points to the fact that while diversification through acquisition fails to offer gains in profitability or increasing returns to shareholders, it is highly effective in the creation of large corporate empires.

In terms of improving the performance consequences of diversification strategy, the first recommendation is for candid questioning of the motives for diversification and a careful assessment of the consequences of diversification for shareholders. Such inquiry may be particularly effective in avoiding one of the most common errors of diversifying companies: Paying over the odds for acquisitions.

The second critical issue in diversification decisions concerns the analysis of competitive advantage. One of the most treacherous areas of strategic planning is forecasting the potential for building competitive advantage across businesses. The analysis of synergy focusses upon the quest for economies of scope through sharing resources and transferring skills. However, for such economies to provide a valid justification for diversification it must also be shown that these economies cannot be obtained simply through cooperation between separate companies. In identifying the potential for exploiting relationships between businesses, it is important to recognize that some of the most important links may occur not at the operational level but at the strategic level. Because there are technological or market links between products or services, it does not imply that diversification can profitably exploit them. The key functions of corporate management in a diversified company are strategy formulation, resource allocation, and performance control. For diversification to build rather than erode competitive advantage, it is vital that corporate management can apply strategies, systems, and styles that are appropriate to the different businesses within the company.

Moreover, for diversification to build competitive advantage it is also necessary that the costs of managing the diversified corporation do not outweigh the benefits that diversification offers through the sharing of resources and skills. To explore this issue further we need to consider the corporate management of diversified enterprises.

Notes

1. Milton C. Lauenstein, "Diversification – the hidden explanation of success," *Sloan Management Review*, Fall 1985, pp. 49–55.

2. Alfred Chandler Jr., *Strategy and Structure: Chapters in the History of the Industrial Enterprise* (MIT Press, Cambridge, Mass., 1962); and *The Visible Hand: The Managerial Revolution in American Business* (Harvard University Press, Cambridge, Mass., 1977).

3. Leonard Wrigley, *Divisional Autonomy and Diversification*, Doctoral dissertation, Harvard Business School, 1970.

4. Richard P. Rumelt, *Strategy, Structure and Economic Performance* (Harvard University Press, Cambridge, Mass., 1974); Richard P. Rumelt, "Diversification strategy and profitability," *Strategic Management Journal* 3 (1972), pp. 359–70.

5. Azar P. Jammine, *Product Diversification, International Expansion and Performance: A Study of Strategic Risk Management in U.K. Manufacturing*, Doctoral dissertation, London Business School, 1984.

6. See, for example, Stephen A. Ross and Randolph W. Westerfield, *Corporate Finance* (Irwin, Homewood, Ill., 1988).

7. See, for example, H. Levy and M. Sarnat, "Diversification, portfolio analysis and the uneasy case for conglomerate mergers," *Journal of Finance* 25 (1970), pp. 795–802; R. H. Mason and M. B. Goudzwaard, "Performance of conglomerate firms: A portfolio approach," *Journal of Finance* 31 (1976), pp. 39–48; F. W. Melicher and D. F. Rush, "The performance of conglomerate firms: Recent risk and return experience," *Journal of Finance* 28 (1973), pp. 381–8; J. F. Weston, K. V. Smith, and R. E. Shrieves, "Conglomerate performance using the capital asset pricing model," *Review of Economics and Statistics* 54 (1972), pp. 357–63.

8. Stephen A. Ross and Randolph W. Westerfield, *Corporate Finance* (Times Mirror/Mosby College, St Louis, 1988), p. 681.

9. Robin Marris, *The Economic Theory of Managerial Capitalism* (Macmillan, London, 1964).

10. David A. Ravenscraft and F. M. Scherer, "Divisional selloff: a hazard analysis," in *Mergers, Selloffs and Economic Efficiency* (Brookings Institute, Washington, D.C., 1987); and Michael E. Porter, "From competitive advantage to corporate strategy," *Harvard Business Review*, May–June, 1987, pp. 43–59.

11. For the UK, see G. Meeks, *Disappointing Marriage* (Cambridge University Press, Cambridge, 1976); for the US see David A. Ravenscraft and F. M. Scherer, *Mergers and Managerial Performance*.

12. Erwin Blackstone, "Monopsony power, reciprocal buying and government contracts: the General Dynamics case," *Antitrust Bulletin* 17 (1972), pp. 445–62.

13. US Senate, Subcommittee on Antitrust and Monopoly Hearings, *Economic Concentration*, Part 1, Congress, 1st session, 1965, p. 45.

14. Michael E. Porter, "From competitive advantage to corporate strategy," *Harvard Business Review*, May–June, 1987, p. 46.

15. Ralph Biggadike, "The risky business of diversification," *Harvard Business Review*, May–June, 1979.

16. The formal definition of economies of scope is in terms of "sub-additivity". Economies of scope exist in the production of goods $x_1, x_2 \ldots x_n$ if:

$$C(X) < \Sigma_i C(x_i)$$

Where, $X = x_i$, $C(X)$ is the cost of producing all n goods within a single firm, and $\Sigma_i C(x_i)$ is the cost of producing the goods in n specialized firms. See W. J. Baumol, John C. Panzar, Robert D. Willig, *Contestable Markets and the Theory of Industry Structure* (Harcourt Brace Jovanovich, New York, 1982), pp. 71–2.

17. For the US see C. H. Berry, *Corporate Growth and Diversification* (Princeton University Press, Princeton, NJ, 1975); for the UK see R. M. Grant, "Determinants of the inter-industry pattern of diversification by UK manufacturing companies," *Bulletin of Economic Research* 29 (1977), pp. 84–95.

18. *American Express Company 1984 Annual Report*, p. 3.

19. *General Electric: Strategic Position – 1981*, Case No. 381–174 (HBS Case Services, Harvard Business School, 1981), p. 1.

20. "Can Jack Welch reinvent GE," *Business Week*, June, 1988, pp. 40–5.

21. See R. T. Pascale and A. G. Athos, *The Art of Japanese Management* (Simon & Schuster, New York, 1981), ch. 3 for a description of ITT's management system.

22. For a description of Hanson's diversification strategy see Michael Goold and Andrew Campbell, *Strategies and Style* (Blackwell, Oxford, 1987).

23. This section draws heavily upon R. M. Grant, "Diversification and firm performance in a changing economic environment," in H. Ergas et al., *Firm-Environment Interaction in a Changing Productive System* (Franco Angeli, Milan, 1988), pp. 49–91.

24. The nature and implications of transactions costs are discussed by Oliver E. Williamson, *The Economic Institutions of Capitalism* (Free Press, New York, 1985), chs 1–3.

25. This argument is stated more fully by David Teece, "Towards an economic theory of the multiproduct firm," *Journal of Economic Behavior and Organization* 3 (1982), pp. 39–63.

26. "3M's stumbling steps into the limelight," *Financial Times*, June 1, 1987, p. 14.

27. "Inside the New In-house banks," *Euromoney*, February 1986, pp. 24–34.

28. A. A. Alchian and H. Demsetz, "Production, information costs and economic organization," *American Economic Review* 62 (1972), pp. 777–95, argue that the collection and processing of information is the basic role of management and provides the primary rationale for the existence of the firm.

29. O. E. Williamson, "The modern corporation: origins, evolution, attributes," *Journal of Economic Literature* XIX (1981), pp. 1558–89.

30. Rumelt, *Strategy, Structure and Economic Performance*.

31. T. Peters and R. Waterman, *In Search of Excellence* (Harper & Row, New York, 1982), p. 294.

32. Ibid., p. 294.

33. See, for example, the studies by Bettis, and Christensen and Montgomery.

34. See, for example, the studies by Michel and Shaked, and Luffman and Reed in Exhibit 12.5.

35. For a discussion of the role of strategic links between businesses in affecting the success of diversification see C. K. Prahalad and R. Bettis, "On dominant logic: a new linkage between diversification and performance," *Strategic Management Journal* 7 (1986), pp. 485–501; and R. M. Grant, "On dominant logic, relatedness, and the link between diversity and performance," *Strategic Management Journal* 9 (1988), pp. 639–42.

THIRTEEN

Corporate Strategy: Managing the Diversified Corporation

Successfully managing large, diversified, multinational corporations is like teaching elephants to dance. The important thing is that, once they start dancing, everyone else has to leave the floor.

Professor C. K. Prahalad (Address to Strategic Management Society, Amsterdam, October 1988)

Introduction

Chapter 12 was concerned with the decision to diversify. We observed that the generally disappointing performance outcomes from diversification were mainly consequences of the difficulties which companies experienced in managing diversified corporations. This chapter is concerned with strategic management in the multibusiness company. As we shall see, corporate strategy is not simply a matter of answering the question, "What businesses should we be in?" Some of the most difficult issues of corporate strategy are concerned with the role and activities of managers at the corporate head office. We shall be concerned with five main areas of corporate-level strategic management.

- the composition of the company's portfolio of businesses (decisions over diversification, acquisition, and divestment);
- resource allocation between the company's different businesses;
- the role of head office in the formulation of business unit strategies;
- controlling business unit performance;
- coordinating business units and creating overall cohesiveness and direction for the company.

Our approach will differ from that taken elsewhere in the book. Until now, we have dealt first with the conceptual and theoretical issues of strategy formulation and then considered the implications of the strategy selected for organization and management. However, in the diversified corporation, the distinction between corporate and business strategy, and the allocation of decision-making responsibilities between corporate and business levels is, in part, a consequence of a company's organizational structure. An appropriate starting-point is the development of organizational structure in the large diversified corporation.

The Structure of the Diversified Company

The evolution of the structure and management of large enterprises

The growth over time in the size and diversity of companies has transformed the structure and the work of top management. Some of the most interesting features of Alfred Chandler's studies of the evolution of large US corporations are the fascinating insights they offer into the strategic and administrative roles of top management[1]. As we observed in the last chapter, the driving force for corporate evolution was technological change and economic expansion which encouraged first horizontal, then vertical, then diversifying expansion. Each of these phases of growth placed increasing strains upon management. Growth in geographic scope and company size created the need for new management techniques; new systems of information, communication and control; and organizational structures which facilitated the increased specialization and coordination required by higher levels of complexity.

Chandler identified two critical transformations in the organization of the modern corporation. The first was the development of the large multifunctional enterprise during the last part of the nineteenth century. The railroad companies (as a result of their rapid geographical expansion), were the first to establish hierarchical organizational structures with management responsibilities specialized by function:

... safe, regular reliable movement of goods and passengers, as well as the continuing maintenance and repair of locomotives, rolling stock ... and other equipment, required the creation of a sizeable administrative organization. It meant the employment of a set of managers to supervise these functional activities over an extensive geographical area; and the appointment of an administrative command of middle and top executives to monitor, evaluate, and coordinate the work of managers responsible for the day-to-day operations. It meant, too, the formulation of brand new types of internal administrative procedures and accounting and statistical controls. Hence, the operational requirements of the railroads demanded the creation of the first administrative hierarchies in American business.[2]

The second development was the emergence during the 1920s of the divisionalized corporation which, over time, was to replace both the centralized, functional structures which characterized most industrial corporations, and the loosely-knit, holding company structure which was a feature of firms which had grown by merger. The pioneers were Du Pont, which adopted product divisions to replace its functional structure in 1920, and General Motors, which arrived at a similar structure but from a quite different starting point.

At Du Pont, it was the strains of increasing size and a widening product range which stimulated the adoption of a divisionalized structure. Under its centralized, functional structure, coordination between the various functional departments for each product area became increasingly difficult, and top management became overloaded. As Chandler observed:

the operations of the enterprise became too complex and the problems of coordination, appraisal and policy formulation too intricate for a small number of top officers to handle both long-run, entrepreneurial and short-run, operational administrative activities.[3]

The solution devised by Pierre Du Pont was to decentralize, to create product divisions where the bulk of operational decisions would be made, leaving the corporate head office the task of coordination and overall leadership.

At General Motors reorganization from a holding company to a more coordinated, divisionalized structure was a response to the acute financial and organizational difficulties which the company faced in 1920. A slump in demand exacerbated the problems of lack of inventory control, absence of a standardized accounting system, lack of information, and a confused product line. The new structure was based upon two principles: the chief executive of each division was fully responsible for the operation and performance of that division, while the general office, headed by the president, was responsible for the development and control of the corporation as a whole including:

- monitoring divisional return on invested capital;
- coordinating the divisions (including establishing terms for interdivisional transactions);
- establishing a product policy.[4]

The main feature of the divisionalized corporation was the separation of operating responsibilities, which were vested in general managers at divisional level, from strategic responsibilities, which were located at head office. The divisionalized corporation represented a reconciliation of the efficiencies associated with decentralization with those resulting from centralized coordination. Exhibit 13.1 summarizes some major features of the evolutionary pattern observed by Chandler.

The theory of the M-form corporation

Chandler's observation of the tendency for diversification to be preceded by the adoption of divisionalized organizational structures has been developed by Oliver Williamson[5] into a more general theoretical analysis of the merits of the multidivisional corporation or, in Williamson's terminology, the "M-form" firm. The efficiency advantages of the divisionalized firm rest on four propositions concerning management and organizations:

1 *Bounded rationality.* Managers are limited in their cognitive, information processing, and decision-making capabilities. Hence, the top management team cannot be responsible for all coordination and decision-making within a complex organization – management responsibilities must be decentralized.

2 The division of decision-making responsibilities within the firm should be based upon *the frequency with which different types of decisions are made.* Thus, decisions which are made with high frequency, operating decisions, need to be separated from decisions which are made infrequently, strategic decisions.

3 *Minimizing the need for communication and coordination.* In the functional organization, decisions concerning a particular product or business area must pass up to the top of the company before all the relevant information and expertise can be brought to bear. In the divisionalized firm, so long as close coordination between different business areas is not necessary, most decisions concerning a particular business can be made at the divisional level. This eases the information and decision-making burden on top management.

4 *Global rather than local optimization.* Functional organizations are likely to give rise to managers, even at a senior level, emphasizing functional interests over the objectives of the organization as a whole. In the multidivisional firm, the locating of strategic decision-making in a general head office means that company-wide interests are given primacy. Also, at the divisional level, the interests of the business and of products are emphasized over functional interests.

Date	Environmental influences	Strategic changes	Organizational consequences
Early 19th century	Local markets. Transport and communication slow. Labor-intensive production.	Firms specialized and focussed upon local market.	No complex administrative or accounting systems. No middle management.
Late 19th and early 20th century	Railroads, telegraph, and mechanization permit large scale production and distribution.	Geographical expansion: national distribution, large scale production. Broadening of product lines. Forward integration.	Emergence of functional organization structures. Top management responsible for integrating the separate functions. Development of accounting systems, MIS and line and staff distinction.
1920s onwards	Excess capacity in distribution systems, increased availability of finance. Desire for growth.	Product diversification.	Increased difficulties of coordination at functional level; top management overload. Functional structure replaced by product divisions. Separation of operational and strategic functions of management. Establishment of general office for strategic management and the provision of corporate services.

Exhibi 13.1 The evolution of the modern industrial corporation

The separation between head office and operating divisions which is the major characteristic of the multidivisional company offers two further advantages over other organizational forms:

- effective allocation of resources;
- superior managerial efficiency.

With regard to allocation of resources, the divisionalized company can operate a competitive internal capital market. While in the functionally-structured company, resource allocation decisions are subject to internal political considerations, in divisionalized companies (such as General Electric, Hanson, and ITT), each business competes for corporate funds on the basis of its past financial performance and the attractiveness of its project proposals. As was argued in the last chapter ("The information advantages of the diversified corporation"), the head office of a diversified, divisionalized company has better access to information on the performance and prospects of its divisions than the capital market does on the performance and prospects of independent companies. As a result, an internal capital market can allocate resources more effectively than the external capital market.

A second advantage of the multidivisional structure which was also mentioned in the last chapter is its ability to deal with the central flaw of the large, manager-controlled corporation, the *agency problem*. How can owners (the shareholders) ensure that their salaried managers will run the company in the interests of shareholders when the incentive and the power of shareholders to discipline and replace managers who are either inefficient or self-seeking is so limited? An advantage of the divisionalized firm, claims Williamson, is that corporate management acts as an interface between the shareholders and the divisional managers and can ensure adherence to profit goals. Because divisions and business units are typically profit centers, financial performance can readily be monitored by head office, and divisional managers be held responsible for performance failures. The ability of head office to replace the managers of underperforming divisions and reward good performance provides powerful incentives for profit maximization. General Electric under Jack Welch, ITT under Harold Geneen, and, in Britain, Hanson under Lord Hanson, and GEC under Lord Weinstock, are all companies where the multidivisional structure has proved to be highly effective in imposing a strong profit motivation among divisional managers.

The proposition that the M-form structure is more efficient for the management of diversified firms has been tested in a number of studies. Most studies have found that among diversified firms, those with multidivisional structures have outperformed the others.[6]

The divisionalized firm in practice

Despite the theoretical arguments in favor of the divisionalized corporation and empirical evidence of its efficacy, close observation reveals that its reconciliation of the benefits of decentralization with those of coordination is far from perfect. Henry Mintzberg points to two important rigidities imposed by divisional structures:[7]

- constraints upon decentralization;
- standardization of divisional management.

Constraints upon decentralization   While operational authority in the M-form firm is dispersed to divisional level, the divisions often feature highly decentralized power which is partly a reflection of the divisional CEOs' personal accountability to head office. In addition, the operational freedom of the divisional management exists only so long as the corporate head office is satisfied with divisional performance. Corporate control is usually so tight that shortfalls in divisional performance precipitate speedy corporate intervention into divisional affairs.

Standardization of divisional management An advantage of the divisionalized form is that, in principle, divisions can be differentiated according to the requirements of their particular business needs. In practice, there are powerful forces for standardization across divisions. The corporate head office is likely to play an important training function and tends to move divisional managers towards overall corporate goals and values. More importantly, the maintenance of control by corporate head office requires the establishment of clearly-defined performance standards, which tend, inevitably, to be quantitative. The need for a common system of divisional appraisal encourages the divisions to seek similar goals and to adopt bureaucratic patterns of organization and management consistent with hierarchically-imposed quantitative goals.

Finally, the tidiness of the multidivisional corporation is most apparent when each division is operationally separate from each other. Then, all interfunctional coordination can take place within each division and the corporate headquarters can devote itself to resource allocation, control, and influencing divisional strategies. Once there are relationships between divisions which need managing, strategic tasks of top management become much more complex.

The Functions of Corporate Management

We have looked at the structure of the diversified, divisionalized corporation and at the separation which it has achieved between strategic and operational management. However, we have yet to discuss what the role and functions of corporate management are. As a starting-point, let us return to the discussion of corporate strategy in chapter 1.

Corporate strategy was defined by the answer to the question, "What business are we in?". It is concerned with issues of diversification, acquisition, divestment, and the allocation of resources between different business areas. These activities form a major part of corporate strategy decisions, but the role and responsibilities of corporate management extend much further. Strategic management at corporate level is partly concerned with shaping the corporate portfolio, but equally important are the administrative and leadership roles of corporate management in terms of implementing corporate strategy, participating in strategy formulation at divisional level, providing the coordination between the various departments and divisions of the company, and providing the sense of cohesion, identity, and direction to the company as a whole, which are the essential ingredients for the success of any organization.

The functions and responsibilities of corporate management in the diversified company can be grouped into four areas:

- managing the corporate portfolio in terms of the businesses included and resource allocation between them;
- formulating business-level strategies;
- providing coordination between the different businesses;
- controlling performance.

We shall discuss each in turn.

Managing the corporate portfolio: diversification, divestment, and resource allocation

The formulation of corporate strategy is primarily reflected in decisions concerning the composition and balance of the corporate portfolio. These include extensions of the portfolio through diversification, deletions from the portfolio through divestment, and changes in the balance of the corporate portfolio through the allocation of investment between the different businesses. While additions to and deletions from the corporate portfolio represent major but infrequent corporate strategy decisions, the allocation of resources between businesses is the primary, ongoing strategic responsibility of corporate management. While resource allocation is primarily thought of in terms of investment funds, the assignment and transfer of senior divisional managers is also a vital corporate management activity. In the next three sections we shall examine some of the techniques used by diversified companies for assisting their resource allocation decisions.

The role of corporate management in the allocation of resources distinguishes the divisionalized company from the holding company. The individual subsidiaries of a holding company determine their own financial policies: They retain profits required for reinvestment and pay the remainder in dividends to the parent company. Within the divisionalized company financial strategy is the preserve of head office: profits are returned to the corporate headquarters which are also responsible for their allocation and for all external borrowing.

Business strategy formulation

While corporate strategy is formulated and implemented by top management, business strategies are formulated jointly by corporate and divisional managers. In most diversified, divisionalized companies initiation of strategy proposals is the responsibility of divisional managers and the role of corporate managers is to probe, appraise, amend, and approve divisional strategy proposals. The extent of the influence of corporate headquarters on divisional strategies depends upon several factors:

- Satisfactory divisional performance encourages a high level of autonomy. Conversely, if a division is performing poorly, then corporate management is likely to intervene more intensively. General Electric's hands-off management of its investment banking subsidiary Kidder Peabody

> lasted until the Wall Street firm was rocked by a collapse of profits and an insider-trading scandal. GE installed a new top management team, reformulated Kidder Peabody's strategy, and imposed a new framework of controls.[8]
>
> • The closer are the interrelationships between divisions, the greater is head office involvement in divisional affairs because of the need for coordination.

Even in companies where primary responsibility for formulating business strategies is at the divisional level, the input of corporate headquarters is likely to be critical. If corporate management is to add value to the diversified corporation, then it can only come through corporate management's contribution to divisional performance. At the same time, if the input of headquarters into business strategy formulation is to be valuable, then it is important for corporate management to understand the business. For this reason it has been argued that, even in the most diversified companies, there must be some underlying similarities which link the different businesses. The mind set and underlying rationale which gives cohesiveness to the diversified company has been defined by C. K. Prahalad and Richard Bettis as the "dominant logic" of the enterprise.[9] They define dominant logic as "the way in which managers conceptualize the business and make critical resource allocation decisions."[10] For a diversified business to be successful, argue Prahalad and Bettis, there must be sufficient strategic similarity between the different businesses to enable top management to administer the corporation with a single dominant logic. For instance, Emerson Electric comprises a number of different businesses (electric motors, air conditioning, electrical appliances, control instruments), but the common goal of being a low-cost producer in each of its businesses provides a unifying thread.[11] The British conglomerate Trafalgar House comprises a range of businesses including Cunard, Ritz Hotel, Express Newspapers, and Cementation Construction and Engineering. Within this diversity are the common threads of mature, capital-intensive businesses, many of them with high-profile images.

Such strategic similarities can promote learning within the company, as strategies which proved successful in one business can be applied in others. At the same time, the tendency for headquarters to encourage uniformity in the strategies applied in different businesses can cause a failure to fit strategy to the circumstances of the individual business. Philip Morris is particularly good at applying similar marketing strategies to its different consumer goods businesses. At Miller Brewing, the techniques of brand advertising, market segmentation, and product differentiation (low-tar cigarettes/low-calorie beers) were particularly effective. Yet at 7-Up a similar strategy proved to be a costly failure.[12]

Coordination

We have observed that, in the conglomerate, the independence of each business limits the need for coordination. The principal coordinating role of a conglomerate's head office is likely to be the production of medium-term forecasts of economic trends and coordinating budgets to ensure that overall investment spending is within the company's financial capacity. There may also be company-wide issues which the different divisions have to face at similar times. Thus, corporate management may intervene to stress the need for cost reduction, for innovation, or for quicker responsiveness to changing customer preferences.

In more closely-related companies such as the highly vertically-integrated oil companies, or companies with close market or technological links (such as IBM, Proctor and Gamble, American Express, and Alcoa), corporate management is likely to play a much greater coordinating role. This is likely to involve not only coordination of strategies but also operational coordination in order to exploit the economies of scope and transferable skills which were discussed in the last chapter. One indicator of the impact of divisional interrelationships upon the coordinating role of corporate management is the size of the corporate headquarters in different types of company. Hanson, a conglomerate with few links between divisions operates with a "hands-off" corporate management style and has fewer than 200 employees in its London and New York head offices. Hewlett Packard, with about the same sales, but with much closer links between its divisions, employs about 3,000 people at its Palo Alto head office. The essential difference is that Hanson's corporate headquarters are concerned only with monitoring subsidiaries' performance, planning acquisitions, group financial strategy, external relations, and a few other functions. Hewlett-Packard's narrower range of activities and close technological links makes it desirable to centralize more activities at headquarters.

The need to marry decentralized decision making with multiple dimensions of coordination gives rise to complex issues of organizational design. Among the organizational devices that have been developed to facilitate coordination in the diversified firm are:

- matrix organization;
- task forces;
- company-wide focal issues.

Matrix organization attempts to resolve the conflicting objectives of decentralization and coordination by superimposing a functional structure onto the basic product-division structure. For example, Hewlett Packard's is organized into product-based divisions. At the same time, the Director of Corporate Manufacturing provides a link between manufacturing managers in each division which permits coordination of manufacturing policies and diffusion of technological development.

Task forces represent a more flexible and less comprehensive mechanism for achieving cross-divisional cooperation on specific issues and areas. For example, Hewlett Packard introduced "total quality control" task forces as a means of implementing its company-wide quality enhancement program. At 3M task forces are used as vehicles for developing and introducing new products.

Corporate head office's identification of company-wide issues can also play a role in encouraging divisional managers to respond to threats and opportunities that affect the whole company. General Electric issued annual "challenges" to its divisional and business unit managers to encourage a particular issue such as cost reduction, innovation, or quality to be incorporated within the annual planning cycle.

Coordination also involves promoting the overall cohesiveness of the diversified company. Coordination is not simply about reconciling inter-divisional conflicts and exploiting synergies between businesses. Similarly, the corporate strategy of a diversified company is not completely described by the portfolio of businesses which the company holds. Unlike the portfolio of securities held by an individual investor or a mutual fund, the diversified firm is involved in managing each of its businesses. Just as the single-business company needs clarity of purpose to provide its strategy with direction and its employees with commitment, so the diversified firm typically needs an identity and a rationale which gives meaning to its strategy beyond the composition of its portfolio. Hence, key roles of corporate management in coordinating the diversified company are:

● providing leadership;
● defining mission;
● establishing a set of values and beliefs which create a unifying corporate culture.

Unity within the diversified company may be achieved partly through strategic similarities (or "dominant logic") between the different businesses. But companies also need a stronger integrating force if they are to develop the loyalty and commitment necessary to mobilize the efforts and talents of their employees. Because of its very diversity, the multibusiness corporation may find it difficult to establish a common culture which bonds the various businesses and the scattered employees to one another. Moet-Hennessy, the French producer of champagne, cognac, Dior perfumes, and horticulture products, is a company which has made great efforts to establish a unifying set of values and traditions: "the common cultural trunk is based upon the permanent search for quality of the products and the management, human relations based upon responsibility and initiative, and rewarding competences and services."[13] A major theme in American Express's "one enterprise" program, aimed at integrating its various financial service companies, has been the development of a common set of values grouped around quality, outstanding customer service, and marketing excellence.

The corporate head office is responsible for setting, monitoring and enforcing performance targets for the individual divisions. Performance targets may be financial (return on invested capital, gross margin, growth of sales revenue), strategic (market share, rate of new product introduction, market penetration, quality), or both. Performance targets may be short-term

Monitoring and controlling performance

(monthly, quarterly), medium-term (annual), or long-term (five-year). The main function of the management information system in a diversified corporation is to enable head office to monitor divisional performance and identify deviations from targets.

Incentives for achieving target performance include financial returns (salary, bonuses, stock options), organizational status (through praise and recognition), and promotion. Sanctions include blame and loss of reputation, demotion, and, ultimately, dismissal. Some diversified companies have proved to be highly effective in using performance monitoring and a combination of incentives and sanctions to create an intensely motivating environment for divisional managers. At ITT, Geneen's obsession with highly-detailed performance monitoring, ruthless interrogation of divisional executives, and generous rewards for success, developed a highly-motivated, strongly-capable group of young, senior executives who were willing to work unremittingly for long hours, and who demanded as high a standard of performance from their subordinates as Geneen did of them.[14] Precise, quantitative performance targets, which can be monitored on a short-term (e.g. month-to-month) basis, can provide an intensely competitive internal environment that is highly effective in motivating business-unit and divisional managers. Hanson's "high-wire" profit targets provide a relentless pressure for cost cutting within its diverse businesses, while PepsiCo's obsession with monthly market share results nourishes an intense and aggressive, marketing-orientated culture. As one PepsiCo executive explained: "The place is full of guys with sparks coming out of their asses."[15]

For companies in rapidly developing and technology-based industries, formulating and implementing appropriate controls is a difficult task. Despite the clarity and measurability of financial and sales targets, they may stunt innovation. One approach to reconciling the unpredictability and long time horizons in technology-based industries with corporate control is for headquarters and business divisions to agree a series of *milestones* which establishes dates for the achievement of particular stages in the development of a new product or a new business. Such milestones might relate to the filing of patent applications, the production of a product prototype, the market launch of a new product, the achievement of particular levels of market penetration and productivity gains. The merit of this approach is that it can marry the motivation and control of short- to medium-term targets with the corporate need for a longer-term development strategy.

General Electric and the Development of Strategic Planning Techniques

The difficulties associated with the management of large diversified corporations have stimulated the development by managers, consultants, and academics of a variety of ideas, structural innovations, and analytic techniques designed to facilitate the process of corporate management. A fascinating feature of these developments in corporate strategy is the large number which have been pioneered by a single company: General Electric. GE has featured regularly among the leading group of *Fortune* magazine's "America's Most Admired Corporations" since its listings began. The key feature of GE's success is its highly-effective corporate management system. The fascination of Japanese executives with GE's system of strategic planning and control has already been commented upon.[16]

GE's innovations were responses to the difficulties it experienced in managing its diverse corporate empire. During the late 1960s GE's problem was that of profitless growth. Yet, because of its diversity (GE competed in 23 out of a total of 26 two-digit SIC industries) and its organizational complexity (GE was organized into 46 divisions and over 190 departments), corporate management was unable to get to grips with the problem of inadequate profitability. As a result, in 1969 GE launched a series of initiatives aimed at developing a more effective system of corporate planning backed by better analytical techniques. Senior managers worked with three leading management consulting companies – Boston Consulting Group, McKinsey and Company, and Arthur D. Little – on the problems of strategic planning, while another group cooperated with Harvard Business School to develop GE's strategic information data base. These initiatives spawned three innovations which were to transform the methods by which GE, and other diversified companies formulated their corporate strategies:

- the strategic business unit;
- portfolio planning models;
- the PIMS data base.

A key feature of McKinsey's recommendations was the creation of a new unit for strategic planning purposes. The Strategic Business Unit (SBU) is a business for which it is meaningful to formulate a separate strategy. Typically an SBU is a business which comprises a number of closely related products and for which most costs are not shared with other businesses.

All three consulting companies developed simple, matrix-based frameworks to be used in evaluating business unit performance, formulating business unit strategies, and assessing the overall balance of the corporate portfolio. We shall consider these portfolio planning models in greater detail in the next section.

From informational and analytical inputs into the corporate planning system, GE developed a data base which comprised strategic, market, and performance data on each of GE's businesses and was later supplemented with data from other companies. The primary purpose of the data base was to enable empirical investigation into the impact of market structure and strategy variables upon profitability.

While GE is known for its techniques and systems of corporate planning, a key feature of GE's strategic planning is the balance it achieves between the discipline of formal systems and the flexibility and opportunism of its top management. Balancing the bottom-up system of strategy formulation is a strong leadership style which has restructured GE's business portfolio (the acquisition of RCA and Kidder Peabody, the exit from consumer electronics and mining) and initiated major strategic shifts including the drive towards global market leadership and the pressure towards cost reduction.[17]

Portfolio Planning Models

Portfolio analysis is probably the best known and most widely applied technique of strategy analysis ever to be developed. The basic idea is to represent the businesses of the diversified company within a simple graphic framework that can assist in four areas of strategy formulation:

- allocating resources;
- formulating business unit strategy;
- setting performance targets;
- analyzing portfolio balance.

Allocating resources   Portfolio analysis examines the position of a business unit in relation to the two primary sources of profitability – industry attractiveness and competitive position – thus enabling its investment attractiveness to be compared with that of other business units.

Formulating business unit strategy   On the basis of a business unit's location in relation to the same basic variables – industry attractiveness and competitive position – portfolio analysis yields simple and straightforward strategy recommendations. For example, the McKinsey matrix offers three recommendations: grow, hold, or harvest. Further analysis may generate more sophisticated recommendations, for instance, suggesting how a poorly-positioned business may be developed into a more attractively-positioned business.

Setting performance targets   To help establish performance targets for individual businesses, standardized procedures based upon a limited number of key environmental and strategic variables can be used to estimate what kind of profit performance can reasonably be expected for such a business.

Analyzing portfolio balance   A single diagrammatic representation of the positions of the different businesses within the company is a valuable means of representing the overall balance, cohesiveness, and performance potential. Portfolio analysis can assist in examining several dimensions of portfolio balance:

- cash flow;
- continuity;
- risk.

Diversified companies often seek independence from the external capital market by achieving a balanced cash flow within the company. This requires that businesses which generate a surplus cash flow to finance businesses which are in their growth phases and which are net absorbers of cash.

To maintain the company over the long term, companies frequently seek a portfolio which is composed of businesses in different stages of their life cycle. As older businesses decline and die, they are replaced by younger, growing businesses.

Managing risk may involve risk reduction through spreading the firm's activities over businesses whose returns are imperfectly correlated.

The McKinsey matrix

One of the fruits of General Electric's collaboration with McKinsey and Company was the portfolio analysis matrix shown in Exhibit 13.2. The two axes of the matrix are familiar: They are the two basic sources of superior profitability for a firm – industry attractiveness and competitive advantage. In the case of the McKinsey matrix the axes are composite variables. Exhibit 12.2 also shows the individual variables which together determine the levels of industry attractiveness and competitive position for a business unit. The strategy recommendations derived from the matrix are quite simple:

- business units which rank high on both dimensions have excellent profit potential and should be "grown";
- those which rank low on both dimensions have poor prospects and should be "harvested";
- in between businesses are candidates for a "hold" strategy.

The value of this technique is its simplicity. Even for a highly complex and diverse company such as General Electric, which in 1980 comprised 43 SBUs, the positions of all the firm's SBUs can be combined into a single display. Thus, while the matrix may be simplistic, its power lies in its ability to display the businesses of the whole company and to compress a large amount of data into two dimensions.

The Boston Consulting Group's growth-share matrix

The BCG matrix follows a similar approach: It combines market attractiveness and competitive position to compare the situation of different SBUs and to draw strategy prescriptions. It differs from the McKinsey matrix in that the two axes measure single variables: *Market growth rate* and *relative*

Exhibit 13.2   The
McKinsey-General
Electric portfolio
analysis matrix

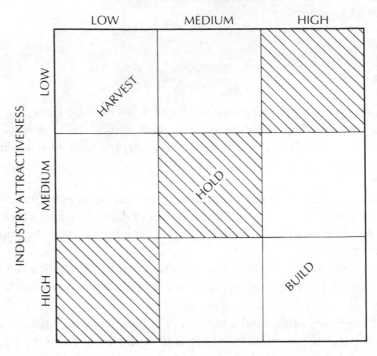

The Criteria

Industry attractiveness

1 market size
2 market growth (real growth rate over 10 years)
3 industry profitability (3-year av. ROS of the business and its competitors)
4 Cyclicality (av. annual % trend deviation of sales)
5 Inflation recovery (ability to cover cost increases by higher productivity and increased prices)
6 importance of overseas markets (ratio of international to US market)

Business unit position

1 Market position (av. US market share; av. international market share; market share relative to three major competitors)
2 competitive position (superior, equal, or inferior to competitors with regard to quality, technology, manufacturing and cost leadership, distribution and market leadership)
3 relative profitability (SBU's ROS less av. for 3 main competitors)

market share (i.e. the business unit's market share relative to that of the largest competitor). This choice of variables reflected BCG's view, first, that growth is the primary determinant of industry attractiveness, and, secondly, that competitive position is primarily determined by market share (because of its link, through the experience curve, with relative cost position). Exhibit 13.3 shows how a company's business units may be plotted upon the axes of the BCG matrix.

The BCG matrix provides clear predictions as to the pattern of profit earnings and cash flow associated with the different cells (see Exhibit 13.4). It also provides recommendations as to appropriate strategies: Milk the cows, invest in the stars, divest the dogs, and analyze the question marks to determine whether they can be grown into stars or will degenerate into dogs.

The BCG's growth-share matrix is even more elementary than the

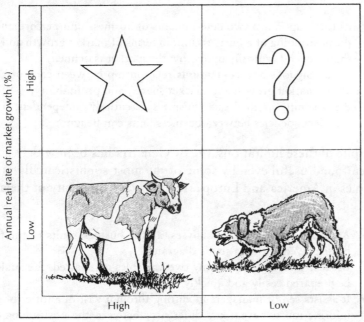

Exhibit 13.3 The BCG growth-share matrix

Note that relative market share measures the market share of the business relative to the market share of the largest competitor, e.g. if a business has a market share of 10 percent, while the largest competitor has 20 percent, relative market share is 0.5.

	High Relative Market Share	Low Relative Market Share
High Annual real rate of market growth (%)	*Earnings:* high, stable, growing *Cash flow:* neutral *Strategy:* invest for growth	*Earnings:* low, unstable, growing *Cash flow:* negative *Strategy:* analyze to determine whether business can be grown into a star, or will degenerate into a Dog
Low	*Earnings:* high, stable *Cash flow:* high, stable *Strategy:* milk	*Earnings:* low, unstable *Cash flow:* neutral or negative *Strategy:* divest

Relative Market Share

Exhibit 13.4 Predictions and recommendations of BCG's growth-share matrix

McKinsey matrix and at best it can provide only a rough, first-cut analysis. Corporate strategy decisions should never be taken by the mechanistic application of such a framework. The major weaknesses of the analysis include:

- its focus upon just two determinants of business unit performance;
- the positioning of a business unit in terms of market growth and market share depend critically upon how the market is defined;
- the ambiguous and contentious relationship between each of the variables (market growth and market share), and profitability;
- the assumption that each business is entirely independent and that interdependencies between business units can be ignored.

But in spite of these limitations, the BCG matrix has been widely used and has been found useful even by some of the most sophisticatedly-managed companies in America and Europe. It is the very simplicity of the analysis which is its strength.

- As with other portfolio analyses, all the business units of the firm can be displayed within a single diagram.
- Because information on only two variables is required, the analysis can be prepared easily and quickly.
- It assists senior managers in cutting through vast quantities of detailed information to reveal key differences between the positioning of individual business units.
- The analysis is versatile – in addition to comparing the position of different business units, the framework can be used to examine the performance potential of different products, different brands, different regions, different distribution channels, and different customers.
- It provides a useful point of departure for more detailed analysis and discussion of the competitive positions and strategies of individual business units.

Some of this more detailed analysis can be incorporated within the framework of the BCG matrix. For example, the movement over time in the positions of different businesses can be plotted, and additional descriptive information can be added (see Exhibit 13.5).

The Application of PIMS Analysis to Corporate Strategy

The development of PIMS

The PIMS Program, we have noted, has its origins in the internal data base constructed by General Electric as a means of testing the reasonableness of the strategic and budgetary plans submitted by operating units. To broaden the data base so that strategy–performance relationships could be better estimated, the project was transferred to Harvard Business School in 1972. In 1975, a separate organization, the Strategic Planning Institute, was founded to conduct the research and to provide advisory services to the member companies. By 1986, PIMS incorporated data on more than

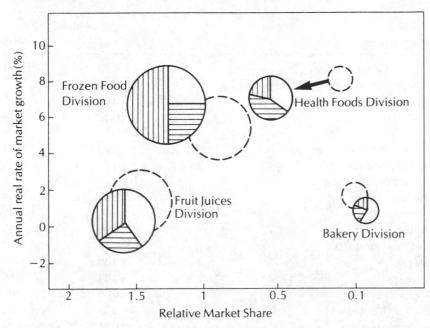

Exhibit 13.5
Application of the BCG matrix to BM Foods Inc.

Note that (a) the continuous circles show the position of each division in 1987, the broken circles show the position in 1984; (b) the sizes of the circles are proportional to sales revenue *at 1987 prices*; (c) the vertically-shaded segments show sales to supermarket chains, the horizontally-shaded segments show sales to other retailers, the unshaded segments show sales to wholesalers and caterers.

2,600 businesses, mostly in North America, but including more than 400 European businesses and over 100 in other regions of the world. Annual data on three sets of variables are included:

- profitability, i.e. pre-tax operating profit as a percentage of sales (ROS) and invested capital (ROI);
- strategy variables (e.g. market share, product quality, new product introduction, marketing, and R&D expenses);
- industry variables (e.g. market growth, life-cycle stage, unionization, customer concentration).

PIMS then uses multiple regression analysis to relate performance to industry and strategy factors. Exhibit 13.6 shows the estimated PIMS equations.

Setting performance targets for business units   One of the main problems which corporate managers face in appraising the performance of its business units is determining what level of performance is appropriate for different types of business. Top management can, of course, set out company-wide performance targets (e.g "Businesses must earn a pre-tax ROI of 20 percent or more") but, while some businesses can easily achieve such a target (e.g. a pharmaceuticals producer), a business located within a depressed industry (steel manufacture, farm equipment) might find such a target impossible.

Applying PIMS to strategic decisions

Exhibit 13.6 The PIMS multiple regression equations: the impact of industry and strategy variables on profitability

Profit influences	Impact on:	
	ROI	ROS
Real market growth rate	0.18	0.04
Rate of price inflation	0.22	0.08
Purchase concentration	0.02	N.S.
Unionization (%)	−0.07	−0.03
Low purchase amount:		
low importance	6.06	1.63
high importance	5.42	2.10
High purchase amount:		
low importance	−6.96	−2.58
high importance	−3.84	−1.11
Exports-Imports (%)	0.06	0.05
Customized products	−2.44	−1.77
Market share	0.34	0.14
Relative quality	0.11	0.05
New products (%)	−0.12	−0.05
Marketing, % of sales	−0.52	−0.32
R&D, % of sales	−0.36	−0.22
Inventory, % of sales	−0.49	−0.09
Fixed capital intensity	−0.55	−0.10
Plant newness	0.07	0.05
Capacity utilization (%)	0.31	0.10
Employee productivity	0.13	0.06
Vertical integration	0.26	0.18
FIFO inventory valuation	1.30	0.62
R^2	0.39	0.31
F	58.3	45.1
Number of Cases	2,314	2,314

For example, if the Real Market Growth Rate of a business was to increase by one percentage point, the equation predicts that its ROI would rise by 0.18 percent.
Source: Robert D. Buzzell and Bradley T. Gale, *The PIMS Principles* (Free Press, New York, 1987), p. 274.

PIMS analysis shows how a business's profitability is determined by some 30 strategy and industry variables. By plugging in the actual levels of a business's strategy and industry variables into the PIMS regression estimates, it is possible to calculate that business's "Par ROI". Par ROI is the normal level of ROI for a business given its profile of strategic and industry characteristics. Hence, Par ROI is a benchmark for the business, it is the ROI which would be expected for a business of this type as indicated by the PIMS data base as a whole. Par ROI can be used to set a target level of profitability for a business, and it can be used as the standard against which the actual profitability of a business is judged. For example, in Exhibit 13.7, Business A earned a higher ROI than Business B, but because Business B is a textile business with a small market share and

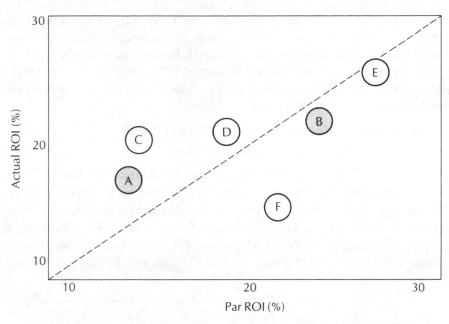

Exhibit 13.7 Using PIMS Par ROI to evaluate business unit performance

unionized employees and Business A had a large market share of the fast-growing medical equipment industry, Business A achieved an ROI well above its par level, while Business B underperformed its par.

Formulating business unit strategy Because the PIMS regression equations estimate the impact of different strategy variables on ROI, these estimates can indicate how a business can adjust its strategy in order to increase its profit performance. The Strategic Planning Institute offers several analyses which indicate the potential for changes in strategy to increase profit performance.

First the PIMS Strategy Report simulates the short- and long-term consequences of changes in the values of different strategy variables for a specific business. It identifies an "optimum strategy" which nominates a combination of market share, investment intensity, vertical integration, and other strategic moves that promises to optimize a given performance measure.

The ability to predict the consequences of different strategy moves is further assisted by the *PIMS Analysis of Look Alikes*. This analysis scans the database for businesses with similar characteristics to that of the business under review. It focusses on the differences between similar businesses which have been successful in achieving a specific objective and those which have not. It highlights opportunities for improving the performance of a business and indicates ways of achieving above average performance.

Allocating investment funds between businesses One of the most difficult areas of corporate strategy is the allocation of investment funds between the different business units. Past profitability is a poor basis for allocation since the correlation between a business's recent level of ROI and the ROI earned on *new investment* is extremely low. Discounted cash flow analysis is excellent for appraising individual projects, but is less useful in allocating funds between whole businesses. A useful PIMS tool is its "*Strategic Attractiveness Scan*". A business unit's investment attractiveness is assessed in relation to:

- estimated future real rate of growth of its market;
- its Par ROI.

The analysis offers predictions as to the "strategic attractiveness" of investment in the business, and the cash flow that can be expected from the business. The underlying rationale for this analysis is that the best predictors of the future returns on new investment in an industry are industry characteristics, the strategic position of the business within the industry, and the expected growth rate of the industry. Exhibit 13.8 shows the framework.

Exhibit 13.8 Using PIMS in allocating resources between business units: The profitable opportunities screen

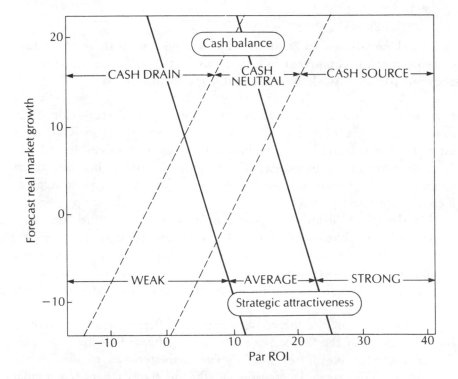

Valuing Businesses and Analyzing Restructuring Opportunities

The McKinsey "Pentagon framework"

Portfolio analysis such as PIMS techniques is primarily useful for assisting resource allocation within the multibusiness corporation. These "strategic" approaches to resource allocation decisions are justified by the fact that the rate of return which will be earned on new investment in a business is likely to bear a closer relationship to the underlying determinants of industry attractiveness and competitive position than to the rate of return currently being earned on past investments in the business. However, portfolio techniques are less useful as a guide to divestment and restructuring decisions. Just as the fundamental criterion for evaluating diversification decisions is whether or not the diversification will add value to the corporate whole, so the fundamental criterion for determining whether or not a particular business should be retained within the corporate fold is the value that the business adds to the corporation as a whole. Valuation of a business also permits the appraisal of alternative strategic options. To the extent that it is possible to predict the implications of alternative strategies for expected returns and risk, so it is possible to evaluate them in terms of their impact on the value of the business.

McKinsey and Company propose five stages in valuing a company and assessing the opportunities for restructuring.[18] They organize their analysis around a "Pentagon framework" (see Exhibit 13.9). The five stages of the analysis are:

- the current market value of the company;
- the value of the company as is;
- the potential value of the company with internal improvements;
- the potential value of the company with external improvements;
- the optimal restructured value of the company.

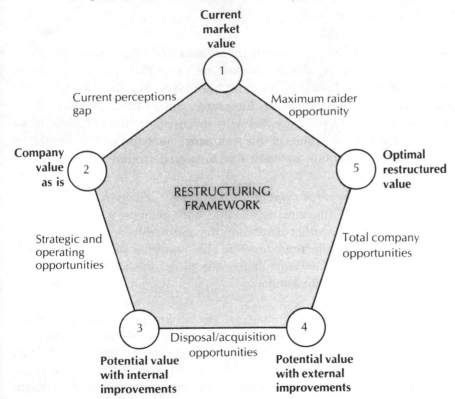

Exhibit 13.9 The McKinsey & Co. pentagon framework for assessing restructuring opportunities

Source: Tom Copeland, Tim Koller, and Jack Murrin, *Valuation: Measuring and Managing the Value of Companies* (John Wiley, New York, 1990), p. 249.

The current market value of the company   The starting-point is the market value of the company which comprises the market value of the company's equity (number of shares outstanding multiplied by the price of the shares) and the market value of the debt (nominal amount of debt multiplied by its market price).

The value of the company as is   The market value of the company will represent the stock market's estimate of the discounted cash flow of the company. To the extent that this is below management's estimate of the discounted cash flow valuation of the company, then management must seek to close this "perceptions gap" through more effective communication with the market. The discrepancy might also justify the company repurchasing its shares on the market. As General Electric chairman, Jack Welch replied when asked about his company's 1989 share repurchase program: "They're the best investment we can find." I shall defer explaining the principles of company valuation until a little later.

The potential value of the company with internal improvements   Within the present portfolio of the company's businesses it may be possible to increase the company's value through operating improvements which cut costs and increase efficiency, and strategic initiatives which enhance cash flows.

The potential value of the company with external improvements   The company may also be able to increase its value through changes in its business portfolio. Poorly performing businesses may have a higher sale price than their contribution to the present value of the company. Businesses whose rate of return is below their cost of capital are likely to be reducing the overall value of the company. Such businesses should be liquidated if they cannot be either sold or turned around.

The optimal restructured value of the company   The potential for value-enhancing internal adjustments together with changes to the company's business portfolio together determine the company's maximum possible present value. The difference between this "optimal restructured value" and the current market value shows the profit potential available to a raider from acquiring the company.

Valuing the company

To determine the value of a company "as is" and to estimate the impact on value of restructuring measures a DCF analysis of the constituent parts of the company is necessary. The valuation of each business unit follows the principles for company valuation outlined in chapter 1 (and in the Appendix to chapter 1 in particular). For the external analyst, a major problem is the paucity of data in corporate financial statements on divisional operations. However, typically operating income and capital expenditure is disaggregated by division which may make it easier to estimate divisional cash flows than divisional accounting returns on assets.

In discounting divisional cash flows it is important to use a cost of capital for the division rather than for the corporation as a whole. Since different divisions typically have different levels of operating risk, so their costs of capital will differ. But the cost of capital to a division is not directly observable. Hence, the appropriate approach to measuring cost of capital is to estimate the risk premium for publicly-traded competitors, whose risk characteristics can be assumed to be the same. From the Appendix to chapter 1 cost of equity (k_E) capital was shown to comprise a risk-free rate of interest (i) plus a risk premium:

$$k_E = i + \beta \, (R_m - i)$$

Where β is the *beta coefficient* or *coefficient of systematic risk* for the company, and R_m is the expected return on the stock market as a whole. The beta coefficient for the shares of similar companies can be used as indicators of the beta for the division of a diversified company. However, some adjustment must be made to take account of any differences in leverage ratios between the competitor companies and the diversified corporation. For example, if competitors have higher debt/equity ratios than those of the diversified corporation, then competitors' greater financial risk will be reflected in a higher beta coefficient than that appropriate for the division of the diversified company.[19]

The McKinsey authors advocate treating corporate headquarters as a separate division. While corporate headquarters is conventionally viewed as a cost rather than a profit center, it is, in principle, possible to measure the value added by the corporate center through economies of scope in the provision of corporate services, the transfer of managerial and technological expertise between divisions, and offering tax-shelter benefits. However, since most of these synergistic benefits are included in the cash flows of the individual business units, separating them is likely to prove a near-impossible task.

Valuation analysis in corporate strategy formulation

Until recently, valuation analysis has been undertaken more by corporate raiders than by corporate managers. The acquisition of R. J. R. Nabisco by Kravis Kohlberg and Roberts, of SCM and Imperial Group by Hanson, and attempted takeover of BAT by Coniston Group were attempts by outsiders to release the value potential from dismantling and financially-restructuring poorly-performing diversified companies. Indeed, it has been the failure of corporate management to effectively utilize the tools of value management which has made so many large diversified companies attractive targets for acquisition and restructuring.

Michael Jensen[20] argues that the wave of hostile takeovers during the 1980s led by takeover specialists such as Carl Icahn, James Goldsmith, Saul Steinberg, and T. Boone Pickens, rather than reflecting myopia on the part of the stock market, was primarily a product of myopia on the part of the corporate managers of the acquired companies. The propensity for managers to invest the free cash flow from their profitable core businesses in diversification rather than distribute it to shareholders resulted in companies growing beyond the size that maximizes shareholder wealth with consequent reduction in valuation ratios.

By evaluating the effects of acquisitions, divestments, and changes in financial structure upon overall corporate value, managers have the ability to improve upon the dismal performance which has characterised so many large diversified corporations both in America and Britain during the 1970s and 1980s.

Corporate Style and Management Systems

We have discussed several areas of strategic management in the multi-business company: Determining the composition of the corporate portfolio, allocating resources between businesses, formulating business strategies, and controlling performance. While all diversified companies address these issues, companies face a range of options as to how responsibilities for these various tasks are allocated between head office and operating units and the nature of the interaction between head office and operating units. A company's choices with regard to these two sets of issues determine the role of corporate management in a diversified company.[21]

The appropriate role for corporate management depends closely upon the way in which corporate management adds value to the individual businesses of the diversified corporation. Michael Porter has identified four concepts of corporate strategy which are defined in terms of the means by which corporate management creates profit within the diversified company.

Porter's "concepts of corporate strategy"

Portfolio Management   The essence of a portfolio management strategy is the acquisition of attractive, soundly-managed companies. The acquired companies are operated autonomously, they formulate their own business strategies, and corporate control is exercised primarily through the allocation of investment funds.

The role of corporate management in pursuing a portfolio management approach is limited to four main activities:

- identifying acquisition candidates and purchasing them at a favorable price (since there are few operating synergies to be exploited, it is vital that the takeover price does not exceed the value of the assets acquired);
- reducing the costs of the acquired companies because of the lower cost of capital of the large, diversified company;
- increasing the efficiency with which investment funds are allocated by using corporate management's expertise and access to information to rigorously review business strategies and project proposals, and to accurately assess the relative merits of alternative investments;

- establishing close monitoring of business unit financial performance, demanding targets of divisional and business unit managers, and an environment of fierce internal competition for investment funds which is conducive to intense and sustained effort by operating managers.

Restructuring   Like the portfolio management companies, a key strategic role of top management in companies which pursue a restructuring strategy is acquisition. However, in addition to the post-acquisition roles of banker, reviewer, and monitor which corporate managers in the portfolio management companies occupy, a restructuring strategy requires much more interventionist post-acquisition management by corporate executives. Intervention takes the form of changing the management of acquired companies, increasing efficiency, and disposing of underutilized assets. For a restructuring strategy to be successful requires, first, that inefficient firms with undervalued assets are available for acquisition, and, secondly, that after successful restructuring the company realizes the return from its efforts by selling off its restructured subsidiaries.

Transferring Skills   Corporate management can add value to its business units by transferring skills between them and thereby creating or enhancing competitive advantage. Examples are Philip Morris's acquisition of Miller Brewing, General Foods, and Kraft with a view to transferring its skills in marketing, new product introduction, and international distribution to the acquired businesses. General Motors' acquisition of Hughes Aircraft and Electronic Data Systems was primarily motivated by the desire to transfer the skills in electronics and advanced technology of these companies back to its core automobile business. For transfer of skills to be effective certain conditions must be met:

- There must be commonalities between the businesses in terms of similar skills being applicable across the businesses and these skills being important to establishing competitive advantage.
- Corporate management must take an active role in the transfer of skills through the transfer of key personnel and the creation of interdivisional working parties.

Sharing Activities   An important source of cost efficiency for the diversified company is economies of scope in common resources and activities. Examples of the exploitation of economies of scope through diversification were discussed in the last chapter. For these economies to be realized, corporate management must play a key coordinating role. This requires involvement in the formulation of business unit strategies and intervention in operational matters to ensure that opportunities for sharing research and development activities, advertising campaigns, distribution systems, and service networks are fully exploited. Porter suggests several mechanisms that can assist collaboration in the sharing of activities:

- a strong sense of corporate identity;
- a clear corporate mission statement that emphasizes the importance of integrating business unit strategies;
- an incentive system that rewards cooperation between businesses;
- interbusiness task forces and other vehicles for cooperation.

Alternative roles for corporate headquarters in the diversified corporation

Porter argues that the potential for management to create value for shareholders increases as a company moves from the loose, portfolio-management strategy towards the more integrated shared-activities strategy. However, the evidence on this point is mixed. A study by Lorsch and Allen compared corporate management practices and corporate-divisional relationships in three conglomerates (which adopted "portfolio management" and "restructuring" approaches) with those of three vertically-integrated paper companies (which pursued "transfer of skills" and "sharing of activities" approaches).[22] The need to manage divisional linkages and coordinate operations resulted in the paper companies showing:

- greater involvement of head office staff in divisional operations;
- larger head office staffs;
- more complex planning and control devices;
- lower responsiveness to change in the external environment.

The administrative burden of coordination imposed by close relationships between the divisions of the paper companies was such that:

the conglomerate firms we had studied seemed to be achieving appreciable degrees of financial and managerial synergy but little or no operating synergy. Some of the firms saw little immediate payoff in this operating synergy; others had met with little success in attempting to achieve it.[23]

A recent study by Goold and Campbell investigated the nature and effectiveness of different "strategic management styles" among a sample of large, British diversified companies.[24] They found that no single style of corporate management was generally superior. Different styles are appropriate to different types of business and different types of corporate management. They focussed upon two key corporate management functions: involvement of corporate head office in business strategy formulation, and the type of performance control imposed by head office. On the basis of these two functions they identified three corporate management styles: Financial control, strategic control, and strategic planning, plus two additional categories – centralized and holding company – which they believed to be largely defunct among contemporary diversified companies. Exhibit 13.10 shows these categories.

The principal contrast is between companies where corporate head office plays an important role in formulating and coordinating business unit and divisional strategies (the strategic planning style) and those where corporate head office concentrates on financial management (the financial control

Exhibit 13.10
Corporate
management styles

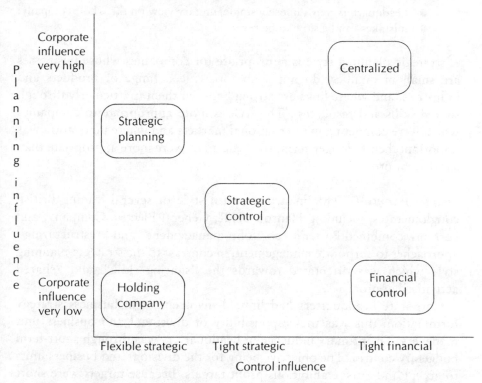

style). A third style, strategic control, identified with ICI, Courtaulds, Plessey, and Vickers, is a hybrid of the other two. It aims to balance a high degree of divisional autonomy with the benefits of head office coordination.

Strategic Planning   A strategic planning style of corporate management was found in British Petroleum, Cadbury-Schweppes, Lex, and STC. In these companies there was substantial involvement by corporate head-quarters in business unit planning. This included intensive discussion between business unit managers and corporate staff as to the content and goals of strategy, and a large corporate role in integrating and coordinating business unit strategies. Because of the involvement of the corporate level and the ability to call upon corporate support, the strategy-formulation process was conducive to adopting ambitious strategies aimed at establishing long-term competitive advantage. This was typically reflected in performance goals that emphasized strategic objectives (market share, innovation, quality leadership, overseas penetration) over financial objectives, and emphasized the long term over the short term. Key drawbacks of the strategic planning style are:

- the lack of autonomy which business unit managers possess can be demoralizing for them;
- the strategy-making process can become slow and cumbersome with resulting loss of flexibility and speed in adjusting to new circumstances and opportunities;

- headquarters may impose a single, unitary view on the whole company;
- mistakes can be slow to be reversed.

A strategic planning style is appropriate for companies whose businesses are small in number, do not span too wide a range of products and industries, and where links are strong between them (particularly through shared skills and resources). The style is more appropriate to companies which were competing in international markets and where innovation was important, hence, longer-term, strategic goals were more appropriate than short-term profits.

Financial control   The financial control style of several leading British conglomerates, including Hanson, BTR, General Electric Company, and Ferranti, combined Porter's "portfolio management" and "restructuring" approaches to corporate management, in contrast to the strategic-planning style which was orientated towards the "sharing skills" and "shared activities" approaches.

Corporate headquarters had limited involvement in business strategy formulation; this was the responsibility of divisional and business unit managers. The primary influence of headquarters was through short-term budgetary control. The objective being for the divisions and business units to accept and pursue ambitious profit targets. Because targets were short term, quantitative, and easily measured they provided strong motivation to managers to increase efficiency and expand business into profitable areas. Careful monitoring of performance by headquarters, with rigorous questioning of managers responsible for deviations from target, maintained constant pressure on divisional management and created a challenging working environment.

Apart from being highly conducive to profitability, the financial control style has three important benefits:

- because of the autonomy it gives to business units, it provides an excellent environment for developing executives with strong entrepreneurial and general management skills;
- by placing strong pressure on business unit managers for profitability it encourages these managers to break away from ineffective strategies at an early stage;
- because the major operating and strategic decisions are taken at business unit level, headquarters staff does not need to have an intimate knowledge of the individual businesses.

The principal weaknesses of the financial control style are:

- emphasis on short-term profitability targets results in a bias against projects and strategies with long lead times and payback periods, and can make businesses vulnerable against competition from rivals with a longer-term strategic approach (in consumer electronics, when GE and

RCA were attacked by Far Eastern competitors they yielded segment after segment on the basis that profitability was depressed until both ultimately withdrew from the industry);

- its difficulty of exploiting synergies between businesses; each business is treated as a single entity and corporate headquarters lacks a mechanism for coordination and cooperation between businesses.

The financial control style is suited to companies which feature:

- wide diversity with many business units;
- investment projects which are mainly short- and medium-term in fruition, and where innovation is relatively low;
- mature industries with low levels of international competition.

Exhibit 13.11 summarizes key features of the two styles.

Subsequent work by Goold and Campbell in collaboration with McKinsey and Company has combined the different strategic management styles with different degrees of divisional linkage to form a classification

Exhibit 13.11
Characteristics of different strategic management styles

	Strategic planning	Financial control
Business strategy formulation	Business units and corporate center coordinate in strategy formulation. Center responsible for coordination of strategies between business units.	Strategy formulated at business unit level. Corporate HQ largely reactive offering little coordination.
Control	Primarily strategic goals with medium to long term horizon.	Financial budgets set which set out annual (and shorter term) targets for ROI and other financial variables.
Advantages	Can exploit linkages between businesses. Can give appropriate weight to innovation and longer term competitive positioning.	Business units given autonomy and initiative. Business units can respond quickly to change. Encourages development of business unit managers. Highly motivating.
Disadvantages	Loss of divisional autonomy and initiative. Conducive to unitary view. Resistance to abandoning failed strategy.	Short-term focus discourages innovation and building longer term competitive position. Businesses may be willing to give ground to determined competitors. Little scope for exploiting shared resources and skills between businesses.

	Strategic planning	Financial control
Style suited to:		
portfolio structure	Small no. of businesses across narrow range of sectors with close interrelations.	Many businesses across wide range of industries. Linkages ideally few.
type of investments	Large projects with long-term paybacks.	Small capital investments with short payback periods.
environmental features	Industries with strong technological and global competition.	Mature industries (technical change modest or slow). Stable industry environment without strong international competition.
UK examples	BP, BOC, Cadbury-Schweppes, Lex Group, STC, United Biscuits.	Hanson Trust, BTR, General Electric Company (UK), Ferranti, Tarmac.

of "corporate parenting roles". In order of increasing corporate involvement in business unit affairs, three "corporate parenting roles" are identified: *controller*, *coach*, and *orchestrator*. Exhibit 13.12 summarizes the main features of each role.

Exhibit 13.12
Corporate parenting roles

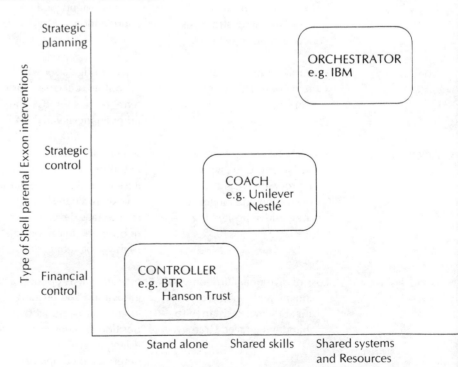

Note that (a) in the *Controller* role, head office has little involvement in the individual businesses except to set targets and monitor their achievement; (b) in the *Coach* role, the operating businesses are separate but gain from sharing knowledge and skills; the corporate role is to encourage each business to develop its full potential through drawing upon capabilities within the group; (c) in playing an *Orchestrator* role, the corporate head office is indispensable in coordinating businesses and ensuring that resources, activities, and systems are shared between businesses.

Sources: Michael Goold and Andrew Campbell, "Corporate strategy: the rationale for a group of companies," (Ashridge Strategic Management Center, 1989) and Nathaniel Foote, "Corporate parenting roles," paper presented at the Strategic Management Society Conference, October 17–20, 1988.

Summary

Most of the strategy analysis which has been developed in this book is simple, straightforward, and common sense. For example, our analysis of business strategy was guided by the underlying principal that, to achieve a position of competitive advantage, a company must match its internal capabilities with external opportunities. Corporate strategy represents by far the most difficult area of strategy analysis in that it lacks such clear guiding themes. The range of activities of the multibusiness corporation is typically the result of a series of historical accidents rather than of a logical plan. The need for a corporate strategy arises, not from the need to survive against competition, but from the need to organize and direct the multibusiness company. In the multibusiness company, sound business strategies are not enough. The corporate management must determine the content of the corporate portfolio; it must decide how and by whom business strategies are to be formulated; it must coordinate the various business strategies; and it must control the performance of each business.

Corporate strategy is complex. The existence of diversified corporations reflects a variety of objectives and rationales: economies of scope, risk spreading, market power, and the quest of size itself. The appropriate corporate strategy for a company must depend upon the reasons for its being. It is not possible to simplify matters by drawing a distinction between the formulation and implementation of corporate strategy. To some extent, corporate strategy is formulated through its implementation. For instance, the composition of the corporate portfolio is determined by the continuous stream of decisions concerning the allocation of investment funds. Finally, empirical evidence offers little clear guidance in formulating successful corporate strategies:

- diversified companies may be more or less successful than specialized companies;
- closely-linked diversified businesses may be more or less successful than conglomerates;
- exploiting shared resources and skills can lead to cost efficiencies and the transfer of competitive advantages, it can also lead to high administrative cost, management inertia, and inflexibility;

- for some diversified companies rigorous financial controls are conducive to high performance, in others longer-term strategic goals are more effective.

The key to the formulation and implementation of successful corporate strategies is *fit*. In determining the composition of the portfolio, the role of corporate headquarters in the formulation of divisional strategies, the organizational structure of the company, and appropriate control systems, there are seven important elements which need to be taken into account:

- the objectives of the company;
- the characteristics of its individual businesses;
- the characteristics of the industries in which they are located;
- the actual and potential links between the businesses;
- the company's primary resource strengths;
- the personalities of the CEO and the top management team;
- the values, traditions, and style of the company; in short, its organizational culture.

Objectives of the company   The corporate strategy issues in a company which has diversified in order to extricate itself from a declining industry (Greyhound, USX) or in order to guard against potential risk (Philip Morris), are different from those in companies whose diversification has been orientated towards vertical integration (Ford Motor Company, Chevron) or exploiting technological linkages (General Dynamics, Dow Chemical). Hence, the starting point for the formulation of corporate strategy is the question "What kind of company are we seeking to become?"

Characteristics of the individual businesses of the company   The appropriate role for corporate strategy within a diversified company depends upon the types of businesses which comprise the company. The better is the performance of a subsidiary or division, the more inclined towards autonomy will corporate headquarters be; the more diverse are the characteristics and needs of the individual businesses, the greater is the need for differentiation of strategies and control systems. If diversification has been through acquisition rather than new ventures, the more appropriate is decentralized strategic decision making which avoids the potential for clashes between different corporate cultures.

Characteristics of the industries in which business units are located   In industries where strategic investments are large (oil, aerospace) and where international competition is strong (automobiles, consumer electronics), the importance and complexity of business strategy decisions is likely to require a substantial involvement by corporate headquarters. In sheltered industries where investments are small and returns are short-term (publishing, restaurants, building materials), strategy decisions are simpler and a high degree of divisional autonomy is feasible.

Actual and potential links between the businesses   The need for corporate management to pursue an active coordination role depends upon the closeness of the links between individual businesses. In the absence of close links, business strategy decisions can be decentralized, and each business can be evaluated as a profit center.

Primary resource strengths of the company   A corporate strategy must recognize and exploit to the full the distinctive competences of the company at both the corporate and the business level. The primary strengths of Philip Morris are its cash flow and its marketing expertise. Its corporate strategy must therefore utilize these resources to lever its competitive position within the different markets in which Philip Morris competes. If General Electric's key competences are its corporate systems and its technological resources, then its corporate strategy must be orientated towards acquiring businesses where GE's corporate systems can be advantageously applied, and ensure the transfer of technology between its businesses.

Personalities of the CEO and the top management team   The corporate style of a company must fit the personalities of the people at the top. The position of Hanson as one of the world's most successful conglomerates is partly due to the fit between the company's arm's-length, financial-control style of management and the backroom style of Lord Hanson and Geoffrey White, neither of whom visits subsidiary companies or gets involved in the details of divisional management. In contrast, the orientation of American Express and Citicorp towards exploiting synergies between their various financial service businesses reflects the hands-on, strong personal leadership styles of their chairmen James Robinson III and John Reed. Of course, this fit between CEO and strategy has its drawbacks: ITT's corporate strategy was so closely matched to the personality and capabilities of Harold Geneen, that the company had enormous difficulty in adjusting to a new chief executive.

Values, traditions, and style of the company   The way in which corporate management manages must be consistent with organizational culture. In an innovation-driven, market-orientated company like 3M, where individual initiative and team work are fostered and rewarded, it is vital that corporate strategy provides the autonomy and encouragement needed to maintain the loyalty, drive, and inventiveness of employees. The successful revival of Walt Disney owes much to the ability of top management team Michael Eisner and Frank Wells to recapture the spirit of inventiveness, imagination, and idealism upon which Walt Disney founded the company.

Notes

1. Alfred D. Chandler, *Strategy and Structure* (MIT Press, Cambridge, Mass., 1962); & *The Visible Hand: The Managerial Revolution in American Business* (Harvard University Press & Belknap Press, Cambridge, Mass., 1977).
2. Chandler, *The Visible Hand*, p. 87.
3. Chandler, *Strategy and Structure*, pp. 382–3.
4. Alfred P. Sloan, *My Years at General Motors* (Sidgwick and Jackson, 1963), pp. 42–56.
5. This section draws heavily upon Oliver E. Williamson, *Markets and Hierarchies: Analysis and Antitrust Implications* (Free Press, New York, 1975) and Oliver E. Williamson, "The modern corporation: origins, evolution, attributes," *Journal of Economic Literature* 19 (1981), pp. 1537–68.
6. See, for example, Peter Steer and John Cable, "Internal organization and profit: an empirical analysis of large UK companies," *Journal of Industrial Economics* 21 (1978), pp. 13–30; Henry Armour and David Teece, "Organizational structure and economic performance: a test of the multidivisional hypothesis," *Bell Journal of Economics*, 9 (1978), pp. 106–22; and David Teece, "Internal organization and economic performance," *Journal of Industrial Economics* 30 (1981), pp. 173–99.
7. Henry Mintzberg, *Structure in Fives: Designing Effective Organizations* (Prentice-Hall, Englewood Cliffs, NJ, 1983), ch. 11.
8. "GE's costly lesson on Wall Street," *Fortune*, May 9, 1988, pp. 72–80.
9. C. K. Prahalad & R. Bettis, "The dominant logic: a new linkage between diversity and performance," *Strategic Management Journal* 7 (1986), pp. 485–502.
10. Ibid., p. 490.
11. "Shades of Geneen at Emerson Electric," *Fortune*, May 22, 1989, p. 39.
12. "Philip Morris Inc." in A. J. Strickland and Arthur A. Thompson, *Cases in Strategic Management*, 2nd edn (BPI, Plano, Texas, 1985).
13. Roland Calori, "How successful companies manage diverse businesses," *Long Range Planning*, 21 (1988), p. 85.
14. Geneen's style of management is discussed in chapter 3 of Richard T. Pascale and Anthony G. Athos, *The Art of Japanese Management* (Warner Books, New York, 1982).
15. "Those highflying PepsiCo managers," *Fortune*, April 10, 1989, p. 79.
16. See chapter 12, "Competitive Advantage from Diversification."
17. "Inside the mind of Jack Welch," *Fortune*, March 27, 1989, pp. 39–50.
18. Tom Copeland, Tim Koller and Jack Murrin, *Valuation: Measuring and Managing the Value of Companies* (John Wiley, New York, 1990) ch. 9.
19. Ibid., pp. 262–9.
20. Michael C. Jensen, "Takeovers: their causes and consequences," *Journal of Economic Perspectives* 2 (Winter 1988), pp. 21–48.
21. In a recent study, Michael Goold and Andrew Campbell, *Strategies and Style* (Blackwell, Oxford, 1987), refer to the corporate management's role as its "strategic management style".
22. Jay W. Lorsch and Stephen A. Allen III, *Managing Diversity and Interdependence: An Organizational Study of Multidivisional Firms* (Harvard Business School, Boston, 1973).
23. Ibid., p. 168.
24. Goold and Campbell, *Strategies and Styles*. For a summary see, Michael Goold and Andrew Campbell, "Many best ways to make strategy," *Harvard Business Review*, November–December 1987, pp. 70–6.

FOURTEEN

Strategies for the 1990s

Frank Popoff, Dow Chemical's chief executive, professed himself at a loss when his 25-year-old son, an M.B.A. candidate, asked what career path to follow. "I said, 'Tom, it's not as simple as it used to be.'"[1]

Introduction

The purpose of this final chapter is to look ahead. Business strategy is a new area of study: before the 1960s it received little systematic attention either by academics or practitioners. Progress has been rapid. Concepts and theories from economics, organizational theory, psychology, and decision theory have been imported, adapted, and augmented to provide a sound analytic foundation. Observation of the relationship of strategies to company performance, and of the strategy formulation process itself, has been valuable, not just in testing theories, but also in developing powerful new ideas. Inductive analysis has proved particularly fruitful: By observing individual examples of success or failure and identifying the strategies and other conditions that appeared to explain the observed performance, illuminating generalizations have been generated. A symptom of recent progress is the increasing rigor and sophistication of strategy analysis. Simplistic analyses lacking strong theoretical foundations such as the

Experience Curve, SWOT (Strengths–Weaknesses–Opportunities–Threats) analysis, and the Boston Consulting Group's growth-share matrix, have given way to less-mechanistic analyses with sounder conceptual and empirical bases.

Yet, despite rapid development of the tools of strategy analysis, the gulf between strategic problems and managers' abilities to find solutions to them remains as broad as ever. The reason is simple: The rate at which the business environment changes and at which new problems emerge, constantly outstrips the rate at which the theories, tools, and techniques of strategic management are developed.

During the current 1990s we can expect a similar pattern of progress: While companies will move at an unprecedented pace at developing solutions to last year's problems, they will be challenged by new and unforeseen problems and issues. In this chapter we shall focus upon three broad sources of change in the practice of strategic management over the next decade.

The first is change in the external environment. The evidence of recent years points towards the rapid pace of environmental change being sustained, if not accelerating over the new decade. In this chapter we will review briefly some key dimensions of environmental change; notably technology, demography, social structure, the economic system, and global ecology.

Next, we will examine some of the forces which will influence company's responses to existing and new challenges. The first of these is the development of new ideas, concepts, and philosophies. New ideas are among the most powerful forces for change even in the hard-headed world of business. Just as Frederick Taylor's theories of scientific management and their popularization by Henry Ford helped revolutionize manufacturing industry during the first three decades of this century, the ideas of W. E. Deming, Peter Drucker, and Peters and Waterman have exercised a worldwide impact on business management during the 1980s. The impact of new ideas on management practice in terms of pervasiveness and speed of dissemination is increasing all the time. An important function of this chapter is to identify and assess recent contributions to management thinking likely to influence management practice during the 1990s.

Companies will also learn from experience. Most of the major advances in strategic management practice have been the result of experimentation and adaptation by pioneering companies. For example, General Electric's development of strategic planning techniques for large, diversified firms; 3M's contribution to the promotion of innovation and "intrapreurship" in the mature corporation; Toyota in manufacturing strategy; Matsushita in globalization strategy. In this chapter we shall identify and discuss novel approaches to strategy which are being developed by pioneering companies of the present.

In short, the purpose of this chapter is to assess current trends and developments in order to predict the issues which strategy will need to address in the 1990s and onwards, and to identify the themes which will characterize the formulation and implementation of strategy.

The Emerging Business Environment

The business environment of the 1980s was dominated by two principal trends: Internationalization and turbulence. The two are linked: intensification of competition as a result of the growth of world trade and the emergence of new manufacturing nations has increased the vulnerability of companies to international economic factors, while increased interdependence through trade and financial flows results in the economic problems of one country being transmitted internationally.

Turbulence has other sources too. One consequence of increased economic interdependence is that divergences between countries' economic policies and economic performances has created instability. Some countries, notably Japan, West Germany, South Korea, and Taiwan, experienced increasing balance of trade surpluses during the 1980s. Others, notably the US together with most of the Third World countries suffered destabilizing current account deficits. Capital balances have been the reverse of current account balances: Japan has huge outflow of capital funds, while the US has been the primary destination.

Both these trends, internationalization and turbulence, have continued into the 1990s. At time of writing, the internationalization of the business environment appears to be accelerating rather than slowing:

- Direct overseas investment is expanding at an unprecedented rate with acquisitions and greenfield investment by Japanese and European companies in the US now being matched by investments by US and Japanese companies in Europe.
- Despite imbalances of trade, there is no evidence of the post-war trend towards freedom of international trade being halted or reversed: despite the call for protectionism in the US and fear of an integrated European Community retreating into "Fortress Europe". The evidence that trade protection is either damaging or ineffective continues to accumulate.
- The increased integration of the socialist world into the international economy opens a vast new set of opportunities for trade and direct investment. The speed at which Western companies are seeking opportunities in Eastern Europe is remarkable: In January 1990, only months after the revolutionary political changes had swept Eastern Europe, both Suzuki and General Motors announced joint ventures to build cars in Hungary, while Fiat was moving quickly to consolidate its position within Poland and the USSR.

The volatility and dynamism of the economic environment shows no sign of abating. At the international level, exchange rates and interest rates appear impotent in resolving trade and financial imbalances. As a result, exchange rates and interest rates will continue to be volatile so long as

The economy: internationalization, turbulence, and growth

such imbalances continue. The free market's capacity to promote gradual adjustment towards equilibrium also seems limited in other areas of economic activity. The gyrations of stock market indices, energy prices, and commodity prices between 1986 and 1990 point to the shakiness rather than steadiness of "the invisible hand".

Yet, despite instability in the financial economy, the "real" economy has shown remarkable resilience to exchange rate, interest rate, and stock market fluctuations. Despite signs of cyclical weakness in the world economy during 1990, most longer-term forecasts were pointing to continuing growth prospects. Naisbitt and Aburdene argue that the combined influences of increased trade, lower taxes, technological change, growing consumer demand in Asia, world peace, and the spread of free enterprise will result in the 1990s being a period of unprecedented global economic expansion.[2] The political convergence of the late 1980s offers a sound basis for economic expansion. The worldwide collapse of Marxist-Leninism and the global consensus around the principles of liberal democracy marks a turning-point in world history and a firm foundation for world economic development.[3]

Technology

Technology is a further source of change which promises to have as pervasive an impact during the 1990s as during the 1980s. As with the previous decade, the continued diffusion of electronics will continue to be the most general feature of technology change during the 1990s. The potential of integrated circuits has yet to be fully realized. While the application of integrated circuits to products is well-advanced, their impact on manufacturing technology, communications, and management will be substantial during the early years of the 1990s.

For example, in manufacturing technology, the cost and the limited availability of factory workers is likely to be an important factor accelerating the adoption of automation. During the 1990s, computer-aided design, robotics, and computer-integrated manufacturing will extend from their present islands of application in electronics, automobiles, and aerospace, throughout much of manufacturing industry.[4]

Similarly, in administration, improvements in communication, data retrieval, data storage, and data-processing capabilities will accelerate the slimming of administrative hierarchies already occurring in most large corporations during recent years. Early stages of this process had their biggest impact on staff engaged in clerical, routine functions. More recent advances, particularly in expert systems and the use of neural networks in artificial intelligence, promise radical consequences for the work and continued existence of middle management.[5]

Among emerging technologies, there are several with potentially huge economic impacts. Optical technology offers an alternative to electronic technology not just in communication, but also in computers themselves through the development of optical microprocessors.[6] There are new materials: most notably the application of ceramics to electronics and engineering, the use of gallium arsenide in integrated circuits, the replacement of metals and plastics with composite materials with superior performance combinations.[7] Superconductivity has revolutionary implications for computing, and for electronics and electrical engineering as a whole.[8] Biotechnology has the potential to revolutionize agriculture and pharmaceuticals, and has possible applications to many other industries. Genetic engineering can produce remarkable productivity gains in raising crops and animals; and, in health care, genetic extracts offer opportunities for the improved treatment of cancer, AIDS, and hemophilia.

As the diffusion of process innovation continues to accelerate and product innovation becomes increasingly attractive as a source of sustainable competitive advantage, so companies must position themselves to exploit technological change. Some of the management implications are explored in the next section.

The new challenges which business managers must cope with are not only within the world of business. As governments increasingly recognize the limits of their capacity for action, so the business sector is increasingly being called upon to respond to broader environmental and social objectives. Increasing public concern over the threat of economic development to the natural environment exerts increasing influence over the technologies and materials used by industry. Apart from specific issues such as the implications of bans on fluorocarbons for the manufacturers of refrigerators, aerosols, and plastic packaging; there are general issues whose impact will be much broader. Even small climatic changes arising from increased carbon dioxide in the atmosphere can have radical effects on industries from agriculture to tourism, and efforts to limit the production of carbon dioxide and other gases will have a great impact on manufacturing industry.[9] Concern over the adverse environmental impact of burning fossil fuels promises revitalization of the nuclear power industry, especially if developments in fusion offer commercial application.[10]

Emerging environmental and social demands on business

Business enterprises will also be changed from within. Organizations will have to adapt to changing attitudes, ideals, aspirations, and social relationships. Just as the era of scientific management through mass production was brought to an end partly through increasing resentfulness of production workers towards the disciplined tedium of assembly-line production, so emerging social trends will have equally powerful effects.

Demographic changes will be particularly important in breaking down traditional career patterns. As the baby-boomers mature into middle age and new entrants into the labor force dwindle as a result of low birth rates and longer time spent in education, companies will be forced to rely increasingly on part-time workers, women, and semi-retired workers. The Hudson Institute estimates that during the 1990s, only 15 percent of entrants to the US workforce will be native-born white males; while more than half will be women, many of them mothers.[11]

Changing life-styles and aspirations

Even among young workers entering the labor force, conventional notions about career patterns are breaking down. Charles Handy anticipates two major trends during the 1990s.[12]

First there is likely to be a resurgence of individualism and decline of corporatism. People increasingly desire the freedom and incentives of self-employment over the security of a cozy corporate niche. Business organizations will rely increasingly on consultants and subcontractors for a whole range of functions and activities previously supplied internally.

Rather than commitment to a career in a particular specialization with a single company, people will increasingly seek to manage "portfolio lifestyles". They will seek to leave the workforce periodically for reeducation, retraining, to take up childrearing responsibilities, to engage in community work, and to explore other activities.

Exhibit 14.1 summarizes some of the predictions for the 1990s and beyond made by leading futurologists.

Exhibit 14.1 Towards the new millenium: a summary of forecasts for the 1990s

The international environment

- Increasing imbalance of population – between 1950 and 2025 the OECD countries' proportion of world population will have fallen from 23 to 12 percent, and Europe will account for 3 percent of world population.
- Widening gaps in living standards between developed and developing countries – 1.5 billion people in "absolute poverty" (income less than $300 per year) by 2000.
- The number of people over 60 years old will increase between 1980 and 2020 in Japan from 15.0 m. to 34.7 m., in USA from 35.8 to 66.9 m., in USSR from 34.7 m. to 69.3 m., in China from 73.6 m. to 238.9 m.
- Explosive and anarchic development of Third World megapolises – Mexico City will have 30 million inhabitants by 2000.
- Lack of international leadership: US and USSR economically weak; Japan unwilling to accept increasing international role.
- Worldwide environmental problems including: inadequacies of water supplies, in developed as well as less developed countries; climatic changes; pollution problems notably problems of acid rain, waste disposal, and nuclear accidents.
- Monetary instability with strong fluctuations in exchange rates.
- Rapid economic growth during the 1990s.

Technology and work patterns

- Increased automation, shift to smaller-scale production, mass production of variety.
- Manufacturing jobs requiring higher skills, but growth in service sector mainly providing low-skill jobs.
- Major breakthroughs in biotechnology; diversification of energy sources through fusion, coal gasification, geopressure; application of superconductivity; new composite materials.

Socioeconomic trends
- Development of a dual economy – a formal economy and an informal economy.
- Declining effectiveness of state-provided services speeds privatization of the provision of collective goods and services (health, education, environment, culture). Nevertheless, the growing problems of health care for the elderly poses an increasing economic drag.
- Emergence of new inequalities in material living standards, security, and social status.
- Democratic processes increasingly influenced by institutionalized pressure groups and increased power of the old ("The grey panthers").
- Increasing leadership role of women in private and public sectors.

Life-styles and living
- Trends towards global uniformity matched by heterogeneity and differentiation of life-styles and a resurgence of cultural nationalism.
- Increased insecurity reflected in regeneration of the family unit.
- Search for new forms of fulfillment – family, children, group life, associations, networks of solidarity and exchange.
- Continued urbanization, with rejuvenation of city centers, and increased social segregation in urban areas.

Sources: Michel Godet (Conservatoire National des Artes et Metiers), "Into the next decade: major trends and uncertainties of the 1990s," *Futures* Vol 20 (1988), pp. 410–23. Hugues de Jouvenel (Futuribles International), "Europe at the dawn of the third millenium: a synthesis of the main trends," *Futures* Vol 20, October 1988, pp. 506–18; John Naisbitt and Patricia Aburdene, *Megatrends 2000*, (William Morrow & Company, New York, 1990).

The Shifting Basis of Competitive Advantage

A critical shift in the strategic orientation of Western firms during the 1980s was away from cost efficiency as the primary source of competitive advantage and towards quality and innovation. During the 1960s and the early part of the 1970s, business strategies were dominated by the quest for cost leadership through large-scale manufacture and mass distribution. The belief that "Big is Beautiful" was nourished by studies which showed minimum efficient plant sizes in most industries to greatly exceed the size of most actual plants, by BCG's demonstration of the cost reductions arising from experience effects, and by evidence of the global convergence of consumer preferences. By the late 1970s, however, excess capacity across much of manufacturing industry, and intense price competition in markets for standardized, mass-produced goods, focussed interest upon the quest for differentiation advantage through quality and innovation.

During the late 1980s concern over quality had permeated every corner of the business world, nourished in particular by evidence that improvements in product consistency and reliability, far from adding to manu-

Themes of the 1980s: quality and innovation

facturing costs, could be achieved simultaneously with cost reduction. US enthusiasm for quality was indicated by the diffusion of *Total Quality Control* programs and by the National Bureau of Standards' inauguration of the annual Baldridge prizes for quality (equivalent to Japan's W. E. Deming Prize).[13]

Interest in innovation had grown in response to the question, "How can the older industrialized nations compete in manufacturing industry?" The rising share of world exports contributed by the newly-industrializing countries had convinced a growing proportion of industrialists that only through innovation could the high-wage countries hope to maintain their preeminence in manufacturing industry. The performance of the US in innovation has been particularly worrying to those who see the industrial future of the US as technology based. Of all patents issued in the US in recent years, the proportion issued to US companies and individuals has been dwindling.[14]

Like quality, the quest for innovation has become pervasive. In some industries, competition has always focussed around research and new product development: Semiconductors, computers, chemicals, and pharmaceuticals, for example. The interesting phenomenon of the 1980s was the increased emphasis on innovation across the industrial spectrum, particularly in mature and service industries. The resurgence of technology-based competition in automobiles, the potential for complex knitwear designs made possible by computer-controlled knitting machines, innovations in sports shoes, and the flood of new financial instruments, all pointed to a resurgence of innovation in industries with traditionally low R&D intensity.

Trends for the 1990s: managing innovation and targeting customer needs

As aspects of quality such as consistency and reliability have become so diffused as to become a prerequisite for competing rather than a source of competitive advantage, so companies are being forced towards a more precise targeting of specific areas of quality and improvement: "How can value be created for customers?"; "In which dimensions of differentiation can a firm excel?"

With regard to innovation, it is becoming increasingly clear that sustained success in most markets is based upon *continuous innovation*, involving numerous small improvements rather than a few major technological advances. The Boeing 747 was introduced in 1970, the Apple Macintosh personal computer in 1984, but despite a rapid pace of technological change in these industries, continual, incremental improvements have extended the commercial success of these products over a number of years. Continuous, incremental innovation across a broad front requires that innovation is diffused across all areas of the company rather than being the preserve of the R&D department. "Make innovation a way of life for everyone," proclaims Tom Peters:

The reality is that millions . . . of innovation/improvement opportunities lie within any factory, distribution center, store, or operations center. And you can multiply that by more millions when you can involve the factory and the distribution center and the store working together as a team. And multiply again when you add in involvement in innovation by suppliers and customers.[15]

The critical challenge for companies during the 1990s is not allocating resources to R&D or even creating innovation, it is managing technology to ensure that technological knowledge can be transformed into competitive advantage. Kim Clark argues that top management is the critical link between technology and strategy; if managers are not conversant with the technologies developed and utilized within their industries, then that link is bound to be weak. Critical elements in the link include the design process, which draws together technology, marketing, and manufacturing; the manufacturing system which executes new product designs; and the information system which distributes knowledge and plays a central role in integrating functions and activities.[16]

In relation both to innovation and quality, firms will need to target more selectively the features and performance dimensions which will be most effective in the market. Manufacturers which have been in the forefront of the application of electronics to major domestic appliances have seen little return for their efforts. Market research shows that customers neither use nor attach much value to sophisticated control and programming features. Competitive advantage in the 1990s is likely to focus much more closely upon understanding of customers' use of products and the aspects of performance which they regard as important. The key to competitive success argues Kenichi Ohmae, head of McKinsey's Tokyo office, is not toe-to-toe battles with competitors, but understanding customers' real needs:

Of course it is important to take competition into account, but in making strategy that should not come first. It cannot come first. First comes painstaking attention to the needs of customers. First comes close analysis of a company's real degrees of freedom in responding to those needs. First comes the willingness to rethink, fundamentally, what products are and what they do, as well as how best to organize the business system that designs, builds, and markets them.[17]

Yamaha provides an interesting example of this approach in practice (see Case Note 14.1).

Time-based advantage

Innovation is intimately concerned with speed. Innovative success in the business world is increasingly based upon cumulative incremental product improvements. Technological leadership therefore becomes dependent less upon fundamental scientific breakthroughs and more upon the ability to speedily implement incremental improvements. Speed also confers other advantages: It reduces costs, alleviates the need for demand forecasting, and permits increased responsiveness to customer requirements. George

---

Case Note 14.1   Yamaha: Innovating with Pianos

By 1988 Yamaha had captured 40 percent of the world piano market. However, demand was declining by an estimated 10 percent each year. There was a stock of some 40 million pianos in customers' hands, mostly unused. What could Yamaha do?

What Yamaha's managers did was look – they took a hard look at the customer and the product. What they saw was that most of these 40 million pianos sit around idle and neglected – and out of tune – most of the time. Not many people play them any more ... No matter how good you are at strategy, you won't be able to sell that many new pianos – no matter how good they are – in that environment. If you want to create value for customers, you're going to have to find ways to add value to the millions of pianos already out there.... What Yamaha did was to remember the old player piano ... Yamaha worked hard to develop a sophisticated, advanced combination of digital and optical technology that can distinguish among 92 different degrees of strength and speed of key touch from pianissimo to fortissimo. Because the technology is digital it can record and reproduce each keystroke with great accuracy, using the same kind of 3.5 inch disks that work on a personal computer. This means that you can now record live performances by the pianists of your choice – or buy such recordings on a computer-like diskette – and then, in effect, invite the artists into your home to play the same compositions on your piano ...

Furthermore, if you have a personal computer at home in Cambridge and you know a good pianist living in California, you can have her record your favorite sonata and send it over the phone, you simply download it onto your computer, plug the diskette into your retrofitted piano, and enjoy her performance. Or you can join a club that will send you the concert that Horowitz played last night in Carnegie Hall to listen to at home on your own piano. There are all kinds of possibilities.

In terms of the piano market, this new technology creates the prospect of a $2,500 sale to retrofit each of 40 million pianos – not bad for a declining industry ... Yamaha started marketing this technology last April, and sales in Japan have been explosive ... Yamaha did not pursue all the usual routes: it didn't buckle down to prune costs, proliferate models, slice overhead, and all the usual approaches. It looked with fresh eyes for chances to create value for customers. And it found them.

Source: Kenichi Ohmae, "Getting back to strategy," *Harvard Business Review*, November–December, 1988, pp. 151–2.

Stalk, vice-president of the BCG, argues that time management is the most powerful new source of competitive advantage and is the basis of the success of many Japanese companies, including Sony, Matsushita, Toyota, Hitachi, and NEC, and some Western companies, such as Benetton, The Limited, Federal Express, and McDonald's: "For these leading competitors, time has become the overarching measurement of performance. By reducing the consumption of time in every aspect of the business, these companies also reduce costs, improve quality, and stay close to customers."[18]

The potential for time reduction is considerable. For many products 19 weeks elapse between a retailer placing an order, it being received by a manufacturer, and the resulting production reaching the retailer. Even in a fast-moving, fashion business such as leisure shoes, the time taken between orders being placed for Nike shoes, their production in the Far East, and shipment to retailers in America and Europe is typically four months.[19] The costs of such delay are high: Sales must be forecast, inventories must be maintained at all stages of production and distribution, customer preferences must be anticipated in advance. Reductions in time can be achieved in all areas of operation, in particular:

Case Note 14.2   Atlas Door

Consider Atlas Door ... its pretax earnings ... were about five times the industry average. In its tenth year it achieved the number one position in its industry ...

Historically, the [industrial doors] industry had needed almost four months to respond to an order for a door that was out of stock or customized. Atlas's strategic advantage was time, it could respond in weeks to any order ...

First, Atlas built just-in-time factories. These are fairly simple in concept. They require extra tooling and machinery to reduce changeover times and a fabrication process organized by product and scheduled to start and complete all of the parts at the same time ...

Second, Atlas compressed time at the front end of the system where the order first entered and was processed. Traditionally, when customers called ... with a request for price and delivery they have to wait more than one week for a response ... Atlas first streamlined, then automated its entire order-entry, engineering, pricing and scheduling processes. Today Atlas can price and schedule 95% of its incoming orders while the callers are still on the telephone. It can quickly engineer new special orders because it has preserved on computer the design and production data of all previous special orders – which drastically reduces the amount of re-engineering necessary.

Third, Atlas tightly controlled logistics so that it always shipped only fully complete orders to construction sites. Orders require many components.

Gathering all of them at the factory and making sure that they are in the correct order can be a time-consuming task. It is even more time consuming, however, to get the correct parts to the job site *after* they have missed the initial shipment. Atlas developed a system to track the parts in production and the purchased parts for each order, ensuring arrival of all necessary parts at the shipping dock in time – a just-in-time logistics operation.

When Atlas started operations, distributors were uninterested in its product. The established distributors already carried the door line of a larger competitor, they saw no reason to switch suppliers except, perhaps, for a major price concession. But as a start-up, Atlas was too small to compete on price alone. Instead it positioned itself as the door supplier of last resort, the company people came to if the established supplier could not deliver or missed a key date.

Of course, with industry lead times of almost four weeks, some calls inevitably came to Atlas. And when they did get a call, Atlas commanded a higher price because of its faster delivery. Atlas not only got a higher price but its time-based processes also yielded lower costs: it thus enjoyed the best of both worlds.

In ten short years, the company replaced the leading door suppliers in 80% of the distributors in the country. With its strategic advantage the company could be selective, becoming the house supplier for only the strongest distributors.

Source: George Stalk Jr., "Time – the next source of competitive advantage," *Harvard Business Review*, July–August, 1988, pp. 50–1.

- product development;
- manufacturing;
- sales and distribution.

New product lead times are the single most important determinant of speed in innovation. During the 1980s, lead times (from concept to market introduction) of Japanese cars was 43 months, in Europe 62 months, and in the US 63 months.[20] Across the whole of manufacturing industry lead times are being cut drastically, Xerox has halved its lead times for new products. Integration of design with manufacturing is critical for speedy new product introduction. At Next Computer integration of computer-aided design with computer-aided manufacturing permits prototypes to be manufactured on the production line. At Northern Telecom engineering change orders for PBXs can be decided and implemented in the manufacturing system within 48 hours.

Just-in-time scheduling combined with a reconfiguring of factory layouts around product-based manufacturing rather than process-based manufacturing can offer remarkable reductions in cycle time: Matsushita reduced the time needed to make a washing machine from 360 hours to 2 hours.

The benefits of time saved in product introduction and manufacture can be dissipated in slow-moving sales and distribution systems. The benefits of speed in ordering and distribution systems are particularly evident in fashion-sensitive industries such as clothing and toys. The success of Benetton and The Gap in fashion clothing owes much to these companies' ability to quickly identify market trends and respond through fast, flexible production arrangements and lightning distribution.

Finally, companies need to integrate their whole organization upon a time-based system of competition. Once all functions and activities are focussed upon and coordinated around the objective of minimizing time, then the goals of cost reduction, technological leadership, and responsiveness to customer requirements can be achieved simultaneously. George Stalk quotes the example of Atlas Door in the market for industrial doors (see Case Note 14.2).

Competitive advantage through intercompany cooperation

The capitalist market system, particularly in its American form, is committed to the notion that competition is the natural state of relations between companies, and it is the guarantor of efficient performance. This view was vividly iterated by Ray Kroc, the founder of the McDonald's burger chain, in an interview in 1972: "This is a rat-eat-rat, dog-eat-dog business. I'll kill 'em, and I'm going to kill 'em before they kill me. You're talking about the American way of survival of the fittest."

To the extent that strategy is concerned with the attainment of competitive advantage, this view of the business world as a battlefield where companies are engaged in eternal conflict for survival and supremacy in the marketplace is implicit in much of the discussion of strategy in this book. Yet, we have also recognized (chapter 2) that competition is not, in most cases, a condition of all-out warfare. *Destructive* competition through which one firm seeks to eliminate another does take place. It normally entails price wars, losses sustained by all combatants, and finally the exit of the losing player. In general, however, competition in the business world is limited both in scope and intensity, and normally involves the coexistence of competitors over long periods of time.

The ambivalent relationship between competitors – competing for customers and resources, while at the same time maintaining a shared interest in survival and the maintenance of industry stability – is becoming more sharply dichotomized. On the one hand, competition is becoming increasingly intense; on the other, firms are increasingly seeking to enhance their competitive positions through cooperative arrangements with one another.

Industry	Pre-1975	1975–7	1978–83	1984–6
Automobiles	1	1	19	21
Communications equipment	6	10	37	53
Communications services	6	14	52	53
Computers and peripherals	8	12	42	53
Electronic components	3	22	46	51
Engines and aerospace	2	8	25	32
Farm and industrial equipment	0	1	7	10
Financial services	16	27	61	79
Heavy machinery	6	15	18	16
Medical products	6	11	24	27
Metals fabrication	3	4	6	6
Metals processing	5	7	9	8
Mining	9	11	18	16
Office equipment	2	12	25	26
Petrochemicals	44	42	95	93
Pharmaceuticals	6	18	60	87
Precision controls	2	3	18	27
Programming – films	2	3	5	7
Programming packaging	0	1	15	25
Software and data bases	2	5	12	24
Steel	5	12	23	29
Videotape and videodisc	5	7	13	20
Total	134	246	630	763

Exhibit 14.2 Joint ventures and cooperative ventures involving US companies, 1975–86

Source: Kathryn R. Harrigan, "Joint ventures and competitive strategy," *Strategic Management Journal*, 9 (1988), pp. 141–57.

Exhibit 14.2 shows the growth over time in the proportions of companies in different industries with joint ventures or other types of cooperative ventures with other companies.

Cooperation as a strategic tool, not just between domestic companies but also with overseas companies, has been pioneered by Japanese firms. Licensing agreements, joint ventures, and technology-exchange agreements played a vital role in closing the post-war technology gap between Japan and the United States and helped Japanese companies gain access to Western markets. In recent years roles are being reversed: Western firms are seeking technology-exchange agreements and joint ventures with Japanese companies in order to gain access to superior product and process technology. The US automakers have been especially prominent in such cooperation. General Motors, in addition to its 41.3 percent ownership of Isuzu and 5 percent stake in Suzuki (from which it buys small cars), operates a jointly-owned automobile plant in California in partnership with Toyota, and formed a joint venture with Fujitsu-Fanuc to produce industrial robots.[21] Exhibit 14.3 shows the network of strategic alliances between GM and overseas automobile manufacturers.

Despite the potential for cooperation to transfer skills and knowledge

Exhibit 14.3 Strategic
alliances between
General Motors and its
competitors

Company	Type of alliance
Japan	
Suzuki	5.1% owned by GM
Isuzu	38.6% owned by GM
Toyota	NUMMI joint venture
Europe	
Lotus (UK)	100% owned by GM
Pinifaria	Joint development of sports car
Volvo	Joint production of trucks
Jaguar	100% owned by GM (Chrysler)
USA	
AMC	GM supplies engines
Korea	
Daewoo	Builds small cars for GM in 50/50 joint venture

Source: "The motor industry," *The Financial Times*, October 20, 1988, section III.

and combine complementary capabilities, most international joint ventures are short lived; mainly reflecting management difficulties, disagreements between the partners, or a reassessment by at least one partner of the desirability of the venture. Joint ventures which share management responsibility are far more likely to fail than those with a dominant parent or with independent management.[22] Other forms of international collaboration display a similar propensity for disagreement and misunderstanding leading to premature divorce. AT&T's collaboration with Olivetti in personal computers, and JVC's collaboration with Thorn-EMI and Thomson in VCRs have failed to satisfy all partners.

The greatest problems arise in cooperation between firms which are also competitors. In cooperative partnerships between Japanese and Western firms, the propensity for the Western company to emerge as the disappointed partner has been noted. A typical scenario is the Western company making available its key resources of technology or distribution to its Japanese partner in return for short-term benefits, only to see its Japanese collaborator reemerge as a resurgent competitor.[23] Such experiences point to Japanese companies' more systematic approach to managing complex relationships which involve both competitive and cooperative dimensions. In the US auto-parts industry, 126 companies entered into joint ventures with Japanese parts suppliers in order to supply the US plants of Honda, Nissan, and Toyota. Conflicting objectives, divergent management styles, disputes over quality and labor practices have meant that almost all these joint ventures are losing money.[24] Yet the picture is not all bleak. Corning Glass, a veteran of international joint ventures, derives over half its profits from joint ventures; Ford's collaboration with Mazda has helped it enter South Korea, as well as enhancing its competitive position within the US and Japanese markets.[25]

During the 1990s, global competition and increasingly costly research and product development will increase the attractions of cooperative agreements. In order to achieve maximum benefit from cooperation, American and European companies will need to adopt more effective strategic management of these arrangements. The key, argue Hamel, Doz, and Prahalad, is to recognize that "Collaboration is competition in a different form."[26] Naturally, one partner will tend to benefit more than the other from collaboration. Hamel et al. argue that the sharing of benefits will depend upon three key factors:

- the strategic intent of the partners;
- appropriability of the contribution;
- receptivity of the company.

Japanese companies have entered partnerships with the clear intent of gaining global dominance; strategic partnerships are just one step on the road to global expansion. By contrast, Western companies have often entered partnerships with the aim of giving up manufacturing to more efficient Japanese producers. The willingness of Western companies to yield major items of value added to former competitors limits their ability to learn from their partners, and is likely to lead to a cumulative abandonment of activities and capabilities.

The ability of each partner to capture and appropriate the skills of the other depend upon the nature of each firm's skills and resources. Where skills and resources are tangible or explicit, they can easily be acquired. Where they are tacit and embodied in people, they are more difficult to acquire. To avoid the unintended transfer of know-how to partners, Hamel et al. argue the need for a "gatekeeper" to monitor and administer contacts with strategic partners.

The more receptive a company is in terms of its ability to identify what it wants from the partner, to obtain the required knowledge or skills, to assimilate, and to adapt them, the more it will gain from the partnership. In management terms, this requires the setting of performance goals for what the partnership is to achieve for the company and managing the relationship to ensure that the company is deriving the maximum of learning from the collaboration.

Closer cooperation between independent companies is also apparent in supplier–customer relations. Changes in manufacturing methods – just-in-time systems, quality enhancement programs, faster new product development – require far closer cooperation between component suppliers and finished product manufacturers. Cooperation between personal computer companies and suppliers of operating system software, between automobile companies and their suppliers, currently involves joint product design, technology sharing, joint production scheduling; all areas of cooperation which a few years ago would only have been conceivable through vertical integration. Where independent companies can cooperate through close, but informal, supplier–customer collaboration, they can gain the efficiency benefits of vertical integration, but without its administrative costs and inherent inflexibility.[27]

Networks Cooperation between companies has conventionally been viewed in terms of bilateral partnerships and agreements. One of the most exciting areas of intercompany relationships during the 1990s and beyond will be wider and more complex cooperative arrangements. Networks of informal cooperation between companies are not new. Complex networks between self-employed crafts people were the dominant organizational form in preindustrial revolution manufacturing. The highly successful Italian clothing industry utilizes complex local networks comprising numerous small firms which share technology, subcontract production between one another, and collaborate in sales and distribution activities.[28] In the securities industry, intense competition between investment banks is matched by close cooperation through syndication of new issues. The construction industry, too, has traditionally featured close networking arrangements between architects, design engineers, building contractors, and specialist subcontractors.

The trend towards networking is a result not only of the opportunities for cooperation between companies in technology, marketing, and distribution, but also of the breakup of large vertically-integrated corporations in response to the need for flexibility and the desire of employees for entrepreneurial opportunity. Apple Computer has only 8,000 employees despite sales of over $4 billion. It is lean because it relies upon a huge network of third-party business partners: Software developers, manufacturers of peripheral equipment, retailers, and providers of business services. This structure permits enormous flexibility, enhances innovativeness, and encourages a wider repertoire of capabilities. Apple's success in desktop publishing owes much to the diverse capabilities which Apple's network could orchestrate.[29]

The potential for networks to displace large, vertically-integrated corporations in the organization of production is one of the interesting opportunities of the next decade. The advent of the factory system caused hierarchies to replace networks during the industrial revolution. The innovations of today in the form of information technology and new financial developments in the areas of venture capital and leveraged buy-outs are encouraging movement in the opposite direction.

Developing Responsiveness and Team Work within the Organization

The changes taking place in the competitive environment, in the strategies which firms adopt, and in the attitudes and expectations of people towards their jobs and towards their lives are having profound implications for the ways in which business enterprises are organized and managed. Among the emergent trends are:

- the breakdown of structural rigidity;
- less distinct organizational boundaries;
- new models of management;
- resolution of the problems of accountability and legitimacy within companies;
- cooperation within the organization.

The breakdown of structural rigidity   The primacy of innovation, flexibility, and customer responsiveness as sources of competitive advantage will necessitate increased job flexibility at all levels, shorter chains of command, greater team work, and increased lateral communication. Achieving these conditions will require the abandonment of many conventional features of established corporations including

- less separation of strategic and operational decision making as strategic decision making becomes more diffused;
- fewer levels of management hierarchy;
- less reliance on rules, procedures, and controls, and more emphasis on initiative and opportunism.

The key symptom of what Tom Peters calls the "flexible, porous, fleet-of-foot organization of the future" is the lack of a meaningful organization chart: It is "a world of ordered chaos, purposeful confusion; a world, above all, of flexibility, adaptiveness and action."[30]

Less distinct organizational boundaries   As firms form closer networking relationships with suppliers, customers, and competitors, and as individuals increasingly seek the freedom of self-employment, so the boundaries of corporations become less distinct. Oliver Williamson viewed the organization of production occurring through the invisible hand of the market or the visible hand of corporate hierarchies.[31] Internal transactions are governed by corporate rules and management direction, market transactions are governed by contracts overseen by corporate lawyers. In the next decade, the distinction between the two will diminish. Ultimately, however, all transactions whether within or between companies involve two individuals and it is the trust between individuals which is the foundation of successful transactions and interactions.

New models of management   Traditional management methods and organizational systems were developed on the basis of the need for order and efficiency in the large-scale production of standardized products. Success in innovation and customer responsiveness in knowledge-intensive companies calls for different approaches to management and organization. Peter Drucker suggests that the organizational models for the future will be those of "professional" organizations today – the symphony orchestra, the university, the hospital.[32] The key features of the information-based organizations of tomorrow, like those of professional organizations today, will be:

- the presence of specialists in operations rather than at headquarters;
- small head office cores;
- operations concentrated in task-focussed teams;
- wide spans of control.

John Sculley uses a similar metaphor to describe the management of innovation:

Many of Apple's leaders weren't leaders at all; they were impresarios ... Not unlike the director of an opera company, the impresario must cleverly deal with the creative temperaments of artists ... He ensures that the setting and stage are conducive to the production of a masterpiece. His gift is to merge powerful ideas and the performance of his artists.[33]

Successfully managing the innovative company of the future, argues Sculley, requires:

- giving people the security that encourages them to strive for the highest challenges;
- giving people direction, not specific goals;
- encouraging contrarian thinking – dissent stimulates discussion, sharper perception, new ideas, and better decisions;
- building an environment that encourages play, interaction, and relaxation;
- avoiding defensiveness, encouraging involvement, and recognizing individuals' contributions;
- giving people the flexibility to structure their own work and making them accountable not for their inputs, in terms of hours spent at the office and so on, but for their *results*.

Resolution of the problems of accountability and legitimacy within companies   American corporations, argues Peter Drucker, have fallen between two unsatisfactory control mechanisms: Professional management tends to be self-perpetuating and self-seeking, while shareholders are overconcerned with short-term returns.[34] One solution to the problem of accountability and the reconciliation of short- and long-term goals is the growing movement in the US to take large businesses private so that ownership is concentrated into a few hands. Although the leveraged buyout movement slowed considerably during 1989–90, the problems of reconciling the interests of managers and shareholders will continue to add appeal to the option of taking companies private.

Cooperation within the organization   Western capitalism's commitment to competition is reflected not just in relationships between companies, but in interpersonal relationships within companies. Just as the pressure of competition between companies can promote efficiency, innovation, and customer service, so competition between individuals within a company can ensure maximum effort and productivity. Such competitive relationships between individuals at similar levels of the hierarchy for promotion to the next stage is a traditional feature of Western, especially American, corporations. However, such internal competition is likely to be effective primarily in hierarchically-structured organizations where individuals work independently and their individual performance can be accurately assessed. If companies are moving from mechanistic to organic structures and operational tasks are increasingly team-based, organizational efficiency is critically dependent upon coordinated, harmonious working relationships between individuals. Incentive systems need to be radically over-hauled: where administrative hierarchies are not clearly defined, promotion to the next level of management is not a particularly meaningful or effective incentive. Where tasks are team-based, then rewards should also be team-based. The kinds of interpersonal behaviors and personality profiles which are conducive to superior organizational performance also change substantially. The aggressive, independent, self-seeking, fast-track individual traditionally sought by corporate recruiters may be uniquely dysfunctional in the company environment of the 1990s. The skills needed for effective teamwork in innovation-based companies are likely to include sensitivity to others, listening, flexibility, and the ability to form meaningful and productive interpersonal relationships with a wide range of different people.

New Models of Leadership

Changes in organization structure, management systems, working relationships, and the types of skills required by employees have far-reaching implications for business leadership in the 1990s. Popular concepts of business leadership remain remarkably invulnerable to the changes which are transforming the corporate sector. In many respects, the resurgence in the cult of the entrepreneur during the 1980s encouraged a revival of older stereotypes of business leaders. The popular images of business leaders such as Lee Iaccoca, Ross Perot, T. Boone Pickens, and Ted Turner are of combinations of the buccaneering industrial barons of the turn of the century, and Hollywood heroes in the John Wayne mold. Iaccoca is a hero straight out of traditional mythology. Banished from Ford, he seeks refuge in a crisis-torn Chrysler. His crusade against inefficiency, incompetent executives, unions, bankers, and government, reveals resourcefulness, initiative, and strength of character. After enormous personal sacrifices, Chrysler emerges renewed and profitable. The triumphant Iaccoca goes on to become a multimillionaire, saves the statue of Liberty, and writes a best-selling autobiography.

The warrior-CEOs are "men of action" – they make the key decisions concerning the strategies of their organizations; they are bold – they launch huge takeover bids and preside over radical corporate restructurings; they are tough and aggressive with intolerance of inefficiency and little respect for the personal feelings of others. Even though few in number, the values and traits they represent are widely accepted. *Fortune* magazine recently lauded seven of "America's Toughest Bosses" characterizing each as "Loose Cannon," "Old Blood and Guts," "Cost Buster," "Detail Monger," "Megabrain," and "Commando."[35]

Unfortunately these characteristics and virtues are singularly inappropriate to the future world of business. Robert Reich observes that:

If the entrepreneurial heroes hold center stage in this drama, the rest of the vast workforce plays a supporting role – supporting and unheralded. Average workers in this myth are drones – cogs in the Big Machine, so many interchangeable parts, unable to perform without direction from above.[36]

Reich goes on to argue that:

If America is to win in the new global competition, we need to begin telling one another a new story in which companies compete by drawing upon the talent and creativity of all their employees, not just a few maverick inventors and dynamic CEOs.[37]

The key element of that story is the role of *collective entrepreneurship*, where the company is being constantly reinvented through the innovations, decisions, and adaptability of everyone in the organization working in cooperation. The hero in this story is not the individual but the team. "The cultural challenge," says Reich, "is to move these stories from the sports pages to the business page."

But the task goes further still. What types of people, with what styles, and what tasks are required as senior managers in the coming years? If decision making is to be decentralized, if employees are to work in cooperative teams, if innovation, seep and customer responsiveness are to be the key goals of strategy, then the traditional CEO as power-broker, police officer, decision maker, and bully is of limited use. Drucker's view of the CEO as conductor of the orchestra, or Peters and Waterman's view of the CEO as coach and cheerleader is closer to the mark. The critical ability of the CEO in the company of the 1990s will not be decision making, but will be to create an internal environment that exploits the capabilities of all employees, that promotes adaptation and customer-orientation, and which facilitates team work.

Summary

This chapter has targeted a few emerging trends in the external environment and in management thinking in order to speculate about the nature of strategic management during the current decade. Amidst all the uncertainties there are at least two sure bets. The first is that most attempts to forecast developments in the business sector in any precise sense will be as erroneous in the future as they have been in the past. The second is that, whatever developments emerge, the future environment of business will be characterized by increased complexity, increased uncertainty, and increased discontinuity. As a result, the demands on management will grow. Major problems are likely to be the reconciliation of planning for the long term with flexibility in the short term, decentralization and individual initiative with coordination and leadership, innovation and customer service with efficiency, and short-term financial performance with long-term competitive strength.

But these problems are also opportunities. The business world of today offers unparalleled excitement, variety, and opportunities for personal development, wealth creation, and the building of meaningful and productive personal relationships. The problems are great, the risks are many, but the opportunities and rewards are boundless. The intellectual structures and organizing frameworks which this provides will at least provide you with a head start in understanding and coping with the business world of the 1990s. Good luck!

Notes

1. "Going global: the chief executives in the year 2000 are likely to have had much foreign experience," *Wall Street Journal*, February 27, 1989, p. A4.

2. John Naisbitt and Patricia Aburdene, *Megatrends 2000* (William Morrow & Company, New York, 1990), ch. 1.

3. Francis Fukuyami, "The end of history?" *The National Interest*, Summer 1989.

4. Bernard Avishai, "A CEO's common sense of CIM: an interview with J. Tracy O'Rourke," *Harvard Business Review*, January–February 1989, pp. 110–17.

5. "Computers that think like people," *Fortune*, February 27, 1989, pp. 90–3.

6. "Computers that do it with mirrors," *Economist*, March 4, 1989, p. 82; "AT&T unveils laser-based prototype chip," *Los Angeles Times*, January 30, 1989, p. D1.

7. "When the heat is on, metal oxides can keep ceramic engines running," *Business Week*, January 30, 1989, p. 69.

8. "Warm superconductors that can really conduct," *Business Week*, February 20, 1989, p. 148.

9. "When the rivers run dry . . .," *Business Week*, February 13, 1989, pp. 95–8.

10. "Making nuclear power friendly," *Economist*, February 18, 1989, pp. 91–2.

11. "For American business, a new world of workers," *Business Week*, September 19, 1988, pp. 112–24.

12. Charles Handy, "Careers for the 21st Century," *Long Range Planning* 21 (3) (1988), pp. 90–7.

13. "Victories in the quality crusade," *Fortune*, October 10, 1988, pp. 80–8.

14. Hans H. Glissman and Ernst-Jurgen Horne, "Comparative invention performance of major industrial countries: patterns and explanations," *Management Science* 35 (1988), pp. 1169–87.

15. Tom Peters, *Thriving on Chaos* (Knopf, New York, 1987), pp. 274 and 277.

16. Kim B. Clark, "What strategy can do for technology," *Harvard Business Review*, November–December 1989, pp. 94–8.

17. Kenichi Ohmae, "Getting back to strategy," *Harvard Business Review*, November–December 1988, p. 149.

18. George Stalk Jr, "Time – the next source of competitive advantage," *Harvard Business Review*, July–August 1988, pp. 45–6.

19. *Nike in China*, Harvard Business School, Case No. 9–386–065 (Boston, Mass., 1985).

20. Kim Clark and Takahiro Fujimoto, "Reducing time to market," *Design Management Journal* (1) (1989), pp. 49–57.

21. "General Motors: what went wrong?" *Business Week*, March 16, 1987, pp. 102–10.

22. J. Peter Killing, "How to make a global joint venture work," *Harvard Business Review*, May–June, 1982, pp. 120–7.

23. See Robert Reich and Mankin, "Joint ventures with Japan give away our future," *Harvard Business Review*, March–April 1986.

24. "When U.S. joint ventures with Japan go sour," *Business Week*, July 24, 1989.

25. "Your rivals can be your allies," *Fortune*, March 27, 1989, pp. 66–76.

26. Gary Hamel, Yves Doz, C. K. Prahalad, "Collaborate with your competitors – and win," *Harvard Business Review*, January–February 1989, pp. 133–9.

27. See Russell Johnston and Paul R. Lawrence, "Beyond vertical integration – the rise of the value–adding partnership," *Harvard Business Review*, July–August 1988, pp. 94–101.

28. G. Lorenzoni and O. A. Ornat, "Constellations of firms and new ventures," *Journal of Business Venturing*, 3 (1988), pp. 41–57.

29. John Sculley, *Odyssey* (Fitzhenry & Whiteside, Toronto, 1987), pp. 97–107.

30. Tom Peters, "Restoring American competitiveness: looking for new models of organizations," *The Academy of Management Executive* 2 (2), 1988, pp. 103–9.

31. O. E. Williamson, *Markets and Hierarchies*, (Free Press, New York, 1975).

32. Peter F. Drucker, "The coming of the new organization," *Harvard Business Review*, January–February 1988, pp. 45–53.

33. John Sculley, *Odyssey*, p. 183.

34. "Peter Drucker's 1990s: the futures that have already happened," *Economist*, October 21, 1989, pp. 19–24.

35. "America's toughest bosses," *Fortune*, February 27, 1989, pp. 40–54.

36. Robert B. Reich, "The team as hero," *Harvard Business Review*, May–June 1987, p. 79.

37. Ibid., p. 80.

Index

Note: page numbers in italics indicate tables and exhibits

Index compiled by Geraldine Beare